SOCIAL ECONOMICS:
RETROSPECT AND PROSPECT

Recent Economic Thought Series

Warren J. Samuels, Editor
Michigan State University
East Lansing, Michigan, U.S.A.

Other titles in the series:

This series is devoted to works that present divergent views on the development, prospects, and tensions within some important research areas of international economic thought. Among the fields covered are macromonetary policy, public finance, labor and political economy. The emphasis of the series is on providing a critical, constructive view of each of these fields, as well as a forum through which leading scholars of international reputation may voice their perspectives on important related issues. Each volume in the series will be self-contained; together these volumes will provide dramatic evidence of the variety of economic thought within the scholarly community.

SOCIAL ECONOMICS: RETROSPECT AND PROSPECT

edited by
Mark A. Lutz
University of Maine

Kluwer Academic Publishers
Boston/Dordrecht/London

Distributors for North America:
Kluwer Academic Publishers
101 Philip Drive
Assinippi Park
Norwell, Massachusetts 02061 USA

Distributors for all other countries:
Kluwer Academic Publishers Group
Distribution Centre
Post Office Box 322
3300 AH Dordrecht, THE NETHERLANDS

Library of Congress Cataloging-in-Publication Data

Lutz, Mark A.
    Social economics : retrospect and prospect / Mark A. Lutz.
        p.   cm. — (Recent economic thought)
      ISBN 0-7923-9004-0
      1. Economics—Moral and ethical aspects.   2. Social values.
    I. Title.   II. Series.
    HB72.L885   1989
    306.3—dc20   89-24461
                                                           CIP

Printed in the United States of America

CONTENTS

LIST OF CONTRIBUTORS

William M. Dugger is Professor of Economics at DePaul University, 25 East Jackson Boulevard, Chicago, IL 60604-2287.

David P. Ellerman is Professor of Economics at Tufts University, Medford, MA 02155, and one of the key staff members of the Industrial Cooperative Association, Somerville, MA.

Amitai Etzioni is Professor of Sociology at George Washington University and Director of the Center for Policy Research, Washington, DC 20052. He is currently Visiting Professor of Ethics at Harvard Business School.

Lewis E. Hill is Professor of Economics at Texas Tech University, Box 4470, Lubbock, TX 79409-4470.

E. K. Hunt is Professor of Economics at the University of Utah, Salt Lake City, UT 84112.

Mark A. Lutz is Professor of Economics at the University of Maine, Orono, ME 04469-0158.

Thomas O. Nitsch is Professor of Economics at Creighton University, California at 24th Street, Omaha, NE 68178.

Edward J. O'Boyle is Professor of Economics at Louisiana Tech University, P.O. Box 10318, T.S., Ruston, LA 71272-0046.

Malcolm Rutherford is Professor of Economics, University of Victoria, P.O. Box 1700, Victoria, British Columbia V8W 2Y2.

Warren J. Samuels is Professor of Economics at Michigan State University, East Lansing, MI 48825.

J. R. Stanfield is Professor of Economics and Colorado State University, Fort Collins, CO 80523.

William R. Waters is Professor of Economics at DePaul University, 25 East Jackson Boulevard, Chicago, IL 60604-2287.

PREFACE

At the very heart of the conception of the present volume lies the conviction that social economics is a highly pluralistic discipline, inspired and enriched by several often radically different world views, Schumpeterian visions, and at times even quite antagonistic social doctrines. Yet, in spite of all these differences, social economists can nevertheless be seen and also approached as some kind of economic brotherhood for various reasons dissatisfied with the austere "value-free" diet offered by the positivistic neoclassical paradigm. What all social economists seem to have in common is a profound interest in values and the process of valuation in order to more fully understand both economic behavior and the possibilities of improving the economic system. Such a distinguishing characteristic is also well articulated and enshrined in Article 1 of the Constitution of the Association of Social Economics where we are told that the aims and objectives of the Association shall be:

1.   To foster research and publication centered on the reciprocal relationship between economic science and broader questions of human dignity, ethical values, and social philosophy, [and to] encourage the efforts of all scholars who are dedicated to exploring the ethical presuppositions and implications of economic science.

2.   To consider the personal and social dimensions of economic problems and to assist in the formulation of economic policies consistent with a concern for ethical values and pluralistic community and the demands of personal dignity.

It is also interesting to note that the pluralistic character of modern American social economics is only two decades old and was not a characteristic when the Association was created almost 50 years ago with an explicit stress on Catholic social doctrine, Christian moral principles, and Christian social philosophy.

One way to capture this new pluralist nature of social economics is to recognize several major threads, strains, or "strands" that make up the fabric of the contemporary school. In this vein, we can distinguish three primary perspectives: a Catholic solidarist strand first articulated in Heinrich Pesch's *Lehrbuch*, and the two secular strands representing Marxist socialism and American institutionalism, particularly of the instrumentalist variety developed by Clarence Ayres.

At the same time, and more controversially, we identified a fourth strand that, for the sake of simplicity, we chose to label "humanistic," since it centers around a "human standard" using personality and moral development as a yardstick in assessing economic institutions. As its key representative we singled out the eminent British social economist John Hobson, while recognizing that the concept of personality can perhaps be even better understood in philosophical terms, particularly the moral philosophy and "deontological" type ethics of Immanuel Kant. The motives for including such a fourth strand are twofold: first, it merely recognizes what has been a primary force for almost 200 years in the history of social economics, and second, it allows us to affirm the simple truth that there is a place for a social economist outside the solidarist, Marxist, or instrumentalist frames of reference.

It should be explicitly mentioned, however, that any categorization or typology, such as the 'strands' or 'veins' one chooses for this book, is by its very nature bound to be highly limited and in many ways even counterproductive. For example, it tends to be exclusionary giving short rift to scholarship that defies being categorized in any of the four boxes. Among others, there are neo-institutionalists (such as Malcolm Rutherford) who appear uneasy about the type of instrumentalist ethics outlined by Clarence Ayres and his follower Lewis Hill. In a similar position, lacking identification with any group, are some of my best friends, such as Jon Wisman and Jim Wible. There are a significant number of social economists who have been working within a research program grounded in the work of Karl Polanyi (such as Ronald Stanfield and his former student Bruce McDaniel) or of Aristotelian ethics (such as Lon Smith). Moreover, there are many prominent contemporary Catholic social economists (e.g., Steve Worland) who would not want to be identified with solidarism, as well as many more neoclassical economists (e.g., Kenneth Boulding) who take values, valuation, and ethics seriously without identifying with any of the four strands. Finally, it is not well suited to accommodate the work of eminent social economists such as Nicholas Georgescu-Roegen and Herman Daly who have been giving primary focus to resource use and entropy. To the extent that the work and stature of all these outstanding social economists ended up being underemphasized or omitted will reflect poorly on this book.

Nevertheless, a beginning had to be made by concentrating on some manageable number of the major currents in the field. The treatment here, although far from comprehensive, can be seen to capture an essential ingredient, perhaps even the very backbone of modern American social economics. To the extent that this project succeeds in working towards a greater mutual understanding among practitioners of four of its 'cardinal strands', the stage is also set for a potential movement toward greater integration, unity, and strength.

The book has been structured to allow for maximum balance among the different viewpoints. The section on the history of the discipline has been left to the Catholic socialist Tom Nitsch and one of the key architects of the "new" pluralist social economics, the former editor of the *Review*, solidarist William Waters. The discussion of the contemporary strands presented by representatives of the instrumentalist, Marxist, solidarist, and Kantian-humanistic camps has been entrusted to (pragmatist) Warren Samuels who graciously agreed to undertake this difficult and challenging task. The policy applications have been left in the hands of the two instrumentalists, Bill Dugger and Ron Stanfield (the latter with strong Marxist sympathies), and also David Ellerman, a neo-Kantian economic philosopher. Finally, the section speculating about the prospects of social economics has been filled with contributions from Malcolm Rutherford, an institutionalist, and myself, an active advocate of a humanistic approach in social economics.

For whatever imbalance and bias that is still manifest, I, the editor, will have to take the blame. Nevertheless, I trust that this book, with all its imperfections, by being the result of "inter-strand" intellectual cooperation, will be able to serve as a significant stepping stone toward greater mutual awareness and respect, and with it, greater unity of purpose in the ongoing construction of a viable social economics. Time will tell. Meanwhile, I'd like to express my deepest heartfelt gratitude to all the participants for the time and energy spent on a project that, initially at least, was bound to look somewhat risky and certainly overly ambitious.

More generally, I want to thank Zachary Rolnick of Kluwer Academic Publishers for agreeing to publish the book, and especially Gail Fernald for her patience and care in enabling it to materialize.

Mark A. Lutz, Editor

SOCIAL ECONOMICS:
RETROSPECT AND PROSPECT

PART I:

SOCIAL ECONOMICS IN HISTORICAL PERSPECTIVE

1

SOCIAL ECONOMICS: THE FIRST 200 YEARS[1]

Thomas O. Nitsch[*]

INTRODUCTION

The history of social economics (l'économie sociale, etc.), like that
of political economy before it, begins with some conceptual or theoretical
reflection on human economic activity, to which a designation is subsequently accorded. As that expression catches on, it comes to be appropriated by diverse views of and approaches to that praxis and discipline,
viz. human economizing and its lore. In modern times, political economy--
l'Oeconomie politique, 1615; Staatswirthschaft, 1755; Economia civile, 1765;

[*]Minimally, the author is obliged to acknowledge here the patient and expert assistance of
colleagues Bruce Malina (Theology) and Andreas Gommermann (Modern Language) in
critical renderings of certain key texts from the Italian and German, respectively.

Political Oeconomy, 1767--began as the designation for the prevailing
school of mercantilism/cameralism, whence being appropriated by Adam
Smith and disciples (1776-1874) to express an entirely different view of
how best to "administer" the national household.[2]

In the case of *l'économie sociale* (from which, in time, came our
social economics), specifically, we have an appellation that has enjoyed now
a 215-year history, to be minimally exact, and has similarly served as the
banner for diverse schools of economic thought. That is, like political
economy, for which it came to be substituted to some extent, it has
signified different conceptions. To some, such as Wicksell (1911/28) and
Rima (1967-86), it has stood for and been conceived to embrace the art
of economic policy or applied political economy. Others, such as Cossa,
Dietzel, and Cassel (1892-1923), have reserved and upheld our economia
sociale, Sozialoekonomik, etc., in just the opposite sense, i.e., as the "pure,"
apolitical, etc. percept-model and science of human economy.

As we launch and conduct our historical excursion--as we trace out
the course of social Economy(ics) from its French origins, via its Franco-
Belgian, Italian, German, and Anglo-American adaptations--we shall work
with a typology developed earlier by the present author, maintaining a
distinction between (1) secular-positive, (2) secular-normative, and (3)
religious-normative adaptations and usages.[3] Otherwise, our basic ordering
will be chronological.

PHASE I -- FROM PHYSIOCRATIC ORIGINS TO J. S. MILL

Here we treat l'économie sociale, whence social economy, in its
physiocratic birth (1736) and baptism (1773), whence its classical confirmation (1836-44) by John St. Mill. For, both substantively and terminologi-
cally, social economy(ics) had its origins in eighteenth century France, with
the physiocrats holding sway there circa 1736-'75. Thus, as Gide informs,

> Dr Quesnay, through his medical studies on "the animal
> economy" [viz. *Essai physique sur l'Oeconomie animale*,
> Paris, 1736] and on the circulation of the blood, has duly
> been found oriented in this direction [i.e. the analogy of
> (a) natural-social laws (order)]; [whence] social economy
> might well have appeared to him, just like animal econo-
> my, as a sort of physiology. Moreover, from "physiology"
> to "physiocracy" is not a very far step.[4]

Essentially what had been "the doctrine of Mr. Quesnay" came to be further elaborated into the system of physiocracy, which would duly be recognized by Adam Smith as embracing the whole "system of civil government." But, three years before that prominent recognition, an otherwise obscure French nobleman baptized that new formulation of the social order in the title of a six-volumes-in-three book published very anonymously at London in 1773. This was the *Elements of Politics; or, Inquiry into the True Principles of Social Economy*, by Le Comte du Buat-Nançay. Garnier (1952) has regarded this as a vaguely titled work by "one of the less brilliant writers of the physiocratic school"; a decade later, Marx (1862-63) derogated it further as a "Glorification of the Landed Aristocracy by Buat, an Epigone of the Physiocrats." While Roscher (1858-56) would further note Buat's *nomenclatural* contribution, Cossa has regarded Turgot's *Reflections on the Formation and Distribution of Wealth* (1769) as "the first *scientific treatise on social economy*."[5]

Yet, as Garnier continues, something was in that name itself. So much so that, 55 years later, the celebrated J.-B. Say, employing that same (physiocratic) organismic construct of an abstract and universal economic society (viz. the physiological analogue), would express his regret that social, rather than political, economy had not been used to designate the science.[6]

Finally, J. S. Mill was to give further endorsement to both the generic effect accorded to l'économie sociale by Buat and the Quesnay-Say abstract, universal-organismic construction in his erudite essay, "On the Definition and Method of Political Economy" (1836-'44) when he wrote:

> [The] laws of society, or laws of human nature in the social state, . . . form the subject of a branch of science which may be aptly designated . . . *social economy*; somewhat less happily . . . *speculative politics*, or the *science* of politics, as contradistinguished from the art. This science stands in the same relation to the social, as anatomy and physiology to the human body.[7]

In the prelude to that definition and distinction, Mill had noted that it was jointly the sufficient universality and simplicity of the results to which those otherwise "general truths" gave rise that justified their being called "*laws* of society."

Thus we have it. The initial conception of social economy qua a positive, theoretical, natural-law science of universal application: the anatomical and physiological study of human societies, le corps social; in Say's subtitular phrase, "the Economy of Societies." At the same time, measuring from Quesnay's seminal essay noted above, we have on record the first 100 years of the discipline. That is, from its birth with Quesnay (1736), its baptism by Buat (1773), and its confirmation by no lesser luminaries than J.-B. Say (1828) and J. S. Mill (1836/44).

We need now to turn to the followers, both true disciples and those who merely come after, alternately deepening and diverting the ruts and tracks now established.

PHASE II. -- THE "NEW" ÉCONOMIE POLITIQUE ET SOCIALE: THE RISE OF NORMATIVE SOCIAL ECONOMICS (1825-73)

The preponderance of our earlier history and meaning are found here. With the publication of his *Nouveaux Principes d'Économie politique* (1919; 2e ed. 1827), J.-C.-L. Simonde de Sismondi helped to usher in our "new" discipline that came to be somewhat uniquely designated "Social Economy(ics)." For though he seems not to have employed that new name himself,[8] Rist informs, in his chapter on "Sismondi and the Origins of the Critical School" (alias "The Antagonists"),[9]

What really interested Sismondi was not so much what is called political economy, but what has since become known as *économie sociale* in France and *Sozial- politik* in Germany.

The critical ideas and antagonistic sentiments that characterized this new wave of political/social economists we shall examine briefly presently. Let us first note here a contemporary of Sismondi, but true *defender* of the faith. This was the noted optimist, B.-C.-P.-J. Dunoyer, whose *Nouveau Traité d'Économie sociale* (1830, 2 vol.) first appeared in 1825 under the more telling title of *Industry and Morality Considered in their Relationships with Liberty*, and, finally, without further incident--the second (1830) edition had been almost entirely destroyed by fire before its publication--in its completed form and third title, *On the Freedom of Labor; or, Simple Exposé of the Conditions Wherein Human Efforts are*

Exerted with the Greatest Effect (3 vol.), in 1845.[10] Of its second edition
Blanqui (1837) has written significantly:[11]

> This excellent work, which has not been put into
> circulation except in a very small number of exemplars,
> belongs to the new French economic school which does
> not separate the progress of industry from that of morality
> and well-being in general.

With these two works, we have early examples of the two branches
into which the *secular-normative* brand of social economy(ics) divided itself,
viz. what we may call the "critical" and the "orthodox" varieties. Both go
beyond the narrow wealth-enhancement concern of the "old" or prevailing
orthodoxy of Smith, Say, and disciples--i.e., "political economy (proper)" as
implied by Rist (supra)--and recognize human well-being as the ultimate
object to be maximized. That is, they are concerned with human material
welfare or well-being, and not merely material wealth. Further, they will
recognize this magnitude to be equally a function of the *distribution* of the
society's stock of wealth and flow of production among its population, as
it is of the mere quantitative enhancement of those two aggregates, even
on a per-capita basis. They want to show how that social distribution
might be improved. Thus, their spirit, again, is *normative* in this regard;
i.e., they are not content, along with Ricardo, for example, to merely
predict *positively* the natural course of the distribution of the social product among the several classes of workers, capitalists, and the landed aristocracy.[12] Finally, this group are wont to include in the arguments of
their individual and social welfare functions the other factors, besides the
usual objects of exchange and consumption, and including especially
education and the formation of the whole person, versus the very "functional" or "vocational" sort advocated by Smith in the opening chapter of
his closing book.[13]

Now, still before we examine some particular specimens, we shall
note the emergence, with the 1832-34/37 works of Ch. de Coux and A. de
Villeneuve-Bargemont in the Franco-Belgian theater, of the other basic
branch of this new wave, viz. the *religious*-normative. This will give us, in
effect, l'Économie sociale qua l'Économie politique chrétienne or otherwise practical Roman Catholicism. As our secular-normative variety will
be seen to divide into both a staunch defense of the classical liberalism of
Smith, Say, and disciples on the one hand, and a radical critique thereof
on the other (e.g., Proudhon, 1846), so will this religious-normative brand

range from the more radically and reformistically critical to the more
conservatively liberal. Whether the basic appeal, explicit or implicit, is to
the natural (temporal) or the supernatural (eternal) law, the practical
(political, programmatic) approaches seem always to divide this way.
Finally, we shall not totally overlook those who carried the banner of the
original, positivistic strain.

The Secular-Normative Vein

Here we encounter defensive, reformist and radical-critical views
vis-à-vis the classical or orthodox political economy: defenders and
deepeners, critical modifiers, and abject negators of that "faith." Thus, as
already noted, Sismondi, as precursor to such more radical critics as
Proudhon, led the reaction to classical political economy on the continent.
Such attacks on the faith brought, in turn, staunchly defensive and
glowingly "optimistic" reactions. To these we now turn.

**The Disciples of Say: From Dunoyer (1825-45) to About (1868/-
'73).** Dunoyer's second effort (1830) proclaims a *New Treatise on Social
Economy*, whence the present writer regards it as his pivotal treatise. Yet,
the third version is the most complete, its author informs; and, he notes
further in that same (1845) "Preface," that, despite the several diverse titles
and imperfections of the earlier editions of his book, its object had
remained singular, unique, and simple. That was, he writes:

> To inquire experimentally as to which conditions, accord-
> ing to which laws, under the influence of which causes,
> men succeed in availing themselves with the greatest free-
> dom--i.e. the greatest power--of those forces--those natural
> faculties--which, put into action, constitute human labor
> [*le travail humain*].

Whence, he refrains, "such is purely that object."[14]
Next (pp. X-XII), the author distinguishes social from political
economy. The latter is the general "study" and "particular investigations"
of which wealth is the exclusive object. "That's it!" he exclaims, and
rhetorizes: "Political economy, economy of society, that is production,
distribution and consumption of wealth [merely]?" But, that "economy of

society" lies on a loftier plane, on a par with "the economy of the human body, or equally the economy of the world."

The influence of Say, à la both the subtitle of his *Traité* of 1803 sqq. (viz. "Simple Exposition of the Manner in which Wealth is Formed, Distributed and Consumed") and the subtitle and opening discussion of the *Cours Complet* of 1828 already noted, is very obvious here. This in turn means a geneological lineage tracing back to Quesnay's seminal 1736 *Essay*.

In furthering this French tradition, the author remains a safe distance from the more purely materialistic thrust of the English school (Smith, Ricardo, Senior). He proposes not a science of wealth but of human society seeking and employing the real means, the true instruments of its general well-being. The anatomical analogy is elaborated. One should speak of "the economy of society" as one does of that of the human body. As the latter is nothing but "the manner in which all therein is ordered for the exercise and growth of its forces," so the former is "parallely the order according to which all therein is ordered and arranged for the exertion and development of the social forces" (p. XI).

The "social forces," in turn, are essentially the *travaux*, the trades, occupations, lines of human labor, and endeavor that constitute industrial society, together with the *arts* that cultivate and empower them. The "science of that economy," then, is simply "the knowledge of those forces and of their means, i.e., . . . of all the travaux of the society and of the conditions to which their power is subordinated" (p. XI). Yet, while these are the real sources and instruments of wealth, that is not the *unique* or sole result of the travaux and their supportive arts. For, while the latter do enrich society directly in the material sense, and especially so when they are pursued in a free and unhampered fashion, they simultaneously and just as positively contribute to the learning, enlightenment, and moral development of the society. It is then "the ensemble of these arts," fostering both the material and spiritual well-being and development of a people, "which l'économie sociale embraces."

Concerning l'économie sociale proper, the author continues:

What social economy should propose for itself is thus . . .
to be aware of those trades which enter into the economy
of society. It is not to occupy itself in a special way with
each one; but it seeks to acquaint itself with the nature of
all, their relations, the influence which some exert on the

others, and the means of power and of liberty of action
which they have in common.

Having thus illustrated how his new treatment of social economy
proposes to improve upon the more narrowly materialistically oriented
political economy, Dunoyer next manifests his disdain for those "writers
who today are designated by the name of socialists, . . . who all pretend
to subject the society to artificial forms," to any and all forms of centralization and intervention by the public authorities (pp. XIIff.).   Alas,
however, those tendencies are the talk of the day, while, "La liberté est un
subject passé de mode."

Thus, social economy appears in Dunoyer's sights as both a
positive and normative science.   As the former, it sheds the light for
stripping away the "artificial forms" noted.   This, in turn, permits the
unshackled operation of those natural social laws and forces that conduce
to the national wealth, health, and well-being.

Gide's treatment of Dunoyer comes partly under the subcaption
of "The Law of Solidarity." Like other "optimists," for example, Bastiat
and his *Harmonies économiques* (1850), he appealed to an harmonious
solidarity among and between the social classes: an essential and socially
efficacious form of cooperation under the appearance of competition.

Equally zealous in this regard was the noted French journalist and
novelist, Edmond About (1828-1885).[15]   In his *Handbook of Social
Economy; or, the Worker's A B C* which appeared in English dress in this
country in 1873,[16] the translator's "Introduction" informs (pp. viiff.) that
the work is specifically addressed to certain Parisian workmen who, in
correspondence with M. About, "avowed themselves innocent of the
doctrines of political economy generally current and accepted among
educated and thinking men." In this context, their spokesman queried the
author, "'Is there no science of Social Economy? . . . Can you teach it to
us?'"

Thus initially inspired, About, says his translator, was further
struck by the idea that "a simple elementary work" such as the workers
(allegedly) sought "might prove useful to others besides working men." He
continues, quoting the author:

> Whether agriculturists, tradesmen, manufacturers, land-
> lords, fund-holders, artists, and men of letters, we all
> produce Social Economy, as M. Jourdain made prose,

without knowing it. Unfortunately we do not always make
it of good quality.

What *is* good, true, right social economy? Essentially, it is the
fact and recognition that the interests of all socioeconomic classes, all
strata of economic society, all occupations and professions, are one. The
rich have just as much need of the poor as the poor have of the rich. To
treat their workers well, see to their education, equip them with the best
tools, etc., is to the self-interest of the rich no less than the benefit of the
poor. And, in this same "interdependence of mankind," the principle of
"self-interest, rightly understood," also applies to the poor person; whence,
the author's text is now summoned, "'the poor man ought to wish for the
opulence of the rich, and do so in his own interest'" (pp. xviii-xix). As
such, "'social economy ascends to such a height that it merges into
universal morality.'" The text is resumed:

> For man's reason is indivisible, and there are no truths
> which cannot be reconciled with each other. What would
> happen if the poor, out of calculation, were to apply
> themselves to enrich the rich? If the rich, out of a wise
> selfishness, were to apply themselves to enrich the poor?
> Who would be the gainer in such an event? Everybody.

The author is quoted to continue and conclude on the equally exuberant
note, viz. the unlimited nature of "the production of useful things"
(Aristotle's *chremata*) despite the fixity of "the area we inhabit," and would
we only cease "fighting each other [and] unite all our efforts against blind
and stupid nothingness!" (cit. orig. text, pp. 122f.).[17]

Positive-Law and Moral-Philosophical Views in England (1842-48).
In the midst of this developing natural-law normativist tradition there
appears to have been a somewhat prevalent positive-law conception in
England. Thus, the *Oxford English Dictionary* (s.v. "Social") informs us
that a certain Arthur Polson, in his article on "English Law" in the *Encyclopaedia Metropolitano* (Vol. II) of 1845, singles out and defines our
term as follows: "Social Economy. -- Laws which directly consult the
health, wealth, convenience or comfort of the public, may properly be
referred to this head." From the title of the article ("English Law"), we

deduce the *positive*-law character of that social economy; and, from the *public* welfare/well-being orientation, its *normative* nature.

Special names and works representing the moral-philosophical as well as positive-law character of social economy(ics) here are (1) the (then) late Samuel Laing of Edinburgh, whose positive-normative definition of social economy (1842) was quoted in a very significant article falling into our next phase; (2) J. S. Mill's confrere, Wm. Ellis, and his *Outlines of Social Economy* of 1846; and (3) William Atkinson and his *Principles of Social Economy* of 1858.[18]

The Radical-Critical *Économie sociale* of P. J. Proudhon (1846). Proudhon's views and *Systéme* are sufficiently familiar as not to require any extensive treatment here. Mainly, we are concerned with his employment of our économie sociale, for that he certainly did in his classic *Systéme des Contradictions Économiques, ou Philosophie de la Misère* of 1846.[19] There, as opposed to the system of A. Smith, Say, Ricardo, et al., founded as it was on private property, egoism, competition, etc., Proudhon seeks and proposes a new and more humanistic socioeconomic order. This would consist in a "recreating of l'économie sociale from bottom to top, . . . constituting a new law, a new politics, of institutions and customs diametrically opposed to the old forms" (I, pp. 2-5, passim). This new socioeconomic system, *socialism*, would instead be predicated upon the principles of equality and fraternity, and would be one of community and association. And, he is quoted in this regard, "The foundation of association is solidarity."[20]

Classical and neoclassical political and social economy sought and would seek, as we so well know, such remedies and antidotes as the preservation of competition, regulation of monopolies, and other forms and measures (including palliatives) of economic politics (à la Cossa). Proudhon, on the other hand, wanted "root-and-branch" relief and change, nothing less than a radical reconstruction of the social economy, and a new science or theoretical system to accompany it.[21]

As opposed to l'économie politique as the extant, reigning economic science, he seemed to reserve l'économie sociale or social economics, if we want, for the socioeconomic order and its science more generically, and thus as open to the new forms and formulae he sought. *Political* economy for him, as for others, it might seem, had too much of the old connotations, mercantilist/cameralist and, to him as to Marx, worst of all, classicist--i.e., the system of Smith, Ricardo, and their "vulgarizers."

Perhaps, to him as well as to Marx, likewise, that "political" bore too much of either or both the bourgeois and statist systemic connotations and even conceptions of human nature. Man's being by nature (and full-fledgedly) a *social* (versus merely a political and/or sociable [geselliges]) animal, the economic system must accordingly be an Économie sociale; or, for Marx and certain others, a gesellschaftliche Wirthschaft, whence Sozialoekonomik, etc.

The Religious-Normative Vein: 1832-73

Here we encounter in a formal, if not official, sense Christian Political and Social Economy proper; and, again, our story begins in France, or in the Franco-Belgian, Roman-Catholic centers of Paris, Louvain, and Brussels. It closes with an entry in a Protestant British journal. In between, we capture the origins and early development of what came to be called Social Catholicism (Christianity); and, of one of its central elements, the doctrine of social solidarity or "solidarism."

The Rise of Catholic Social Economics: De Coux and Villeneuve-Bargemont (1831-37). Like any doctrine, Social Catholicism and its pivotal solidarist tenet are found rooted in antiquity. There is birth, rebirth (sometimes in baptism), and so on. Catholic social economics was born and even baptized in the works of two devoted French noblemen-scholars in the 1830s.[22]

Charles de Coux, in the opening of his introductory lecture at Paris (1831/32), informed his audience how, at a certain point in his intellectual development,

> I entered into a new order of ideas, and soon recognized
> that Catholicism contains in its practical consequences the
> most admirable system of social economy which has ever
> been given to the earth.

In tracing out "the temporal results of each of its precepts," the lecturer continued,

> I learned to discern in the doctrines of modern economists
> the true from the false, because I soon noticed that the
> science which to them is so dear ceased to be true, that

is, it is no longer universal when it departs from Catholic teachings.

The author seeks a unified, universal society, based upon Catholic/Christian social principles, recognizing the importance of material wealth or richesses, but stressing as much or more the "moral or social wealth" comprised by the virtues--charity, honesty, self-sacrifice, etc.-- embodied in the "spiritual" aspect of the human populace. Private property is upheld as proper and essential to such social economy, but competition--between men and machines, among workers, international, free, and universal--is regarded as deleterious.

The influence of Say is particularly apparent. Utility or usefulness, coupled with natural scarcity, are just as much determinants of national wealth as labor and capital costs of production. Thus, all free gifts of nature must be reckoned as part of the national patrimony, along with produced wealth. And, while the "industrial school" (Smith et al.) might purport to distinguish carefully between nominal price and the real value of goods, they implicitly confuse that valeur d'échange with the true value or valeur d'utilité in reckoning national wealth. Finally, the author insists, giving full weight to the *utility* criterion requires recognizing the moral virtues as a component part of the true wealth of a society.

Like any other such critique, de Coux's was a melange of (1) negation and abolition of what was false and wrong regarding the extant theoretical and real-world systems, (2) affirmation and preservation of what was true and right therein, whence (3) transcending and superceding that system with something different and better. *His* social economy was to be that something new and improved. The term itself, however, only appears in that early part of the *Essais*, though we are otherwise apprised of his *Course on* or *Introduction to l'Économie Sociale* at Louvain (cf. fn. 24 infra), wherein he besought the restriction of economic freedom and competition, for example.

A further insight into de Coux's meaning of social economy is provided in the heart-and-core of his "Second Essay," "On Moral and Material Wealth," which presents a two-way classification, distinguishing on the one hand between (1) productive, (2) exchangeable, and (3) latent wealth; and, on the other, between (1) common, (2) individual, and (3) social or moral wealth (pp. 76-77). First of all we note, the discussion *is*, following Smith et al., about the *wealth* of nations; although, in the first part of that Second Essay there is much recognition of the poverty, misery, etc., of the proletarian class versus the affluence of the capitalists and others in present-day society, under the prevalence of the industrial system. In a sense, moral or social wealth might translate into moral or social economy. That is, the difference between de Coux's social economy and the political economy of that industrial school, would be the focus on the spiritual nature and moral character of the real wealth of the nation. Here he writes (pp. 85-86):

> *Social or Moral Riches* have it in common with individual riches that they consist in qualities at once personal and intransmissable. They differ in that the advantages which ensue from their existence constitute a form of wealth of which the least part returns ordinarily to the producer.

Further, when we read in the introductory essay about higher planes of economy--domestic, whence national and political (= international)--and sociability, the highest levels of both being universal, with the necessary glue and supervision provided by the Catholic faith and fatherly eye of the Holy See, we obtain some idea of the true social economy of a united human family, such *social* universality, unity, etc., being prominent recurring themes.

We now note how de Coux attempted to simultaneously negate, preserve, and supercede the principles of the industrial system (school) of Adam Smith (et al.), in terms of his own vision of social economy. Thus, for example, he would *negate* or *reject* egoism, materialism, greed, fraud, and deceit along with unbridled competition in the marketplace, the strict labor-cost theory of value, the dominance of industry over agriculture, Say's Law, labor as a mere instrument of production, and exchange-value or marketprice as the sole gauge of the true wealth of a society.

At the same time, de Coux would *preserve* or otherwise affirms and upholds (1) private property, along with civil rights, as the foundation and necessary requisite for individual freedom; (2) the view of capital as nothing but stored-up labor; (3) that human effort is productive--is true labor--whenever its product is humanly *useful*; (4) the socioeconomic classes, and hence (5) the division of labor and (6) market-exchange, but with (7) positive laws prohibiting competition from autodegenerating into monopoly.

Finally, our faithful Catholic social economist would *replace*, *transcend*, etc., reigning prevailing socioeconomic institutions and/or politicoeconomic theorems as follows: (1) egoism and personal-interest by

Christian charity and the general-interest; (2) the greed, fraud, etc. with
self-sacrifice and social justice; (3) the concept of wealth = material riches
with true wealth = material + moral riches; (4) the principle of competition and class antagonisms with Christian solidarity (his "higher sociability,"
"universal unity," etc.); (5) the exclusive labor (or labor + capital) - cost
theory of value with a more general utility theory, thus recognizing that
material wealth = natural + produced riches; (6) the overemphasis on
manufacturing etc. with the restoration of agriculture to its primus inter
pares stature; (7) Say's Law with (à la Sismondi) the observed tendency of
production to outstrip consumption; (8) the natural tendency of wages to
decline as the productivity of the workers increases with a policy of
maintaining wages to prevent the immiseration of the working class and
the tendency noted in (7); and (9) the concept that progress consists
merely in the quantitative amassment of ever more national wealth with
the recognition that true social well-being (and social economy) is as much
a function of (concerned with) the distribution of riches, which is--in turn
--essentially a matter of human institution and *not* natural law.

Following squarely in the footsteps and right on the heels of de
Coux, the Vte Alban de Villeneuve-Bargemont (1784-1850), likewise a
student of his French forerunners Say and Sismondi,[23] essentially advances
their doctrine. More openly patriotically and sectarianly critical of the
English systems of political and industrial economy and society, he upholds
both the institution of private property as the foundation of economic
freedom and adds to the British (Smithian, Ricardian) "principle of labor"
in the production and augmentation of wealth that of Christian charity in
its distribution and use. To him, the British systems, theoretical and
praxeological, advanced the wealth of the nation at the totally uncon-
scionable expense of simultaneously increasing the poverty and misery of
the producing masses. Adam Smith had inquired into "the Nature and
Causes of the Wealth of Nations"; that was the object of *his* "Political
Oeconomy." V.-B. gave us a treatise on 'the Poverty of Nations,' of *its*
nature and causes, and on the means of its amelioration and prevention--
his Économie politique chrétienne.

He also gave us further directions and more explicit dimensions of
économie sociale. Of course, as he used the term it would designate
Christian political economy, in contrast and substantial opposition to that
of Smith and company. But, at the same time, it was simultaneously (1)
more open to and allied with the cognate disciplines of the philosophy of
civilization, "statistics, legislation and the moral sciences related to the
causes of indigence" (p. 18); (2) always founded on "education and

religion" (p. 186); and (3) stimulative of both "labor and charity," with this latter--and most crucial--aspect elaborated as follows (p. 410a):

> True social economy is that which excites at once labor and charity, which rightly counsels less the production of wealth than the distribution and general diffusion of well-being, which prescribes setting limits on needs instead of multiplying them indefinitely [the Aristotlian approach], which assigns just proportions to the extension of industry [cf. Sismondi, esp.], and finally, which is applied principally to the development of national industry, viz. that which is exerted on the products of the soil.

> [Whence:] That political economy, of accord with the Christian philosophy, conduces to liberty, dignity, the comfort of all men, the maintenance of the social order, and consequently to the most perfect civilization.

As opposed to this are "the other economic and philosophic theories" which,

> in making us view wealth and enjoyments as the sole end and destiny of man, in exciting and multiplying the needs fashioned [cf. Galbraith's "synthesis of demand"], in suffocating charity, in giving to industry an unlimited extension, succeed in concentrating wealth and luxurious refinements with a few individuals, but rain misery, brutality [l'abrutissement] and servitude on the masses, and resolve in anarchy or in despotism (p. 410a).

In large part echoing and enhancing the concerns and strictures of de Coux, Villeneuve-Bargemont denounces over and again the "insatiable egoism," materialism, "spirit of commerce," and "universal competition" in the "system of manufacturing" tending to concentrate economic gains in "the hands of the entrepreneurs," "the monopoly of land" and industrial concentration, growth of manufacturing at the expense of neglect of agriculture, focus on production without limit, displacement of workers by machines, lowering of wages, "constant stimulation of needs," and the moral degradation of the human being upon which the "English system"

rested or otherwise entailed. The current "revolution," our critic charged
(p. 23), "communicates to economic systems that aridity of heart, that
absence of humanity [and, elsewhere, "contempt for human nature" (p.
12b)] and charity, that egoistic materialism which came to be revealed in
France as well as in England: the application of the school founded by
Smith."

When all is said and done, the author concludes (p. 624a),

> All is explained, for us, by the interlinking and the
> power of the principles which subordinated the social and
> material order to the eternal laws of the moral and reli-
> gious order. Labor and charity have appeared as the two
> great bases of human societies, as the sole elements of
> general happiness, elements united by Providence, and
> which cannot be separated without destroying the harmony
> and the economy of the social universe.

The Social Economy of La Sagra, Aug. Ott, and Le Play.
Following closely on the heels, if not squarely in the footsteps, of our two
earlier pioneers is a Spaniard and two prominent Frenchmen now to be
briefly considered.

Ramon Dionisio La Sagra y Périz (1798-1871) wrote and presented
his "Social Economy" first at the Ateneo in Madrid, lecturing and writing
"more than 30 works in the social sciences," including his *Lecciones de
Economía social* (Madrid, 1840).[24] This economía social, we are further
told, was to be a science of human happiness serving as a guide for
governments. Among the thinkers noted as influencing his doctrines are
Villeneuve-Bargemont and Proudhon. In 1848, one account informs, he
travelled to Paris "to participate in the discussion of social questions,
thence adopting a great part of the theories of Proudhom [*sic*]."[25]

La Sagra wrestled with the problem of private property in land.
At first he felt that "'the destruction of landed property would bring about
that of society itself,'" we are told. "Afterwards," that account (*EUI*)
continues,

> La Sagra had to abandon his faith *in the liberal constitu-
> tion of landed property*, regarding it the cause of nearly all
> the economic evils afflicting modern society, and recom-

mending . . . the constitution of collective ownerships in
favor of the disinherited classes and future generations.

Thus Sagra's program, originally predicated simply on the principle
of Christian love and advocating educational and moral improvement,
finally called for a complete organization of society along collectivist lines,
including the abolition of interest and debt-redemption, and of private
property in land.

Besides La Sagra we also point to the Frenchman Auguste Ott (b.
Strasbourg, 1814), a somewhat more radical-reformist disciple and ally of
the "associative socialist" Buchez (Rist).[26] Because of the affinity of his
*Traité d'Économie sociale; or Political Economy Coordinated from the
Viewpoint of Progress* to Sismondi's work, Cossa informs, Ott has been
grouped with the "semi-socialists." Though a Protestant, Ott professed "an
elevated spiritualism which only separated him from the Catholics in
dogmatic questions" (*EUI*). In 1836, we are relatedly informed, Ott joined
Buchez and "adopted his ideas on the alliance of Catholicism and the
Revolution," plunging into German philosophy and, following Buchez'
example, involving "himself in the political movement culminating in the
revolution of 1848" (*GDU*).

After 1848, this Christian social economist, it is further noted
(*GDU*), "devoted himself more especially to labors on economic and moral
questions," thus producing his *Traité d'Économie sociale* of 1851 (22d ed.,
1892), contra liberalism (*GDU*; *EUI*), *Travail et Liberté* of 1870, etc.

But it is for his *Treatise on Social Economy* that Ott is chiefly
recognized, and in regard to which Cossa notes the special usage of "the
expression *social economy* [by] Ott, disciple of the socialist Buchez [to
connote] the intent of *reform*, which they regard as properly the chief
inspiration of economists" (*Intro.*, 70/58f.).

Finally, we come to our eminent *Économiste social exemplaire*, the
Norman Pierre-Guillaume-Frédéric Le Play (1806-1882). For Frédéric Le
Play is the first of our group to constitute a true social economist in the
dual sense of both a positive investigator and normative advocator: an
extremely serious and meticulous student of what is, and an equally
studious and, shall we say, realistic visionary and counsellor as to what
might be and how. He is also the first of our lot to establish a following
and found a school proper--or, indeed, two such, according to his dualistic *économie sociale*.

While there is thus some question as to where to place Le Play according to our secular/religious-normative/positive categories, it seems sufficient that Gide treats him and his school--though with some reservation--under the rubric of "Doctrines Inspired by Christianity," while his *La Réforme Sociale* of 1864 is generally regarded as his crowning glory. Whence, we treat him here, and confine our attention primarily to some chief points or observations conveyed *in* his foremost "doctrinal" work.[27] Nor do we wish to overlook the organizational and administrative prowess for which Le Play is generally recognized. He organized the social-economy exhibits at no less than three Great Expositions (Paris, 1855 and 1867; London, 1862) and founded in April 1856 the Société Internationale des Études Pratiques d'Économie Sociale, whose monograph series *Les Ouvriers des Deux-Mondes* (1858ff.) and fortnightly *La Réforme Sociale* (1881ff.), again, well reflect the dual interests of their founder. But here we focus on the Social Economy of Le Play as elaborated in the *RS* of 1864.

The primary and pivotal social unit or cell, according to Le Play, was the family. Social analysis, from which comes reform, begins there. Reform is stressed, and carefully distinguished from revolution. Reform is considered, steady, gradual, and hence permanent; revolution, abrupt, unruly, misfounded, misfocused, and hence ephemeral. The point is made with the French revolution of 1789. The chief culprit there, he emphasizes, was that most pernicious and misleading idea of the late eighteenth century, still borne by the conventional wisdom, of the "original perfection" of man; whence, once beyond that (purely chimerical) "state of nature," man's corruption could be attributed only to governments or other social institutions (*RS*, pp. 7, 12). Accordingly, by abolishing those institutions, in the long run, human perfection could be regained. Le Play found this philosophy blinded to the "organic infirmities of human nature," whence it has always "led, in treating social questions, to erroneous conclusions" (p. 7). The gravest of the latter is its "considering of moral progress as a necessary consequence of material progress" (p. 7).

Le Play's introductory chapter, devoted to "The Preconceived Ideas and the Facts," proclaims in its opening section (#1, p. 1) that "The Urgency of Reform is Signaled in France by the Antagonisms and the Instability which Agitates the Social Body [le Corps Social]." Thus launched, the discussion here focuses on the "social problems," essentially matters of "social organization," with which "social science" must deal. These are characterized as the "social antagonisms, discords, disorders, strife, and struggle" of modern times which have replaced the "harmony, solidarity, and peace" of earlier days. The task of *la réforme sociale* is to regain that social Eden, one might say, within the modern context.

When egoism, tyranny, etc., corrupt the classes dirigeantes and cause the clergy, rulers, employers, and others, to abuse their power and authority, to weigh down the governmental, religious, and industrial processes with overextended bureaucracies, etc.; when all sense of the special paternal predilection of self-denial is lost (p. 7)--then we have the moral decadence which leads inexorably to material decline.

Social reform *is* moral-material reform; and, in that order only. Here, Le Play places himself squarely in the camp of Hegel, Max Weber, and the other idealists of the nineteenth and twentieth centuries, as well as that of the social doctrine of the Roman Catholic Church.

In discussing the relation and the difference between the physical sciences and moral science, as these pertain respectively to the material and social orders, Le Play asserts that in the former new inventions leading to measurable progress are integral, while in the latter only discovery of extant and immutable truth(s) is possible. In an Aristotelian world, everything pertaining to the physical order and its sciences ("the multitude of primordial elements" etc.) is infinitely variable (modifiable, recombinable, etc.). The object of the moral sciences, on the other hand, is singular and invariable--"the soul and its relations with God and humanity"; thus, in contrast to all the progress made in the realm of physical science, in "the domain of moral science [all] the innumerable thinkers . . . have had nothing to add to the Decalogue of Moses" (pp. 8-10). This is all to refute the popular belief (cf. #2, p. 7) that the key to human progress is to be found "in the changing of doctrines" rather than in "a better practice of the known verities" (#3, p. 11).

Le Play's program of social reform is erected directly upon the foundation of his social system, with its focus--again--on the family. The following sequential seven categories constitute the terms of analysis in *RS* as per its "Tableau Méthodique": I. *Religion* (the first foundation of societies); II. *Private Property* (the second foundation); III. the Family, as "fortified by religious freedom and private property" (the true social unit); IV. *Labor* (the principal auxillary of the moral order; but wealth, its fruit, often a stumbling block); V. the *Association* (the Community and the Corporation); VI. *Private Relations* (inequality, poverty, patronage, etc.); and VII. Government (public life as divided judiciously between the community, the province, and the State) (p. XIII).

In the "Conclusion," we are told (#68), "Reform will not be accomplished except by the action simultaneously of the law and the morals (manners, customs [moeurs])."[28]   This, then, is the program submitted by Le Play; from his positive, empirical-theoretical analysis to his normative science as applied in social reform--this, integrally, *his* "Économie Sociale."

An English-Protestant Terminus (1873).   Very brief note must at least be made here of Millicent Garret Fawcett's review of W. F. Rae's translation of "Edmond About's Social Economy" which appeared in the *Congregationalist* (Vol. II, pp. 15-20) of 1873.   While the reviewer makes no attempt to conceal various reservations about the author and his work's French exuberance and pretensions, she appears quite sincere and even-handed in regard to its positive contributions.   In particular she finds the two chapters in the original work--*Handbook of Social Economy* (1873)-- on Liberty and Co-operation especially worthy of favorable note, the former in its dealing with the dangers of "paternal government" and the latter--recognizing France as the birthplace of the cooperative movement- -on the "very sound practical advice to workmen . . . contemplating the establishment of co-operative manufacturing societies" (p. 20).   Otherwise, we are apprised (p. 18),

> The general reader [will] find the well-worn subjects of
> social and economic science, such as free trade, paternal
> government, almsgiving, gambling, the functions of money,
> and the benefits conferred by society on the individual,
> treated with an [atypically] airy freshness.

With respect to this writer's conception of social economy, she takes no exception to the (actual/implicit) distinction made by the French author between that and political economy, the latter being (apparently) reserved for the "received doctrines," and the former being regarded as more generic, open to the truth, and broadly concerned with both "the social and economic problems of the day."   Recognizing About minimally as "a writer on Social Economy," while finding his prescription of en-lightened and self-interested solidarity between workers and capitalists unduly effusive and cumbrously absurd, the reviewer thus further recog-nizes this solidaristic optimism as characteristic of the French brand of l'économie sociale.

The Continuing Secular-Positive Tradition: Europe, 1840-73

Our examples here, a not-too-small but compact lot, are Italian and German. It is they who carried on and variously further developed that original (positivistic physiocratic) tradition, and to whom we turn now briefly.

Antonio Scialoja (opp. prin. 1840-48). Scialoja (1817-1877), Cossa informs, was among those who used that "expression *economia sociale*" to refer to "*rational, pure, scientific* economy(ics)."[29] In his *Principii d'Economia sociale* (1840) "as in his other works" (e.g., *Trattato elementare de Economia sociale*, Turin, 1848), Rabbeno further informs, "Scialoja stoutly upheld the principles of liberty, at a date when Naples was the stronghold of absolutism and protection."[30] According to Cossa, again, Scialoja's chief claim to fame in the area of economic theory was the spreading "in Italy of the theories of Malthus and Ricardo." The well-spring of this dissemination was his *Trattato* noted above, first published at Naples, with a second edition appearing in 1846 and French translation in 1844. It was upon taking the chair in economics restored at Torino (Turin) that Scialoja published the *Elementary Treatise on Social Economy(ics)* (1848), which reputedly enjoyed a wide popularity (Cossa). As opposed to a contemporary at Sienna, for example, who "demonstrated the economic importance of the *religious* element" (Cossa), Scialoja's *Principles* (reportedly) stuck to "the principal arguments of economics and finance," further emphasizing the importance of mathematics in economic inquiry and "the expediency of using them, especially in the theory of value" (Rabbeno).

We turn now briefly to *I Principi della Economia sociale* itself, second edition.[31] Noting (p. v) the other adjectives ("public" and "political") applied to our science, Scialoja obviously prefers *social* economy(ics). The following excerpt (pp. ix-x) from his "Preliminary Discourse on the Nature [etc.] of Economic Science" should explain that terminological preference.

> The society is an organized and living body; constant laws emerging from its very nature consequently remain to regulate its life. The sciences which contain the description of these laws are specifically political and social sciences. Economy, already known as political from

polis (city), *civil* from civitas, or also *national*, and which
I along with many others prefer to call *social*, is as the
base of the cognate sciences. It contains the history of
those *organic manifestations* of the society, which constitute its life of conservation. It seeks the origin, nature,
implication and consequences of the principle nutritive of
social life and reparatory of the forces of the great body
called SOCIETY. It supposes knowing only the organs,
and nothing else; while the other political sciences
suppose more than this knowledge, in addition to the
economic laws.

Could one ask for a clearer, more physiocratic conception of
economia sociale?

H. Eisenhart (1844). Most significant in regard to our present
German exemplar is the fact that Dietzel, in his prominent *Theoretische
Socialökonomik* (1895), equates Eisenhart's title "*System der Volkswirthschaft, oder ökonomische Socialtheorie*" with "the name 'Socialökonomik,' or
'Socialwirthschaftslehre.'"[32] Now, as already explained elsewhere,[33] that
very Germanic Volkswirthschaft or roughly People's-economy is to be
taken as a positive-scientific paradigm, supposedly referring to phenomena
which would spring up spontaneously regardless of political system, etc.--
comparable to Tönnies' Gemeinschaft (versus Gesellschaft), and representing perhaps a more purified/universalistic version of Hegel's "civil
Society" or "bürgerliche Gesellschaft" as abstracting (especially) from any
extant "political State" ("politischer Staat"). The Volkswirthschaft, that is,
is looked upon as a purely natural-social order (organism/mechanism). To
study what it is and how it works is not to pass judgment; if it ails, or
otherwise can be improved, that may be another matter--especially for
Cossa's politica economica.[34]

Albert E. F. Schäffle (1831-1903). Albert Schäffle's *Das gesellschaftliche System der menschlichen Wirtschaft*, or *Social System of Human
Economy*, appeared in its third edition at Tübingen in 1873, which may be
compared with the title of *Die Nationalökonomie* under which the first
edition was published there in 1861. His later work, *Bau und Leben des
Sozialen Körpers* (1875-78), further brings out the physiocratic/Sayian

character of his social economy but with his earlier emphasis on such a "social system of *human* economy."[35]

Eugen K. Dühring (1833-1921). Eugen Dühring seems to have gained his reputation primarily as the able student of the "optimist(s)" List (and Carey) and critical historiographer of economic doctrines. In this latter regard, his name crops up consistently with that of Eisenhart in Cossa's *Introduction*. His principal works are his *Critical History of National Economy and Socialism* (1871-79) and *Course in National and Social Economy* (1873-92). In the former, Rist tells us,

> Dühring . . . has insisted on the fact that protectionism [as advocated by List] is not an essential element, but only a momentary form of the higher principle of national economic solidarity which is the fundamental conception of List, and which must survive protectionism.

As the "only true successor . . . of List and Carey," Rist goes on to add, "he has developed [their ideas] with much talent in a remarkably scientific spirit. Only," the same continues very significantly, "that which he admires in the two writers is not their protectionism, but their effort in going beyond the simple phenomena of exchange to seize the material and moral forces which underlay the prosperity of a country." The key elements the present writer would note here are that "national economic solidarity," "scientific spirit," and "moral and material forces" as characteristic of Dühring's social economy(ics). In the closing breath of the footnote in question, Rist remarks, "He [Dühring] has published a most interesting *Kursus der National und Socialökonomie* (Berlin, 1873)."

Schumpeter's account, which is the most extensive and glowing of the work of Dühring as such, notes the latter's prominence, originality, etc., in such intellectual spheres as "the history of the anti-metaphysical and positivist currents of thought," the "philosophy of life" (D's "'person-alism'"), and "his social philosophy--or system of social reform" which Dühring labeled "'societary.'"

An Italian Finale. We wind up here with an otherwise somewhat motley group whose common nationality is Italian, significant works fall within the present time-frame (1827-76), and social economy(ics) is essentially of the secular-positive variety. Otherwise, that *economia sociale* ranges from (1) the sociological/historiological emphasis(es) of S. Cognetti de Martiis and R. Schiatrella (linked with Schmoller and Knies in Germany), (2) the puristic/rational-scientific accents of De Augustinis, G. G. Reymond, and Antonio Ciccone, combined with (3) the (further) scientific-optimistic/practical-individualistic and "free-trade" bents of the *liberals* Reymond and De Augustinis. A final figure, Fedele Lampertico, we mention chiefly for the "Germanic" title of his work cited (*fn. infra) and for *his* being the mentor of our Guiseppe Toniolo (infra)--as, for example, Reymond here was the foremost disciple of the noted Francesco Ferrara (1810-1900), the *successor* in turn of our Ant. Scialoja (supra).[36]

Conclusion

Dühring has accentuated the call for "national economic solidarity" and recognition of the "moral and material forces" at work beneath the façade of the marketplace. Ciccone has traversed beyond the "natural laws" of pure economics to the normative concerns of economia sociale and practical applications of economic science. We are now set to turn to what might be thought of as the *true era* of social economy(ics) proper, with the continued growth and even mushrooming of all three branches: (1 and 2) the secularly positive and normative; and, especially with the promulgation of the Leonine *Rerum Novarum* of 1891 and men and works leading up to and descending (cascading!) from it, (3) the religious-normative.

PHASE III. -- THE "EXPLOSION" OF SOCIAL ECONOMY(ICS): 1876-1935

We now embark upon much more familiar waters in much better-known vessels. The authors Cossa (now on his own account), Dietzel (similarly), Wieser, Weber, Cassel, and--exactly 200 years after its baptism by du Buat--J. E. Elliott (1973) of the secular-positive strain greet us. In the secular-normative group are found the equally prominent names of Walras, Hobson, Wicksell; whence, the Americans falling just beyond the pale and therefore *not* treated but merely mentioned now, J. M. Clark (1936), O. Lange (1945/46), and H. R. Bowen (1948).[37] Foremost, we come to that most conspicuous, *religious*-normative tradition which, especially by virtue of official sanction, accelerated during this period. In that *official*, Vatican, Papal tradition, it is launched by Leo XIII and that First Great Social Encyclical Letter, *Rerum Novarum: On the Condition of Labor* of 15 May 1891, which is revised "Forty years after" by Pius XI in his almost equally celebrated *Quadragesimo Anno: On Reconstructing the Social Order* of 15 May 1931. Significantly, in these two connections especially will appear the names--"Jesuit" and otherwise--of Toniolo, Antoine, Pesch, Fallon, von Nell-Breuning, Dempsey, and Mulcahy--among others. Now, to our task.

Continuation of the Secular-Positive View

We begin the present section where we terminated the preceding, on the secular-positive note; and, here big names and personages are encountered immediately.

Luigi Cossa (and Son) in Italy (1888-93). The one who strove the mightiest and most diligently (no thanks to a particular translator!) to define and advance this conception of his *economia sociale* was Luigi Cossa (1831-1896). To him, the designation of social economy(ics) should be reserved for the "rational, pure, scientific" form of our discipline. Consistently, he poses that *pure rational science* of social economy(ics) against the *art* (or *applied* science) of economic policy (politics)--i.e., *economia sociale* versus *politica economica*. The two of these combined constitute the complete discipline commonly known as political economy --his *economia politica*, and not *politica economica*, which latter his translater (*Intro.*, 1893) insists on misrendering "political economy."

To Cossa, *social economy(ics)* is not a physical or biological science, nor is it social physiology or otherwise sociology. At the same time, the validity of certain physical- and biological-scientific *analogies*, including the biological or organismic view, is upheld. Social economy qua sociology is rejected on the grounds of the half-baked nature of the latter at the then-present juncture. And, while social economy *is* properly an "ethical (moral) science," because it deals with human beings who are sensate, rational, etc., it is not to be confused or equated with la morale or etica.

To Cossa, furthermore, social economy(ics) is more a deductive than an inductive science, particularly regarding the theory of exchange and distribution. Economic policy (politics), on the other hand, being an art (applied science) associated with legislation, regulation, public administration, and finance, etc., is mainly served by the process of induction.[38]

The Austro-Germanic Group: From Wagner to von Wieser and Cassel. We have already noted how Rau's *Grundsätze der Volkswirthschaft* (1826; '33) has been more recently (*EUI*) rendered into the Spanish as *Principles of Social Economy*; and have suggested that the same might have been done with Carl Menger's even more prominent classic of the same title published at Vienna (Wm. Braumiller) in 1871. For that latter purported to explain the pure principles underlying the behavior of "economizing men" in any society, regardless of political system, etc.--i.e., of the so-called natural economy. Menger, that is, essayed a pure, universalistic, positive-scientific analysis of human or people's economy. In this tradition, after Menger would come Eugen von Böhm-Bawerk and, importantly for our purposes, F. F. von Wieser, whence Max Weber. In Germany, and then in Sweden, we include in this camp as followers or fellow travelers such notables as, first, Adolph Wagner, whence Heinrich Dietzel (and Karl Diehl), and--finally--Gustav Cassel.

We begin with Adolph H. G. Wagner (1835-1917) and his *Grundlegung der politischen Oekonomie* (3d ed., 1892), originally a revision of Rau's *Grundsätze* published (1876) under the title of *Allgemeine oder theoretische Volkswirthschaftslehre*, whence (2d ed., 1879) as an independent work.[39]

In the *Grundlegung* (1892) itself, Wagner addresses the question of "Social Economy [Sozialökonomie] as an Independent Science" (pp. 65ff.) as a followup to his consideration of the other "standpoints" and "approaches," viz. those of "Socialism," "the German historical national-economic," "Katheder-socialism," "State-socialism," and "the new theoretical, especially in Austria" (pp. 37-65). Here, much in the fashion of Cossa, Wagner seems to find social economy a more neutral form generically comprehending all those various ideological and methodological viewpoints than the usual political economy, while indicating its separate existence "als einer *eigenenselbständigen* Wissenschaft" with its own objectives, tasks, and methods. Similarly, while it belongs to the social and political sciences, it is not "eine *Soziologie* oder eine Sozial- oder Gesellschaftswissenschaft in a strict sense" (pp. 65ff.).

What was Wagner's program? Where does he stand vis-à-vis the competing schools and viewpoints or approaches? What is *his* Sozial-ökonomik? Basically what Wagner proposes and promises is a "new ground-laying [a refoundation] of political economy"; or, in a word, the formation of "a genuine Social-economy"--'eine wahre Sozialökonomie' (p. 19). We might say that Wagner attempts to erect from the ruins and remains a new and (shall we say?) transcendent social economics. That is, with *his* "sublation"--involving a (new) "*National-economic* inquiry into the economic legal-order (viz. the whole governing system of private law) and into the *organization of the Volkswirthschaft* (viz. the interrelationship between "private and common economy," paying special attention to the question of "'freedom and property' [as considered from] the Volks-öconomie and social-political [standpoints]") (p. 19)--a new synthesis is formed, with a different "qualitative" outlook on the old "quantities" of production, distribution, etc. "On the basis of these criticisms and investigation," we are told (Walker, p. 19),

> [Wagner] erected what he called a true social economy, giving special attention to three problems, namely: (a) The interrelations and interaction of psychological and purely economic and technical forces, of moral and religious influences and of habit and custom in the formation of human motives and of the motive forces of economic life; (b) the distinction between purely economic and historical-legal points of view, and between absolute, purely economic categories, and those of a variable, historical-legal character; and (c) the distinctions and the relations between the problems of production and those of distribution and the dependence of these problems and of the methods of their correct solution upon different social conditions due to differences in legal relations, in the treatment of personal freedom, in the relations between private and public property contracts, &c. &c.

In all of this, it seems safe to say, Wagner took an extreme middle-of-the-road position and approach, though an expectable leaning toward the social--if not socialistic--on balance can be detected. His respects are duly paid to all schools and viewpoints; his system, accordingly, is highly eclectic. As between the classical and Austrian abstract-theoretical approaches on the one hand, and the historico-institutionalist on the other, by avoiding the excesses of either he found accommodation with both (Walker, p. 260). And, most importantly, we are further informed (p. 260),

> Between the classical economists and the socialists, Wagner [also] steers a middle course. In political economy, everything turns on the relation between the individual and the community. The truth in regard to this relation, he believes, leads neither to socialism nor to individualism, but to a compromise between the two. True science and rational practice he says, will avoid both extremes, but "sie haben doch . . . anzuerkennen dass das Sozial-princip das Vorherrschende ist und sein muss und soll" (*Grundlegung*, 3d ed., p. 23).[40]

Whichever school or viewpoint(s) Wagner veered more toward, it seems obvious here that *his* social economics was essentially of the positive variety, whether it was in search of more fundamental natural-static economic laws or of a better understanding and explanation of human-economic phenomena as they transpire at any particular time and place and/or as they unfold and develop over time and space.

Heinrich Dietzel's *Theoretische Socialoekonomik* (1895) and very explicitly "*theoretical* Social Economics" must be understood within the framework of the collective Wagner-Dietzel-et al. *Lehr- und Handbuch* enterprise noted in footnote 39 and in contrast to Wagner's own "*genuine* Social Economy" just presented. However, Dietzel both chooses the title *Social Economics* for his work (in preference to the originally assigned theoretische Volkswirthschaftslehre) and, carefully distinguishes that conception from those he holds to be conveyed by the more common designations of the day, viz. "Political Economics, National Economics [and] Volkswirthschaftslehre."

Suffice it to say that Dietzel's theoretical social economics is very, very pure--unabashedly puristic, one might say. All of the other conceptions--again, those conveyed by the qualifiers "national," "political," "Volks," or "people's"--are too concrete or reality-laden; and therefore too restricted in their application.[41] But human economy (cf. p. 57) as a social (societal) phenomenon transcends nation-states, polities, and Volks-schaften, whence the theory thereof must be more abstract and universal in nature than the offerings going under those other banners. Thus, abstractly and universally there is "(a) social economy"--"(eine) gesellschaft-liche Wirthschaft"--Dietzel is (in effect) saying; and, its equally pure, universal, and *positive* science is--again--"*theoretische Sozialoekonomik.*"

Dietzel's focus on the highly rarified, universalistic character of the theory of human economy is best brought out in his argument for the superiority of "Social-" over (even) "*Volks*wirthschaft" (pp. 58-59). Unlike, and perhaps actually in objection to, Eisenhart's equation of the two, Dietzel stipulates and explains the distinction as follows:

> Folk economy and social economy are entirely different formations [Gebilde]. There are as many folk economies as there are "lawfully ordered, politically formulated spheres [Kreise] of human life" ([Karl] Knies) [*Das Geld*, 1873ff.]; but social economy, just as the theory presupposes, has no such existence at all. Yet, within and overarching all real folk economies there are also in reality social-economic spheres [socialwirthschaftliche Kreise], drawn and formed by virtue of the economic motive, and extending as far as economic need has woven the commercial web [das *Verkehr*snetz].

Finally, and most subtly in this regard, Dietzel notes that both the "folk" and "social" economy are *organisms*, yet even in this similarity they remain "thoroughly different constructs" (p. 59). He elaborates:

> The individual economies constituting the members of commercial society stand in a relationship of mutual dependency and conditionality. They are joined together by a real, never-seen and ever-changing whole, within which every individual economy lives its particular life, but--intertwined in the "orphic chain" of the economic cycle [Konjunktur], whose waves disregard states and folk economies and reach as far as the social economy stretches at the moment--is continuously influenced by all the changes in the life of the rest, as they in turn influence it in its activity and inactivity.

May we conclude here that no more abstract, pure, positive, universal construct of social economy and conception of social economics can be found than that described by Dietzel in his "Einleitung" of 1895?

The next pair cross the Austro-Germanic boundary, and provides us also with a highly positivistic though more or less pure or narrow conception of social economy(ics). They are Friedrich Freiherr von Wieser (1851-1926), and the renowned German economic sociologist, Max Weber (1864-1920), whose Hauptwerke--for our purposes--first appeared at Tübingen in 1914 and 1922, respectively. We take them up in turn in this chronological order.

Friedrich Wieser, as Menger's successor at Vienna and cofounder --with Böhm-Bawerk (1851-1914)--of the Austrian school of economics, is primarily known to us for his contributions to the marginal utility theory of value and distribution. Here, we are interested in his conception of, and contribution to, *social economics* per se, seen in his *Theorie der gesell-schaftlichen Wirtschaft* which first appeared in 1914.

The second (1924) edition of Wieser's *Theory of Social Economics* was rendered (and, not insignificantly, misrendered) into English and published in this country in 1927, almost exactly a year after the author's death, under the simple title of *Social Economics*. In his "Foreword" to this translation, Wesley C. Mitchell opens with the proposition that "Wieser's *Social Economics* holds a place in the literature of the Austrian School such as John Stuart Mill's *Political Economy* holds in the literature of classical theory" (p. ix). That is, it was the final summation, system-atization, and extension of the work of that founding triumvirate. Yet, Mitchell adds, Wieser's endeavor stands above Mill's in that it was "the first systematic treatise upon economic theory *at large* produced by the Austrian School," whereas Mill's effort had been preceded by other such comprehensive attempts; at the same time, Mitchell peradventures, "Wieser's economic work is also more original than Mill's" (p. ix; emphasis added). To this we add a further difference, that while Mill (et al. until Marshall) clung to the designation political economy of his forebears and their precedents dating back to 1615, von Wieser parts nomenclatural company with his more remote and immediate predecessors (Rau, 1826/'33; Menger, 1871) and replaces the popular indigenous German Volks-wirtschaftslehre with "the Theory of Social Economy."[42]

The task of encapsulating Wieser's *Theorie* and social economics is significantly alleviated by the recent appearance of several significant studies by Ekelund et al.[43] Here, we seek merely to add perhaps another perspective. Basically, which is intended as no surprise, Wieser's theoreti-cal contribution is the rounding out of (the) pure (simple) economy by its social embedment. That is, in addition to the pure or simple economy of the market-system founded on the principle of "utility" or *Nützlichkeit*, Wieser has added the all-important further social force or principle of "power."[44] Utility, law, and power ("right and might"), accordingly, become the organizing and directing principles of the gesellschaftliche Wirtschaft, as revealed and set forth by the *Theorie* thereof, viz. *Social Economics*.[45]

We will now content ourselves here with a brief analysis of the contents of Wieser's *Theory of Social Economics* (1924/'27). The body of the work is divided into four parts, as follows:

I.   Theory of the Simple Economy--beginning with the organic roles of "purpose and power" (Zweck und Kraft) in human economy, whence "the simple natural-economic process"; and, ending with the concept of "economic value" (pp. 17-107/18-146).

II.   Theory of the National Economy (Volkswirtschaft).

III.   Theory of the Public Economy (Staatswirtschaft).

IV.   Theory of the World Economy (International Economics), commencing with the notion of "National Economic Unity" or die Einheit der Volkswirtschaft and ending on the note of "National Economic Solidarity" or Die volkswirtschaftliche Solidarität (pp. 303-21/435-62).

Parts I and II, comprising some 90 percent of the text, constitute the typical introductory (and, of course, mainly micro-) economics textbook of that (interwar) era. Part III is, as its title suggests, and as Musgrave (1959) would later regain, the "Theory of the Public Household," versus the traditional "Public Finance." Finally, we note the inclusion of the modern macro- topic of the balance of payments and that of international economic development in that Book (Part) IV on the "Theory of World-Economy."

We here let Max Weber (1864-1920) and his work in question serve as a footnote and followup to Wieser. If, as Schumpeter claims (*HES*, p. 21n), Weber did more than anyone else to establish the designation social economy(ics) in Germany, it had to be by virtue of that compendious *Grundriss (Outlines) der Sozialoekonomik* which he initiated and edited. His own contribution on *Economy and Society* of 1922,[46] as the title suggests, was one of the more sociological parts of the overall enterprise. With Wieser's own *Wirtschaft und Gesellschaft* formerly partially and now fully available in English dress, we here content ourselves with a selective glance at the contributors and contents of the *Grundriss* or *Outline* itself, to give a better idea of what *Weber* had in mind regarding the nature, scope, etc., of social economics. These include, out of some 56 contributors, the following (and we translate) major divisions and individual contributions: I--Historical and Theoretical Foundations (Pt. I, opp. per Schumpeter et al.; Pt. II, per Wieser), 2d eds., 1924; II--The Natural and Technical Relations (2 pts.), 2d ed., 1923; III--Weber's *Economy and Society*, 1922; IV--Specific Elements of Modern Capitalist Economy (2 pts.), in preparation; V--Goods-Exchange (4 pts.: Trade, Banking, Securities Exchange, Commerce), in preparation; VI--Industry, Mining, and Construction, 2d ed., 1923; VII--Land- and Forest-economic Production Insurance, n.d.; VIII--Foreign Trade Policy, publication undetermined; and, IX--untitled: (Pt. I, The Economic Stratification in Capitalism; Pt. II, The Autonomous and Politically Social Domestic Policy), both in preparation.

Thus, one can readily find in this enterprise that social economics is covered, it seems, from its most social-theoretical to its most applied- and practical-economic.

Finally, there is no better way to wrap up the present Austro-Germanic viewpoint and group than with the Swede Gustav Cassel (1866-1945). Thus, in the "Preface to the First Edition" of his *Theoretische Sozialoekonomie*, we read in a later (1932) English translation,[47] Cassel had informed:

> I call this work *The Theory of Social Economy*. The meaning of this is that I intend to treat the economic relations of a whole social body as far as possible irrespective of its extension, its organisation, its laws of property, etc. The ultimate aim of economic science must be to discover those necessities which are of a purely economic nature and which cannot be arbitrarily mastered by the will of men.

It is in this manner that Cassel stipulates the "positive" character of *his* "Theoretical Social Economy," while at the same time issuing his own *prescriptive* statement regarding the "normative" applications of such "pure" economic science, to wit:

> An intimate knowledge of these necessities is the first condition for Social Reformers being ever able to produce something more than cheap speculations on the economic organisation of the future or costly disturbances of the very delicate machinery of present economic life.

His own effort, thus, is of a purely positive character, to serve as the proper basis for normative assessments and policy-engineered economic change.

A. S. Johnson (1922):   A Solitary U.S. Example?   Alvin S. Johnson's *Introduction to Economics* is perhaps singular in espousing the present conception of social economics in this country during the period in question.   There, at the end of his first chapter devoted to "The Nature of Economic Science,"[48] we find the following summation:

> The key to an understanding of the existing commodity system is to be found in the laws governing the prices of commodities and services.   The prices of goods are for the most part beyond the control of individuals; they may be said to be determined by society as a whole. The laws of price are therefore properly described as social laws; and the body of thought dealing with these laws is known as social economics.

We could go on to note the apparent if not obvious influences of Say (*Cours complet*, 1928), the historical school, and even J. S. Mill and Walras, and perhaps especially Marx on the author's thought in regard to (among other things) economics as properly a "practical 'social' science," the dynamic nature and historical relativity of economic life (p. 14), market-exchange (Marx's commodity-production) and the "formation of classes based upon economic function" as "the fundamental characteristic of the modern economic system" and "natural result of the modern conditions of production" (pp. 15, 19), respectively.   With these considerations surrounding the author's further focus on the rule of competition under restraint of monopoly in the marketplace (pp. 17-18), he arrives at his proposition (#19) that "the laws of price are the governing principle in modern economic life"; whence, his initial finding that, since "almost all prices . . . are set by society, . . . the laws of price are properly called *the laws of social economics, or of political economy*" (p. 21; our emphasis).

The Neoclassical (et al.) Secular-Normative View

Here, as indicated earlier, social economy(ics) comes veritably into its own. It is the French variety, inaugurated by Sismondi, and now to be reinaugurated by Walras. Essentially, in the Anglo-American sphere, it is the "welfare economics" initiated by A. C. Pigou, converted into perhaps broader scope and christened "social economics" in this country by J. M. Clark, and so recognized by both a respected economist and prominent English-language lexicon in the mid-1940s.[49]   Thus did Oskar Lange, in his noted "Scope and Method" article (1945), having distinguished "Economics [as] a *social science*," differentiated it from "*economic sociology*," and delineated the turf of "*theoretical economics* or *economic theory*" (whose object is "*economic laws*") and "*applied economics*" ("economic history . . . and institutional economics," largely), which all deal--one way or another--with empirical reality(ies), arrive at a special "branch of economic science" which, in a way, brings all the former (positive) forms to bear on the socially *ideal*. The *norms* ("social objectives" and "rules for their attainment) being given, the 'ideal' use . . . of scarce resources" is then determined, in this view.   Then, Lange notes,

> The use of resources empirically observed may be compared with the "ideal" use and measures may be recommended to bring the actual use into closer correspondence with the "ideal" one.   This provides the subject-matter for another branch of economic science, usually called *welfare economics* (also normative economics or social economics).[50]

There, we have Lange's version: social economics = normative or welfare economics, theoretical and applied, analysis and policy--as well as a branch of economic science.

We now turn to Walras and commence our review of the members of this school.

Marie Esprit Léon Walras (1834-1910).   In his 1890 lecture on "The School of LePlay," Claudio Jannet alludes (*Quatre Écoles*, p. 22) to "the eminent professor of Lausanne . . . whose *Éléments d'Économie politique pure* are universally known and appreciated today." It was this same Léon Walras, we know, who took the Tableau Économique of

Quesnay, rough-hewn, biologico-arithmetic analogue that it was, and transformed it into the physico-mathematical construct of his "General-Equilibrium System," Newtonian-mathematical analogue that it was. Yet this celebrated and unfortunately confining opus of the founder of the Lausanne school came midway in a career beginning (for our purposes) in 1860 and culminating (likewise) in 1898. The *Éléments* (1874 sqq.), if one wants to make them so, *are* the "pure, unadulterated Walras." But, they are anything but the exclusive and complete Walras, and are certainly not his own last word on *his* "system." For us, "the essential Walras" is the one depicted in the following account.

(1)   Much as the religious-normative social economics, to be considered later, took the essential form of Christian political economy, Walras' initial (secular-normative) effort is entitled *L'Économie politique et la Justice*, and is billed further as a "Critical Examination and Refutation of the Economic Doctrines of M. P.-J. Proudhon, preceded by an Introduction to the Social Question." It was published at Paris in 1860; where, at the College of France, we are further informed, our author was exposed to a professor "who treated generally of the principles of political economy put in relation to morals in that which concerns poverty" (p. I).

This, of course, is exactly the social question that was concurrently being addressed, not only by the poor, beseiged--from both sides!--Proudhon and others, but by what came to be called social Christianity (Catholicisme) as well. From a more purely "economic" viewpoint, it was the question of *repartition* or *distribution*. This was, indeed, a *social* issue. For, as none less than J. S. Mill had recognized (1848 sqq.) "the Distribution of Wealth . . . is a matter of human institution solely," much as the principles regarding the *production* thereof might "partake of the character of physical truths"; and, foremost among those distributive institutions was "property."[51] That point, and the nature, object, etc., of social economy-(ics) is originally spelled out in Walras' *Éléments pure*, which made its debut at Paris and Lausanne in 1874.

In the *Éléments* specific distinctions are made and maintained between the several component disciplines of Walras' *system* of "Political and Social Economy." First, there are those "pure elements" regarding the production and exchange of wealth under a hypothetical regime of free competition, economics qua a physico-mathematical science. Second, there is l'Économie politique appliquée, the theory of the economic production of wealth in reality. Third, there is l'Économie sociale, to which we now turn.

The *Éléments* of Walras' social economy(ics) constitute the "theory of the distribution of wealth via property and taxation." And, since property is predicated on appropriation, and such acquisition is essentially a moral phenomenon, "the theory of property is essentially *une science morale.*" The author continues:

> Justice consists in rendering to each one that which is his due; and, if ever a science, by consequence, has had justice for a principle, it is assuredly that of the distribution (*repartition*) of social wealth, or, as we call it, *l'économie sociale* [*Éléments* (1874), pp. 42f.; emphasis added].

Social economy is further distinguished from the "theory of industry" as an "applied science." The latter "fixes and determines the relations among men considered as workers devoted to particular occupations, with a view toward the multiplication and the transformation of social wealth, or the conditions of an abundant production of social wealth among men in society. In contrast, the theory of property fixes and determines the relations of men considered *as moral persons* among themselves with regard to the appropriation of social wealth, or the conditions of an equitable distribution (repartition) of social wealth among men in society" (*Éléments*, p. 43).

(2) In lieu of his originally planned "Éléments," likewise, of "Applied Political Economy" and "Social Economy," Walras left us his *Études* or *Studies* thereof, appearing in 1898 and 1896, respectively. The *Études d'Économie sociale*, a collection of "works, memoirs and articles" published, and presented, over the period 1860-96, are regarded by the author as "sufficiently developed indications of the most important points . . . of an economico-social doctrine which [he] taught from 1870-1892 at Lausanne."[52]

The constituent essays or studies are organized under the four basic topics of "I. Inquiry into the Social Ideal," "II. Property," "III. Realization of the Social Ideal," and "IV. Taxation." The concluding section of that last part (IV) is entitled "France and the Social Question," under which such issues as the nationalization of land, collectivism versus liberalism, etc., are addressed. At the end (p. 462), Walras calls on the youth of his day "to uproot political economy and social science from the abject and miserable condition of servants entirely of bourgeois conservatism and financial feudalism."

(3) In concluding his lesson on "the Theory of the Distribution of Wealth, or Social Economy" in the *Éléments* (1864-1925/'51), Walras raises the "question of the relation of morals and political economy," or "of ethics to economics" (Jaffé, 1954). There, he notes two opposing viewpoints. The first is that of his earlier target, Proudhon. In his *Economic Contradictions* of 1847, says Walras, Proudhon "upheld a contradiction [*antinome*] between justice and (individual, private) interest." The second was that of the unflagging optimist, Fr. Bastiat, who, "in his *Harmonies économiques*, sustained the opposite." Neither, Walras thought, effectually substantiated his position. With this, Walras drops his brief with Proudhon, promising to resume and defend Bastiat's thesis in a different manner subsequently.

(4) Now, we can recognize Walras' social economics as of the secular-normative or moral-scientific liberal, reformist, interventionist variety. In this *secular* vein, he served to establish social economics as "*the* Theory of the Distribution of Wealth," qua science morale (1874, p. 39). With pure and applied economic theory serving the maximal production and optimal exchange of wealth, *l'Économie sociale*--via the instrumentalities of property and taxation--would serve a just and equitable distribution thereof.

We are now also able to glean from this respected authority the meaning of moral in a (then) contemporary prominent reference-work account of "Économie sociale" (*GDU*, VII [1870], p. 133). Namely, it means moral in the *philosophical* or secular sense, much as Adam Smith and J. S. Mill were moral and social philosophers. Moral and social *philosophy*, that is, as opposed to *theology* as the hallmark of our social Christianity (Catholicisme) presented in section III.C.

Two American Exemplars: Denslow (1888) and Gunton (1887-1900). In his *Principles of the Economic Philosophy of Society, Government and Industry* (1887-97), V. B. Denslow (1834-1902) notes (p. 1) that "the term Political Economy has been applied indifferently to the science, the philosophy and the art of economy, whether as practiced by individuals, by society, or by the state." By the author's sights (p. 1),

> Political Economy treats of the duties of Government to the people as respects their social well-being, and

of the natural laws, principles and truths which apply to
society as an organization that subsists by material means,
growing if they are supplied and dying if they are withheld.

To justify this definition, Denslow cites (p. 1n) Aristotle (actually
pseudo-Aristotle, *Oeconomica*, Bk. I), and goes on to show that political
economy is both a science and an art. In the former regard, for example,
it provides Comte's "sociology [with] its first principles"; while, as an art,
it has "the practical aim of [enabling] its students to judge or predict . . .
the consequences which will ensue to the material welfare of the people
from certain courses of governmental or social action" (pp. 7-8). This art,
then, is properly regarded as "economic statesmanship" (p. 8), and may at
least be roughly equated with Cossa's Politica economica, for example.

In the ensuing discussion (pp. 9-19) the author undertakes a
critique of "the metaphysical [alias laissez faire] school of economists, then
notes the decline of the latter and the ascendency of the 'Historical
Method,'" and, finally, the "Relations of Economics to Ethics." Here, it
seems, the term social economy--which now appears for the first time--is
used in the sense of "the economic life of society." Thus we are told, for
instance, of the "difficulty [which] arises in the effort to compare our
[politicoeconomic] life with [that] life in the middle ages, in which the
church ruled, or with any other unlike *form of social economy*" (p. 20; our
italics).

Next, in terms of the economics-ethics connection, we are first
informed that

> there is still a very large following for those who discuss
> questions of *social economy* from the *ethical standpoint*,
> i.e., who assume that it is much easier to know and to do
> what is right, than to find out what is profitable to society
> in the utilitarian sense (p. 22; our italics).

In between these two appearances, the author introduces the
question of interpersonal obligations, the respective duties of the social
classes, etc. (pp. 20-21). Here, shall we say, "principles of *social economy*"
are suggested to the effects (positively-normatively) that, (1) in the
economic progress of society, as individuals' ability to fend for themselves
advances, "moral obligations to provide for others contract as [such]
economic competency is diffused"; whence, (2) one can conclude with

Professor Sumner that "the social classes owe each other nothing"; and, thusly (3) a new extension of "the *laissez faire* doctrine" emerges, viz. "'Not merely should the state let the social classes alone, but the social classes should let each other alone.'" But, the author retorts, "human nature rebels against this utter excision of moral obligations from social economy"; rather, somewhere between that "ultra-*laissez faire* view" and "the opposite theory that the state should be everybody's guardian in all things," lies the appropriate compromise.

In resolving this question of the proper role of the state in human society, Denslow notes, arguments will come from both the moral and economic standpoints. Either way, given that "society [is] an organism," sometimes healthy and diseased at others, with "health in some parts and disease in others," we are confronted here with the "peculiarity that 'in the diseases of the body politic the physicians and nurses are themselves parts of the diseased organism'" (p. 21). To the author, this is the pressing question and essential problem of social economy, in both its positive aspects of what the true realities and tendencies are and its normative dimension of the nature and extent of the constituent moral obligations.[53]

Contemporaneously and somewhat more prominently in the United States, George Gunton (1845-1919) published first his *Principles of Social Economics Inductively Considered and Practically Applied* (1891), followed in due course by the *Outlines of Social Economics* (1900) co-authored with Hayes Robbins. Gunton is billed there as--among other things--author of *Wealth and Progress* (1887) and *Trusts and the Public Interest* (1899); Robbins, as "Dean of the Institute of Social Economics."[54] Guided by our criterion of social economics being that which one who professes to be doing it *by name* does, Gunton must certainly be counted among our leading exemplars of this period, and--as well--as somewhat unique and otherwise worthy of special note in any history of economics.

In the *Principles* Gunton distinguishes his system from the pack in the following terms. "Instead of a system of *'commodity'* economics which justifies human degradation as a means of cheapening wealth," he informs (p. x), "we have a system of *social* economics, which shows that the most effective means of promoting the industrial welfare of society on a strictly equitable basis, must be sought in influences which elevate the social life and character of the masses." In the later *Outlines*, we are further informed (pp. 1-2), the subject matter of what now must be regarded as modern social economics stretches way beyond the bounds of the original political economy of the pre-nineteenth century, "and now includes not merely the economy in public revenues, but the economy of the production and distribution of wealth, and, finally, everything which affects the industrial and social welfare of the community." "Social economics," the author(s) notes, "includes all questions which affect the industrial and social welfare of the people." Finally, "the welfare of the people [being] the point of view from which all industrial and social problems should be decided," the authors go "one step farther" (p. 3) in stipulating that

> the welfare of the public is best reflected in the welfare of
> the great wage-earning class, and their welfare is indicated
> by in general the amount of wealth and comfort and
> advantages of higher civilization that can be obtained for
> a day's work.

Whence, "Wealth of itself is of no account unless it is consumed and broadens the civilization and happiness of the community" (p. 3). Certainly our two pioneering Catholic-social or Christian-political economists (de Coux and Villeneuve-Bargemont), along with the early Fathers and later Doctors of the Church, not to mention Sismondi, Proudhon, and that ilk, would heartily concur in that final statement.

As an economist proper, Gunton would be most acclaimed for his low-wage/underconsumptionist theory of economic overproduction and stagnation; whence, by corollary, his high-wage/full-consumption prescription for sustained economic progress. This central theme is introduced early on in his *Wealth and Progress*, with the title of Chapter II actually constituting the working hypothesis: "Increased Consumption by the Masses the Real Cause of Improved Machinery." That is, given "improved machinery" as the efficient cause of labor productivity, the author holds, it is not a high propensity to save but rather a high propensity to consume which--via the induced-investment principle--promotes this cause; and, in turn, the higher the earnings of labor and the more leisure time they have for spending them, the higher that overall propensity to consume, and so on. The reader will quickly note, no doubt, the very Keynesian nature of this argument; and, perhaps, recall also Keynes' argument for a more equal distribution of national income on grounds of economic efficiency (i.e., full employment) as well as social justice.

J. A. Hobson (1914/33). In his *Work and Wealth* (1914 sq.),[55]
John Atkinson Hobson (1858-1940) finds orthodox political economy and
economic science sorely lacking in terms of any meaningful normative
content. It could measure material wealth with its money yardstick and
system of market-values at any given time; it could estimate real national
income, and even quantify its distribution. But, given the organic nature
of human society, it provided no concept, measure, or operational means
insofar as the corresponding "'organic welfare'" was concerned. Truly
human economy, individual and *organically* social, had to be achieved and
conducted as an art, he held. The same was "rational economy" (Aristotle
would have said "prudential *techne*"), and needed a "science" thereof, for
which the designation "social-economics" was suggested. Here (pp. 9-10),
the author quotes Ruskin's "famous declaration that 'There is no wealth
but life,'" and notes "the truly scientific service rendered by Ruskin towards
the foundation of social economics."

Throughout, the author's emphasis is on "human economy" (e.g.,
pp. 37, 80, 105, 107, 164, and 219), "human utility" (disutility) and "human
cost," individual and social, and as opposed to (more narrowly construed,
or 'strictly') "economic" utility/cost, enjoyed and suffered in consumption
and production, simultaneously in a full-fledged, integrated and "organic"
general-equilibrium or total-system analysis. Again, that organic connection, especially, between individual and social economy within this system
of human economy is focal (e.g., p. 27). Our concern, of course, is with
the author's conception and practice of social economy, which continues
to be exhibited throughout the work. Two connections only shall we
single out in this regard. The first is that very crucial Chapter XII on
"The Human Law of Distribution" (pp. 159-89). There we are informed
(pp. 163-64), for example, that this law involves merely the distribution of
Wealth, vis-à-vis its production and consumption, so as to maximize the
difference between the related human costs and human utility. In this
context, we are further instructed, for instance, that it is a "human
economy" to impose saving for investment in "socially necessary capital" on
the upper income groups, whose human sacrifice or cost would be zero or
minimal; and, also, for example, that "true social economy [requires of
labour and capital] that each should contribute in accordance with its
ability." Later in this same connection (pp. 166-167) it is noted that "a
society based in sound social economy" will secure equality of opportunity
of (i.e., remove all artificial barriers to) entry into all occupations and
professions in order to eliminate and prevent scarcities "which have no
natural basis" (pp. 166-167). Here, especially, Hobson refers to "the dif-

ference between the salary [alias "'the economy of high wages'"] versus the 'commodity' view of labour" on the part of employers and others, a distinction which seems to relate to Gunton's (supra) distinction between "*social* economics," which seeks to promote aggregate material well-being via the "elevation" of the working class, versus the "'*commodity*' economics," which "justifies human degradation" as the necessary cost of "the industrial welfare of society" (as we noted). Finally, in this regard, we are instructed (pp. 168-170) how "the organic law of distribution in regarding needs will . . . take as full an account as it can both of the unity and the diversity of human nature." Among other things, this same law would involve the minimization, if not total elimination, of "individual 'rents'" (p. 169). The residual existence of such (factor) rents, in turn, would mean that "the selfishness of individual man [versus 'the altruism of social man' (?)] might give a slight twist to the application of the social policy of distribution according to needs, [but] would not impair its substantial validity and practicability" (p. 170). Significantly, the conclusion is then reached in this regard that

> this law of distribution, operative as a purely physical economy in the apportionment of energy for mechanical work, operative as a biological economy through the whole range of organic life, is strictly applicable as a principle of social economy. Its proper application to social industry would enable that system to function economically, so as to produce the maximum of human utility with the minimum of human cost.

Here, then, we have--it seems--all the several humanly relevant forms of economy(ics): the physical-mechanical, the biological-organic, and the simply *social*. Here, perhaps, we also note a certain triangularization, if one wants, a triangular interface, of and between the Walrasian "pure," physiocratic "organic," and Walrasian (et al.) "social" forms or constructions of human economy.

Fetter (1915-25), Carver (1919), Chapin (1917), and Jones (1920). Somewhat less illustrious than Hobson, there follow in the Anglo-American strain, if indeed one exists, the several authors and their respective pronouncements on social economy(ics) presented now. The first two of these treat of social versus or vis-à-vis political (etc.) economy or economics in general; the second two, of social economy(ics) proper. All fall into the narrow temporal confines of this decadal period, capped off merely by Fetter's sixth reprinting. Thus, in his popular *Economic Principles*,[56] Frank A. Fetter (1863-1949) draws the distinction (Vol. I, pp. 512-513) between "Business Economy and Social Economy" in the following manner:

> Not without reason it has been made a reproach to economic writers that they often have confounded business incomes (and especially those of a limited, influential, class in society) with general social welfare, and have identified individual acquisition with social production. Business economy has been mistaken for *true political economy*, commercial profits for social welfare. The right understanding of *the nature of value and capital* makes possible a clearer distinction between *business economy and social economy*. Men can not to-day, in view of the truths set forth above, cherish the error that 'whatever is, is right' in the distribution of incomes. . . . We must recognize further that the law of value is not necessarily the law of justice, that the incomes resulting from values in the world as it is do not always meet an ethical test (our emphases).

Four years after Fetter's first edition appeared that of the *Principles of Political Economy* by Thomas Nixon Carver (1864-1961).[57] Economy and economics occur and pertain to both the "private" and "public" levels or spheres, this work commences (p. 2). Whence, "public economics" or "political economy," in its turn, divides into "(public) finance" and "Social Economy." The former consists in the "management of the income and expenditure of the government"; the latter, in "promoting the general social well-being," and thus with "getting [and] utilizing social income" (P. 2). Subsequently (p. 8), under "Social well-being," in terminology reminiscent of the tripartite French model of Économie: privé/public/sociale, we are informed of a "branch of public economics which is broader than public finance," and transcends that of the individual family. Again, "this branch . . . deals with the general problem of *social wealth or well-being*," whence "with the income and expenditure of *the people as a whole*. This is called *social economy* or *social economics*," the author restates (our emphasis). And, while a knowledge of both "public finance and private economics" has its obvious value, it is that social

economics which constitutes "the most important study for the *real* states-
man or nation builder," which "in a democracy" means everyone (p. 8, our
emphasis).

Thus, from these two Americans, we get a sort of micro- and
macro-normative conception of social economy(ics), respectively; in the
next two examplars, one American and the other British, we obtain two
other and slightly different perspectives of social economy(ics) proper.
These are, respectively, F. Stuart Chapin's *Historical Introduction to Social
Economy* and Harry Jones' simply *Social Economics*. Chapin is given as
a professor of sociology and economics at the time of his publication;
Jones, as a "lecturer in Social Economics in the University of Glasgow"
when his work was being prepared.[58] If we take Chapin's historical essay
first, we find his use of the title "social economy" in a positivistic sense to
be generic enough to embrace modes or stages of development of human
economy not aptly embraced by the more popular descriptive of "political
economy," though we are left to infer this.   At the same time, the
fundamental normative thrust is clearly indicated by the author when he
describes his work (p. vii) as an introductory history jointly of "social
development [and] the evolution of industry," consisting "of a series of
brief essays on the contrasting types of industrial organization which have
existed at different historical periods, and an account of *the private and
public efforts made to relieve the poverty of each period*" (our emphasis).[59]

Jones' work, on the other hand, is rather similar in character, but
with a more applied-contemporary inclination.   That is, it is more along
the specific lines of a study in modern industrial organization cum a
normative, industrial-welfare sociological dimension.   It is described by its
author as "a brief survey of the most important and urgent problems of
[post-war] economic reorganisation" whose brevity, further, is offered in
"apology for [among other things] the absence of any attempt to justify the
choice of title" (p. vii).   And, by way of further explication, he continues,

> I have endeavoured to emphasize the interrelationships
> of individual economic and social problems in such a way
> as to bring out the central economic problem, which may
> be crudely described as *the reconciliation of individual
> ambition and social welfare* (pp. vii-viii; our emphasis).

This author's secular-solidaristic brand of social economics
becomes eminently clear when he opens his book as follows:

The organisation of economic society is based upon co-operation. Co-operation is anterior to and more fundamental than competition. Competition is not the negation of co-operation; it is the form of expression which the co-operative principle assumes at a certain state of economic development.[60]

With these shades of Rousseau, Marx, and even Hobson, we conclude this social economists' social economics.

Wicksell, Gide, and Amadeo (1911-37). In the "Introduction" to his *Lectures on Political (National) Economy*,[61] Knut Wicksell (1851-1926) addresses "the division of the subject" (p. 5). That "which first suggests itself"--he begins--"is into 'theoretical' and 'practical' political economy--economics in the narrow sense and national economic policy." The latter, he further notes, is properly subdivided "into two parts: [1] an application of the theory *founded on existing conditions*, and [2] a *critical examination* of the *foundation* itself."

Following further elaboration, the author concludes preliminarily, "We thus arrive at the following division of our subject":

(1) *A theoretical part* (pure, general or theoretical economics), comprising a statement of economic laws [etc. which must] necessarily proceed from certain *simplifying assumptions*.

(2) *A practical part* (applied economics, particular problems of the consumption, distribution and production of goods) comprising the application of these laws to various fields . . . in the *concrete economic life of society*.

(3) *A social part* (social economics or economic policy), comprising an investigation into the question how these economic laws and practical precepts should properly be applied in order to obtain *the greatest possible social gain*, and what changes in the existing economic and legal structure of society are necessary to this end.[62]

Wicksell himself notes that "this division of the subject accords with that used by Walras in his *Éléments [etc.]*, though it is not always based on the same reasons."

In the later (1921-26, for example) editions of his prominent *Principes d'Économie politique*, Charles Gide (1847-1932) had come to make a similar three-way division of his subject.[63] First, recognizing "Economic Science" as that one among "*the social sciences*" which, while focusing on the "same social man," "has as its [special] object only those relations among men living in society which tend to the satisfaction of their needs, to their well-being, to the extent which that well-being depends on the possession of material objects" (pp. 1-2), Gide goes on to elaborate as follows (pp. 2-3):

> On the one hand, *pure* political Economy (which is also called *Economics*) studies the economic relations which are formed spontaneously among men living in society, as one would study the relations which are formed within any body whatsoever. It does not propose to judge them, either from a moral or practical point of view, but only *to explain that which is*. Thus, it proclaims itself to be constituted as an exact science and even claims to be able to employ the mathematical method.
>
> On the other hand, *social Economy* studies rather the voluntary relations which men create among themselves--under the form of association, of legislation or institutions whichever--with a view toward ameliorating their condition. It proposes to investigate and assess the best means for attaining that end. Thus, it partakes rather of the character of the moral sciences in investigating *that which should be*, and of the character of the arts in investigating *what needs to be done*. Accordingly, it is designated sometimes, above all by the German economists, under the name of "social Politics" [*Politique sociale*].

Having thusly distinguished and delineated these two subdisciplines of Économie politique, Gide hastens to drop a footnote at that last point (1926, p. 3n; 1924, p. 2n), stressing that "Social Economy or social Politics is not to be confused with *applied* political Economy." The latter, he notes, "indicates the best practical means of increasing the wealth of a nation, such as banks, railways, monetary or commercial system, etc.--while social Economy seeks above all to render men happier, in their procuring not only more comfort, but more security, more independence and more leisure; and, consequently, is concerned especially with the working class." Indeed, the author concludes, "these two (and we interject 'Walrasian') sisters," l'Économie politique *appliquée* and l'Économie ou Politique *sociale*, "live in two different and hardly sympathizing worlds: the one in the world of affairs and the other in the committees of social reform." Thus, Gide would beg to differ somewhat with Wicksell and those who follow him in equating what we might call the normative or moral science and advocative art of "l'Économie (et Politique) *sociale*" with what amounts to the applied science and art of economic policy and govern-ment--viz. Cossa's Politica economica, as we have seen.

We conclude here with a follower in Gide's conception of social economy(ics). Romulo Amadeo, in his *Political and Social Economy* (2d ed., 1937),[64] while following very closely the Walrasian definition of "pure economy(ics)" (p. 11), holds to an almost Thomistic or "social-Catholic" view of the parent discipline itself. As opposed to the earlier tendency to use "social" and "political" interchangeably,[65] the author informs that while political economy has been primarily concerned with "the organization of the solely material elements and with the production of wealth of a given country," social economy has to do with "the organization of all the elements of the society"; accordingly, it is broader than political economy, to the point of being "confused with Sociology" (p. 13). Thus, while this author next notes both the Walrasian and Gidean narrower focuses of social economy(ics)--qua that part of political economy concerned with distribution, the diminution of social injustices, and the betterment of the working classes; whence, with the voluntary arrangements which men establish for these purposes--his conception is at once more generic as equally normative.[66]

Religious-Normative View: Social Christianity/Catholicism from Apple to v. Nell-Breuning

Here at the very outset (Apple, 1887) we will encounter a degree of Christian solidarity--an ecumenical spirit and oneness of mind--totally unsuspected at least by the present writer. At the same time, the reader is apprised that no attempt is made here to include other, non-Christian conceptions or formulations of social economy(ics); while, even within the

Christian sphere or orbit, attention is further focused on Social Catholicism. We trust most readers will agree that, under the circumstances,
such delimitation is legitimate.

What the Roman Catholic Church regards as the "Great Social
Encyclical," Pope Leo XIII's *Rerum Novarum: On the Condition of Labor*,
was issued on 15 May 1891. However, while this may have marked the
beginning of *official* Social Catholicism in its modern phase, this move-
ment--qua Catholic social economics, Christian political economy, etc.--
began in a de facto sense over a half-century earlier. Men, professedly or
otherwise Catholic (Christian), could only vent their moral concern--if not
outright indignation--over the extent to which Adam Smith's "great body
of the people, the labouring poor" had been immiserated by the very
system he and his followers otherwise espoused and defended. Labor, as
Marx put it, had been ground down under "the juggernaut of capital."

It was this existential situation, Leo XIII would note, that literally
cried out for attention and redress. But it was more than that he hastens
to add (cf. *RN*, ##1-3).[67] Antithetical ideological responses of earlier
vintage (Sismondi and Proudhon, LaSalle, Marx) had seized the moral- as
well as positive-scientific initiative, and had advanced a new ideological
thesis, against which the Church would rise up as primary antithesis.
Significantly, until Leo XIII and *Rerum Novarum*, official Church silence
had not been broken. The multifaceted concern which had been exhibited
on the part, especially, of Catholic social thinkers and activists bore no
obvious or recognized authority, whence the moral issue was less clear.

Thus, in this category of our subject and stage of its history, this
"First Great (or 'Silence-Breaking') Social Encyclical," together with its
"revised edition" in the form of Pius XI's *Quadregesimo Anno: On Reconstructing the Social Order* which appeared exactly "Forty years (later)" on
15 May 1931, are pivotal. They stand, respectively, as (1) the solid
launching pad of official Social Catholicism a decade and a half or
quarter-way into our period, and (2) a "booster stage" a half-decade from
its forward terminus of 1936. The transitional figure would be Pius XII
(1939-58), whose official pronouncements on l'économie sociale represented both the final restatement of traditional Social Catholicism to that
point and the platform from which would be launched the new wave
thereof with John XXIII, Vatican II, Paul VI, etc.[68]

But all that falls way beyond the temporal scope of our study;
and, maintaining both our basic chronological ordering and at least initial
spirit of ecumenism, we shall now commence with a Protestant-Christian

view (brand) of social economy(ics); and, at that, one so forceful that it even comes to smack of a religious-*positive* stance!

Th. G. Apple, DD., LL.D. (1887). By the present writer's sights, no more representative example of Christian (and even Roman-Catholic!) solidarism can be found than Thos. G. Apple's "The Ethical Constitution of Social Economy," which appeared in the *Reformed Quarterly Review* in 1887.[69] Positive-scientifically, the author espouses an organismic conception of human society and social economy which is as physiocratic-Sayian-etc. as one might hope to find in such abstract form and brief scope; moral-theologically, this organic social economy is held to be ordained by God, of divine creation and authorship, and--apart from special modifications and adaptations--humanly immutable in its essential form. Thus, referring to the developmental dialectic of individuation-collectivization, separation-combination, differentiation-integration, etc., holding throughout the divinely ordained natural order, the author observes (p. 21; our emphasis):

> Looking now at human existance, we find the same general law referred to in the constitution of *the social economy*. Humanity is *an organic unity* which unfolds itself through subordinate organisms, such as race, nation, family, and reaching its final individuation in individuals, or single personalities. The *right study* of this economy [we christen "Christian social economics"] must begin with the study of these two factors in their antithetic and reciprocal relation, the *general life* and the *individual life*; and the progress of civilization must be determined by the degree in which these two factors advance in right relation to one another. The *social economy of the world* crystallizes, or rather organizes, itself by the mutual operation of these two laws, and its progress is graduated by the degree in which these two factors advance in actualizing the full meaning of all that is originally contained in the idea of humanity.

Pivotally, echoing Le Play contra Rousseau et al., our Doctor of Divinity will note that in the societal hierarchy "the idea of the state [like that of the family and other collectivities] has its origin, not in any

external social compact, . . . but in this innate or inherent mutual relationship between . . . the generic and the individual life of man" (p. 22).
Whence, the author continues, proceeding from "the archetype of the
world" via Adam, the family, state, and race,

> we reach, in the social economy, a complex organism in
> which individual men are embraced, and by which they
> attain their growth and perfection [*n.b.* Man, the Social
> Animal]. The organization of the social economy, then,
> is divinely ordained in the constitution of humanity, just
> as really and truly as the individual person is created from
> the same divine source. Within certain limits man may
> determine the particular form of this social economy, but
> in its fundamental constitution it is just as truly deter-
> mined and ordained of God as the solar system, with its
> planets revolving around their sun.

In the midst of such positive supernaturalistic determinism, one
may wonder where is there any room for the voluntarism required of any
moral activity and normative science thereof? But, however that may be,
our unswerving author here is certain of one thing, that one way or
another Christianity holds the key to *the social problem*. For, "it is really
only in the nations of Christendom that the rights of man, as man, have
come to be regarded as sacred, . . . only there that man's personality is set
forth as an end in itself" (p. 23). But, he continues (p. 24),

> the social problem has to do not only with the rights of
> the individual. If we regard humanity as an organism, we
> must find another law, according to which the individual
> is attracted to the social order in which his life must find
> its completion. This law of attraction grows out of his
> social nature, . . . It is this social relation [into which
> "every one is born"] that he is drawn out of his narrow
> egoity, . . . If we consider the true nature of marriage, we
> shall find that its deepest moral and spiritual significance
> lies in that . . . communion of being by which the selfish
> principle is broken in upon and the unselfish principle has
> scope for its exercise. The same principle operates in the
> unselfish devotion of parent to child. . . . The family
> widens into the State, where . . . room is made for love

of country--patriotism--which is still farther removed from
the egoism of . . . individual life.

Again echoing such of our earlier social economists as Le Play
and Chateaubriand ("Économie sociale," *GDU*) on the fundamental role
of marriage, parenthood, and the family in human society, our author
proceeds to the level of the state. Thus, as if to complete the program of
de Coux, Apple reminds that this otherwise sovereign institution itself "is
only an integral function in a still broader organism--the race." He
explains (pp. 24f., our emphasis):

Man's social nature cannot complete itself until it feels
the throbbings of that humanity which comprehends *the
whole brotherhood of man*, in the bosom of which the
highest of all inspirations of *his social nature* become
realized in philanthropy. In this sphere we have such
universal interests as science and art, which know no
national limitations, but bring all men into *one common
brotherhood*.

Thus, in the language of the Roman encyclicals, the state itself is an
intermediary structure, subsidiary to the universal family of humankind;
and, there yet (but cf. Jno. XXIII, *PT*, 1963) being no such universal
political authority, the Church thus fills that void.

Next, the author cites (pp. 25-26) the generally accepted remedies
which Christianity had provided in earlier times for returning the health
of the social body: (1) setting "forth the true basis for the institution of
the family by restoring the relation of marriage to its original character";
(2) resting "the parental authority . . . in God, giving the parent, not
absolute, but delegated, control over the child"; and, similarly, (3) asserting
"the divine authority of the State, [distinguishing] here also between the
ultimate and the relative authority." Again, this is surely a program to
which no pontiff or other Roman prelate up to John XXIII could object,
at least "for starters." It is to such, advanced four years prior, that an
official pronouncement like *Rerum Novarum* can only be regarded as a
thunderous echo and hearty seizure of the mantle.

Cl. Jannet (1890; 1893). We turn now to the leading representative of Le Play's school in France. Among other things, Claudio Jannet (1844-1894) was Professor of Political Economy at the Catholic Institute of Paris; and, while author of many works on social-economic issues, he is chiefly reputed by Gide, for example, for his lecture on "The Catholic School" in Jannet et al., *Quatre Écoles d'Économie Sociale* (1890), to which we shall add his *QJE* article "On French Catholics and the Social Question" (January 1893), penned and published just *after* the promulgation of *Rerum Novarum.*[70]

Jannet opens that first of those four lectures at the Swiss Christian Society of Social Economy by stipulating (p. 4) "the grave problem posed today in all countries enjoying a certain degree of civilization, in the United States as in Europe"; namely,

> the question of the relations of the classes among themselves, or, putting it more clearly, that *question of the rich and the poor* which, thanks to Christianity, humanity has no more known since the stormy days of Athens and Rome.

In explaining "how the School of F. Le Play conceived the means of resolving . . . that grave question," Jannet turns to the master's "capital work," *La Réforme sociale* of 1864. That work, he notes, is where "Le Play would state the conclusion of the vast inquiry which he would pursue after a half-century of traversing the world and traversing history" (pp. 4, 9-10). Chief among Le Play's "master ideas," according to Jannet, is the recognition that

> The end of the activity of human societies is less the development of wealth in itself than the attainment of well-being for men. Well-being supposes daily bread; but it does not exist without social peace. The true criterion of the well-being of societies is contentment, the acceptance of their plight [sort] by men; that is peace among the classes, peace in the family, in the workshop and in the State, that peace which the Savior has brought to men! (p. 10.)

If that was the gospel of Le Play according to Jannet, we may now turn to one of the latter's latest "epistles," published only a year or so before his death. Here, the impetus given to the Catholic social movement perhaps makes its debut. The author's self-assigned task is to "indicate in a general way the practical methods commended by French Catholics for the amelioration of the material and moral conditions of manual laborers" (p. 137). Subsequently, noting the material progress but warped distribution of the fruits thereof brought on by the industrial revolution and development of manufacturing, the author indicates the accompanying shift of popular concern from the political to the economic: "the working classes . . . will henceforth be far less interested than their ancestors . . . in purely political questions [and] will be preoccupied more and more with the relations of capital and labor"; whence, "more frequent . . . conflicts between these two necessary factors of production" should come as no surprise (pp. 138-139). The sad fact of the matter, the author continues, "is that the diminution of the Christian faith," wrought by "the false science of the English deists and the French encyclopaedists of the eighteenth century and [by] the agnostics and materialists of the present century, makes these conflicts more bitter," and leads to the seduction of the masses by the anarchical parties that rise to this occasion (p. 139).

But there is no need to despair because of the "great hope of peaceful solution of the social question [found in] the religious revival, to which Leo XIII has given a powerful impulse by showing the affinity existing between the aspirations of the working-men of to-day and the permanent teachings of Christianity" (p. 139). At the same time, Jannet must add, the promulgation and acknowledgment of those teachings does not put the system on a new course by automatic pilot, for "practical methods of combating existing evils and promoting the welfare of the people" must be employed.

The author recognizes and elaborates four types of implementational methods, beginning with (1) "State intervention in the organization of industry [necessitated by] the impulse of original sin constantly lead[ing] to new manifestations of the exploitation of man by man," and by the inability of "society [to] rely simply on the free play of private interests for its suppression"; this, however, with the understanding that, in prevailing against "private initiative," the state "should not undertake . . . to assure the national good by subordinating individual interests" [So much for any preferential option for the common good!] (pp. 139-140). Examples of such "State action" include factory legislation, special protection of women laborers, working-time maxima and wage-rate minima, and the insurance of workmen "against the principal risks of life" (pp. 141-146). In these cases, the state should intervene when no appropriate private or otherwise subordinate mechanism exists; for instance, in the case of the insurance just noted, government compulsion of employer-worker provision is preferred to direct public-budgetary intervention.

Next comes "(2) action of employers," reflected (in France) by "the moral reconciliation which is spontaneously taking place between employers and employed, [especially] where socialist politicians have not sown prejudices to excite evil passions," and taking the form of the employer's moral obligation, qua "Patron," to take "as much interest as possible" in *everything* tending to improve "the material and even the moral condition of the workmen" (pp. 139, 146).[71]

Third, there is "(3) benevolence . . . springing from charitable impulse and from pious zeal for the material relief and moral elevation of manual laborers" (p. 139). Thus does that uniquely French *patronalism* embrace both (2) and (3) methods here. But, we are informed here, *patronage* "only accomplishes its full results when it is Christian" (p. 149).

Fourth and finally are "(4) associations of workingmen based upon co-operation and mutual aid" (p. 139), to which are added "trade associations" (p. 152). Here we find the outlines of what the present writer has elsewhere alluded to as the Franco-Vatican model of the national economy, the tripartite paradigm that might be conceived as a circle with three radii drawn from the central core to the circumference, yielding the three forms of économie: *privé* (households and firms), *publique* (government), et *sociale*--that so-called "dynamic third sector," particularly of the mutual-aid formations, worker/employer organizations, and so on.

Jannet closes on a hopeful note regarding the interplay of political, religious and scientific forces. The spreading "influence of democracy and . . . the gospel"--especially given the "great impulse" the latter has received "from the encyclical published by Leo XIII in 1890" [sic] (p. 161)--can only improve the plight of "the weak." But democracy itself must be predicated on a properly instructed "sovereign people," the task of those "two great forces [of] science and religion . . . co-ordinated with one another under the supreme law of Christ" (p. 161).

Ch. Antoine, S.J. and the *Cours D'Économie Sociale* (1896-1905). Charles Antoine (1847-1921) was initially a Jesuit Professor of Moral Theology and Social Economy whose *Course in Social Economy* (1896-

1921) did just that.[72] It was intended to be a didactic exposition, focusing on the "social question," and aimed at all those who needed to know and do something about it. As such, the discipline it treated represented the confluence and collaboration of three otherwise separate and distinct disciplines: moral theology, natural law (philosophy), and political economy. At the same time, finding his tripartite *économie sociale* an integral discipline unto itself, but subordinate to both la morale and la politique, Antoine thus parts company with Degas, for example, who held that politics, whence political economy, was (were) a branch(es) of "particular ethics."[73]

Social economy, in turn, is a branch of social science. The object of social science is the society, in both its variable or contingent aspects (phenomena, relationships) and in its more durable or immutable elements. The former involve the empirical tasks of observation and description; the latter, "the researching and establishment of general laws, the principles and the causes of societies" (p. 1).

In this definition, nature, and scope discussion, the author notes the error in drawing any direct relationship between pure science (theory) and art. The middle ground, often neglected, between pure (speculative, contemplative) science and "art which executes" is "practical science [which] considers its object as applicable in action; art directs the execution of labor"--we are informed (pp. 10-11/12).

As to the relationships between morality and economics, ethics and political economy, on the one hand, and social economy and politics or the "science of government of the society," on the other, Antoine is very clear and firm. Political economy is a *human science*, it is not merely "the science of wealth *en soi*"; human economic life in society involves *"free activity"* directed toward the immediate object of wealth; hence, the relationships involved are subject to "the moral law" (pp. 8-9/10). As between economics or social economy and politics, on the other hand, the latter pertains to the overall "temporal prosperity" of the society, which latter in turn is a function of its "intellectual and moral progress, as well as its material development or the social wealth" (p. 11/13). In fine, the moral law is concerned with man's ultimate (spiritual) welfare, whence all temporal things ("here below") are subject to that transcendent concern; but, in the temporal order, politics is superior to economics, since its end is more inclusive or perfect, i.e., the total-temporal--and not merely material--well-being of man.

If our Italian exemplar, Toniolo (infra), was a material contributor to the formulation of *Rerum Novarum*, our erstwhile French Jesuit here was--one is tempted to say--a "slavish" follower of Leo XIII and his encyclicals. This is brought out most clearly in the author's methodological discussion, where he describes "The Role of Deduction" in economic science (p. 13):

> With the aid of the deductive method political economy establishes or receives: 1st) the superior rules of morality which direct man towards his ultimate end, obligatory moral laws; 2nd) the general means for producing and acquiring wealth, e.g. the importance of diminishing the costs of production for raising profits, i.e. laws of pure economy; 3rd) the immediate rules of human activity which depend on two precedents--example: the employer [*sic*; not *patron*] can utilize the labor of children, provided that their physical health and morality would be safeguarded [sic!]--practical laws of social economy.

Next, we are told,

> The sources from which the Christian economist will draw the principles of deduction are: the treasury of dogmatic truths, the teaching of the Church manifested principally in the magnificent encyclicals of Leo XIII, the theories of natural law and the applications which have been made of them by moral theology (p. 13).

Thus we have "moral theology," itself the synthesis of "divine revelation" and "the natural light of reason" (philosophy), and officially established as "tradition" in the papal encyclicals, firmly tied into Antoine's *économie sociale* via the deductive method employed therein. While the author concludes this discussion in turn with "the Role of Induction [in] social economy" and "the laws of political economy," we return to his "Preface" and program. What is his design beyond the proper instruction of those who need to deal with "the social question"? "For the rest," he admits,

> if this book has one pretention, even remote, of innovating or overturning blindly the existing order of things, it would be to return our society to its normal type, and thence to revive the traits which it still guards of a past

less advanced in industry, the sciences and commerce, but
more clear on the true laws and true duties (p. VII/IX/-
III).

"We believe," the author goes on to observe, "with Leo XIII, that social
reform consists 'in rendering to the society its natural form, in restoring
it to the principles which give it life'" (pp. VII-VIII/IX-X/III). And quoting from Leo XIII's *Immortale Dei* (1885) where the pontiff recounts that
"'time . . . where the philosophy of the Gospel governed the States,'"
Antoine informs that "many of these *Christian politico-economic* theses
sustained here are not of accord with the official teaching of political
economy in France" (locc. cit.). But, "they are defended by the new
school" [to which Gide in his 1890 lecture gave the name of "the Solidarity
school"], represented by Gide, et al. and by Catholic scholars like Father
H. Pesch.

Specifically, that *new* school espousing such *old ideals* is constituted of the social-Catholic viewpoint and peopled by Pesch et al. It holds
"that between socialism and the liberal school there is room for a way very
large, very clear, very sure, and in our opinion the only sure one, that
from which the French revolution has made us deviate" (p. IX/XI/V).
"'The fundamental error of the French revolution,' Mgr. Freppel has well
said, 'is in not conceiving and not admitting any intermediary organism
between the individual and the State.'"

Here we have, from our French priest citing a local ordinary and
theologian-apologist, the kernel of Social Catholicism/Christianity, that
"third sector" or middle way between unbridled economic individualism and
full-fledged collectivism/statism. This *is* Économie social catholi-
que/chrétienne, the Franco-Vatican model.[74]

G. Toniolo and the *Trattato Di Economia Sociale* (1907-9).
Reputed collaborator of Leo XIII and ("probable") contributor to *Rerum
Novarum*, exemplary Catholic layman (nominated to sainthood in 1951),
"mentor of Italian Catholics and [widely considered] one of the most
illustrious teachers of Catholic social thought," Giusseppe Toniolo (1845-
1918) is primarily recognized for his *Treatise on Social Economy* (2 vols.,
1907/'09), and even more particularly (scientifically) its noted Volume I,
Introduction.[75] Dedicated to his revered former mentors at Padua, Angelo
Messedaglia and Fedele Lampertico, and written while he was professor at
Pisa, this first volume is a critical exposition of the nature, scope, method,

history and premises of "economic science" or social economy, including its organic position in the hierarchy of the sciences and disciplines.   In Volume II, *Production*, the particulars of that science--and Toniolo insists that it is "a *true* science [and] not simply a *scientific discipline*" (p. 28)--are examined: "the causes and laws of the production, exchange, distribution (composing the *active order* par excellence) and (as the purely *final* order) the use or application (i.e., consumption) of wealth in social human satisfactions, which constitute the end of civilization." In that last part are treated also "the complex problems which go under the title of the 'social question'" (p. X).

The *Introduction to Social Economy* opens (p. 3) with the following "summary concept" of its title:

> Social economy (others say political) is *the science of the social order of wealth*. It studies . . . the activity of the people in effectuating their material well-being, serving the superior ends of civilization.

Thus, as we shall see, being one of the social sciences, it is accordingly inferior to ethics, for example, and superior to the physical sciences. But where does economic science or social economy stand within the system of the social sciences? According to his organic conception of the constitution of human society, Toniolo distinguishes first between and further partitions three social sciences (pp. 4-5):

> I. *Civil.* -- Concerned with the society as a moral, primitive and universal community of men, comprised of (A) the science of the social constitution, viz. of the arrangement [structure] of the social body in its organic elements and institutions (individuals, families, classes, nations and humanity), and (B) the Science of Social Life, comprised in turn of (1) "social biology (physiology)" and (2) "social psychology."
>
> II. *Political.* -- Concerned with the ruling and coercive arrangements [power structure] of society, i.e. of the State as the exterior guardian of the spontaneous moral order, consisting in (A) "political science 'proper'," viz. the science of the public or political constitution, and (B) the science of public administration, or of the activity

of the State in supporting the conservation and progress of the society.

III. *Ecclesiastical.* -- Treats of Religion as a formation of "external society," viz. as "the Church among men," immediately ordinated to the interior and supernatural ends of men, comprised in turn (similarly) of the sciences of (A) the social constitution of the [usually Catholic] Church, and (B) the life or function of the Church in conducting its "magisterial and ministerial" roles in the cohabitation of society and progress of the civilization.

Then, finally, comes "IV. *The social economic science,* which investigates the forces, institutions and processes of the people in the order of wealth, as the material means to the ends of civilization" (p. 6). And, here the author sums up:

> There is a trifold order of principal social doctrines (civil, political and ecclesiastical), of which the first deliniates the organic constitution of human society, which is immediately founded on the nature of man and of things, and is directly addressed to the ends which Providence assigned down here to the consortium among men, and in respect to which the others represent an aid and complement; the second designates the ulterior social device, to which--thanks to the juridical-political human authority--is delegated the extrinsic and coercive security (the State); the third, perfecter of the final social ordering, which . . . directs and raises the other two forms of society to the supernaturally supreme ends.

"Finally," Toniolo notes in this context,

> to these three principal concentric circles of social existence and life, which constitute the *intrinsic and immaterial* ordering of human society is joined a fourth circle of *extrinsic* organizing and activity, that which furnishes the *external material means* of wealth, serving all the preceding forms of the social constitution and life.

Social economy thus constitutes a doctrine of useful material means, and quasi the external and sensible covering of the intrinsic content, component of the pyramid of the social sciences.

"V. Yet," we are informed, "atop these individual hierarchical groups of social sciences [is] a comprehensive or synthetic science, which is *Sociology,* i.e. the *'General doctrine of the society and of civilization.'* Coordinating into unity the responses of all the social sciences," he continues, "this one shows by that harmonic labor the multiple forms of social constitutions and life (activity) confering the supreme end of effectuating successively civilization." And, finally, *"La Civiltà* in fact is the ultimate end of human convivience down here" (p. 6).

As such, then, social economy, in a sense the "material basis" of the social sciences which sociology in turn synthesizes, is (like them) not one of "the *rational-speculative* (or philosophical) *social* sciences, which occupy the apex of this hierarchical pyramid, in that they designate the essence and the end of the society, and the duties or obligations deriving therefrom"; this is the province rather of "social ethics and social law" (p. 4). Rather, social economy sociology, etc., are *"rational-positive* social sciences, which study the society (economy) as a totality of *facts,* viz. as a system of forces, orderings and activity converging on that end, or in other words the society in its concrete constitution and its life" (p. 4).

Otherwise, we are further apprised of social economy, (1) that its nature and significance are both theoretical and practical, but limited; (2) that it is more analytically defined as "the science which studies human society, revolving on its activity in procuring and enjoying the usufruct of wealth for all the legitimate ends of existence, for recognizing the rational positive order of utility, subordinated to the moral order directing that application to the greater common good" (p. 18); (3) that is "aim" qua the "wealth" and "material well-being" of society is such insofar as these are subservient to the *"ultimate moral good"* (pp. 21-22); (4) that it may be subdivided into (a) "the *Science of social Economy,* which studies the *theoretical* order of the causes and laws of wealth in universal human society" (p. 22), and (b) "the *Science of economic Administration,"* which subdivides into (i) "the Science of *economico-social* administration" and (ii) "the Science of *economico-financial* administration" (pp. 23-24); (5) "in respect to its object," it is both a *moral science,* a *social science,* and a *hedonistic science,* whence distinct from Ethics, Law and *"la scienza politica"* (pp. 25-28); (6) that, since its aims or objectives are proximate and subservient to the ultimate ones, "it is not a *teleological doctrine*," concerned with "ultimate reasons and ends," but is rather a *deontological* science, "examining one of the orders of facts from which the universe results" (p. 31); and, finally, (7) within the hierarchy of the sciences, again, social economy is inferior to philosophy and ethics, for example, but superior to the natural sciences and that of technology and other instrumental knowledges in general, and "private economy" in particular, while holding a "concomitant" relationship to the other *"positive social sciences and disciplines"* (pp. 34-46).

The really tough questions regarding social economy as a science of material means to higher ends are raised in relating economics as a speculative science to ethics (pp. 38-39). Thus, should it focus on "individual or social well-being, that of the short- or the long-term"; and, does that well-being consist "in the absolute quantity of wealth or rather in its proportional distribution? and according to which distributive criteria?" he queries (p. 39). Different emphases give rise to different perspectives on these questions. Thus, if *liberty* is regarded as "the end and hence the supreme good of humanity, we have an individualistically liberal Economics; if it is *social solidarity*, we will have an *authoritarian* pantheistic Economy (of the State); if it would be *material equality*, there would be a socialist (collectivistic) economy" (p. 139).

And, here, we must recognize and respect social economy, as a *positive* social science, as likewise having become imbued with "an *organic* character" (p. 41). Such *"Science of the social constitution* studies the society as it comes to be comprised *in its organism"*; whence, "Economics, as it accepts from this the concrete notion of the personal autonomy of the family and of property, essentially *ethico-private* institutions, as it takes therefrom the concrete notions of the other *institutions of a collective or social character*, such as the classes, the nations, the human family at large," this constitutes that *"Economia sociale"* to which "an *organic* character" is attributed (p. 41). And, it is this social economy which must interpolate between those different levels of interest, duly respective of all, individual or private, class, national, and humanitarian. It must avoid the extremes and erroneous assumptions regarding the nature of the social organism of the competing schools and varieties of economic thought: (1) the *atomistic* view of "(liberal) *individualistic economy(ics)* [that] the society is by nature nothing but a sum of individuals"; (2) of *socialism*, "which refuses to recognize [its] substantially irreformable nature [etc.]"; and, (3) of "*politico-sociological* (or social political) *economy(ics)* with its state-worship, [holding] that the society is a concrete entity furnished of its own life, independent of the individuals which compose it" (p. 41). Rejecting the errors and upholding the truths of these vying doctrinal views, true social economy will steer the middle course, we may infer, giving due recognition to the autonomy of the individual and individuality of material well-being, to the organic conception of society as more than a mere collection of individuals and the common or collective good as more than the mere sum of private goods, and to the legitimacy of the social institutions such as the family, property, the classes, state, etc.

The "Final Relationship" considered by Toniolo here in his "study of the relations among the orders of truth" is that which "Economy(ics) has with *religious doctrine*" (pp. 47-49). "The question is replicated today," he notes, "in the discussion of a Christian Social Economics"--viz., "una Economia sociale christiana (Villeneuve de Bargemont, Périn, and the modern school of ethico-Christian economists)." Basically, Toniolo's response to this (and subordinate) question(s) is that we have here two different orders of truth: "The doctrine of faith [qua] a system of truths founded directly on divine authority and transcending science"; and the latter, "a system of truths founded directly on reason." Accordingly, the relationship between the two is *extrinsic*. Negatively, this relationship requires that economic science not contradict religious doctrine; positively, "superior truths can give light to the methodological investigation of the truths proper to science" (p. 47). In a word, he notes, "*Christian science* in general does not signify anything other than 'a system of rational doctrines which does not contradict the faith and can be harmonized with it'" (pp. 47-48). "This is valid as well for Economy(ics)," we are there assured.[76]

Moreover, Toniolo continues, the *christian civilization* embodies in itself "the ideal and positive type (model)" by which to judge definitely the legitimacy of *economic* laws; it prefixes for them "a final criterion of evaluation," a nonarbitrary one "which gushes forth and is elevated in the center of the real and historic life of humanity." The result of the advances of critical history, the author concludes, the economist must take this "supreme positive criterion" as given (p. 49).

Thus we have what amounts to the very positivistic brand of religious-normative social economics of G. Toniolo. But the story of the Catholic religious perspective does not stop here. Instead we have a veritable burst, guided by three Jesuits, to continue construction of the new school of thought ushered in here by Jannet and Antoine. We conclude here with a Jesuit triumvirate, stepping-stones, as they might be called, to and in the present.

Pesch and the *Lehrbuch* (1905-26). The first is the noted German scholar, Heinrich Pesch (1854-1926), variously described by Mulcahy (1952; 1967) as "the first economist to construct an economic theory on the foundation of Aristotelian-Thomistic philosophy," "a commentator on *Rerum Novarum* . . . and the sourcebook of *Quadragesimo Anno*" and founder of the Catholic-social doctrine of "Solidarism."[77] Of his learned treatises, the compendious *Lehrbuch der Nationaloekonomie* (5 vols., 1905-26) stands out as his true Hauptwerk.[78] There, in the first two volumes, we are treated with such vital information as the origin of the "solidarity-concept," prominently associated with the name of de Coux's successor at Louvain, Ch. Périn (I, pp. 414f.) and the related clamor, especially on the part of the "Social Catholics," for a "New Social Economy(ics)" to replace the old orthodoxy (and oppose socialism/Marxism), along with the author's own proposal of "a solidaristic Labor-system" (II, pp. 194-213ff.).

The *Lehrbuch* is an invaluable sourcework for the student of Catholic social economics in its formative period, and touches on many of the topics and ideas which have been near and dear to our heart--e.g. National-oekonomie as a (preferred) synonym for Volkswirthschaftslehre, and the latter versus Volkswirthschaft (I, pp. 456-57ff.), etc. But here we narrowly confine our attention to just one crucial question of the nature and scope of (Catholic) social economy(ics) itself, and its relation to the loftier or superior disciplines of ethics, theology. Does Christianity/Roman Catholicism itself contain or propose any particular economic system or doctrine?

Here, in the "Foreword" to the 2d/3d editions of his Volume II (1924), Pesch announces "up front," for example, that "Solidarism is not a theological, but a social-philosophical System, [that] the social Labor-system is an economic [volkswirthschaftliches] system"--i.e., solidarism, as a doctrine, is a social-ethical and not a moral-theological one; and, as a praxeological matter, solidarism is an economic and not a religious system or institution. Then, in Volume III (1926, p. 547) comes the further emphatic pronouncement:

> Der Katholismus gibt der Welt kein Wirtschaftssystem, er
> ist an keine bestimmte Wirtschaftsverfassung gebunden
> und bindet an kein bestimmtes Wirtschaftssystem. --

[Catholicism gives to the world no economic constitution, and is bound to no definite economic system.]

Elsewhere (III, p. 61n) he explains:

> If occasionally the expression "christian" or "Catholic" economics [Nationaloekonomie] is used, this can be misunderstood. Economics [Die Nationaloekonomie] is a *natural* discipline, it has to do with a *natural* ordering of economic life, therefore with "natural ethics" [mit der "Ethica *naturalis*].

Fallon and the *Principes* (1921-44).   With that all-too-brief treatment of Pesch, we turn to the next stepping-stone to the present, the Louvain philosophy professor, Valére Fallon, and his "well-blessed" *Principes d'Économie sociale.*[79]   Very significant here is the commendation of the fifth (1935) edition received by the author from the then Secretary of the State of the Vatican, "E. Card. Pacelli," subsequently (1939-58) Pope Pius XII, specifically for the good his work had done in conveying the teachings of "the Encyclicals 'Rerum Novarum' and 'Quadragesimo Anno'" (p. VII).

Fallon explains his preference for *social* over *political* and *national* economy(ics) in both positive and normative terms. On the positive side, he notes that one could drop "the restrictive qualifier of political, and say most briefly *economy* or *economics*, as one says biology or botanics" (p. 2). But, in choosing social over political and/or national economy, one has at once a more generic descriptive, which "neither excludes the economic phenomena of the familial order nor those of the international order"; and, more positively, he notes (p. 2),

> It underscores besides a characteristic of economics which, without being of universal verification, is encountered to some degree in the majority of cases, that of science which considers men living in relations or in society.

"Above all," he continues, now introducing the normative dimension, the decisive reason for adopting *social* was that "it marks the preoccupation, which is ours, of enlarging the field of economy(ics) proper for specifying the data and researching the solutions of the *social questions* posed by modern economic evolution" (p. 2, our emphasis).

At the same time, in this dualistic positive/normative vein, Fallon notes (pp. 5-6) that in addition to being both a "*theoretical* and *practical*," "*psychological* [and] *social*" one, economics is also a "moral Science." Firstly, the author explains,

> Economic activity, as all human activity, is subjected to moral precepts. La morale (Ethics) *orients, elevates, sustains* and *restrains* the economic activity of man.

Secondly, since "the object of economy implies the free intervention of man," so that "the conclusions and laws of that science have not the rigor of physical and mathematical laws; they are [thus] of certainty moral laws."

Von Nell-Breuning, Pius XI and Social Economy (1931-36). We close here with our third Jesuit and stepping-stone in the present, Oswald von Nell-Breuning (1890-). Father Nell-Breuning and Franz H. Mueller are the two surviving pupils of Pesch himself, and have contributed significantly to the development and dissemination of his doctrine. But, here, it is primarily for the translation of the former's 1932 commentary on *Quadragesimo Anno* by the American Jesuit, Bernard W. Dempsey, that we make this last (transitional) stop.

Father Nell-Breuning's *Die Soziale Enzyklika: Erlauterungen zum Weltrundschreiben Papst XI uber die gesellschaftliche Ordnung* appeared in Koln in 1932. A more literal rendering of his title would be *The Social Encyclical: An Explanation of the Circular-letter to the World of Pope Pius XI on the Social Order*; and, while that original German title is not to be found in the present English translation, *Reorganization of Social Economy: The Social Encyclical Developed and Explained*, we may presume the author approved of this variation.[80]

There are two points of interest in the discrepancy between these two titles. One, perhaps minor to the present audience, is the fact that the original German title makes explicit that this encylical or circular-letter was addressed not only to "The Patriarchs, Primates, [etc.]," as such were usually addressed, but also to "All the Faithful of the Catholic World."[81] The second, and somewhat more significant one for a history of social economics, is that, for the main title itself, Dempsey substitutes *Reor-*

ganization of Social Economy as a surrogate for the popular title of the encylical itself, *Restoring (Reconstructing) the Social Order*.

The essential phenomenon involved here is the official Church's virtually interchangeable usage of the terms "social," "temporal," "material," etc. (cp. Hegel's Realphilosophie). Thus, the so-called "*social* encyclicals" have always addressed essentially *economic* conditions and issues, viz. "the *social* question" qua essentially an *economic* one. By the time of *QA* and the "second and a half" great social encyclical, *Divini Redemptoris: Atheistic Communism* (1937), it is true, "social economy" in the vernacular and even official Latin versions had crept in; as, likewise in the case of Pius XII's vernacular allocution to the (French) International Union of Catholic Patronal Associations (7 May 1949), where l'économie sociale appears in contradistinction, for example, to l'économie nationale.[82]

Yes, the central message, the new dimension of *QA* was the *restoration* (Italian, restauizone; official Latin, instaurandum) of the social order (l'ordine sociale; socialem ordinem); and, just prior to that (#75), for example, we read of "the social economy be[ing] rightly established" ("l'economia sociale veramente sussiseterà"; "res economico-socialis et vere constabit") etc., and of the (necessary) "social organization (constitution) of economic affairs (life)"--i.e., "la constituzione sociale del fatto economico"; "sociale rei oeconomicae constitutione" (#75).[83]

Here we have, then, with Pius XI, von Nell-Breuning, et al. the final official and scientific, dogmatic- and moral-theological word(s) on the truly Christian social economy (social-economic/economic-social order); and, such doctrinal, normative pronouncements and analysis (science) is what we mean here by Roman Catholic social economics--i.e., that is what Pius XI, Nell-Breuning, and others are doing.

Nell-Breuning's social economics consists in expert commentary, in this case, on Pius XI's pronouncements on social-economic reconstruction (renewal, etc.); much as, for further example, Mueller's has consisted in the continuation and furtherance of Peschianism, along with the work of von Nell-Breuning, etc.[84]

Again, this is Christian social economy á la Roman Catholic social economics, official and otherwise, up to the end of our period and even down to the present day.

CONCLUSION

We have witnessed the development of social economy(ics) in three different modes of existence over its first 200 years. The story began with the birth of the secular-positivistic conception in the form of Quesnay's 1736 *Essai physique sur l'Oeconomie animale.* This was a conception that came to be baptized *l'économie sociale* by the Count of Buat-Nançay in 1773, whence to be confirmed by Say (1828) and J. S. Mill (1836-44), no less. With various twists and turns, it picks up a considerable Italian and Germanic-Austrian following (including historical, sociological/sociophysiological, and universalist/abstract-theoretical emphases) over the ensuing 100 years. Authors such as Scialoja (1840/'48), ... , Cossa (1888-93), Wagner (1892-1909), Dietzel (1895), Weber and Wieser (1914-24), and Cassel (1918-32) stand out here. Such a conception has remained in the form of *social* versus *individual* economy à la Elliott (1973) and economia *sociale* qua sociology in the *Cambridge Italian Dictionary* (1962 sq.). This also, one can note finally, is both the oldest and least recognized conception of social economics by those who diligently have searched for its identity and inquired after its roots. Today, its members have found a home in the Austrian strand in contemporary economic thought.

With equally variegated stripes, the second, "secular-normative" conception of social economics appeared on the scene. The birth thereof is marked with Sismondi's *New Principles of Political Economy* (1819/'27), a work rather critical of the *old* principles thereof (Smith, Say, and company), and regarded as the first exemplar of l'économie sociale French style (Gide and Rist; Ekelund and Hebert). The defensive counterrevolution came with a work by Say's disciple Dunoyer, who felt that the old principles needed at least a new banner: for example, his *Nouveau Traité d'Économie sociale* of 1830. The last of such disciples was Edmond About and his *Social Economy* of 1873. In addition to various positive-law/moral-philosophical views of social economy, particularly in Britain around mid-century (1840-60), we made special note of Proudhon's radically new économie sociale (1846), a system which would replace the old political economy "root and branch"; and, then, of the all-too-neglected system of Léon Walras, viz. économie sociale qua "essentiellement une science morale," developed over the period 1860-96, as both a response to Proudhon and major reform of the classical and capitalist systems. Those who succeeded in the Walrasian strain included most prominently Gide and Wicksell in the first quarter of the present century, and as later documented by Amadeo (1937). Others, especially in the Anglo-American theater, and ranging from mainline, neoclassical welfare-economic to humanistic-critical conceptions, included Denslow and Gunton (1887-1900), Hobson (1914/'33), Fetter and Carver (1915-25), Chapin and Jones (1917-20). Meaningfully, the modern/contemporary synthesis of the antithesis-thesis struggle that held sway in this particular arena over that roughly 100-year period of 1825-1925 will be found most prominently in works like J. M. Clark's *Preface to Social Economics* (1936), H. R. Bowen's *TOWARD Social Economy* (1948), and many of the authors and articles peopling and filling the pages of our two major journals, the *Review of Social Economy* (1943-) and *International Journal of Social Economics* (1974-).

This brings us, finally, to the third, last, and perhaps most distinctive variety of social economics, the *religious-normative*. This is the story we just completed. It is well embraced by the century of the time demarcated conveniently by the publicational dates of 1832-34/37 and 1932/36. The former refer to the pioneering works in this tradition, those of de Coux and Villeneuve-Bargemont; the latter, to the German Jesuit von Nell-Breuning's commentary on Pius XI's *Quadragesimo Anno: Restoring the Social Order* of 1931 and its English translation (1936) by the American Jesuit B. W. Dempsey. Departing from the classical works of Smith and Say especially, and noticeably reflecting the critique of Sismondi, for example, our two French pioneers adopted the English principle of labor, upheld the institution of property, and coupled these together with the Christian (Roman-Catholic) principle of charity to advance a true social economy which was on balance more concerned with the distribution of well-being than with the mere production and accumulation of wealth. As opposed to the egoistic materialism and unbridled laissez-faire of the Smithian or English system, and the concept of human nature upon which they were predicated, this explicitly Christian political economy sought restraints on competition and advanced the figure of l'homme social who would practice self-denial in service of the public good. A partnership between the state, what came to be called voluntary associations, and the private sector as such was advanced to ameliorate and eventually eliminate the misère publique which was plaguing France and Europe as the British systems of political and industrial economy was taking hold there.

A central element, if not the fundamental characteristic, of this movement was the principle of solidarity and related doctrine of solidarism. Initially, perhaps, a more positivistic (natural-law) conception, but increasingly and more significantly as a matter of divine (biblical) revelation and moral theology, this tenet was advanced both in condemnation of the existing social-economic order and also in opposition to the socialist, communist, and especially Marxist analyses and resolutions thereof. Reform, restoration, etc.--versus uprooting, revolution, etc.--were the remedies emphasized by the majority adherents to this viewpoint, lay (Le Play, Jannet, and Toniolo), clerical (Antoine, Pesch, Fallon, and von Nell-Breuning, for instance) and magisterial (Leo XIII and Pius XI most prominently). Nor, as the periodical literature on social economy well reveals, were the rather strict and dogmatic views on the true nature and proper functioning of the temporal, material, or social order restricted to Roman Catholicism. In fact, one of the most theocratic and solidaristic pieces encountered (Apple, 1887) appeared in a Reformed-Church journal. And, there are many others, prelates (e.g., von Ketteler of Mainz, Freppel of Angers) and otherwise who figure so prominently in this tradition. But, the present is a history of *social economics* as such, and not of Social Catholicism/Christianity as such;[85] whence, we focused on Social Catholics (and others) who purported to be doing l'économie sociale, gesellschaftliche Wirtschaftslehre, etc.

Is there a bottom line, a final word with which we can capture or recapture the distinctive difference between l'économie sociale, Sozialoekonomik, etc., as it (they) developed out of and in opposition to the original political economy, Volkswirthschaftslehre, etc., of the classical and neoclassical (Austrian) pure, positive varieties? It would be redundant merely to repeat the distinctions and definitions advanced by Lange (1945-46), Bowen (1948) and others of more recent vintage. At the same time, despite the efforts of Cossa, Cassel and the like, that normative, moral-philosophical, and even theological perspective and concern have remained and prevailed in social economics. Importantly, this has meant a preoccupation with the question of a just or equitable distribution of economic well-being, versus the efficiency issue of maximizing the stock of wealth, flow of real income or production, etc. Orthodox (classical-neoclassical) political economy or simply economics has always been normative in the sense of pursuing the goal of wealth and especially welfare maximization in the Pareto-optimum sense. Social economics has also always been concerned with the efficiency criterion of well-being; but, in addition, its bottom line has rested as well on the *equity* criterion. And, when a tradeoff between the two presents itself, social economics does not shy away or beg the question.[86]

Second, as opposed to the mechanical paradigm or mechanistic approach which came to characterize pure or straight political economy and economics, social economics has always inclined to the physiological analogue or organic paradigm. The former runs in terms of equilibria and gravitational movements; the latter, in terms of flows and functional ties between the major parts of the social-economic anatomy. This, most importantly, has given rise to that idea (doctrine) of solidarity(ism) also so distinctive of l'économie sociale as handed down from Quesnay to Gide, Toniolo, Leo XIII, . . . , John Paul II (*Laborem Exercens*, 1981) and, qua Solidarnosc in the politicoeconomic arena of Poland today.

The Catholic Church--Roman-Catholic social economy(ics)--for one has always held fastidiously to the naturality, or otherwise legitimacy or necessity of (1) the classes, (2) the State, and (3) private property. Marx, an adopted social economist if not a natural-born one,[87] envisioned the "sublation" or *Aufhebung*--i.e., the simultaneous abolition, preservation, and transcendence--of all three. In the *Principles* (1848-71) John Stuart Mill, never so adopted, wrote prophetically, perhaps, of the realization of that principle of "association" so fundamental to both the secular- and religious-normative versions of social economics as follows:[88]

> The form of association . . . which if mankind continue to improve, must be expected in the end to predominate is not that which can exist between a capitalist as chief [patron?], and work-people without a voice in the management, but the association of the labourers themselves in terms of equality, collectively owning the capital by which they carry on their operations, and working under managers elected and removable by themselves.

If that makes one more convert, and/or encourages one more adoption, the ranks could suffer a worse recruit.

Notes

[1]The present text is based on an approximately 200-page manuscript constituting the first rough draft of a book-length work to be published in the near future. As editor, I would like to add the following comment. The present version of this chapter is the result of an almost supernatural effort on my part to keep it from filling the entire book. Earlier drafts started out with over 200 pages and had to undergo several rounds of painful and heartless trimming. In the process, it was unavoidable to eliminate valuable material and dozens of personal comments by the author enriching the general text. I very much regret this type of censorship and will have to take the blame for whatever distortion and impoverishment resulted. Considerations of length also prevented us from constructing the usual bibliography at the chapter's end. I apologize to the reader but would like to also add that in spite of everything I consider this chapter a (perhaps even *the*) most valuable contribution to this book. To labor over it was both endless agony and a rare privilege.

[2]Ordinarily, the dates in parentheses refer to the publications of pertinent works, including of authors or personages cited. Here, for example, the first (implicit) reference was to Antoyne de Montchrétien's *Traicté de l'Oeconomie politique*, published at Rouen in 1615; the others to noted works by von Justi, Genovesi, and Jas. Steuart. Otherwise, when particular individuals are being introduced (e.g., de Coux infra), the birth-death dates are given in full digits (viz. 1787-1864)--versus the partial digits for two editions of Wicksell's Lectures (1911/28) and first-latest of Rima's Development below, for example.

[3]Nitsch, "Social Economics: A Typology," ASE/WEAI, San Francisco, July 1-5, 1986; "Social Economics: From Search for Identity to Quest for Roots," *International Journal of Social Economics*, 14:3/4/5 (1987), pp. 70-90.

[4]Charles Gide and Charles Rist, *Histoire des Doctrines économiques*, 7e édn. (Paris: Recueil Sirey, 1947), p. 8; et cf. idem, *A History of Economic Doctrine*, 2nd Engl. ed., trans. R. Richards and E. F. Row (Boston et al.: D. C. Heath, 1948), p. 27 (hereinafter, G&R, 1947 and 1948, respectively).

[5]See / cf., in turn: (1) Smith, *Wealth of Nations* (1776-1889), ed. E. Cannan (New York: The Modern Library, 1937), p. 643; (2) Louis Gabriel le Comte du Buat-Nançay, *Éléments de la Politique, ou Recherche des vrais Principes de l'Économie sociale*, à Londres, M.DCC.LX-XIII; (3) Jos. Garnier, "De l'Origine et la Filiation du Mot Économie politique et des divers autres Noms donnés à la Science économique," pt. I, *Journal des Économistes*, XXXII (Mai-Août 1852), esp. 306; (4) Karl Marx, *Theories of Surplus-Value* (1862-63), Pt. I (Moscow: Progress Publishers, 1963), p. 381; (5) Wilhelm Roscher, *Grundlagen der Nationaloekonomie* (1858 sqq.), 18te Aufl. (Stuttgart, 1886), pp. 35f.; (6) A.N. Rugina, "Who Was the First Social Economist in Modern Times?" ASE/ASSA, New York, Dec. 27-30, 1988; and (7) Luigi Cossa, *Introduzione allo Studio dell'Economia politica*, 3.a ediz. (Milano: Ulrico Hoepli, 1892) / idem, *Introduction to the Study of Political Economy*, trans. (sometimes erroneously) by Louis Dyer (Macmillan, 1893), pp. 289-90/264-65.

[6]"The *political economy* is no other thing than the economy of the society. The political societies that we call nations are living bodies, just like the human body. The study which has been made of the nature and functions of the human body has created an ensemble of notions, a science to which we have given the name of *physiology*. The study which has been made of the nature and function of different parts of the social body likewise has created an ensemble of notions, a science to which we have given the name of *political economy*, and which we perhaps had done better to name social economy." Jean-Baptiste Say, *Cours complet d'Économie politique practique; l'Économie des Sociétés*, Vol. I (Paris: Rapilly, 1828), pp. 1-2.

[7]John Stuart Mill, "On the Definition of Political Economy; and on the Method of Philosophical Investigation in that Science" (1836; the later 1844 version, no. V in Mill's *Essays on Some Unsettled Issues in Political Economy*, reads instead: "and on the Method of Investigation Proper to It"), as in *Collected Works of John Stuart Mill*, Vol. IV (University of Toronto Press, 1967), pp. 320, 309.

[8]Cf. J.-C.-L. Simonde de Sismondi, *Nouveaux Principes d'Économie politique, ou de la Richesse dans ses Rapports avec la Population*, 2e éd. (Paris: DeLaunay, 1827; 2 vol.), passim, but esp. Vol. I, "Avertissements" on the Second and First (1819) Editions, pp. i-xxiv, and Chap. II, "Division of the Science of Government. High Politics and Political Economy," p. 11, where "économie politique," "économie domestique," etc., are defined and distinguished.

[9]G&R (1948), p. 192. That Sismondi *did* social economy(ics) in our new sense, and even set afoot the earlier branch thereof (the secular-*normative*), is further indicated and documented both in his own day and more recently. Thus, for example, his colleague and editor-to-be, M. Mignet, in closing his eulogy read at the public sitting of the Academy of Moral and Political Sciences on 17 May 1845, remarked as follows: "With these noble sentiments [viz. "the love of justice, and a passion for the good"] he has imbued politics, history, *social economy*; to make these contribute to the cautious progress of the institutions of state, to the instruction and well-being of nations." And, the editor of the present volume, Mark Lutz, develops the thesis of Sismondi's *New Principles* as "The Roots of Social Economics."

Cf. Mignet (ed. etc.), *Political Economy, and the Philosophy of Government; a Series of Essays Selected from the Works of M. de Sismondi*, trans. from the French, etc. (London: John Chapman, 1847; reprint ed., New York: Augustus M. Kelley, 1966), p. 24; and M. A. Lutz, "On the History of Social Economics: the British Contribution," *International Journal of Social Economics*, 7:5 (1980), pp. 241-44ff.

[10]Vide Charles Dunoyer, *De la Liberté du Travail, ou Simple Exposé des Conditions dans lesquelles les Forces humaines s'exercent avec le plus de Puissance*, Tome Premier (Paris: Guillamin, 1845), "Preface," incl. esp. fn. 1, pp. XVf.; et cf. "Dunoyer (Barthélemy-Charles-Pierre-Joseph), French economist and administrator, member of the Institute," etc. in the *Grand Dictionnaire Universel de XIXe Siècle* (hereinafter, GDU) Vol. VI (Paris: Librairie classique Larousse et Boyer, 1870), pp. 1397-98, which gives, inter alia, the full title (etc.) of Dunoyer's first edition, "*Industrie et la morale considerées dans leurs rapports avec la société* (in-80)."

[11]Adolphe Blanqui, *Histoire de l'Économie politique en Europe [etc.]* (Paris: Guillamin, 1837), pp. 390-91.

[12]Contrast especially N. Wm. Senior, *An Outline of the Science of Political Economy* (London, 1836; reprint, New York: Augustus M. Kelley, 1938f.), esp. pp. 1-3.

[13]Smith, op. cit., pp. 734-40, esp. 737f.

[14]Dunoyer, *Liberté du Travail* (1945), p. V. For a more extensive treatment of the "Social Economy" of Dunoyer "the Optimist," cf. G&R (1948), pp. 331-53 passim, etc.

[15]See, Francesco Casnati, "About, Edmond," in the *Enciclopedia Cattolica* (Citta del Vaticano, 1949), Vol. I, col. 113; et cf., e.g., "About (Edmond-Francois-Valentin)," in the *Larousse du XXe Siècle* (hereinafter, *L.XX.S*), Vol. I. (Paris, 1928), p. 18; whence, for a more extensive account, the *Enciclopedia Universal Ilustrada: Europeo-Americana* (Madrid: Espasa-Calpe, Vols. as dated; hereinafter *EUI*), I (1958/08), pp. 614ff.

[16]About, op. cit., "Translated from the Last French Edition" by W. F. Rae (New York: D. Appleton and Co., 1873), 284 pp. A. de Foville, "About, Edmond," in *Palgrave's Dictionary of Political Economy*, ed. Henry Higgs, rev. ed. (1925-26) reprint (New York: Augustus M. Kelley, 1963; hereinafter *PDPE*), Vol. I, p. 2, cites *"le Progrès* (1864) and *l'A B C du travailleur* (1868)" as first among the "genuine didactic works" of this acclaimed novelist and "inimitable romance writer."

[17]While this same optimism will characterize the religious writers next examined, it seems safe to say that About's inspiration was otherwise. One of the accounts noted (*Casnati*, loc. cit) informs of his tirades against temporal power and Roman corruption, and of calumnious and irreverent affirmations against Pius IX, for instance.

[18]Cf. (1) F. B. Sanborn, "Our Progress in Social Economy since 1874," *Journal of Social Science*, Vol. XXXV (1902), p. 50; (2) F. Y. Edgeworth, "Ellis, William (1800-1881)," *PDPE*, I, 693f.; and, (3) on Atkinson and his title re in documenting the non-novelty of the designation "'Social-economics' or Social-economic theory," Heinrich Dietzel, *Theoretische Sozialoekonomik* (Leipzig: C. F. Winter, 1895), p. 54.

[19]"Solidarité," *GDU*, XIV (1875), p. 840.

[20]Thus, for example, in his chapter (III, Vol. I) on "The Division of Labor," he devotes a whole section (II.) to the "Impotence of Palliatives" *as proposed by* "MM. Blanqui, . . ., Dunoyer" et al. for the same amelioration of the well-recognized ills wrought thereby (pp. 105ff.).

[21]P.-J. Proudhon, op. cit. (Paris: Guillaumin et Cie., 1846), 2 vols.

[22]C. de Coux, *Essais d'Économie politique*, or as per paper-cover, *Discours prononcé à l'Ouverture d'un Cours d'Économie politique* (Paris: Bureaux de l'Agence générale pour la Défense de la Liberté religieuse / Lyon: Sauvignet et Cie., 1832), "Introduction to a Course on Political Economy," pp. 1-52, and "Second Essay: On Moral and Material Wealth," pp. 53-111; M. le Vte. Aban de Villeneuve-Bargemont, *Économie politique chrétienne, ou Recherches sur la Nature et les Causes du Pauperisme en France et en Europe, et sur les Moyens de le Soulager et de le Prévenir* (Bruxelles: Meline, Cans et Compagnie, 1837; "Préface," Paris, 13 May 1834), 676 pp.

Of de Coux (1787-1864), we are informed as follows: (1) by Cargan of his initial "radical" associations (e.g., F. de Lamennais) and efforts (*L'Avenir*), wherein he condemned the industrial system "for its exploitation of labor" and advocated a syndicalist (versus state-interventionist) approach to the setting of fair wages and prices, whereafter, (1830-32), he took a post at Louvain (1834-45), "giving a *cours d'économie sociale* and a *cours d'économie politique*"; (2) by Fallon, that, "in his *Introduction to Social Economy*, he besought a limitation of economic freedom and of competition"; and, (3) Pesch, that, to his successor to the Chair of Political Economy at Louvain, Ch. Périn, can be traced the origin of the "Solidarity-principle." Cf. (1) E. T. Cargan, "Coux, Charles de," *New Catholic Encyclopedia* (McGraw-Hill, 1967; hereinafter *NCE*), Vol. IV, p. 401; Valère Fallon, S.J., *Principes d'Économie sociale*, 6e ed. (Louvain et Bruxelles, 1944), p. 517; and, Heinrich Pesch, S.J., *Lehrbuch der National-oekonomie*, I. Bd., 3te/4te Aufl. (Freiburg im Briesgau: Herder & Co., 1924), "Solidarismus," esp. p. 415.

On the place and role of Villeneuve-Bargemont in the founding and early development of Catholic socioeconomic thought, and his being "sublated" (*aufgehoben*) in the central doctrines of Leo XIII's RN, see/cf. (1) Mary I. Ring, S.N.D., *Villeneuve-Bargemont: Precursor of Modern Social Catholicism, 1784-1850* (Milwaukee: Bruce Publishing Co., 1935), passim; (2) Melvin J. Williams, *Catholic Social Thought* (New York: Ronald Press Co., 1950), passim; and, (3) Georges Goyau, "Villeneuve-Barcemont [sic], "Jean-Paul-Alban, Vicomte de," *The Catholic Encyclopedia*, Vol. XV (New York: Appleton, 1912), p. 431.

[23]On Sismondi's influence on V.-B.'s *Écon. pol. chr.*, and his favorable impression of at least "ten chapters of the book of M. de Villemain [*sic*], a Christian political economist," see in turn G&R, *History*, tr. R&R (1948ff.), p. 210; and J.C.L. Simonde de Sismondi, *Political Economy, and the Philosophy of Government; [etc.]*, trans. etc. Mignet, (London, 1847; reprint ed., Augustus M. Kelley, 1966), "Extract from the Private Journal [etc.]," 14 March 1835, (p. 452), which continues, "The principal idea, of mixing charity with political economy, is as beautiful as true." However, as usual, there is a critical "*aber*" here, viz. V.-B.'s error of "confounding religion with Catholicism, and that with the sacerdotal spirit. He would put all public charity in the hands of the priesthood, and at the same time would give them all political power." Cp. here de Coux's ridiculing of Sismondi's attack on ecclesiastical celibacy on the one hand, while "demonstrating on the other that it would not but be to the health of the society the interdicting of the marriage of the poor!" (*Essais*, p. 49).

[24]Cf. variously here the following: (1) "Sagra (don Ramón de La)," *GDU*, XIV (1875), p. 47; (2) "La Sagra (Ramon de)," *EUI*, XXIX (1925/,58), pp. 901f.; and (3) C. Bernaldo de Quiros, "Sagra y Périz, Ramón Dionisio de la (1798-1871)," *Encyclopaedia of the Social Sciences* (New York: Macmillan, 1931; reprint, 1939), Vol. XIII, pp. 506f.

[25.]The *GDU* notes here that, "at the time of the events of February 1848, Mr. de la Sagra came to Paris and involved himself actively in the social movement, whence he participated in a lively fashion in the ideas of Proudhon and supported with all his efforts the establishment of a People's Bank" (1).

[26.]Cf. (1) "Ott (Auguste)," *GDU*, XI (1874), 1556:3/4; (2) "Ott (Augusto)," *EUI*, XL (1919/'58), 1054; (3a) Cossa, *Intro.* (1892), pp. 70, 406-7; (3b) ibid., tr. Dyer (1893), pp. 58-59, 389; (4a,b) Rist, in G&R, *Hist.* (1947, tr. 1948), qua cit.; and, cf. (5) H. Pesch, *Lehrbuch*, I (3te u. 4te Aufl., 1924), for citations of an Adolf (Ad., A.) Ott--pp. 176, 281, 283, 440n, 495n, and 526n--who wrote articles on "Liberalism" and "Individualism" for the *Staatslexikon der Gorres-Gesellschaft* (5 vols., 1887-97), III:2,4, and published a book on *Thomas Aquinas and Mendicancy* (*Thomas von Aquin und das Mendikantentum*, 1908); also, an article in the *Theologische Revue*, 1904, No. 8, cited regarding Christian revelation and the social and economic order (p. 526n).

[27.]This is certainly not to denigrate his contribution to our now firmly developing discipline of social economics in the form of his purely sociological (or socioeconomic) *magnum opus*, the *European Workers: Studies on the Labor, Domestic Life and Moral Condition of the Working Populations of Europe*--and especially as that was "Preceded by an Exposition of [that all-important] Method of Observation"--of 1855.

Vide: F. Le Play, *Études sur les Travaux, la Vie domestique et la Condition morale des Populations ouvrieres de l'Europe precedées d'un Exposé de la Méthode d'Observation* (Paris: L'Imprimerie imperiale, MDCCLV), esp. the "Table des Matières" and "Introduction"; et idem, *La Réforme sociale in France deduite de l'Observation comparée des Peuples européens*, 2 vols. (Paris: Henri Plon, 1864), Vol. I, esp. "Table Methodique" and "Introduction"--hereinafter, *OE* and *RS*, resp.

[28.]Here we make a brief note of a critical comparison (difference) between the leading idealists of our concern, Le Play and the Roman Catholic magisterium, along with the more purely secular figures of Hegel and Weber, and the realists Adam Smith and Karl Marx especially. The question, of course, is the direction of the dialectic in the Aufhebung/thesis-antithesis-synthesis process. With Hegel, as with Weber's *Protestant Ethic and the Spirit of Capitalism* (1904-5; tr. 1930/'58), Le Play above, and more recently Pope John Paul II in his *Sollicitudo Rei Socialis: On Social Concern* (30 Dec. 1987), change begins with the *Idea*, the "inner conversion," if one wants. With Smith and Marx, it begins with the *Real*; the process is from *real(ity) -> ideal(ity)*. In the first chapter of the last book of his *Wealth of Nations* Smith posited ever so significantly that "the understandings of the greater part of men are necessarily formed by their ordinary employments"; Marx would say, of course, by the "mode of production" or Produktionsweise. Marx, thus, as we know and he said in his "Foreword" to the second edition of *Kapital* (1873), had to stand Hegel on his head to upright the dialectic. If we take, as I have, the three constituent works of the Smithian system--*The Theory of Moral Sentiments* (1859ff.), the *Lectures on Jurisprudence* (1759-63), and the *Wealth* (1776-89)--we can distill from them Adam Smith's "realism" or "materialistic determinism" in the following formulation: (the Wm.-Robertsonian) "Mode of Subsistence" (commerce, agriculture, shepherding, hunting/gathering) -> Customs and Manners -> Reason/Under-standing -> Moral Sentiments (Morality). With Le Play, Weber, and others, we begin with the Reason-Morality combination and work the other way; the spiritual or inner conversion comes first--though, of course, very real and *material* institutions (e.g., religion, the Church) are employed in effectuating such "changes of mind and heart." Cf. Nitsch, *On the Smithian vs. Unsmithian Nature of Marx's Concept of Alienation* (Omaha, NE: College of Business Administration, Creighton University; Fall, 1982), n. 10, pp. 58f.; and, William Robertson, *The History of America*, Vol. I (London: W. Strahan [and] T. Cadell, 1777), p. 324.

[29]Cf. Cossa, Intro. (1892 / tr. 1893), pp. 70/59 (here) and 509/490f. (below)--et passim (for more).

[30]Ugo Rabbeno, "Scialoja, Antonio (1817-1877)," *PDPE*, III, 366.

[31]Ant. Scialoja, op. cit., 2a ed. (Turino: Pomba, 1846), locc. cit.

[32]Heinrich Dietzel, op. cit., I. Bd. (Leipzig: C. F. Winter, 1895), p. 54.

[33]Nitsch, "Social Economics: From Search for Identity to Quest for Roots; or, Social Economics: The First 100 Years (or So)," *International Journal of Social Economics*, 14:3/4/5, esp. pp. 71-72, et op. al.

[34]Given this brief elaboration of an otherwise very complex subject matter, we might appreciate, for instance, why the prominent *Enciclopedia Universal Ilustrada* (XVIII:2a, 1958, p. 2824) renders the title of Karl Heinrich Rau's celebrated *Grundsätze der Volkswirthschafts-lehre* (1826; 2te Aufl., Heidelberg, 1833) as "Principios de Economia social"; while at the same time, we might further note, as this was the "First Volume" of Rau's more generic *Lehrbuch der politischen Oekonomie*, the same (Spanish) account renders that as his *"Tratado de Economía política."* Thus, the problem is in rendering Volkswirthschaftslehre, the solution here--again--being "Principles of Social Economy."

Finally, though it falls outside our time-frame here, we might conveniently note that Carl Menger's even more famous *Grundsätze der Volkswirthschaftslehre* (Wien, 1871) might just as correctly have been rendered *Principles of SOCIAL Economics* as simply *Principles of Economics* when translated by Dingwall and Hoselitz (Glencoe, 1950), the exception being that, at least in Anglo-American circles, the "social" was no longer necessary.

[35]Israel Kirzner, *The Economic Point of View* (Princeton, NJ: D. Van Nostrand Co., 1960; passim), calls attention to the *human focus* of Schäffle's earlier (1861-73) work, while Pesch (*Lehrbuch*, I, 82ff.) indicates its (author's) theoretical-sociological character (proclivity).

[36]Since our source is essentially Cossa (*Intro.*, 1892/'93, passim), we mainly note further here the major works of these men (which we translate), to wit:
1. De Augustinis, (a) *Istituzioni de Economia Sociale*, Naples (Porcelli), 1837;
   (b) *Elementi de Economia Sociale*, 1843.
2. Cognetti, *On the Relation between Social Economy and History*, Florence, 1865.
3. Schiatarella, *On Method in Social Economy*, Naples, 1873.
4. Reymond, *Studies on Social and International Economy*, 2 vols., Turin, 1860-61.
5. Ciccone, *Principles of Social Economy*, 3 vols., 1866-68; 3rd ed., 1882-83.
* Lampertico, *Economy of the People and the State* (cp. the German, *Volks und Staatswirthschaft*) Vols. I-V, Milan 1874-84.

The exception singled out here is Cossa's "Nestor among Italian economists," the Neopolitan Antonio Ciccone (1808-1893). Importantly, besides his *Principii d'Economia sociale* (1866-83), we are told (*Intro.*, 1892/'93, pp. 517f./499), "[Ciccone] left behind valuable memoirs on the 'natural laws of economy(ics)' (1883), 'value' and 'wages' (1888), 'old-age pensions' (1882) and others of more considerable dimensions . . . on 'beneficence' and 'poverty' (1874) and his Milan prize-winner on the 'social question' (1884)."

Thus did Cossa's veritable *leader* among those contemporary Italian economists expand the scope of *his economia sociale* beyond the purely positive-scientific concern with those (physiocratic) "*leggi naturali dell' economia*" to matters of obviously *normative* import, including no less than what was to become that famous *social question* itself.

[37]See: John Maurice Clark, *Preface to Social Economics*, ed. M. Abramovitz and E. Ginzberg (New York: Farrar & Rinehart, 1936), subtitled "Essays on Economic Theory and Social Problems"; Oskar Lange, "The Scope and Method of Economics," *Review of Economic Studies*, XIII:3 (1945-46), where an excellent explication of "social economics" qua "*welfare economics* [alias] normative economics" is provided (pp. 21f.); and Howard R. Bowen, *TOWARD Social Economy* (New York: Rinehart and Co., 1948), where the holistic or comprehensive and normative or welfare-economics conceptions of social economy are described (p. v) and essayed (passim). Perhaps underrecognized in this (secular-normative) modern American group is Raymond T. Bye, whose "Criteria of Social Economy," *Amer. Econ. Rev.*, XXXIV:1, Suppl. Pt. 2 (March 1944) and *Social Economy and the Price System* (Macmillan, 1950) are at least worthy of mention in this connection.

[38]To conclude Cossa's last word on the relationships involved here between the severally designated disciplines of "political economy" (*economia politica*), "economic policy (politics)" (*politica economica*), and "social economy(ics)" (*economia sociale*), we correct the mistranslation of Dyer in the *Introduction* (1893, p. 57; et cf. the *Introduzione*, 1892, p. 66) at the conclusion of chapter IV ("Characterisation [Carattebe] of Political Economy") of the "Theoretical Part" as follows:

> Social economy, being a science, must defend its universal character and maintain strictly its independence of any and every practical purpose, while its truths must once and for ever renounce all claims to immediate and universal application. Economic policy (politics) being an art (applied science) must preserve its connection with the various sciences that supply it with rules to work by; from these it must formulate precepts which shall be adapted to circumstances, and sufficiently elastic to suit varying cases.

Finally, again, political economy is the discipline (art/science) which has embraced--often without distinguishing and differentiating--*Cossa's* economia sociale and politica economica.

The presentation above pertains especially to chapters II-VI of the "Theoretical Part" of the *Introduzione* of 1892. One might want to see/cf. the following works by Cossa and his son Emilio: (1) L. Cossa, *Guide to the Study of Political Economy*, trans. anon. (London: Macmillan, 1880; Ital. orig. *Guida*, 2a ed., 1871), "Gen. Pt."; (2) idem, *Economia Sociale* (8th ed., 1888), 9th ed. 1891; (3) E. Cossa, *Forme Naturali dell'Economia Sociale*, 1890; (4) idem, (we trans.), *The Phenomena of Public Finance in their Relationships with Social Economy(ics)*, Milan, n.d. [cit. *QJE*, VII (1893), 501].

[39]This *Ground-laying of Political Economy*, in turn, was the First Major-section of a collaborative enterprise (in union with Dietzel and others) under the collective title of *Lehr- und Handbuch der politischen Oekonomie*, and was to be subdivided into Part (and Volume) I on the *Fundamentals of the Volkswirthschaft* and Part (and Volume) II on *Volkswirthschaft and Law, especially Property-law or Freedom and Property [etc.]*; whence, according to the same "Plan des Gesammtwerks" (1892), Dietzel was to follow with the Second Major-section, *Theoretische Volkswirthschaftslehre* (cf. infra). Finally, as announced there, there were to be three more major-sections entitled, subdivided (for our purposes), and authored as follows: III. *Practische Volkswirthschaftslehre*, Part I--Commerce and Commercial Policy [Verkehrswesen und Verkehrspolitik], Wagner; IV. *Finanzwissenschaft*, Wagner; and V. *Literary History of Political Economy*, unassigned. Cf. Wagner, *Grundlegung*, 2te Aufl., I. Hbd. (Leipzig: C. F. Winter, 1892), pp. 1-3.

[40]The last sentence in translation: "You have to . . . acknowledge that the Social-principle is, must and will be *dominant*."

[41]In particular, national economics could hardly apply to any social system of human economy before the appearance of nation-states; or, to that contemporarily existing in the absence of such geopolitical boundaries. political economy confounds the art with the science, while even the latter--properly designated political *economics*, and granted that the state (*polis*) has existed (almost) universally since antiquity--is too politische, staatliche, i.e., not economically pure enough.

[42]F. F. von Wieser, 1st op. cit., 2te Aufl. (Tübingen: J. C. B. Mohr [Paul Siebeck], 1924; 1te Aufl., 1914) = I. Abt., II. Teil, *Grundriss der Sozialökonomik*, bearb. J. Schumpeter, Max Weber (ed. etc.) et al.; and, Friedrich von Wieser, 2nd op. cit., trans. A. Ford Hinrichs, with a Preface ("Foreword") by Wesley Clair Mitchell (New York: Adelphi Co., 1927), xxii, 470 pp. In this 2nd ed. (trans.), we note the citations of (esp.) Dietzel's *Theoret. Socialök.* (1895) and Weber's own *Wirtschaft und Gesellschaft* = III. Abt., *Grundr. d. Sozialök.* (1922) at pp. 17, 149, 437, e.g.

[43]Cf. Robert B. Ekelund, "Power and Utility: The Normative Economics of Friedrich von Wieser," *Rev. Soc. Econ.* XXVIII: 2 (Sept., 1970), 179-96; idem and Mark Thornton, "Wieser and the Austrian Connection to Social Economics," *Forum for Social Economics*, 16:2 (Spring 1987), pp. 1-12; Warren J. Samuels, "Introduction," Wieser, op. trans. Kuhn, cit. infra.

[44]Th. O. Nitsch, Review of *The Law of Power* (*Das Gesetz der Macht*, 1926) by Friedrich von Wieser, trans. W. E. Kuhn, etc., in *The Journal of Economics*, IX (1983), 226-28.

[45]In light of that background, we might further observe that Wieser's social economy, his theoretical construct significantly in the fashion established by Dietzel and followed by Cassel (cf. his *Theor. Sozialökon.* of 1918/'23 cit. p. 16/17) for example, similarly transcends all the special and concrete forms, forms at least *meant to be* "real." Thus, when Wieser wrote of the "classical theory (pushing) into the connections of the Volkswirtschaft" (p. IX), and the translator misrenders that latter "social economy" (p. xix), the translation is confusing the real-life context to which Wieser held classical economics to be restricted with Wieser's own universalistic, generic construct of the social economy, *die gesellschaftliche Wirtschaft*.

[46]Max Weber, *Wirtschaft und Gesellschaft* (Tübingen: J. C. B. Mohr [Paul Siebeck], 1922 = III. Abt., *Grundriss der Sozialokonomik*; ibid., 2te Aufl. (Tübingen: Mohr [Siebeck], 1925; 2 vols., 892 pp.), Parts "I. The Economy and the Social Orders and Forces" (Chaps. I-IV), "II. Types of Communal and Social Formations" (Chaps. I-VIII), and "III. Types of Herrschaft" (Chaps. I-XI).

[47]Gustav Cassel, *The Theory of Social Economy*, trans. S. L. Barron, New Rev. Ed., trans. 5th German ed. (New York: Harcourt, Brace and Co.; 1932), pp. vii-viii; et cf. idem, *Theoretische Sozialoekonomie*, 5te Aufl. (Leipzig: A. Deichertsche Verlagsbuchhandlung Dr. Werner Scholl, 1932).

[48]Johnson, op. cit. (1910), rev. ed. (1922), reprint ed. (Port Washington, NY / London: Kennikat Press, 1971), p. 23.

[49]"*Social economy*," stipulates *Webster's Second Unabridged* (1943), "[is] that branch of social science dealing with proposals for wider diffusion of material welfare; --called also *social economics*." When we "see ECONOMICS" as instructed in that place (s.v. "social"), we are informed first that "*economics* [or] political economy [*qua*] the science that investigates the conditions and the laws affecting the production, distribution, and consumption of wealth, or the material means of satisfying human desires," is divided into both "a *theoretical* branch concerned with the investigation of said laws, and a *practical* branch, showing the application of these laws to the problems of government." Then, the nomenclature:

> To this latter branch, the name of *applied political economy* or *national economy* is sometimes given. Writers who deal with wealth chiefly in its relation to THE CONDITION OF THE PEOPLE sometimes designate their subject as *social economy* or *social economics* [OUR emphasis].

Here, then, we have a specimen of popular wisdom, if one wants, of the nature and scope of social economy(ics) in its heyday in this country, at least. As evidence of this heyday situation, one searches in vain in *Webster's Third Unabridged* (1961-81) for a separate existence of social economy(ics), under either rubric, i.e., social or economy(ics).

[50]Lange, art. cit., *Rev. Econ. Studies*, XIII (1945-46), sec. I, "The Subject Matter of Economics," esp. 21f. Appropos the distinction by Lange between economic science and economic sociology, one is obliged to make at least brief mention here of a special brand of social economy(ics) qua what amounts to (Christian) secular-normative industrial sociology, as contained in the three contributions of F. B. Sanborn in the *Journal of Social Science* of the American Social Science Association over the period 1880-1902, viz.: (1) "Report of the Social Economy Department, . . . 1879," Vol. XI, May 1880; (2) "Phases of Social Economy," Vol. XXXI, Jan. 1894; and (3) art. cit, our n. 18 supra.

[51]John Stuart Mill, *Principles of Political Economy with Some of Their Applications to Social Philosophy* (5th ed., London; New York: D. Appleton and Co., 1868), Vol. I, pp. 257ff. (Bk. II. Chap. I, ##1,2,ff.).

[52]The works of Walras referred to above are as follows: (1) *L'Économie politique et la Justice*, (Paris: Guillaumin et Cie., 1860); (2) *Éléments d'Économie politique pure ou Theorie de la Richesse sociale* (Lausanne: F. Rouge / Paris: Guillaumin et Cie. / Bale [et Genève]: H. Georg, 1874); (3) ibid., 3d éd. (Lausanne: F. Rouge / Paris: F. Pichon / Leipzig: Duncker & Humblot, 1896); (4) *The Elements of Pure Economics or the Theory of Social Wealth*, trans. from the "Edition Définitive (1926)" by Wm. Jaffé (Homewood, IL: Richard D. Irwin, 1954); (5) *Études d'Économie Sociale (Theorie de la Repartition de la Richesse sociale)* (Lausanne: F. Rouge / Paris: F. Pichon, 1896); (6) *Études d'Économie politique appliquée (Theorie de la Production de la Richesse sociale)*, 2e éd. (Lausanne: F. Rouge et Cie. / Paris: F. Pichon et R. Durand-Auzais, 1936 [orig., 1898].

The concluding essay in that last (1898) work was apparently freshly written. Entitled "Sketch of an Economic and Social Doctrine," it may be considered the author's final word on his system as a whole. It is subdivided as follows: I. (The) Distinction between Pure Science, Moral Science, Applied Science and Practice; II. (The) Pure Science of Man and Society; III. (The) Pure Science of Social Wealth; IV. (The) Moral Theory of the Distribution of Social Wealth; and, V. (The) Applied Theory of the Production of Social Wealth / Stabilization (Regularisation) of Variations in the Value of Money; and, VI. French Politics: the Prayer of the Free-thinker.

Most importantly, that section IV opens as follows: "A general-rational cénonique [= "commonic(s)" qua an "abstract science . . . comprehending pure ethics and pure economics" (pp. 450f)], pure mathematical economics: such are the two indispensible disciplines for the theory of the distribution and of the production of social wealth." These are the "two preparatory sciences," which he "approached consecutively": "first the Theory of Property, . . . in considering it as an applied moral theory for elaborating the point of view of *justice*, and such as figures in my *Études d'Économie sociale* [1896]." We only note further here that, whoever would elaborate the social economy(ics) of L. Walras would have to pay careful attention to this last word (1898).

[53]Van Buren Denslow, op. cit. (New York: Cassel & Co., 1888), loc. cit.

[54]See/cf. Gunton, chronologically, as follows: (1) *Wealth and Progress* (New York: D. Appleton and Co., 1887; 7th ed., 1897), esp. the "Preface," pp. vii-viii, where "the principles of social economics" are promised and defined; (2) the *Principles* itself (New York / London: G. P. Putnam's Sons / The Knickerbocker Press, 1891), locc. cit.; (3) *Trusts* (New York: Appleton, 1899), esp. pp. iii, 1 and 32f-33; and, (4) the *Outlines* with Robbins (New York: Appleton, 1900), being essentially a popular version "especially adapted for study clubs [et al.]" of the earlier *Principles* (p. iii).

Gunton may well have edited/published the *Social Economist* (9 vols., 1891-95) whence *Gunton's Magazine* (14 vols., 1896-1902) containing his and other articles on "Social Reform(s)," "(The) Social Education Congress, Paris, 1900" etc., as per *Poole's Index*, Vols. I-VI. His earlier *Wealth and Progress* both provided a solution to "'the labor question'" and promised a second volume on "the principles of social economics" ("Preface," pp. v-vi, vii). The former consisted in what we might call the demand-side argument that higher wages and enhanced leisure time (shorter working hours, etc.) are the necessary and sufficient conditions for the successful (profitable) employment of more machinery (capital). The other book "devoted to the principles of social economics," he promised, would include "the principles of social progress in general, the principles of economic production [and] economic distribution, and the principles of practical statesmanship or applied economics" (p. viii). This closing equation of "practical politics" and "applied economics" should be rather familiar by now. The subsequent *Principles of Social Economics [etc.] with Criticisms on Current Theories* is valuable as a further statement of the author's 'low-wages/lack-of-leisure, etc.' underconsumptionist theory of "Business Depressions" (Part IV, Chap. V), etc. in the carrying out of the program earlier promised. A cursory examination of this work will reveal that, like many which preceded and followed it, while explicitly normative in its basic object, it purports to be equally positive in its argument; and, here even, when resting on induction from real-world conditions instead of on deduction from (Gunton would say *spurious*) "natural laws."

[55]J. A. Hobson, op. cit. (1914), reprint ed. (New York: Augustus M. Kelley, 1968), loc. cit.; and/or ibid., rev. ed. (London: George Allen & Unwin, 1933), loc. cit. For more on Hobson's (contributions to) social economy and humanistic economics, including references to his other works--especially his *Ethics and Economics* of 1928--see, most recently, M. A. Lutz and K. Lux, *Humanistic Economics: The New Challenge* (New York: The Bootstrap Press, 1988), p. 124 (quotation from op. cit., 1929, regarding economic security and "social solidarity"), "Appendix II," et passim; and, earlier, H. R. Bowen, *TOWARD Social Economy*, pp. 24n, 28n, 36n, 222 and 242, regarding the purposiveness (hence "organic" nature and "biological import") of human society, man's "conscious control . . . over human institutions [and their] 'laws'"; and "economic values" versus "ethical values," "wealth" versus "welfare," etc.

[56]Fetter, op. cit. (New York: The Century Co., 1915 sqq.), Vol. I, locc. cit.

[57]T. N. Carver, op. cit. (Boston et al.: Ginn and Co., 1919), loc. cit.

[58]Cf. Chapin, op. cit. (New York: The Century Co., 1917), "Preface" and locc. cit.; Jones, op. cit. (London: Methuen & Co., 1920), loc. cit.

[59]This particular normative concern coupled with a reformist thrust is further conveyed by the author when he writes (p. x):

> we believe that the poverty of to-day is a by-product of our industrial system, and not a necessary element in it. We do not believe with the ancients that 'the poor we have always with us.' By far the larger part of the poverty of the present is a product of social maladjustment, an incident in an industrial awakening and manufacturing growth that has been more rapid than adaptation in methods of distributing wealth and sharing the costs of progress. A passing of the emphasis from the ancient alleviative to modern preventive and constructive methods of dealing with poverty exemplifies a fundamental reversal in point of view.

[60]Jones, *Social Economics* (London: Methuen & Co, 1920), p. 1. Jones further maintains that "economic development," itself, may be regarded simply as the increasing complexification in the mode of cooperation, "with the consequent emergence of new economic functions" (ibid.). This increasing complexity and the emergent new functions are mirrored in many of our social problems; whence, he concludes this catena,

> The heart of a social problem resides not in difficulty of function so much as in the responsibility of every part for the welfare of the organic whole (ibid.).

Finally, while "co-operation may be a temporary and simple supplement to individual economy," it was nonetheless the very essence of that most primal form of "a body economic, with interdependent members, [viz.] the village community" (p. 2). Here, there was cooperation "based upon the appeal to individual gain"; here, too,

> There were rich and poor, and class distinctions: but there were no conflicts between 'capital' and 'labour,' for capitalists and wage earners . . . did not yet exist (ibid.).

[61]Wicksell, *Lectures on Political Economy*, trans. E. Classen, ed. etc. Lionel Robbins (New York: Macmillan, 1934), Vol. One, locc. cit.

[62]Subsequently, Wicksell expresses the need to note further at that point that

> the third main division (or Social Economics) would include, as its last section, a theory of public finance--which is usually treated nowadays as a separate science, as a study of particular financial legislation--though in essence it undoubtedly constitutes a part, growing more important and extensive every day, of political economy (p. 8).

For the most part, we are informed, he followed Walras, who also, we recall, treated "public finance" (qua "taxation") as an integral part of économie sociale.

[63]Gide, op. cit., Paris, 1884; 25e éd. (Paris: Société Anonyme du Recueil Sirey, 1926), pp. 2-3; *Principles of Political Economy*, trans. 3d ed. E. P. Jacobsen (Boston: D. C. Heath, 1891), pp. 2-3, where the *science* or "purely theoretical side of political economy" versus the *art* or "practical nature" thereof is explicated, but no mention of économie sociale is to be found; and, ibid., trans. 23d (1921) ed. E. F. Row (Boston, 1924; reprint ed.; New York: AMS Press, 1971), p. 2.

[64]Amadeo, *Economía Política y Social*, 2a. Ed. (Buenos Aires, 1937), loc. cit.

[65]A prominent case in point is Joseph Garnier's own *Traité d'Économie Politique, Sociale ou Industrielle*, further described as a "Didactic Exposition of the Principles and Applications of *that* Science," 7e éd. (Paris, 1873; 1st ed., 1845).

[66]For a contemporary manifestation of Wicksell's conception, cf. I. H. Rima's *Development of Economic Analysis* (Irwin, 1967; 4th ed., 1986), Chap. 1, "Early Impediments to Economic Inquiry: Dominance of the State"; but, cp. her remark (4th ed., p. 396) regarding J. M. Clark's "new type of economics, which he designates as social economics" with our "First 200 Years" here told.

[67]Cf. Leonis XIII, Pontificus Maximi, *Acta*, Vol. XI (Romae: Typographia Vaticana, 1892), "Litterae Encyclicae, *De Conditione Opificum*," pp. 97-144; and, idem, "On the Condition of Labor," trans. etc. in *Five Great Encyclicals* (New York: Paulist Press, 1939 sqq.), pp. 1-30 (##1-45).

[68]Cf. Nitsch, "Social Catholicism, Marxism and Liberation Theology (etc.)," *International Review of Economics & Ethics*, 1:3 (1986), esp. pp. 52-74; idem, "Social Catholicism, Marxism and Solidarism: Views on Human Nature and Values," *Forum for Social Economics*, 17:1 (Fall 1987), pp. 1-19; et fnn. 23 and 31 supra, for example.

For the latest, very heavy, and *official* emphasis on this Roman-Catholic, moral-theological doctrine on human-social solidarity, or human beings' natural/supernatural sociality, see John Paul II, *Sollicitudo Rei Socialis: On Social Concern*, 30 Dec. 1987 (Washington, DC: United States Catholic Conference, 1988; Publication No. 205-5), esp. ##39-40; and, cf. National Conference of Catholic Bishops, *Economic Justice for All: Pastoral Letter on Catholic Social Teaching and the U.S. Economy* (Washington, DC: NCCB, Nov. 1986), ##185, 186 et passim.

[69]Thos. G. Apple, D.D., LL.D., op. cit., Vol. 34 (1887, Philadelphia: Reformed Church Publishing House), pp. 20-32; and, cp. esp. Rev. W. Rupp, "Christianity and the Problem of Social Economy," ibid. 33 (1887), 23-44, which may have served as a prelude. Rupp's essay presents a clear notion of the transcendence of Christian social over orthodox political economy, which latter is (implicitly) regarded as both responsible for and apologetic of the system wringing misery on the working masses. Seemingly contrary to Apple, Rupp holds human nature, hence social economy, reformable; but, like Apple and others, he opposes alike the social Darwinism of the evolutionists, abolition of private property, and extensive state intervention of the communists and socialists. Yet, while the "natural law of competition" rendering the increasing pyramiding of wealth must be superseded by the ethical rule of Christian social economy, the state can help redress this maldistribution via taxation, for example, "What is required [for] the happiness of a people, and the safety of the social system," Rupp holds, "is not merely the accumulation of national wealth, but also a fair and equitable distribution of it" (p. 35).

Further, while not so focally as in Apple's argument, the organic view of society--"the social organism"--is maintained here. A truly organic social economy, driven by the Christian spirit of brotherly love and quest for justice, is one where cooperation and altruistic sharing will supersede competition and selfish piling up; and, in its vigorous development will hasten the day when "oppression and wrong will no longer exist, the contest between labor and capital will have ceased, and 'liberty, fraternity and equality' will no longer be an empty phrase" (p. 40). Withal, the Church must continue its special mission of catering to the daily needs of the poor; but, recognizing this as ameliorating symptoms merely, it must respond to the challenge of the "socialist agitators [that] what the poor require is not charity but justice" (p. 38). In the pursuit of justice, however, the Church's role seems to remain here much more that of pricking the consciences of the rich and powerful than of conscientizing the poor and powerless.

Finally, in unison with (1) the early Fathers of the Church (cf. Malina & Nitsch, 1986-87) et al., the here-styled "lords of Mammon" are indicted for "reaping the fruits . . . of the sweat and toil of thousands of others, to which they are not entitled" (pp. 35f); and, (2) the current Pontiff (*SRS*, 1987) the root of it all--"the [basic] cause of poverty" for Rupp and ultimate source of alienation and oppression for John Paul II--is "sin," viz. man's alienation from God.

[70]Jannet, lec. cit. ("Prem. Conf."), *Quatre Écoles d'Économie Sociale*, lectures given in the gymnasium of the University of Geneva, under the auspices of the Swiss Christian Society of Social Economy (Paris: Librairie Fischbacher, 1890), pp. 1-54; idem, "French Catholics and the Social Question," *Quarterly Journal of Economics*, Vol. VII (Jan., 1893), 135-61. The most complete listing of Jannet's works encountered in the present study is that by the *EUI*, XXVIII, Pt. 2 (1926), where we find such additional entries as (1) *De l'État présent et de l'Avenir des Associations coopératives* (1867), (2) *L'internationale et la Question sociale* (1871), (3) *L'Institutions sociales et le Droit civil à Sparte* (1874), (4) *Les E.-U. contemp.* (1875), (5) *Le Credit populaire et les Banques en Italie* (1885), (6) *Les Precurseurs de la Réforme sociale* (1889), (7) *Les Faits économiques et le Mouvement social in Italie* (1889), and (8) *Le Capital, la Speculation, et la Finance au XIXe Siècle* (1892).

[71]*Patronage*, the author notes, is peculiarly French, "a natural consequence . . . of that peculiar trait of . . . *bonhomie*" (p. 146). It was originally "an affair of custom," not institutionally formalized; whence, Le Play, in his extensive studies throughout Europe (1829-64), "recognized that everywhere these customs were assuring a social peace unknown where business managers had organized their relations with their employees solely upon the basis of the law of supply and demand" (p. 147).

[72]Le R. P. Ch. Antoine, S.J., *Cours d'Économie Sociale* (Paris: Guillaumin et Cie., 1896), locc. cit.; idem, sans "S.J.," op. cit., 3e éd. (Paris: Felix Alcan, 1905), locc. cit.; et ibid., 6e éd., updated by Henri du Passage, S.J. (Paris: Librairie Felix Alcan, 1921), locc. cit. The joint paginal citations will be given in the chronological order, 1896/1905/1921.

[73]Ch.S. Devas, *Political Economy*, 2d ed. (London, et al.: Longmans, Green, and Co.; 1901), p. 1.

[74]While Pesch (infra) may protest and proclaim that Catholicism presents the world no economic system or system of economics, his claims are hard to take seriously when one peruses such a work as the present and that of Toniolo next examined; and, when one considers seriously the "middle way" provided and prescribed by Pesch himself (infra).

[75]Prof. Giuseppe Toniolo of the University of Pisa, *Trattato di Economia Sociale / Introduzione* (Firenze: Fiorentina, 1907), locc. cit.; ibid, *La Produzione* (1909), which opens with the ontological proposition that "The *operative order* follows the *constitutive order* because . . . being is prior to operating, the organism is prior to life," etc. (p. 1); and ends (Chap. XIV) with a discussion of "The Laws of Coordination or of Solidarity among All the Industries" (pp. 302ff.). Cf. (1) E. A. Carillo, "Toniolo, Giuseppe," *NCE*, XIV, 198; (2) Serafino Majeretto, "Toniolo, Giuseppe," *Enciclopedia Cattolica*, XII, 305-8; and, (3) anon., "Toniolo (José)," *EUI*, LXII, 733-35.

[76]Moreover, as a living force, religious doctrine (Christianity) invades the human intellect (as dogma), affects the human will (as precepts of conduct), and actually forms part of "the society and collective life (as ecclesiastical organization and action)" (p. 48). Religious doctrine thus exerts a positive influence on both *scientific thought* and "the varied forms of *human-social* activity. From these relationships between the history of the religions and the same *economic science* and *life*," he continues, "[several] postulates as directive scientific

criteria are drawn." Thus, (1) "In the logical subordination of Economy(ics) to philosophy, Christian ethics . . . must be taken as the highest and surest expression of rational ethics. . . . (2) Christian morality, with the dogma which it inspires (dogmatic theology), coupled with the juridical applications which it confirms (canon law), as they came to unfold it in the historico-living organism of the Catholic Church, . . . must be considered by the positive-empirical scientist as the most potent factor in stirring up the economic energy of the people. . . . (3) Finally," the author notes, "the scientific acceptance of the fact of Christianity with its doctrines, . . . involving the recognition of the other solemn historical fact of the *christian civilization* which was generated thereby, and of its pre-eminence over all the other forms of civil progress by virtue of the harmonious, continued and universal development of all the specializations of collective human activity, including the economic, under the fertile predominion of the reason of the spirit; comprising thusly in its very self the normal law of social evolution" (pp. 48-49).

[77]Richard E. Mulcahy, S.J., *The Economics of Heinrich Pesch* (New York: Henry Holt and Co., 1952), passim; idem, "Solidarism," *NCE* (1967), XIII, 19-20; et cf. idem, "Pesch, Heinrich," ibid., XI, 195.

[78]Pesch, op. cit., as follows (vols.): (I) *Grundlegung*, 3te/4te Aufl. (Freiburg im Breisgau: Herder & Co., 1924; 1st ed., 1905); (II) *Allgemeine Volkswirthschaftslehre*. I, 2te-4te Aufl. (1926); and (III) ibid. II, 2te-4te Aufl. (1926) -- pp. cit. Other notable works of Pesch include his *Liberalismus, Sozialismus und christliche und sociales Arbeitssystem* (1922) -- as per Mulchay (1952) and art. "Pesch, Heinrich," *Brockhaus Enzyklopadie* (Weisbaden, 1972), XIV, 424.

[79]Fallon, S.J., op. cit., 6e éd. (Louvain / Bruxelles / Namur, 1944; 1st ed., 1921), locc. cit.; from the "Pref.": "This work exposes the principles of political economy and of social ethics [la morale sociale]" (pp. XIII).

[80]Nell-Breuning, op. cit. (Koln: Katholische Tat-Verlag, 1932), 2d ed. (1950); idem, op. cit, trans. Dempsey (New York / Milwaukee / Chicago: Bruce Publishing Co., 1936), p. vii et passim; et. cf. "Nell-Breuning, Oswald von," in *Brkhs. Enzyk.*, XVII (1971), 287-88.

[81]Raymond J. Miller, C.Ss.R., *Forty Years After: Pius XI and the Social Order / A Commentary* (St. Paul, Minn.; 1947), p. 1 et passim; other English translations of the text of *QA* employed here are found in Gerald C. Treacy, S.J., ed., *Five Great Encyclicals* (New York: The Paulist Press, 1939 sqq.); and Joseph Husslein, S.J., *Social Wellsprings*, Vol. II (Milwaukee: Bruce Publishing Co., 1949 sqq.).

[82]Cf. Pius XI, "Litterae Encyclicae . . . de ordine sociali instaurando [etc.]," *Acta Apostolica Sedis* (hereinafter, *AAS*), XXIII:6 (1 Iunii 1931), esp. p. 202; idem, "Lettera Enciclica 'Quadragesimo Anno' / Della ristaurazione dell'ordine sociale [etc.]," *La Civiltà Cattolica* (hereinafter, *Civ. Cat.*), 1931:II (30 maggio 1931), esp. p. 410; et ibid. as in Miller et al., opp. cit., par. ##75,76; whence, idem (Pius XI), "Litterae Encyclicae . . . De Cummunismo Atheo," *Divini Redemptoris*, *AAS*, XXIX:4 (31 martii 1937), esp. p. 80 ("Leo XIII de oeconomicis socialibusque rationibus deque operariorium causa"); idem, "Let. Enc. . . . 'Del Comunismo Ateo,'" *Civ. Cat.*, 1937:II, p. 14 ("31. -- Sull'ordine economico-sociale [etc.]"); ibid., Engl. trans., as in Treacy and/or Husslein, op. ed. (#31/#30 = "the social-

economic order"; and, Pius XII, "Alloc. 'Ad Delegatos Sodialitatis, etc.'," *AAS*, XXXXI:II (1939), pp. 283-86 passim.

[83]Enc. cit., Engl. trans. (##75, 76); Ital. version, *Civ. Cat.*, 1931:II, 410; official Latin, *AAS*, XXIII (1931), 203.

[84]In the pre-Vatican II era, von Nell-Breuning continued to build on the Peschian and *QA* bases, for example, in his nominally Weberian but substantively very moral-theological *Wirtschaft und Gesellschaft*, I (Freiburg: Herder, 1956), opening with the fundamental question of the Christian social order, e.g.; and, post-Vatican II, cf. his *Beschlüsse des Zweiten Vatican. Konzils* (1967), e.g. Franz H. Mueller's earlier *Heinrich Pesch and His Theory of Solidarism* (St. Paul, 1941) and more recent "Comparative Social Philosophies: Individualism, Socialism, Solidarism" (*Thought*, Sept. 1985, 297-309) are notable. In that last we note in the present connection, the following homage and information (pp. 298-99): "'Tell me,' the great Oswald v. Nell-Breuning used to say, 'what your image of man is, and I will tell you what your notion of social order is.'" Whence (p. 299n): "O. von Nell-Breuning, S.J., now a retired professor at Sankt Georgen, the Jesuit Graduate School of Philosophy and Theology at Frankfurt/Main, was largely influential in the preparation of the Encyclical of Pius XI, *Quadragesimo Anno*."

[85]Cf. esp. M. J. Williams, op. cit. (n. 24 supra) for perhaps the most exhaustive coverage of the "social Catholics," though our prominent Toniolo is excluded from the "Index of Names" if not as well from the pages of the text.

[86]As a classic example, cf. Richard A. Musgrave, "Efficiency vs. Equity in Public Finance," *Review of Social Economy*, XXII:1 (March, 1964), 1-6.

[87]"Karl Marx--Social Economist," ed. Wm. R. Waters, *Rev. Soc. Econ.*, XXXVII:3 (Dec., 1979), 261-387.

[88]Mill, *Principles of Political Economy* (1848; 7th ed., 1871), ed. Sir Wm. Ashley (London, 1909; reprint ed., New York: Augustus M. Kelley, 1969), pp. 772-73.

2

EVOLUTION OF SOCIAL ECONOMICS IN AMERICA

William R. Waters

I

If one accepts the premise that the development of social economics in the United States can be examined by investigating the research of the membership of the Association for Social Economics and its publication in the *Review of Social Economy*, two phases in its history stand out.

First, from the origin of the ASE in 1941 as the Catholic Economic Association until 1965, social economics in America existed as two separate, incompatible schools of social thought, both represented in the *Review*. Broad conventional economics, with a strong emphasis on policy based on Christian ethical foundations, was one kind, and social Catholicism, or solidarism, imported into this country from Germany and Italy by the Roman Catholic clergy was another. During the course of this first phase, social Catholicism weakened, so that by the end of the period its influence was almost nonexistent. Goetz Briefs, an influential proponent of it, resigned shortly after he served as president in 1956 because he believed that the Association had cut itself away from its solidarist roots.

The second phase in the history of social economics in America, as reflected in the *Review*, began around 1965. As a new editor in that year, I made a concerted effort to retain and revive social Catholicism as an important influence. At the same time, the *Review* was opened to what earlier would have been considered foreign ideologies by the Catholic membership. The ideologies were American institutionalism (recruited strongly by Ludwig Mai in Texas), a personally humanistic (rather than the traditionally deterministic) form of Marxism, and much later, a deontological economics based on Kantian ethics as an alternative to the utilitarianism of conventional economics. There was understandably some resistance to this influx, but surprisingly--unlike the incompatibility of conventional social economics to social Catholicism--there occurred a mixing of the four strains and a promise of an eventual synthesis. It began as a common stand against conventional economics; whether it will develop into a new synthesis of social economics is too early to say.

In this second phase of the history of American social economics (from 1965) there appeared another strain which differed in its aims from those of social Catholics, institutionalists, neo-Marxists, and Kantians. For want of a better name it is referred to here as resources economics. While the four humanistic ideologies focused most sharply upon the role of the worker in the production process with an emphasis upon human dignity and its related social morality, resources economics sought space in the *Review* for another reason, to argue that the premises of conventional economics lead to an irresponsible and catastrophic squandering of the earth's resources. Since there is no incompatibility between the humanistic strains and resources economics, as evidenced especially in the work of Schumacher, a blending is not inconceivable.

The two phases in the history of social economics as reflected in the *Review* (1941-1965 and 1965 to the present) are of approximately equal length. An overview of each phase follows.

II

Two Americans, both Jesuits from the Midwest, were leaders of the social economics movement and stand out in the first phase of its history in this country. Thomas F. Divine, the convenor of the committee of economists who established the Association in New York in 1941, championed orthodox economics as an autonomous science. He recognized social economics as broader than conventional economics and as valid only in policy matters. In the first convention proceedings message on the origin of the Association he wrote: "Its primary aims are scientific discussion of the problems of economic policy, the solution of which requires a knowledge both of economic science and of Christian social principles and the formulation of sound and practical programs of Christian social policy" (Divine, 1944, p. 103).

Bernard W. Dempsey, educated at Harvard under Schumpeter and a student of the work of Heinrich Pesch, accepted the premise of the autonomy of the science of economics, but he did not agree that the orthodox version that Divine championed explained the economy in a sound and effective way. He contended that economic organization is based on cooperation, which along with competition and authority form the three pillars of a "functional economy." This view is very different from conventional economists, who emphasize only competition. Dempsey's vision was essentially that of the 1931 social encylical, *Quadragesimo Anno*, which in turn came from the thought of Heinrich Pesch. Over time the Divine position won out, so that gradually the social Catholicism of Dempsey, Briefs, Mulcahy, Baerwald, and Mueller, as well as of Gundlach and von Nell-Breuning who wrote for the *Review* from Europe, lost much of its influence. More and more the social economists of this country became conventional economists (albeit with a Judeo-Christian ethic) dedicated to economic problems of labor, big business, international relations, and other topics of interest to all policy-minded economists. The issues important to Dempsey and social Catholicism were given less and less attention.

The Orthodox Position of Divine

In 1948 Divine wrote what he called an *apologica pro scientia sua* in which he showed himself to be a faithful disciple of Lionel Robbins. He defined economics as dealing with human conduct in the administration of scarce means for the attainment of alternative ends and purposes. Economics has two parts: the first is the positive science that is concerned not with value judgments but "with how men do act, and with the consequences of their action, not with how they should act" (Divine, 1948, p. 113). "The so-called economic motive is at the core of the science. The assumption of rational conduct [that] conforms rather closely with the conditions of economic life . . . is to economics what the law of gravity is to physics" (Divine, 1950, pp. 85, 88). Thus the scientific part of economics has an ethical neutrality. The other part, social economics, is economic policy concerned not with theory but with action; concerned "with prescribing what should and should not be done; with passing value judgments upon economic ends, institutions, behavior, etc. . . . If used in this sense economics patently cannot be divorced from ethics" (Divine, 1948, p. 114).

More and more, the *Review* came to reflect this orthodox view. Economics, with its emphases on efficiency and equity rather than on the reconstruction of the social order, and economic policy based on Christian ethical principles, rather than a different economics, became the norms. Writers showed great interest in the worker receiving his just share and expressed their views regarding other ethical problems. They were generally satisfied with the science of economics and concerned themselves with applications. Articles by Raymond J. Saulnier, David McCord Wright, and Edward H. Chamberlin illustrate this.

Saulnier of Columbia University, a past president of the Association and former chairman of the Council of Economic Advisors during the Eisenhower Administration, discussed such topics as the transitional requirements for European military governments to achieve social stability (Saulnier, 1945) and the institutional changes affecting the exercise of monetary controls due to the war (Saulnier, 1947). Wright of McGill University and Chamberlin of Harvard made contributions to the *Review* in which they criticized social Catholicism and supported the Divine position. Chamberlin, commenting on Wright, agreed that as central planning systems "vocational associations [a focal point of social Catholicism] are likely to impede growth . . . major reliance must be put upon the 'external pressure' of competition and the pricing system subject to substantial qualifications and safeguards" (Chamberlin, 1956, p. 61; Wright, 1956, p. 39). In short, the conventional economic view was represented by Divine, Saulnier, and others who dealt with economic problems without questioning the validity of the dominant paradigm, and by Wright, Chamberlin, and others who criticized the solidarist view until solidarist submissions to the *Review* became fewer and fewer.

The Solidarism of Dempsey

In the first issue of the *Review* in which Divine recognized the legitimacy of conventional economics as a valid science based upon rational principles of behavior, Dempsey introduced the diametrically opposed economics of the encylicals concerned primarily with the rehabilitation of social institutions to improve human efficiency and social order. He believed that unless human society develops a truly social and organic body, and unless land and labor combine cooperatively for the common good, society will be unable to produce an adequate output or form socially just institutions for integral human development. This view came directly from *Quadragesimo Anno* of 1931 and *Divini Redemptoris* of 1937. Both pure market and centrally directed economies are deficient. Their initial philosophies approached the problems of commutative and distributive justice, respectively, but these approaches are limited. Liberalism focuses upon satisfying the demands of commutative justice in requiring equivalence in exchange between free and equal parties. The other, socialism, seeks resolution to the problems of distributive justice requiring a more just distribution of society's output. But these social philosophies and the economics associated with them ignore social justice, which is more or less exclusively associated with solidarism. In its narrower and more useful sense, social justice means the obligation to reconstruct economic institutions so that they will reflect human dignity and produce effectively for the common good. This narrow meaning of social justice, sometimes termed constructive justice, is in counterdistinction to social justice in the broader or general sense of a just society whose social institutions are structured and operate so as to permit the satisfaction of individual and community rights (McKee, 1981, p. 3).[1] Social justice in the contributive or reconstructive sense is germane to social economists of the solidarist persuasion who contend that if there is to be social justice in the general sense, there is a responsibility to apply social justice in the narrow sense, that is, there is an obligation to reconstruct the social order (Dempsey, 1944, p. 17).

Dempsey characterized this solidarist kind of economics as dynamic, social, and corporative equilibrium (Dempsey, 1944, p. 18): dynamic because of its reconstructive (social justice) function, social because its end is the common good of society, corporative because the economic unit is the industry organized as a social economic corporation (the vocation group), and equilibrium because the cooperation among the units establishes a harmonious social order. Obviously, Dempsey was critical of contemporary "scientific" economics. He believed that economics as taught to Americans has been a lineal descendant of eighteenth century French liberalism. The descent was direct but the offspring of this liberalism split into two branches, the Ricardian and the Marxist, both priding themselves on the scientific and objective character of their analyses. Social Catholicism, on the other hand, goes back much further historically to Aristotle and Aquinas. Heinrich Pesch, the early twentieth century German Jesuit, wrote thousands of pages (as yet unavailable in English) to develop it. His influence upon Catholic social philosophy and the social encylicals was substantial. Articles in the *Review* in this first period in the development of social economics in America reflect his influence. The best summary still is Richard Mulcahy's 1952 work on the economics of Pesch. Three pillars of the paradigm (solidarity, production for need, and self-regulation by groups) give us a conception of its vision of an effective and just economy:

· While vocational groups (self-governing, autonomous groups organized by their members to deal with their problems) are essential, the vital factor of the system is the solidarist spirit motivating the men in those institutions. It is an ideology, aspiration, or attitude "without which neither their economic system nor any other can succeed" (Mulcahy, 1952, pp. 10, 179). Great benefits are possible if a spirit inspires "the producer to seek his profit in the creation of new utility rather than in a difference between prices and real exchange value, and to consider the welfare of the nation above his subjective, private gain" (Mulcahy, 1952, p. 100). "What is required is that the instinct of self-interest be regulated and ordered so that both the individual and the community be satisfied" (Mulcahy, 1952, p. 165).

· The economy has a goal beyond the marketplace aims of individuals. In the words of Pesch, "the securing of the supply of goods required for the providing for needs takes the first place" (Mulcahy, 1952, pp. 13, 61). This is in the Aristotelian tradition in which the end of the economy is production for social need, a tradition that has been lost in contemporary economics.

· The competitive price is the optimum price but a paradox emerges. Competition leads to its own destruction, to bigness, to monopoly, to cartels, to oligopoly. So Pesch looked to the establishment of order in the market--the regulation of competition (Mulcahy, 1952, p. 71). The regulatory factors which establish order and approximate the competitive price are individuals in consumer organizations, the state as the regulator of last resort, and the vocational group--that ideal self-regulator offering a better measure of the interests of their members than the state (Mulcahy, 1952, pp. 100, 186).   In short, the social Catholic or solidarist vision includes the spirit of solidarity, production for need, and self-regulation by groups.

That the influence of this kind of economics waned in America was evidenced by the diminishing importance of the *Review*, but not before some great contributions.   For example, Solterer, in a 3000-word book review of von Mises' *Human Action*, gave credit to John R. Commons for identifying the substance of the three kinds of justice--commutative, distributive, and social; they pertain to bargaining, rationing, and managerial activities respectively.   He took the last of these, managerial activities creating wealth, as equivalent to social justice in its reconstructive or narrow sense.   This is of some importance because it is an early instance of the integrating of social Catholic and institutional thought.   He quotes Commons thus:

> These three units of activity exhaust all activities of the
> science of economics.   Bargaining transactions transfer
> ownership of wealth by voluntary agreement between legal
> equals.   Managerial transactions create wealth by com
> mands of legal superiors.   Rationing transactions appor
> tion the burdens of benefits of wealth creation by the
> dictation of legal superiors (Commons quoted by Solterer,
> 1950, pp. 127-128).

Another contribution is von Nell-Breuning dealing with the troublesome issue of the vocational groups and the determination of price. He said that ideally society should be organized from the bottom up according to the principles of subsidiarity which implies a decentralized regulation of economic variables. Yet the principle of competition should be accepted to the extent that it does not lead to self-destruction (Nell-Breuning, 1950, pp. 90-91).   In another contribution, Becker stressed "the gentle but effective law of Christian moderation" that is a central focus of *Quadragesimo Anno*.   This law, he said, is an economic as well as ethical doctrine and as such is related to the economic problem of how to narrow the gap between wants and resources generally (Becker, 1952, pp. 66-67). Still another contribution, by Ederer in his review of Mulcahy's *Economics of Heinrich Pesch*, distinguished between the social philosophies of individualism, collectivism, and solidarism and the economic systems of capitalism, socialism, and the social system of labor (Ederer, 1953, p. 88).

Ederer insisted that solidarism is a social philosophy, not an economic system. This is an important distinction, but his label for the solidarist-inspired economic system, "the social system of labor," while it is interesting and does capture the system's essential nature of pertaining to the socially productive function of the sacred person, is awkward and has not become popular.

There were other *Review* articles before 1965 concerning the development of social Catholicism, but their number eventually decreased. The flourishing of solidarism in America ebbed.

III

A second stage in the history of American social economics as reflected in the *Review* came about from a combination of circumstances that pushed social economics into new directions. First, as the new editor in 1965 I expressed interest in two approaches: the theory of social economics--inquiry into "the very principles that shape the economic sector"--and social architecture--"the strategy of reform and efficacy of plans for the best social system" (Waters, 1965, p. 115). Both of these are inimical to mainstream economists; the first because practitioners of a science do not find it necessary to investigate the basic principles of their paradigm, the second, social architecture, because while economic scientists describe, analyze, and apply their discipline they are not involved, qua scientists, in the strategy of reforming the science. Here was a not-so-subtle commitment by the *Review* to (1) a reconstructive (solidarist) approach and (2) a sociophilosophical inquiry.

A second circumstance that influenced direction was the decision of the membership in 1970 to change the name of the organization from the Catholic Economic Association to the Association for Social Economics, thus sending a message that *Review* pages were available to all scholars interested in broad social economics and not just Catholics. A third was the decision to advertise the *Review* by exchanging ads with other social science journals. Still other changes made the *Review* better known: getting approval to abstract articles in the *Journal of Economic Literature*, launching the Potter Award in 1975 to encourage young scholars to submit their research to the editors of the *Review*, and expanding the board of associate editors to include a variety of social economists. The results were that submissions increased, the number of *Review* pages doubled (and then doubled again), and research submitted was varied including conventional, solidarist, institutionalist, neo-Marxist, neo-Kantian (or deontological), and resources economics. Most of these kinds of social economics were new to the old members of the Association. What helped to make the ideologically diverse pieces compatible was a common, personally humanistic base--what Pesch referred to as the solidarist spirit motivating men. Institutionalist and neo-Marxist articles in the *Review* tended to be more humanistic than their deterministic counterparts published elsewhere. Each of these four kinds of social economics requires some explanation.

American Institutionalism

It is not surprising that institutionalists were drawn to write for the *Review*. Both Pesch's brand of economics and American institutionalism were and are related to German historicism. Early institutionalists Richard T. Ely and Simon Patten were educated in Germany. Moreover, Dempsey recognized the affinity of institutionalism and solidarism in the first sentence of his work on the economics of the encyclicals in the first issue of the *Review*: "The economics of *Quadragesimo Anno* is, in the first place, obviously an institutional economics, very much in the same sense as John R. Commons used the term. It is concerned primarily with the rehabilitation of social institutions such that human economic efficiency can be maximized . . ." (Dempsey, 1944, p. 12). Also, as mentioned above, Commons' work was used by the solidarist Solterer in 1950. The great flood of institutional contributions, however, came after 1970. Since then the influence of John Maurice Clark and the Veblen-Ayres wings of American institutionalism has become more and more commonplace in the *Review*.

The work of John Maurice Clark has played an important and continuing role in the development of social economics in the last two decades due, among other things, to the contributions of a number of writers in the *Review*, George Rohrlich especially. A small sample of Clark's influential insights follow.

Clark was very concerned with the destructiveness of rampant self-interest. He felt that a new balance was needed between narrow self-interest and community responsibility (Rohrlich, 1984, p. 226) and that its recrudescence could bring an end to further social adaptation. "The health of the voluntaristic system would have begun to go downhill because it had reached the limits of its capacity, not for production but for voluntary social adaptation" (Rohrlich, 1977, p. 331, quoting Clark).

Clark offered a sustaining theme for social economics. Again it was Rohrlich that stressed the point. What made Clark the social scientist par excellence, said Rohrlich, "was his abiding concern with society in all of its aspects . . . and his unbending resolve to view economic knowledge not as an end in itself but as a tool in our pursuit of a good society" (Rohrlich, 1981, pp. 344-345).

Stanfield stressed Clark's vision of the dichotomy between technological and institutional aspects of human societies. We are not making sufficient institutional adjustment to the innovations in technique, organization, and manipulatory knowledge (Stanfield, 1981, pp. 280, 287).

Benz mentioned Clark's surprising solution to the weaknesses of the free enterprise system and competitive market structure, both of which Clark loved, as ". . . the cooperative movement and an 'effective competition'. . ." (Benz, 1981, p. 320).

Economists of the Veblen-Ayres wing of American institutionalism were more frequent contributors to the *Review* than the followers of Clark. Hans Jensen is surely one. To Jensen all of the great founders of economics (but not their successors "with the possible exception of the followers of Smith") were devisors of "theories for the purpose of finding cures for the social disease of poverty" (Jensen, 1977, p. 256). In effect, almost all the great economists were social economists. Their economics was reconstructive--Dempsey's word for solidarist economics. This kind of contribution was integrative of institutionalism and the more traditionally personalist economics peculiar to the *Review* in the early years. Jensen selected, among others, the archetype of mainstream economists Leon Walras to demonstrate that he especially was a social economist. To Walras there were two criteria of human welfare: the useful, meaning material well-being, achieved through the attainment of maximum utility, and the good, meaning just. "To point out how these goals may be achieved is the task of that branch of economics which Walras called 'social economics'" (Jensen, 1977, p. 241).

William M. Dugger, an influential leader among both institutionalists and social economists, did much to integrate the two. In a popular *Review* article, he discussed what social economics is. It is value-directed: ". . . [W]e employ and we need value premises in making observations of facts and in analysing the causal interrelation" (Dugger, 1977, p. 301, quoting Myrdal). It is ameliorative: ". . . [C]ooperation does not arise

from a presupposed harmony of interests, as the older economists believed.
. . . [I]t arises from the necessity of creating a new harmony of interests
--or at least order, if harmony is impossible" (Dugger, 1977, p. 304,
quoting Commons).   It requires action: Myrdal, who acted in many
capacities in Sweden and the United States to deal with poverty, is a role
model. It is holistic: The only demarcation of subject matter is what is
relevant and less relevant.   Finally, it is organic: Since social economics
deals with people and their institutions it is organic, not mechanistic--again
Commons is mentioned as one who claimed that society is more than the
sum of isolated individuals, being a multiple of cooperating individuals
(Dugger, 1977, pp. 306-307).

      No one has explained basic differences between mainstream and
social economics more persuasively than Dugger.   There is an irreconcilable difference between the two at what Finn called the most elemental
level of scientific methodology--"the ground of explanation" (Finn, 1987).
At this level, sciences treat either the whole of visualized reality or a
specified part.   Mainstream economics very clearly opts for the part.
Social economics opts to treat the whole.   The difference is not, as is
commonly understood, at the second level of method--"the mode of
production," which may be induction or deduction.   One may notice the
similarity between Dempsey and Dugger in this matter of treating the
whole.   Another similarity is that Dempsey also explains solidarism as
reconstructive, a characteristic that subsumes both the ameliorative and
action requirements stipulated by Dugger.   Dugger and other institutionalists differ from social Catholics, however, in that their writings
contain little discussion of the role of human dignity and personal
uniqueness in the philosophical premises of economics.

      Other institutionalists contributed to a developing social econom-
ics. Only a small sample of these contributions is possible here due to
space limitations. For example, concerning the role of government in the
economy, Samuels said that in mainstream economics government is placed
in a role of aberrational exception. This is distortive to economic reality
because government's impact on the economy has long been ubiquitous
(Hickerson, 1981, p. 212).   Khalil, in an article contrasting Sir James
Steuart's concept of the role of government in the economy with that of
James Buchanan, explained Steuart's realistic conception of the functioning
of the public innovator and the need for a spirit of the people that
government facilitates (Khalil, 1987, p. 131). Both the Samuels and Khalil
works expose the dominant bias against government and toward market
liberalism in mainstream economics. Hickerson wrote an article directed

against another bias of mainstream economics that analysis is limited to means, ends being given. He argued that both traditional social economics and institutionalism require full integration of means and ends (Hickerson, 1986, p. 278).

Additionally, Cochran, a member of the Veblen-Ayres group, disputed the view of the harmonious automaticity of the system. Like the solidarists, he denied that "what is good for society is simply good for the individual as measured by the market, which is merely an extension of the natural law" (Cochran, 1974, p. 180). Rather, he contended, the economy is a product of institutional, historical, technological, and social forces, not the product of an unseen hand of divine origin. Thus the economist has a moral responsibility to help society see where it might go and understand what its alternatives are. Economics is therefore a moral science (Cochran, 1974, pp. 186-187).

Finally on this limited list of integrating components of developing social economics emanating from institutionalism is one of Stanfield's contributions. He said that our developing social economics requires a new microeconomic orientation, a return to the micro level to evaluate specific institutions and to take a critical attitude toward extant institutional configurations (Stanfield, 1975). Indeed, as we shall see, one of the major new directions of social economics as reflected in the *Review* is a treatment of collegial participation in economic enterprise.

Neo-Marxism

Ironically, the first appearance of the Marxists in the *Review* was an article that did not mention Marx. E. K. Hunt argued in 1971 that the institutional influence of German-educated Simon Patten early in the twentieth century was profoundly conservative; i.e., his vision of a sound economy was as a coalition of government, big business, conservative labor leaders, and liberal intellectuals of which Kaiser Wilhelm and Bismark would have been proud. The economic ideology of the early New Deal, which inspired the enlightened, socialized capitalism of the National Recovery Administration (NRA) was disseminated by social innovators Rexford Tugwell and Francis Perkins, who were protégés and devotees of Patten, along with General Hugh S. Johnson of the WWI War Industries Board and Raymond Moley, spokesman for big business. Hunt said: "It is not surprising that [Patten's] ideas came directly from Germany, a country in which the liberal tradition had really never taken root" (Hunt,

1971, p. 140). So we have here a Marxist writing for social Catholics who, because they have an intellectual heritage from the German historical school, might unfortunately be inclined to see promising social economic development in big corporate welfare systems. His implication was that the liberal individualist roots which spawned laissez-faire attitudes in France and Britain and that were precursors of Marxian scientific socialism are, after all, more valid than the reactionary statism and institutionalism that come from Germany.

Though market liberalism and Marxism are both children of the Enlightenment, there is no commingling of them in the *Review*. On the other hand, there is some integration of neo-Marxism with American institutionalism and with its cousin social Catholic solidarism, notwithstanding the diversity of origins. For solidarists to have an open mind about Marx would require proof that an element of moral evaluation exists in Marx's work. If, as it appears especially in his mature works, there is a strong determinist flavor--that is, the economy operates and evolves automatically according to the law of nature--then there is little hope of integration. Elliott has written extensively in the *Review* to show that there is an ethic in Marx's explanation of evolving economic systems, that his work is not wholly deterministic. In 1979 Elliot pointed to Marx's strong normative tone and the moralistic words he used: capitalism contains creative powers, produces new and varied human needs, and brings capabilities from such institutions as capital-labor relations, private property, and market exchange processes. Marx also spoke of alienation of labor and dehumanizing conditions. So while the moral dimension exists, it must be recognized in a very special and careful way--remember that Marx rejected the dominant view of the antinomy between is and ought (Elliott, 1979, p. 272).

In the concluding remarks of the Association's conference on "Community Dimensions of Economic Enterprise" in Milwaukee in 1984, Elliott again argued that Marxism is ethically based. Marx spoke of a genuine community of "fully associated men," "associated producers" organizing work, and production "under conditions most adequate to their human nature and most worthy of it" (Elliott, 1984, quoting Marx). Finally in what might be his best work on the subject of Marxian scientific analyses and moral evaluation, Elliott pointed to Marx's view of man's moral capability to ameliorate, to shorten and lessen birth pangs and to rise above his class perspectives (Elliott, 1986, pp. 130-131, 144).

Hunt contended that there is a compatibility between the Veblenian and Marxian paradigms. In an article on the normative foundations of social theory, Hunt defined social economics as having these characteristics: it recognizes innate traits of human nature that include universal needs and a degree of malleability to attain them; it is normative in that it can judge a comparative superiority of one society over another in achieving universal needs; and it is critical in addressing society's historical genesis, relative adequacy, probable course of future development, and possibilities for change. Conventional economics does not have these characteristics (Hunt, 1978).

A great force for integration is Nitsch, who has written for years to show commonalities and differences of solidarism and Marx. Recently, after long study of the sources of sociophilosophical systems, he concluded that in all three--social Catholicism, Marxism, and solidarism of the Gide type--human dignity is taken as an end-value. This includes "human life, living, being and becoming, and the fullness, perfection" (Nitsch, 1987, p. 1). The human being in all of these is to be regarded as subject and not object, and is in some sense even sacred. All else, he follows with, is instrumental.

Deontological or Kantian Economics

The influence of Immanuel Kant has come to the literature of social economics only recently. Kantian economics finds a welcome place in the Association and the *Review* because of the similarity between Kant's social ethical principles and those of Christianity as found in social Catholicism.[2] Some practitioners prefer to call it deontological, stressing the obigatory nature of the underlying intrinsic human rights. Three eminent social economists (Lutz, Ellerman, and Etzioni) have explained how economic behavior and institutions may (should?) be based on Kant's moral principles.

Lutz was the first to introduce Kant in the *Review*. He did it in the context of a critical review of the instrumental value theory of American institutionalism. He asked, Is instrumentalism "consistent with the demands of personal dignity," one of the explicit aims and objectives of the Association for Social Economics as defined by the Executive Council in 1970? His answer was no.

> Intrinsic human dignity demands a view of Man as being
> by birth equipped with an integrative and spiritual center
> transcending space and time. The notion of conscience is

an integral part of this view. It goes without saying that all this would be flatly objected by Dewey and Ayres and most likely by Tool (Lutz, 1985, p. 168).

Lutz contended that emphasis on human dignity is not only explainable within the framework of scholastic natural law doctrine "but also by Kantian ethics stressing dignity and ultimate worth of all human beings" (Lutz, 1985, p. 167). He briefly described the relevant ethical framework of Kant: man is a rational agent with Free Will and an affinity to God; he is unique and as an end-in-itself attains dignity; he has no price--anything that has a price has an equivalent which would contradict the element of uniqueness in the original premise (Lutz, 1985, p. 168).

Ellerman's argument against the immorality of the employment contract was probably inspired by Kant. He contended that the employment contract is a part of the heritage of capitalist liberal thought. To one who accepts an inalienable rights theory as natural law, such a contract is legalized fraud on an institutionalist scale. A person cannot be used to further another person's ends--his uniqueness precludes this. A person may not alienate his basic right--such an agreement would put a person in the legal role of a nonperson and would therefore be naturally invalid (Ellerman, 1986, pp. 37-38).

Using a Kantian ethic, Etzioni contemplated a future Kantian socioeconomics. If one assumes a utilitarian ethic, as conventional economics does, society should be free from interventions by authorities that reduce the sum total of human happiness--the moral position is the general welfare attained by maximizing satisfaction. Individuals in such a society seek but one reality (Etzioni, 1987, p. 38). On the other hand, to assume that in addition to seeking utility there are moral obligations is to change the nature of economics. Should the economist assume the Kantian ethic that each person is endowed with basic rights that cannot be traded off (alienated) for the sake of enhancing the total welfare, a new theory of economic behavior surfaces. This theory must account for factors that enhance and weaken the conventional rules of the game; for example, it calls for reanalyses of property rights, limited liability, rights and obligations of workers and owners, productivity, saving, work incentives, debt transactions, and so forth (Etzioni, 1987, pp. 37-46).

The influence of Kantian moral premises has just begun. Its future as an important variant of social economics, or as an enrichment to a developing integration of the competing strains of humanistic economics, is unpredictable but promising.

Resources Economics

This kind of economics, which has as its theme the preservation of physical resources and the tragic potential of pollution and deprivation should society's output not be managed wisely, is of a different order than solidarism, institutionalism, neo-Marxism, and deontological economics. The latter variants of social economics are concerned essentially with what economists term the factor of labor--the role of humans in the production function. Resources economics, on the other hand, focuses upon land--the factor of physical endowment. But because resources economics has become such an important part of the *Review* it requires some mention here. It became a popular part of the *Review* because it is an alternative economics, critical of conventional economics. Another reason, perhaps, was that is was drawn to the *Review* by Rohrlich's call for an integration of social ecology and economic science (Rohrlich, 1973); authors seek out journals publishing articles of related interest, and Rohrlich's article was a magnet for economists to submit their work on the condition of the environment and the renewal processes of humanity's production and consumption activities. The emphasis of the Rohrlich article, unlike the resources economics articles that came later, was not on the fragility of our natural heritage but on what ecologists call the "web of life" in which organisms seek adjustment to one another and struggle for existence. To Rohrlich, this meant self-renewal and continued equilibrium of society in the broadest sense including "the key areas of health, education, [and] socialization . . ." (Rohrlich, 1973, p. 36). Works by Georgescu-Roegen, Daly, and many others followed.

Georgescu-Roegen's article introduced bioeconomics to *Review* readers, a discipline spotlighting the origin of the economic process and the problem of mankind's existence "with a limited store of *accessible* resources, unevenly located and unequally appropriated." With this approach two pillars of standard economics became inappropriate: the principle of discounting the future, and the principle of rational behavior--that of maximizing utility ("whatever that may mean") (Georgescu-Roegen, 1977, pp. 361, 375).

Daly's contribution calls attention to "an extreme overemphasis in conventional economics on the circular flow and a correlative underemphasis on the linear throughput (Daly, 1985, p. 246). He contended that both are important. In the empirical reality, the flow of exchange, which is circular, is coupled with a physical flow of matter-energy (the throughput), which is linear. The latter begins with the depletion of low-entropy resources from the environment and ends with the pollution of the environment with high-entropy wastes (Daly, 1985, p. 279). The effects of this incomplete and unbalanced conventional macro theory (which is the "regnant Keynesian-neoclassical synthesis") are "the fallacy of misplaced concreteness, the evasion of ethical issues and the apotheosis of economic growth (which) have become a way of life" (Daly, 1985, pp. 295-296).

IV

This final section summarizes the great progress of social economics in this country but also recognizes the barriers and limitations it faces. Progress is occurring even though there were several emotionally charged controversies that arose as serious barriers to a synthesis of the various strains--those of O'Boyle and Stanfield on the solution to the problem of widespread devaluation of human life; of Lutz and Hill on the issue (mentioned above) of human dignity in instrumental value theory; and of Scaperlanda and Lutz on the question of whether Maslowian-type humanistic economics is authoritarian and related to the secular humanism of Lamont and Huxley (Scaperlanda, 1985, 1986a, 1986b; Lutz and Lux, 1986). No doubt there will be others. Progress continues even though social economics may be, by its nature, a limited alternative to the dominant paradigm it criticizes so strongly. After all, social economics is more social philosophy than economic analysis; yet out of this constrained intellectual environment there is rising a practical social economics richer than any of the past. This richness is evident especially in two areas that contrast with conventional economics. First, social economics develops the role of cooperation as a complementary organizing principle to competition, and second, it starts with the wise insight that the economic decision-maker is a unique, socially oriented person rather than a utility-calculating individual. We turn first to one of the controversies and then to the recent contributions in the two areas of cooperation and economic decisionmaking.

The controversies were inevitable. It is not possible to synthesize portions of Pesch, Veblen, Marx, and Kant without giving offense. Only the O'Boyle/Stanfield debate will be dealt with here to illustrate the controversial nature of the subject matter. O'Boyle criticized the secularism of American institutionalism as personified by Stanfield in a leading 1975 *Review* article for which the author won the first Helen Potter Award (O'Boyle, 1978). He charged that Stanfield's interpretation of the widespread and substantial devaluation of human life wherein human beings are viewed less and less as persons and more and more as objects (Stanfield, 1975) is substantively deficient and inadequate because Stanfield's solution is that the artist and scientist be called upon to restore the social order. O'Boyle contended that the key agent is the steward (and the parent and healer) who represents the function of carer in society. The artist and scientist are not the key agents. The function of caring is an obligation in contributive justice for all human beings (O'Boyle, 1978, p. 208). Stanfield viewed the criticism as unwarranted. He was being used as a straw man. After all, the hallmark of Marxist and institutionalist thought is "the primacy of society and the pivotal importance of cooperation and responsibility in socioeconomic behavior." Moreover, the Marxian concept "of commodity fetishism is related to degradation of human relationships in a social order founded upon commodity production" (Stanfield, 1978, p. 209). Implied here is the difference between the social economic strains of Judeo-Christian and Kantian humanists, on the one hand, and the Marxists and institutionalists that come out of a secularist tradition, on the other. It is clear that the groups will never be fully reconciled. Rohrlich was as successful as anyone in restraining the disputants. He said we should look to what is integratable in the two, rather than the differences (Rohrlich, 1980, p. 218). Rohrlich suggested two commonalities: (1) sound economics must be "need-based" in contrast to the established "want-based" of conventional economics; and (2) society must be reconstituted to reform degrading objectification of human labor and interpersonal relations. He recognized that O'Boyle would not accept the second as adequate; giving primacy to society, rather than to the individual, is no solution. O'Boyle, Rohrlich contended, "affirms the primacy of the spiritual through service to others." Still, Rohrlich believes, to dwell upon commonality appears significantly more important to the development of social economics than the differences between the strains (Rohrlich, 1980, p. 220).

With all of the controversies, the integrative tendency persists. As Lutz wrote, ". . . we reach out to our critic (Scaperlanda) to jointly help regenerate a social economy rich in social tissue and community spirit" (Lutz, 1986, p. 186).

The current direction of social economics and its greatest progress might be in the two areas of economic cooperation within the firm and the person as economic decisionmaker. A few notes about the development in each are offered in conclusion.

Cooperation or solidarity is the hallmark of traditional solidarism. The eminent European social ethicist Johannes Messner said in an article on Pesch that the fundamental law of both the social and economic order is the principle of solidarity (Messner, 1976, p. 118). Since 1980, when Jonathan Boswell wrote on economic cooperation this key element has blossomed to make integrative behavior and structure the focal points of developing social economics. Boswell did several things in the article: he gave a short historical description of the role of cooperation in the economy citing Boulding who said that there are three organizing principles of human activity--coersion, exchange, and integration (classified kinds of integration or cooperation, cooperation inside the enterprise, between firms, and social cooperation); and developed the latter form in the article (Boswell, 1980, p. 157). Social cooperation in business, he said, is that form of integration wherein "business institutions freely and deliberately pursue social ends." His findings suggested that the overall effects of business social cooperation in Britain may have been considerable: underpinning habits of commercial trust, encouraging rapprochements with organized labor, reinforcing national economic identity, and mitigating the problem of unemployment (Boswell, 1980, p. 162). Social cooperation, as opposed to the other two kinds, is essentially the discipline of business ethics and as such is important, but it is not the forte of social economics, since business ethics does not have much to do with contributive social justice or the reconstruction of the economy. The other two kinds do. Cooperation among firms is in the tradition of Pesch and Dempsey. There is great promise for this. Surprisingly, however, little has been accomplished in recent years. Edward O'Boyle is one of a few who recognized its great value to social economic reform. (Compare O'Boyle, 1986.) An example for both the common good and mutual advantage of the parties was TopNotch, a combine of construction firms and unions in the Indianapolis area described in Lohman and Mayer in 1984. To make progress in this area means developing a theory of reconstruction using vocational groups, finding case studies that may be emulated (another example is the project Pride in St. Louis) and analyzing the resistance to it from prevailing antitrust laws and the dominant ethos that says only competitive exchange is the legitimate organizing principle.

While social cooperation (business ethics) has been of limited interest to social economists and cooperation among economic organizations is just beginning to be considered seriously, cooperation within the firm has taken off. Much of this has been due to the success of the cooperative movement in Mondragon, Spain, and the competitive edge of collegial production in Japan and Sweden. We can do no more here than list a few of their significant contributions from the *Review*.[3]

Severyn Bruyn, one of the leading scholars in this area, says that social economy is the systematic study of how a society organizes its natural resources, the key concepts being social governance and social development (Bruyn, 1981, pp. 81, 84). In an important contribution to this area, he examined the phenomena of self-management; the new class of professionals and their role in business; community self-studies to promote integration; self-study by firms; and resistance to self-management by the "new class," elected officials, trade associations, and unions (Bruyn, 1984).

Briefs and George dealt with the topic of hierarchic versus collegial participation. It is an essential requirement, Pesch said, solidarity being not only a fact but an ethical requirement. It arises because the individual is totally dependent on the help of others. But it does not follow that the work process should be completely collegial and democratic--there are both advantages and disadvantages to full worker participation in the firm's decisionmaking. Economic advantages of the peer group mode are: it provides for the engaging of workers' capabilities. ("To work is to function as a person," Briefs quotes Pesch as saying.) Work consists in applying human capabilities, i.e., ". . . mental or physical powers, in the individual's or society's service" (Briefs, 1984, p. 297); it performs better in shock situations; it is more compatible with local innovativeness; and it performs better in local decisionmaking. On the other hand, it is less efficient in assigning duties and other matters related to leadership (Briefs, 1984, p. 311). George, like Briefs, is tentative. Reformers must be careful not to throw out hierarchy and expect great things from self-management. This propensity to collegial management may be an unrecognized allegiance to the questionable social philosophy of classical liberalism (George, 1984, p. 416).

Erteszek devised a wholly new institutional construct on the principles of enterprise solidarity for his California manufacturing firm. This "common venture enterprise" recognizes that the firm is a community as well as a business, that employees are investing talent that is as significant as investment in capital, and that the firm must plan for full employment as well as for profit--unemployment being a moral as well as an economic issue (Erteszek, 1982, pp. 324, 326).

Finally, the work of Booth in this area is impressive (Booth, 1985; Booth and Fortis, 1984). His emphasis is upon the effectiveness of the cooperative as a legal form of enterprise. While cooperatives are considered as alien by many Americans, their values, says Booth, are in fact, rooted in Western societies, especially in the ideals of democracy, property ownership, and payment of value created in production to those carrying out the tasks (Booth, 1985, p. 309). Cooperatives outperform their capitalist counterparts, says Booth, something Americans are unaware of and when they find out about it they are surprised (Booth, 1985, p. 311; Booth and Fortis, 1984, p. 341). A number of indications are given to demonstrate this statement. The cause of this greater productivity is that the producers internalize the enterprise objective as their own so there is a huge degree of work effort. Also, solidarity and fellowship act to generate social pressure on group members to maintain high levels of work. But, for all this the producer-cooperative form of organization is not widespread--the institutional support is lacking. Technical assistance from small-business developing centers and institutes for employee ownership are needed; as are centers for entrepreneurship where business ideas may be catalogued. Also, state support of funds and assistance is required, not unlike what the land grant universities supplied in research and development to the agricultural sector of the economy for more than a century in this country.

The last contributions to social economics to be mentioned here are those treating the person as decisionmaker in the social economy. In an article on the necessity for and the limits to the social welfare state, Rauscher referred to solidarism as a discipline based on the understanding of man and society. An earnest acceptance of the concept of the person, he said, leads to the desire to build an economy upon certain qualities: liberty, private initiative, personal responsibility, and self-reliance, on the one hand, and solidarity and justice, on the other (Rauscher, 1978, p. 347). Many social economists complain that conventional economics encourages the development of the first group rather than the second. Social economists of a solidarist persuasion seek to remove this imbalance by building upon a social philosophy of personalism. The contributions of Danner, Stikkers, Davis, and O'Boyle come to mind. Danner's work, based upon Mounier and Scheler, distinguishes between the concepts of person and individual, the former having a genuine social dimension, whereas the individual in economic literature is restricted to self. "A person is poised between offering his own absoluteness and moving toward union with others. . . . The absolute dignity of the person is the transpersonal movement toward community with others and the attainment of absolute values" (Danner, 1984, pp. 80-81). Stikkers applied Scheler's notions of person and community to social economics in more detail--these were insights that were of great influence to Goetz Briefs and other earlier solidarists but were somehow lost to contemporaries. Scheler's social ethics helped (and help) in overthrowing the philosophical premises of classical economics including the metaphysics of Newtonian mechanics, the epistemology of British empiricism, Hobbesian utilitarianism, the deistic theology of the invisible hand, and classical liberalism (Stikkers, 1987, p. 224). Scheler's sociology of knowledge demonstrated (1) the invalidity of economists abstracting from such aspects of society as politics, religion and education, and (2) the difficulty of being objective since all knowledge is conditioned--including data and the laws (Stikkers, 1987, p. 226). An important part of Scheler's thought is that bourgeois society, of which the science of economics is a part, drags down spiritual values to the levels of usefulness, efficiency, and market value. It is, Scheler claims, a perversion to subordinate vital values to utility values. Is profit-seeking a perversion? How ethically legitimate is the pursuit of gain? This was a question taken up by Danner (1984) and Davis (1987) in the light of the soundness of philosophical principles underlying personalism and social economics. Danner (1984) contended that the notion of economic gain if properly conceived in moderation, justice, and the spirit of poverty functions effectively and morally as a principle of action in the social economy. Davis developed the idea contending that the pursuit of gain can only be deemed acceptable when infused with social concern for justice and the individual dignity of others. It is acceptable as a principle of action only if interdependent upon the good of other individuals (Davis, 1987, p. 311).

The man or woman in the economy is a broad concept in social economics. Broader than that of conventional sense which limits the economic decisionmaker to a welfare maximizer--the individual seeking the greatest satisfaction by finding the biggest difference between benefits and costs when consuming, working, and investing. Social economics is concerned in addition with welfare from the work process itself. A *homo laborem exercens* realizes his (her) humanity through work. It is the way the individual fulfills the calling to be a person. This being so labor has priority over capital, the worker has primacy over work in the objective sense (Schotte, 1984, pp. 346-349). Solidarity arises out of work. It has the characteristic of uniting people--it consists of power to build a community. Moreover, the essence of man the worker is to create. O'Boyle stressed this quality of person as creator in an article on the destructiveness of unemployment. It is the knowledge that through work man shares in creation that supplies the most profound motive for undertaking work (O'Boyle, 1985, p. 342, referring to John Paul II). Lack of it destroys man the builder-creator. The very essence of man is to create (O'Boyle, 1985, pp. 342-343).

Social economics in America is prospering. The areas of greatest current interest are cooperation within the firm and the role of the unique person in the economy. We can expect social economists of all of the strains we have examined--social Catholics, institutionalists, neo-Marxists, Kantians, and resources economists--to continue to have a scholarly interest in them. There is promise that their continued integration will develop a widely accepted social economics.

Notes

[1]Social justice is a very helpful but ambiguous term. It is used in both broad and narrow senses. In the broad sense that the institutions of society and their operation must be just, it is synonymous with what Aristotle called legal justice and medievalists called general justice. It is more useful in the narrow sense of an obligation to contribute to society to make it just--to reconstruct it (see Solterer, 1950). Social justice focuses on obligations and opportunities for *production* for the common good and visualizes an environment for individuals to begin contact with the social economic (vocational) groups (Dempsey, 1944, p. 17). Sometimes social justice is confused with other narrow forms of justice: namely, commutative and distributive. Often it is used with no precise meaning at all. Arnold McKee's two papers in the *Review* are an excellent introduction to the subject (McKee, 1981, 1984).

[2]There is no point here in contrasting differences between Catholic and Kantian social policy. One thing that might be mentioned, however, is the *general* character of the Kantian treatment of social ethics as contrasted with the practicable *special* treatment by Max Scheler, a German ethicist influential to Catholics. Henry Briefs suggested this difference in casual conversation.

[3]See Waters (1984) for an edition of the proceedings of the Association for Social Economics' Conference on Community Dimensions of Economic Enterprise devoted to cooperation within the firm.

References

Becker, J. M. 1952. "Economic research and the social encylicals," *RSE* 10 (March).

Benz, G. A. 1981. "The theoretical background of John M. Clark and his theory of wages," *RSE* 39 (December).

Booth, D. E. 1985. "Problems of corporate bureaucracy and the producer cooperative as an alternative," *RSE* 43 (December).

Booth, D. E. and L. C. Fortis. 1984. "Building a cooperative economy: a strategy for community-based economic development," *RSE* 42 (December).

Boswell, J. S. 1980. "Social cooperative in economic systems: a business history approach," *RSE* 38 (October).

Briefs, H. W. 1984. "Solidarity within the firm: principles, concepts and reflections," *RSE* 42 (December).

Bruyn, S. T. 1981. "Social economy: a note on its theoretical foundations," *RSE* 39 (April).

_____. 1984. "The community self-study: worker self-management versus the new class, *RSE* 42 (December).

Chamberlin, E. H. 1956. "Professor Wright on the pluralistic economy," *RSE* 14 (March).

Cochran, K. P. 1974. "Economics as a moral science," *RSE* 32 (October).

Daly, H. E. 1985. "The circular flow of exchange value and the linear throughput of matter-energy: a case of misplaced concreteness," *RSE* 43 (December).

Danner, P. L. 1982. "Personalism, values and economic values," *RSE* 40 (October).

_____. 1984. "The moral foundations of community," *RSE* 42 (December).

Davis, J. B. 1987. "The science of happiness and the marginalization of ethics," *RSE* 45 (December).

Dempsey, B. W. 1944. "Economics implicit in the social encylicals," *RSE* 1-2 (December).

Divine, T. F. 1944. "The origin of the Catholic Economic Association," *RSE* 1-2 (January).

_____. 1948. "The nature of economic science and its relation to social philosophy," *RSE* 1-2 (September).

_____. 1950. "On the assumption of 'rational conduct' in economic science," *RSE* 8 (September).

Dugger, W. M. 1977. "Social economics: one perspective," *RSE* 35 (December).

Ederer, R. J. 1953. Review of Mulcahy's *The Economics of Heinrich Pesch*, *RSE* 11 (March).

Ellerman, D. P. 1986. "The employment contract and liberal thought," *RSE* 44 (April).

Elliott, J. C. 1979. "Social and institutional dimensions of Marx's theory of capital," *RSE* 37 (December).

_____. 1984. "Recapitulation and prospects: worker ownership and self government," *RSE* 42 (December).

_____. 1986. "On the possibility of Marx's moral critique of capitalism," *RSE* 44 (October).

Erteszek, J. J. 1982. "Corporate enterprise and Christian ethics," *RSE* 40 (December).

Etzioni, A. 1987. "Toward a Kantian socio-economics," *RSE* 45 (April).

Finn, D. Rush. 1987. "Where are economic explanations persuasive? A view from social economics," *RSE* 45 (April).

George, D. 1984. "Worker self management versus the new class," *RSE* 42 (December).

Georgescu-Roegen, N. 1977. "A bioeconomic viewpoint," *RSE* 35 (December).

Hickerson, S. R. 1981. Review of *Law and Economics: An Institutional Perspective* (edited by Warren J. Samuels and Allan Schmid), *RSE* 39 (October).

_____. 1986. "Instrumental justice and social economics," *RSE* 44 (December).

Hill, L. E. 1977. "Social and institutional economics: toward a creative synthesis," *RSE* 35 (December).

Hunt, E. K. 1971. "A neglected aspect of the economic ideology of the early New Deal," *RSE* 29 (September).

_____. 1978. "Normative foundations of social theory: an essay on the criteria defining social economics," *RSE* 36 (December).

Jensen, H. E. 1977. "Economics as social economics: the views of the 'founding fathers,'" *RSE* 35 (December).

Khalil, E. L. 1987. "Sir James Steuart versus Professor James Buchanan: critical notes on modern public choice," *RSE* 45 (October).

Lohman, J. and H. C. Mayer. 1984. "Top notch is more than a slogan," *RSE* 42 (December).

Lutz, M. A. 1985. "Pragmatism, instrumental value theory and social
      Economics," *RSE* 43 (October).

_____. 1986. "Instrumental value, and social economics: a rejoinder to
      Lewis Hill," *RSE* 44 (October).

Lutz, M. A. and K. Lux. 1986. "Neo-humanistic economics: a comment,"
      RSE 44 (October).

McKee, A. 1981. "What is 'distributive justice?'" *RSE* 39 (April).

_____. 1984. "Beauchamp and Donaldson on economic justice," *RSE* 42
      (April).

Messner, J. 1976. "Fifty years after the death of Heinrich Pesch," *RSE* 34
      (October).

Mulcahy, R. E. 1952. *The Economics of Heinrich Pesch*. New York:
      Henry Holt & Co.:

Nitsch, T. O. 1987. "Social Catholicism, Marxism and solidarism: views
      on human nature and values," *Forum for Social Economics* (Fall).

O'Boyle, E. J. 1978. "On caring and the restoration of social order," *RSE*
      36 (October).

_____. 1985. "On reconstructing the foundations of policy toward the
      unemployed," *RSE* 43 (December).

_____. 1986. *Cooperation at the Supra-Firm Level: Illustrations*. Un-
      published.

Rauscher, A. 1978. "Necessity for and limits to the social welfare state,"
      RSE 36 (December).

Rohrlich, G. F. 1973. "The potential of social ecology for economic
      science," *RSE* 31 (April).

_____. 1977. "Beyond self-interest: paradigmatic aspects of social
      economics," *RSE* 35 (December).

_____. 1980. "Social economics approaches to teaching, policy analysis,"
      RSE 38 (October).

_____. 1981. "John Maurice Clark's unmet challenge," *RSE* 39 (Decem-
      ber).

_____. 1984. "Community--the submerged component of economic
      theorizing," *RSE* 42 (December).

Saulnier, R. J. 1944. "Postwar international monetary institutions:
      discussion," *RSE* 1-2.

_____. 1945. "The transition to peace under military government," *RSE*
      3 (December).

_____. 1947. "Institutional changes affecting the exercises of monetary
      controls," *RSE* 5 (June).

Scaperlanda, A. 1985. "Is neo-humanistic economics the new paradigm for social economics?" *RSE* 43 (October).

_____. 1986a. "Neo-humanistic economics and social economics, revisited," *RSE* 44 (October).

_____. 1986b. "On social economics: response to Lutz and Lux," *RSE* 44 (December).

Schotte, J. P. 1982. "The social teaching of the church: Laborem Exercens, a new challenge," *RSE* 40 (December).

Solterer, J. 1950. "The entrepreneur in economic theory," *RSE* 8 (March).

Stanfield, J. R. 1975. "On the crisis of liberalism," *RSE* 33 (October).

_____. 1978. "On liberation and capitalism: a reply," *RSE* 36 (October).

_____. 1981. "The instructive vision of John Maurice Clark," *RSE* 39 (December).

Stikkers, K. W. 1987. "Max Scheler's contribution to social economics," *RSE* 45 (December).

Waters, W. R. 1965. "On the theory of social economy," *RSE* 23 (September).

_____, editor. 1984. *Community Dimensions of Economic Enterprise, RSE* 42 (December).

Wright, D. M. 1956. "Dynamic relations in a pluralistic economy," *RSE* 14 (March).

PART II:

THE FABRIC OF CONTEMPORARY SOCIAL ECONOMICS

3

CATHOLIC SOCIAL ECONOMICS: A RESPONSE TO CERTAIN PROBLEMS, ERRORS, AND ABUSES OF THE MODERN AGE

Edward J. O'Boyle

> *Theology does not grow grain.*
>
> Heinrich Pesch

> *For though economic science and moral discipline are guided each by its own principles in its own sphere, it is false that the two orders are so distinct and alien that the former in no way depends on the latter.*
>
> *Quadragesimo Anno*

Catholic social economics is an amalgam of economic science and moral discipline in which economics is perceived as (1) one of several distinct sciences that study man and (2) dependent on moral discipline in order to address the problems, errors, and abuses that beset man in the Modern Age. Each of these distinct sciences has its own unique perspective on man. In economics, the focus is upon man the worker and man the consumer. By focusing on a different aspect of man, each science develops its own special body of knowledge which defines its domain or, as John Henry Newman puts it, the boundaries of its province (Newman, 1947, p. 336). Since these sciences are intertwined around the same subject, each may contribute something instructive to the others. Because man is one and not several, there is a need to reconcile any differences in views held about man not only within a given domain but also across domains, and to work out any implications for theory and applications[1] in each of the affected sciences. Strictly speaking, none of the several sciences alone has the wherewithal to develop the knowledge necessary to answer the three questions that are most central to each one. Who is man? What is man? Whose is man? In that most important sense, each one including economic science is dependent on moral discipline.

Each of the several sciences to some extent depends additionally on moral discipline to help determine whether a specific action of man is morally good, morally bad, or morally neutral. In this regard, philosophy instructs economic science as to the meaning of justice in economic matters. Even so, justice is not sufficient to remedy the ills of man in the Modern Age. Theology also informs economic science that charity is needed to unify man in the economic order. Significantly, this instruction occurs by means of the papal encyclicals.

According to Catholic social economics, man's end in the economic order and the proper goal of the economy is to provide for man's own material needs. This end, however, is only intermediate. Man's final end reflects the fact that man is more than mere material being. We elaborate further on this matter and the others mentioned above later in this chapter.

For our purposes here, the following reduced-form description of Catholic social economics is sufficient: a distinct sphere of economic theory and economic applications that is moral, anthropocentric, teleological, and intertwined with several other spheres (see Figure 3-1).

FIGURE 1. CATHOLIC SOCIAL ECONOMICS: ECONOMIC SCIENCE
INSTRUCTED BY MORAL DISCIPLINE

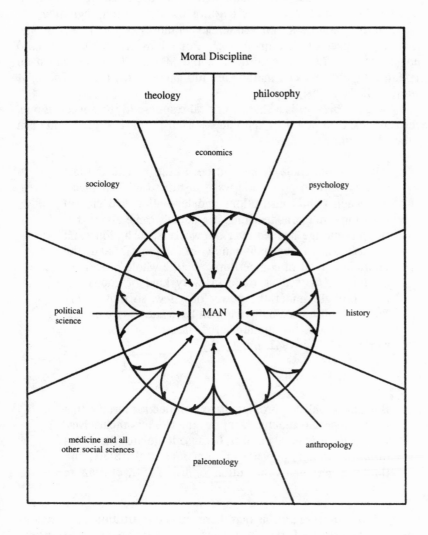

ORIGINS AND LINEAGE

We date the beginnings of Catholic social economics (most especially the moral-discipline component) from Pope Leo XIII's encyclical *Rerum Novarum* (1891). Some may argue for an earlier beginning, but no student of Catholic social economics would deny the powerful and long-lasting impact of that encyclical. Pope Pius XI in *Quadragesimo Anno* (1931) calls Leo's encyclical ". . . the Magna Charta on which all Christian activities in social matters are ultimately based (*Encyclicals of A Century*, c. 1942, p. 204).[2]

Rerum Novarum is a sharply critical response to the abuses of man under capitalism (in practice) and under socialism (in theory). Capitalism is indicted as follows:

> After the old trade guilds had been destroyed in the last century, and no protection was substituted in their place, and when public institutions and legislation had cut off traditional religious teaching, it gradually came about that the present age handed over the workers, each alone and defenseless, to the inhumanity of employers and the unbridled greed of competitors. . . . the whole process of production as well as trade in every kind of goods has been brought under the power of a few, so that a very few rich and exceedingly rich men have laid a yoke almost of slavery on the unnumbered masses of nonowning workers (*EC*, c. 1942, pp. 10-11).

Socialism is scored as well:

> But [the socialists'] program is so unsuited for terminating the conflict that it actually injures the workers themselves. Moreover, it is highly unjust, because it violates the rights of lawful owners, perverts the functions of the State, and throws governments into utter confusion (*EC*, c. 1942, p. 11).

Rerum Novarum affirms that there are two institutional protections against the oppression of the working man by more powerful persons and institutions in society: private property and private associations.

> Let it be regarded, therefore, as established that in seeking
> help for the masses this principle before all is to be
> considered as basic, namely, that private ownership must
> be preserved inviolate (*EC*, c. 1942, p. 19).

Indeed, elsewhere in the letter Leo XIII called this right "sacred" (*EC*, c. 1942, p. 44).

Private associations, especially though not exclusively unions, are vigorously reaffirmed in *Rerum Novarum*.

> In summary, let this be laid down as a general and
> constant law: Workers' associations ought to be so
> constituted and so governed as to furnish the most
> suitable and most convenient means to attain the object
> proposed, which consists in this, that the individual
> members of the association secure, so far as possible, an
> increase in the goods of body, of soul, and of prosperity
> (*EC*, c. 1942, p. 52).

As with property, association is by natural law a right of man (*EC*, c. 1942, p. 48). These two rights, along with man's end in the economic order, it seems, are closely interconnected. Does it not follow that, if man has a right to acquire and hold property, he also has a right to one of the means--association with his work mates--that allows him to acquire more property and thereby to provide more adequately for his own and his family's material needs?

Leo XIII's concerns extend beyond the rights of the working man, encompassing the duties of the poor and the working class along with the obligations of the rich and employers. Among those duties we find the mutual obligation of workers and employers under the principle of equivalence. Leo's "to perform entirely and conscientiously whatever work has been voluntarily and equitably agreed upon . . . [and] . . . to give every worker what is justly due him" (*EC*, c. 1942, pp. 22-23) corresponds to the much more familiar and widely accepted "a fair day's work for a fair day's pay" that expresses in part the meaning of justice in the modern work-place.

Directly in line with *Rerum Novarum* are two other papal letters: Pius XI's *Quadragesimo Anno* (1931) and John Paul II's *Laborem Exercens*

(1981). The first is noteworthy in part because for the first time the principle of subsidiarity is affirmed officially by the Vatican.

> . . . just as it is wrong to withdraw from the individual and commit to the community at large what private enterprise and industry can accomplish, so, too, it is an injustice, a grave evil and a disturbance of right order for a larger organization to arrogate to itself functions which can be performed efficiently by smaller and lower bodies . . . of its very nature the true aim of all social activity should be to help individual members of the social body, but never to destroy or absorb them (*EC*, c. 1942, p. 224).

In addition, for the first time Pius XI calls for a reconstruction of the economic order based on the establishment in the workplace of private associations including as members both workers and employers to complement rather than replace the separate private associations already in place for these two parties.

Laborem Exercens repeats *Rerum Novarum*'s general condemnation of capitalism and socialism, reaffirming the need for private associations in the workplace[3] as set forth originally in *Quadragesimo Anno*, and articulates a new vision of man as a co-creator of the universe through his daily work. Further, *Laborem Exercens* sees man's labor as a small part of the Cross of Christ thereby connecting man more intimately to the redemption and the resurrection (*Laborem Exercens*, 1981, pp. 57, 63).

This encyclical is a prime example of moral discipline instructing economic science as to man's authentic nature. It confirms that this instruction continues even today and that Catholic social economics has boundaries and content that are not fixed rigidly once for all. We return to both *Quadragesimo Anno* and *Laborem Exercens* later.

The economic-science component of Catholic social economics is anchored firmly in the work of the German Jesuit economist Heinrich Pesch (1854-1926). His five-volume magnum opus, *Lehrbuch der National-okonomie*, is regarded as a commentary on *Rerum Novarum* and a sourcebook for *Quadragesimo Anno*. Not surprisingly, Leo XIII wrote *Rerum Novarum* and Pesch took up economic science as a response to the same thing: the miserable conditions of the working class.

Since it originated as a response to a crucial problem of the Modern Age, we find it convenient to present the whole of Catholic social economic thought in the context of a response to the problems, errors, and abuses of that age. We do not mean to suggest thereby that Catholic social economics is entirely reactive.

In Pesch's case a four-year period of study in England in the 1880s sensitized him to the miseries of the working masses. This experience prompted him some years later to undertake a formal program of study in economics (Mulcahy, 1952, pp. 2-3). In addition to the *Lehrbuch*, Pesch produced more than 100 other publications before his death in 1926. Thus, from the very beginning, a concern for the working man and for conditions in the workplace has been a dominant theme of Catholic social economics.[4]

The centerpiece of Pesch's life work is his social system of labor which occupies the middle ground between the problems, errors, and abuses of individualism in unrestrained capitalist economies and of collectivism in socialist economies. Pesch's system more commonly is called "solidarism" and is more aptly described as an architectural sketch for a reconstructed economic order than a set of detailed blue-line drawings.

The absence of detail to Pesch's system is of no crippling consequence since Catholic social economics insists that, without exception in economic affairs, man is far more important than the system. Man truly is; economic systems are a manner of speaking.

> Everything contained in the concept of capital in the strict
> sense is only a collection of things. Man, as the subject
> of work, and independently of the work he does--man
> alone is a person (*Laborem Exercens*, 1981, p. 31).

Moreover, the economic system is to serve man and not man the system and since man's material needs may be different in different places, times, and circumstances, some differences in the details of solidarist economic systems are desirable, if not necessary.

Pesch directly influenced a small group of fellow Germans known as the "Study Group" or "Study Circle." They were Gustav Gundlach, Oswald von Nell-Breuning, Franz Mueller, Wilhelm Schwer, Paul Jostock, Goetz Briefs, Heinrich Rommen, and Theodor Brauer (Mueller, 1940, p. 337). Gundlach and von Nell-Breuning both were Jesuits.

Pesch's influence extended to the United States partly as a result of the immigration of some members of the Study Group. Among his American admirers were several fellow Jesuits including notably Richard

Mulcahy and Bernard Dempsey. Mulcahy authored the only book-length commentary on Pesch's work in English which is all the more significant because only a very small portion of Pesch's work (none of *Lehrbuch*) has been translated into English. Dempsey's *The Functional Economy* owes much to the work of Pesch and is one of the finest examples of scholarly work in the Catholic-social-economics tradition.

Clearly the economic-science portion of Catholic social economics is Jesuit in origin and Jesuit or Jesuit-inspired in development. Today the two are appreciably diminished. Perhaps this reflects the vocation's crisis in the Jesuit order, the laicization (some would say the secularization) of the American Jesuit colleges and universities, the logical positivist bias in conventional economic science, the subordination of labor economics to most other subspecialties among many conventional American economists, or some other reason(s). Whatever the reason(s) for the decline of Catholic social economic thought and the role of the Jesuits within that scholarly tradition, today there are no American universities including Jesuit institutions that offer a doctorate in economics with a concentration in Catholic social economics. The future of Catholic social economics in the United States at best is uncertain.

ERRORS CONCERNING MAN'S NATURE

For Catholic social economics, the most egregious error of the Modern Age relates to the nature of man. Of all modernist errors this one has the most profound significance for Catholic social economists.

This error has two major forms: capitalist man and socialist man. Capitalist man is by nature entirely individual. Capitalist man has intelligence and free will. He is self-made and self-determining--a unique being whose uniqueness is supported physically by his fingerprints, for example, and by his dental prints. The rugged individualism of capitalist man means that he belongs to no one other than his creator--himself. For capitalist man, personal freedom is the ultimate principle.

Socialist man, in contrast, is by nature entirely social. Socialist man has intelligence and is determined by his environment. Some would insist that socialist man has free will. Others would argue that he is entirely determined by his environment. In a physical sense, his social nature is reflected in his human sexuality, for instance, and in his faculty of speech. To the extent that socialist man is determined by his environment and the state controls that environment, socialist man is a creature of the state and belongs to the state. For socialist man, the common good is the ultimate principle.

Conventional economics appears to hold two radically different views of man. *Homo economicus*, on the one hand, is pure reason. Every act and decision is subjected to a rational scrutiny to determine how many units of utility the initiator may expect to accumulate. Hedonistic man, on the other hand, is a physical object that operates on the sensate level: seek pleasure, avoid pain. Hedonistic man is completely embodied; *homo economicus* is entirely disembodied.

While capitalist man and socialist man both have one-dimensional natures, solidarist man's fundamental nature is twofold: a being who is, at once, individual and social. Catholic social economics rejects out-of-hand individualism's conception of man as self-sufficient and self-determined and collectivism's view of him as a lesser part of a greater whole. Rather, solidarist man is simultaneously "an independent free being *and* a dependent social being . . ." (Schuyler, 1953, p. 226; emphasis in the original). For solidarist man, justice and charity are the ultimate principles. More about these later.

Pesch rejects the *homo economicus* of conventional economics. Instead, he affirms that

> Individuals are human persons, subjects (bearers) of the same metaphysical human nature by reason of which all persons are ordained to all values pertaining to humanity, including economic values. This identity of relationship establishes between all persons a bond of mutual recognition of personal value. Moreover, since all persons are limited in their capacities and are individually-qualitatively different, there is need for the relations of giving and receiving, the relation of exchange in all efforts to achieve human values,--including economic (Gundlach, 1951, p. 185).

Reflecting its deep rootedness in scholastic philosophy, Catholic social economics sees man as a body-soul composite. It is the body that gives man his materiality. Without embodiment, man could no more work than an angel could play the piano. Indeed, without his body, man would not have to work because he would have no material needs. Without ensoulment, on the other hand, which supplies him with intelligence and free will, he would not be free to rationally choose or reject God.

Lacking that freedom, man is reduced from a creature made in the image and likeness of God to the status of a slave.

In the words of Thomas Aquinas, man is the "crown of creations." Leo XIII affirms this view as follows:

> The soul bears the express image and likeness of God, and there resides in it that sovereignty through the medium of which man has been bidden to rule all created nature below him and to make all lands and all seas serve his interests (*EC*, c. 1942, p. 39).

Catholic social economics insists that economic science and economic systems preserve and protect this view of man. Any failure in this regard is a capital offense against man, calling for a revision of economic science, a reconstruction of the economic order, or both.

This error with regard to man's authentic nature carries over into economic science in ways that are subtle and in places where it is not expected. If man is seen as completely disembodied, for example, his decisions in the marketplace are interpreted in terms of reason but not emotion. If he is seen as wholly embodied, his needs are reduced to the purely material. In poverty studies, if man is perceived as having only an individual side to his nature, poverty is defined and measured in absolute terms. If he is seen as a social being, however, poverty is defined and measured in relative terms. A solidarist perspective as to man's nature would argue that poverty is to be handled in both relative and absolute terms corresponding to man's dual nature. Pesch employs such an argument in addressing the issue of the minimum wage (Mulcahy, 1952, pp. 126-127).

Additionally, note the reduction of man to object in conventional economics. Instead of referring to workers as persons as does the solidarist Dempsey,[5] conventional economists more and more label them "human resources." Finally, note how man is removed significantly if not entirely from the language of conventional price theory. "Equilibrium" construes the market relationship in terms of two objects: quantity supplied and quantity demanded. "Agreement" construes the same relationship in terms of two parties: buyers and sellers. "Agreed price" is more appropriate for a science that is anthropocentric than is "equilibrium price."

CAPITALISM'S CENTRAL PROBLEM AND ABUSE

The market system is widely acclaimed for the efficient manner in which resources are reallocated in a capitalist economy from uses where they no longer are needed to uses where they are. Imbalances in the product market and the resource market are eliminated by freely fluctuating prices that clear a market of a shortage through a price increase and of a surplus through a decrease. The efficiency of capitalism's markets in allocating resources is admired even further because this outcome proceeds automatically from the interaction of individual buyers and sellers each one of whom is pursuing his own self-interest. No central authority is necessary; the invisible hand is sufficient.

Leo XIII and Pesch had no difficulty seeing the central problem of capitalism at least in its relatively early, unrestrained competitive form: the enrichment of a relatively small number of persons and the impoverishment of the rest. This problem transforms in more mature capitalist economies where the masses achieve a much higher living standard. First, entrepreneurship continues apace in advanced capitalist systems in largely unpredictable fashion, creating new economic opportunities for some persons and destroying old enterprises for others. Second, markets perform the resource allocation function by threatening to idle any resource for which (whom) the price (wage) is set above the market rate (Becker, 1965, p. 292). For these two reasons even advanced capitalist systems inevitably instill a sense of insecurity, greater in some than in others, that is virtually universal. Even young, healthy, well-educated, highly skilled, ambitious, and gainfully employed workers know that in capitalism the opportunity to amass a fortune carries with it the risk of losing everything. In unfettered capitalism, it cannot be otherwise.

The special abuse of man under capitalism derives from the market system itself wherein decisionmaking is overly decentralized. Unrestrained capitalism exposes man to the special abuse of economic anarchy, that is, a dysfunctioning market that is not automatically self-correcting and that is especially destructive because the parties involved are panicked by their own fear. Examples of economic anarchy in a capitalist system include bank runs, price wars, and stock market collapse. For sure, the risk of economic anarchy is very small. However, for any given human individual the damage may be devastating. We explicitly differentiate abuse from insecurity because the former has a zero-sum characteristic whereas the latter has a negative-sum quality.

SOCIALISM'S CENTRAL PROBLEM AND ABUSE

The foremost problem of socialism is a failure to understand properly and fully the precise origins of capitalism's critical dysfunction. *Laborem Exercens* highlights a part of this flaw in socialist thought:

> . . . merely converting the means of production into State property in the collectivist system is by no means equivalent to "socializing" that property. We can speak of socializing only when the subject character of society is ensured, that is to say, when on the basis of his work each person is fully entitled to consider himself a part-owner of the great workbench at which he is working with every one else (*Laborem Exercens*, 1981, p. 37).

Leo XIII in *Rerum Novarum* vigorously condemns the socialist solution of seizing all private property:

> . . . the fundamental principle of Socialism which would make all possessions public property is to be utterly rejected because it injures the very ones whom it seeks to help, contravenes the natural rights of individual persons, and throws the functions of the State and public peace into confusion (*EC*, c. 1942, p. 19).

It was Pesch who identified more precisely the core dysfunction in the capitalist economic order and the defect in the socialist remedy. The dysfunction, asserts Pesch, does not derive from private ownership of the means of production but from defective regulation of economic affairs (Mulcahy, 1952, p. 171).

Capitalism organizes economic matters on the basis of a single principle--competition. According to *Quadragesimo Anno*, the concentration of power which characterizes the capitalist system "is a natural result of limitless free competition" (*EC*, c. 1942, p. 234). Socialism errs by removing competition entirely as an organizing principle and replacing it with the organizing principle of intervention. Removing the competitive organizing principle leads to socialism's thoroughly documented problems with production incentives. Plainly, need fulfillment, when it is made independent of work, no longer serves as an incentive for maximum work effort. Equally plainly, a reintroduction of the competitive principle is necessary.   What is not clearly evident is that these two organizing principles, even when they order economic affairs in tandem, are not sufficient. We return to this point later.

As with capitalism and its special abuse of economic anarchy, socialism exposes man to its own special abuse--economic tyranny. This abuse originates in a decisionmaking process that is overly centralized. Following *Laborem Exercens*, the state claims for itself monopoly control of the means of productions wherein man's rights in the workplace and his basic human rights are violated (*Laborem Exercens*, 1981, pp. 36-37) presumably in the service of some higher good. The slave labor camps of National Socialism in Germany are a prime example of this sort of tyranny. To a less extent, so too is the use of the *nomenklatura* in Poland wherein the managers of economic enterprises are appointed on the basis not of their competency in management but their loyalty to the Communist Party. The elimination of this practice is one of the chief goals of Poland's Solidarity movement (*World Affairs*, 1982, p. 29).

The special abuses of economic anarchy and economic tyranny both originate in the economic decisionmaking process. It follows that the reduction and, for sure, the complete elimination of both abuses call for a reform of economic decisionmaking. Catholic social economics identifies in general what reform is required. We return to this reform later.

FREEDOM, JUSTICE, AND MAN'S FINAL END

Earlier in this chapter, we stated that in Catholic social economic thought man's end and the goal of the economy are to provide for man's material needs. There are two distinct aspects of those needs: (1) the need for income that is sufficient for human well-being and (2) the need for work itself.

For some time, Catholic social economists were not fully agreed as to which need is the more important and where reconstruction of the economic order should begin. Seen from the perspective of the economy, this disagreement reduces to the relative importance of consumption versus production.   By connecting human work to the Act of Creation and making the former a continuation of the latter, *Laborem Exercens* persuasively settles this disagreement in favor of production. We add here, following Pesch on the minimum wage, fulfillment of man's need for work itself presupposes that his need for an adequate income has been met.

Even so, man's material needs are only an intermediate end. As a more nearly ultimate end, Pesch considers individual freedom and rejects it on grounds that unlimited and unrestrained freedom fosters self-love and brutal self-seeking and thereby tends to undermine the stability of the state. Pesch holds instead that justice--the virtue of rendering to another that which is owed--is the higher end and that the practice of justice is necessary for the existence of authentic freedom. Freedom, in turn, is necessary to efficiency in the economic order (Mulcahy, 1951, p. 162).

Catholic social economics asserts that in the economic order there are three principles of justice corresponding to three critical relationships. Over the years there has been some confusion as to the proper name for each of the three but none as to their content.

We have already made reference to the first principle of economic justice--the principle of equivalence. This principle sets forth the mutual obligation of buyer and seller in the marketplace (employer and employee in the workplace). Both parties have the same two obligations: (1) to exchange things of equal value and (2) to impose equal burdens on one another. Any failure with regard to one or the other by either party makes for an exchange that violates justice. Examples of violations of the principle of equivalence include counterfeiting (goods or money), embezzling, and check forging, all of which are condemned by the law. A violation that is not prohibited by law or that falls in the "gray" area between, frequently is called a "ripoff" by the party that is victimized.

The second principle of economic justice is distributive justice. This principle sets forth the obligation of the person with superior responsibilities to those who are his subordinates. The superior's duty under distributive justice is to see that the burdens and benefits are distributed among his subordinates in some equal fashion. This principle attacks such arbitrary and capricious practices as racism, sexism, and nepotism. Justice in this regard is an obligation of the superior to eliminate favoritism in his relationship with his subordinates. Of the three principles of economic justice, this one may be the most widely known.

The third and final principle of economic justice is contributive justice. This principle sets forth the obligation of the individual to the group (whether the group is private or public). Insofar as the individual derives benefits from the group, he has an obligation to maintain and support that group. Examples as to how this principle is violated include tax evasion, industrial spying, and regularly disrupting the workplace by such behavior as reporting to work late or "goldbricking." Catholic social economics stresses the importance of contributive justice in particular because it is so often ignored or disregarded by modern man.

While justice is seen as a higher end than either freedom or providing for human material needs, Pesch does not see it as man's final end. Rather, man's final end is twofold, reflecting his individual nature and his social nature: (1) individual perfection in union with God and (2) social perfection by means of a cooperative effort with other men in order to promote the welfare of the entire human community. Of the two, individual perfection is primary but depends importantly on social perfection (Schuyler, 1953, p. 231).

ECONOMIC COMMUNITY AT THE SUPRA-FIRM LEVEL

While strongly endorsed and encouraged by Catholic social economics, economic community--the deliberate and systematic molding of individual workers into an effective team for the accomplishment of a common task--at the intra-firm level clearly is not unique to Catholic social economics. At that level, the need to unify individuals into work groups is self-evident even if it is not always apparent as to how this is best accomplished. In this regard, Catholic social economics instructs and is instructed by the real world in areas such as employment security, labor-management relations, gain sharing, and participative management.

At the supra-firm level, however, Catholic social economics rightfully may claim a much larger share of the credit for the development of economic community since the 1930s. As in many other areas, Catholic social economic thought is heavily indebted to Pesch who laid the original foundations with his social system of labor.

Pesch's social system of labor is a proposal to prevent the degeneration of workable competition wherein the market price departs significantly from the just price (as determined by the principle of equivalence) and to ward off the worst ends of socialism. Pesch's system is grounded firmly in the principle of subsidiarity, a threefold solidarity, and man's dual nature as individual being and social being.

The principle of subsidiarity limits a larger, more powerful unit of society to those functions which small, less powerful units are unable to do at least as well as the larger unit even with its help. This means developing a sense of economic community through the establishment of forums or councils located in the economic order midway between the state, on the one hand, and private enterprise, on the other.

Pesch's threefold solidarity refers to the natural oneness among mankind in general, the oneness among citizens of the same nation, and the oneness among persons with the same production problems.[6] In what follows we focus entirely on unity among persons with the same production problems mainly because that is where our experience lies.

At the intra-firm level, workplace is an identifiable place or network of places that are more or less permanent. At that level, the concept has concrete meaning and is expressed in ways such as the paper mill, the bag plant, the foundry. Whatever the specific identifying expressions used, at the intra-firm level the workplace has meaning that is widely understood and accepted. Typically, control of the workplace at the intra-firm level is the responsibility of a private business organization that owns and manages the workplace for the good of that individual organization. Even in those instances where there is government intervention in the workplace, we refer to this as "private-individual control" as long as intervention is subordinate to competition as an organizing principle.

At the state or public-authority level also, workplace is identifiable, more or less permanent, widely understood, and accepted. Cape Kennedy, Baltimore Harbor, and O'Hare Airport are examples of this type of workplace. At this level, control of the workplace is in the hands of a public authority which sees to it that the facility is used for the good of all. Clearly, any private organization using the facility is subordinate to the designated public authority. Even when the physical facility is owned and managed by a private organization, we refer to this as "public control" provided competition is subordinate to intervention as a regulator of activity in the workplace.

If one's chief frame of reference is the form of property ownership, private and public are the two main alternatives available. If one focuses instead on decisionmaking in the workplace, a third option opens up. In general, decisionmaking may be organized so that problems and issues are addressed by many persons acting as independent individuals or acting as a group. A group, in turn, may be private (an association of private individuals acting as one), or public (the state). We refer to these three alternatives as: private-individual decisionmaking in the workplace, private-group decisionmaking, and public decisionmaking.[7]

Seen from the perspective of control of decisionmaking in the workplace, private-group control is distinctly different than private-individual control and public control; it is not a blending of the two. More often than not, however, private-group decisionmaking suggests a cartel-like organization. In principle and in practice, though, this need not be so.

Private-group control of decisionmaking directs the individual members of the group toward the common good through voluntary agreement on the responsibilities of the various members of the group itself. The individual members are functionally related to one another through some direct interest in the production of the same product or service. They form into a group in order to deal with workplace dysfunction that each one is unable to deal with alone.

Both the common good and individual responsibility are clarified and specified in terms of reducing, eliminating, or preventing specific dysfunctions in the workplace that affect the various members of the group. Cooperation means a willingness on the part of the individual to voluntarily moderate self-interest in order to deal with the dysfunctions that each one alone cannot deal with satisfactorily. By giving concrete and intertwined meaning to the common good, individual responsibility, and cooperation, private-group decisionmaking provides tangible expression to contributive justice. As Dempsey states, contributive justice operates on the acceptance of an individual philosophy of "being responsible" (Dempsey, 1958, p. 485).

Cartels are much different. Cartel members are mindful of opportunities, that is, they see an opportunity to enhance personal gain and seize it. The members are takers and exploiters; they are self-serving. The individual belonging to the cartel is encouraged to be irresponsible in that a cheater is rewarded because he is able to continue production without the help of the other group members.

Private-group control, as Catholic social economics construes it, means that the members are mindful of dysfunctions in the workplace, that is they see common problems and seek common solutions. They are givers and contributors. They practice the social charity that *Quadragesimo Anno* says brings about a union of hearts and minds (*EC*, c. 1942, p. 252) even if they cannot articulate its meaning and trace it to its origins. The individual members are encouraged to be responsible in that cheaters are not rewarded since they cannot continue production without the help of the rest of the group. In short, the most fundamental difference between a cartel and a solidarist private group is in the shared values of the individual members.

If one accepts subsidiarity as a valid socioeconomic principle, it follows that in the case of workplace dysfunction which the individual is not able to address satisfactorily alone, help is to be sought first through a private group and, only if that fails, from the state. In that sense, supra-firm refers to a private group that is intermediate between the individual and the state. Table 3-1 compares and contrasts the three alternative methods of control of dysfunction in the workplace.

To be an authentically separate level of decisionmaking, the supra-firm level private group must be independent of the larger and more powerful public authority, that is outside the direct control of the state. Additionally, the solidarist private group must be voluntary (so as not to usurp control from a member of the group that is functioning satisfactori-ly) and representative of the various private-individual organizations that are linked in the workplace (so as to know more precisely its own domain). Furthermore, the supra-firm level private group should be supportive but nonintrusive in the sense that if an individual member encounters organization-specific dysfunction in the workplace and asks for assistance, the group should be ready and willing to provide whatever help it can to deal with the dysfunction in a satisfactory fashion.

At the supra-firm level, the workplace has tangible substance just as it does at the intra-firm level and at the public authority level. Nevertheless, at the supra-firm level, the workplace is not as identifiable and permanent as it is at the other two levels. This is so because the typical workplace is identified with and has permanency because of property ownership. At the supra-firm level, control of the workplace proceeds not through owning property but through sharing problems.

Thus, the workplace at the supra-firm level may be defined as any work site(s) where dysfunction is occurring which cannot be managed satisfactorily at the intra-firm level and where the immediately affected individuals voluntarily request assistance from a private group of indivi-duals all of whom are familiar with the work site(s), understand the dysfunction occurring there, and have some direct interest in the product or service produced there. An interdependence exists at the functional level which in Catholic social economics is called "organic." This work is particularly instructive as to the nature of economic communities at the supra-firm level. The solidarist private group is to the economic order what the vital organ is to the human body. Just as vital organs in the human body are specialized cells with a specific function that is essential to physical health and well-being, so, too, solidarist private groups are specialized sets (usually, in an industry sense) of private individuals to provide for the well-being of the economic order. Dysfunction is as inevitable in the economic order without solidarist private groups as illness is in the human body with a failing or missing vital organ.

TABLE 3-1.

DYSFUNCTION IN THE WORKPLACE: THREE ALTERNATIVE METHODS OF CONTROL

Type of Control Over Workplace	Central Purpose	Dominant Organizing Principle	Dominant Form of Property Ownership	Economic Justice Principle	Scope of Dysfunction
private-individual control	individual good	competition (excludes other two)	private	equivalence	dysfunction is specific to individual firm
private-group control	common good	cooperation (includes other two)	private	contributive	dysfunction is common among firms with shared workplace but outside their control at firm level
public control	common good	intervention (excludes other two)	public	distributive	dysfunction is common across firms & industries but outside their control at supra-firm level

Solidarist private associations do not abound in the United States. We complete this section on economic communities at the supra-firm level with an example from St. Louis. Some of the information below comes from the author's own fieldwork.

PRIDE was formed as a voluntary association of various private parties in the St. Louis construction industry in 1972. More particularly, PRIDE is an industry council that is organized locally and operates mainly at the local level and to a lesser extent at the substate regional level.

Its origins are several and varied. First, in 1972, the industry felt a need for market recovery and market preservation. Second, the Business Round Table pointed out that labor-management relations need not be strictly adversarial. Third, there had been persistent complaints about union labor relative to jurisdictional assignment, late starts, coffee breaks, and early finishes. Fourth, a particularly difficult strike involving fitters had taken place in 1963. Fifth, a users council had been established among area firms that use the services provided by the construction industry. Sixth, Anheuser-Busch had made a decision, based on a very negative experience with fitters on a company work site, not to build or expand in St. Louis in the future. Finally, some contractor members of Associated General Contractors, an association of union contractors, had been working non-union jobs. Plainly, the industry was run through with workplace dysfunction.

Critical to the establishment of PRIDE is a *Memorandum of Understanding* that was signed voluntarily by five private parties in the industry: users, designers, contractors, craftsmen, and suppliers. The preamble is instructive:

> The parties signatory to this Understanding recognize the problems confronting the construction industry in the Eastern Missouri Area and pledge their cooperation and support to the provisions of this Understanding and other mutually agreed upon policies and programs which will tend to eliminate these problems and promote a healthy growth of the construction industry in this area (*Memorandum of Understanding*, 1972, p. 2).

The *Memorandum of Understanding* sets forth in detail the obligations of each party to the group. Users accepted four specific obligations. Designers affirmed responsibility in four specific areas, while contractors set forth five areas for which they have responsibilities to others in the industry. Craftsmen accepted six obligations as did suppliers. Contractors and unions set forth three where the responsibilities are shared.

Other than the preamble, PRIDE's *Memorandum* is simply a statement enumerating the specific obligations of the various constituents in the industry. The *Memorandum* makes no reference to rights or to the state. PRIDE functions as a private group without government fiat and without government funds.

PRIDE operates through pre-bid and pre-job conferences to address dysfunction in the workplace before the construction gets underway. In addition, a board of directors meets on a monthly basis to discuss other problems and issues. The meeting is chaired by two persons, one of whom represents the building contractors with the other one representing the building trades.

The co-chairmen of PRIDE are absolutely vital and are further evidence that the "who" of any organization is the most important determinant of its effectiveness. Both derive their authority from two sources. Each one represents a crucial constituency and each one has technical competency. As to the effectiveness of PRIDE in dealing with workplace dysfunction, between 1972 and 1981, more than 300 restrictive work rules were eliminated and there was only one jurisdictional strike. Before PRIDE it was not unusual to have three or four such strikes every month (Ross, 1981, p. 92).

A supra-firm level industry council such as PRIDE is not, in principle, restraint of trade because it seeks positive-sum outcomes whereas restraint of trade leads to zero-sum outcomes. Solidarist private-group decisionmaking seeks the common good mainly by promoting efficiency and by averting the twin abuses of economic anarchy and economic tyranny. Insofar as it achieves that end, it should not be broken up by antitrust law enforcement. The law should follow reason, and in this case reason argues that the industry council is needed to promote the common good.

FINAL REMARKS

Catholic social economic thought is a response to the problems of capitalism's excessive individualism and socialism's excessive collectivism.

Excessive individualism means that capitalism in effect uses the threat of economic insecurity to allocate resources and thereby puts man at risk of not being able to provide for his material needs. Capitalism is unstable because of necessity the capitalist economic order makes man insecure.

Excessive collectivism means that socialism seizes complete control of the means of production under the mistaken notion that man's economic insecurity derives from the institution of private property. Socialism is unstable because it denies man what is rightfully his under natural law in order to provide for his material needs.

Catholic social economics asserts that two reforms are needed to deal with the twin evils of excessive individualism and excessive collectivism. The first reform must take place in the social order, the second in man himself.

The organizational reform calls for the establishment and development of industry councils that are intermediate in the economic order between the smaller, less powerful private enterprises experiencing economic dysfunction and the larger and more powerful state. Dempsey's description of the role of such councils or associations is particularly apt.

> Such associations are the economic organs in the body politic; they are the vertical girders furnishing structural balance in the social edifice along with the horizontal, geographic, political framework (Dempsey, 1958, pp. 430-431).

The moral reform of man himself is a reform of his conscience that encourages him to act according to the demands of justice and charity. *Quadragesimo Anno* describes the need for this reform in eloquent language.

> . . . dead matter leaves the factory ennobled and transformed, where men are corrupted and degraded (*EC*, c. 1942, p. 250).

From the perspective of Catholic social economics, the means of production are privatized under capitalism and nationalized under socialism. In contrast, solidarism socializes man himself. This socialization is a demanding task. Man is challenged to reject the one-dimensional nature imposed on him under capitalism and under socialism, and to become all that he truly can be as an individual being and as a social being.

Catholic social economics frequently is criticized for its idealism. However, unless man responds affirmatively to the challenge to become all that he truly can be, he will remain vulnerable to the insecurity and anarchy of capitalism and to the loss of what is rightfully his and the tyranny of socialism.

Notes

[1] We employ "applications" here rather than "policy" because in our mind the former includes the latter and allows us to differentiate applications in the private sector from public-sector applications (or what is commonly called policy).

[2] Hereafter referred to as simply *EC*.

[3] Called "intermediate bodies" by John Paul II (*Laborem Exercens*, 1981, p. 37) because in the social order they are to be positioned between the person and the family on the one end and the state on the other end. In the United States, they are called variously economic communities, industry councils, or supra-firm level cooperative organizations.

[4] For example, Joseph Becker, S.J., a charter member of the Catholic Economic Association (called the Association for Social Economics since the mid-1960s) and a nationally prominent specialist in unemployment insurance has stated that his central professional interest during more than 40 years of scholarly work has been "the alleviation of the scourge of unemployment" (*Review of Social Economy*, April 1984, p. i). Leo Brown, another Jesuit who was a charter member of the Association, was a nationally known and respected labor mediator.

[5] See chapter 13 of Dempsey's *The Functional Economy* which is entitled "the worker as person" (Dempsey, 1958, pp. 241-265).

[6] Earlier in Catholic social economic thought, "vocational group" was the operative term. Today "industry council" seems to be a much more appropriate term in the United States.

[7] We recognize that this simplification disregards important differences within these three alternatives. Even so, this simplification is very helpful in the exposition of cooperation at the supra-firm level.

References

Becker, J. M. and others. 1965. "Policy recommendations," *In Aid of the Unemployed*, edited by J. M. Becker, Baltimore, MD: The Johns Hopkins Press.

Dempsey, B. W. 1958. *The Functional Economy.* Englewood Cliffs, NJ: Prentice-Hall.

Encyclicals of a Century. circa 1942. Derby, NY: Daughters of St. Paul.

Gundlach, G. 1951. "Solidarist economics: philosophy and socio-economic theory in Pesch," *Social Order* (April).

Laborem Exercens. 1981. Boston, MA: Daughters of St. Paul.

Memorandum of Understanding. 1972. St. Louis PRIDE, reaffirmed and revised in 1977 (brochure).

Mueller, F. 1940. "The solidarist middle road," *Central-Blatt and Social Justice* (February).

Mulcahy, R. E. 1951. "Economic freedom in Pesch: his system demands, but restrains, freedom," *Social Order* (April).

_____. 1952. *The Economics of Heinrich Pesch.* New York, NY: Henry Holt and Company.

Newman, J. H. 1947. *The Idea of a University.* New York, NY: Longmans, Green, and Company, New Edition.

Ross, I. 1981. "The new work spirit in St. Louis," *Fortune* (November 16).

Schuyler, J. B. 1953. "Heinrich Pesch, S.J.: 1854-1926," in *Social Theorists*, edited by C. S. Mihanovich. Milwaukee, WI: The Bruce Publishing Company.

World Affairs. 1982. "The first solidarity congress." (Summer).

CATHOLIC SOCIAL ECONOMICS: A RESPONSE TO CERTAIN PROBLEMS, ERRORS, AND ABUSES OF THE MODERN AGE: COMMENT

E. K. Hunt

Unfortunately, I find little in "Catholic social economics," as characterized by O'Boyle, with which I can agree and only a few principles, theoretical or normative, that I could embrace. In common with Marx, Veblen, Dewey, James, and Ayres, I do not believe that knowledge about the institutional causes of the misery of the disadvantaged or about the institutional changes that would improve the plight of the disadvantaged comes from supernatural sources. O'Boyle's "Catholic economics" seems to me to be more properly labeled "Papal economics." Within the traditions of the Catholic church, I would argue that contemporary "liberation theology" contains the seeds of a genuine social economics but Pope Leo XIII's encyclical *Rerum Novarum* is in many important respects merely an extension of the centuries-long tradition of the institutional, official

Catholic church identification with and alignment with the social and
economic institutions that perpetuate wealth, privilege, and power,
generating many of the worst ills of the disadvantaged.

To say that property is natural is to be obscurantist. Human
beings are social animals. We interact with our natural environment only
by interacting with other human beings. Those rules, principles, or guidelines that regulate the ways in which we socially interact with our
environment and in the process delineate the differential privileges and
sanctions that such social interactions involve, can be properly called the
rules, principles, or guidelines of property. In any law school library
Professor O'Boyle will encounter thousands of books that codify and
enumerate the hundreds of thousands of federal, state, and local laws that
represent the concrete manifestation of "property" at present in our own
country. Are they all "natural"? Will those laws that are repealed next
year become "unnatural" at that time? Are conflicting state laws on
property rights evidence that what is natural in one state is unnatural in
another? And are we to make such judgments based on a medieval
theology written before the types of property laws characteristic of modern
capitalism were even in existence?

With this approach, Papal economics seems to me to be the
antithesis of social economics as defined by either Professor Hill or myself.
I believe that many of the laws of private property that characterize
capitalism are the very source of much of the misery of the disadvantaged
in a capitalist society. If this is true, then an analysis based on medieval
theology that fails to analyze either the concrete consequences of existing
property laws or the probable consequences of changes of these laws but
simply defends the status quo by stating that property is "natural" must
be characterized as asocial if not antisocial.

I take exception with nearly every single characterization of
socialist ideas that Professor O'Boyle gets from Pope Leo, gets from Pesch,
or asserts himself. These are, in my view, manifestations of that general
approach of defenders of the status quo of capitalism that proceeds by
distorting the arguments of the critics of capitalism. Socialists have
traditionally been preoccupied with the problem of the paradox of the individual and the social side of human beings. The apparent purpose in
denying this for Leo, Pesch, or O'Boyle appears to be an *ad hominem*
dismissal of socialists in order to avoid engaging in a detailed debate over
the "naturalness" of all forms of capitalist property.

To say that socialism inherently involves a tyranny and that that
tyranny is exemplified by "National Socialism in Germany" involves a naive

misinterpretation of facts at best or willful deceit at worst. Despite the name, the "National Socialists" supported and had the support of capitalists and right-wing conservatives in Germany. They were fiercely *opposed* by German socialists (although not, interesting enough, by the upper hierarchy of the Catholic church), and before they ever thought of exterminating Jews, they exterminated socialists. To call them an example of socialism is incredible. Not only did the Nazis hate and kill socialists, they accepted the argument of Leo, Pesch, and O'Boyle that capitalist forms of private property were sacrosanct.

The principle reason, however, that I do not see O'Boyle's version of Catholic economics as social economics is that it does not identify the source of economic or social problems as institutions that need to be changed. In general, it accepts nearly every aspect of the institutional status quo and sees most problems as arising from individual moral failure. If people would merely act in a more moral manner, individually, then the institutions of capitalism, exactly as they now exist, would be very nearly ideal. I do not think it would significantly distort the conclusions of this approach to call it a first cousin of the neoclassical doctrine of laissez-faire. The Catholic doctrine is laissez-faire with morally uplifted business, government, and union leaders. As such I cannot imagine that it will ever provoke the hostility of the more thoughtful element among the rich and powerful. A devotee of the doctrine, however, seems to be doomed to the frustrating existence of the proverbial Puritan in Babylon.

CATHOLIC SOCIAL ECONOMICS: A RESPONSE TO CERTAIN PROBLEMS, ERRORS AND ABUSES OF THE MODERN AGE: COMMENT

Lewis E. Hill

Many roads lead to the same destination. In this excellent article, Professor Edward J. O'Boyle follows one road to the goals of social economics. His road runs back through the Jesuit tradition of social economics and the Dominican tradition of philosophy to Saint Thomas Aquinas. In the article that it has been my privilege to contribute to this book, another road has been followed to these goals. My road runs back through institutionalist economic thought to Thorstein Veblen and through pragmatic and instrumentalist philosophical thought to Charles Sanders Peirce. Clarence Edwin Ayres was the economic philosopher who synthesized these lines of intellectual thought into contemporary institutionalist-instrumentalist economics. The purpose of this comment is to respond to O'Boyle's essay from an institutionalist perspective and to compare and to contrast the Catholic and the institutionalist approaches to social economics.

The Catholic approach to social economics is very different from the institutionalist approach to social economics. Nevertheless, it has always been my conviction that these two approaches are entirely consistent with one another. Indeed, it seems to me that each approach makes its own special contribution to the richness and to the diversity of the tradition of social economics. The comprehension and understanding of social economics has been enhanced by the combination of these profound but diverse traditions of scholarship. This diversity, however, should not be allowed to obscure a basic agreement on some fundamentals of social economics.

Professor William M. Dugger has written a very insightful article in which he specifies five identifying characteristics of social economics, which are relevant to both the institutionalist and the Catholic approach to social economics. According to Dugger, social economics is *value-directed* rather than value-free, and *ameliorative* rather than conservative or revolutionary. He believes that social economists are inclined to be *activists* rather than to react passively to economic conditions, and that they seek to understand the economy through a *holistic* rather than a reductionist approach. Finally, social economists conceive the society as an *organic whole* rather than as a haphazard collection of unrelated events and atomistic tendencies (Dugger, 1977, p. 300).

It has been my conviction for a long time that the institutionalist-instrumentalist approach to social economics meets all of the criteria that Dugger has specified in his article. This argument is fully developed in my major contribution to this book, and it would serve no useful purpose to repeat it in this comment. It is also my firm belief that the Catholic approach, which O'Boyle has so ably described in his essay, is in full compliance with all of Dugger's specifications. Clearly, Catholic social economics is firmly grounded on the normative values of the Judeo-Christian tradition. It is equally clear that the immediate and intermediate objectives of Catholic social economics involve the amelioration of the abuses that plague the modern economy. The Papal Encyclicals and Heinrich Pesch's *Lehrbuch* proclaim a clarion call for social economists to become activists in support of their socioeconomic objectives and goals. Catholic social economists have always sought to analyze the economy from a holistic rather than a reductionist approach. Moreover, a very long tradition in Catholic scholarship calls for the conception of the society and the social economy as an organic whole. Both institutionalist and Catholic social economics exhibit many similarities and share all of Dugger's identifying characteristics of social economics.

While there are many areas of agreement between Catholic and institutionalist social economics, there are also some important differences of emphasis between the two approaches to social economics. Catholic social economics has a profoundly religious orientation and is based on intensely metaphysical preconceptions. Catholic social economists emphasize ultimate goals which are explicitly metaphysical and teleological in their fundamental nature. Methodology tends to be de-emphasized in social economics. In sharp contrast, institutionalist social economics is clearly secular in its orientation and is completely devoid of explicitly metaphysical preconceptions, although it is my belief that some metaphysical preconceptions are clearly implied by the institutionalist approach. Most institutionalist social economists would deny the idea that goals should be metaphysical or teleological, insisting that goal achievement involves nothing beyond the physical forces in the natural universe. Their emphasis is on solving practical problems in order to achieve immediate objectives. The solution of these problems and the achievement of these objectives are sought through the application of the pragmatic epistemology and the instrumentalist methodology.

Catholic social economists place a heavy emphasis upon the free will with which God has endowed the human species. They see free will as a reflection of the image of God in which man was created. Conversely, Catholic social economists reject the interpretation which holds that human history is fully determined by the inexorable movement of broad cultural forces which are beyond human control. They find this doctrine of cultural determinism to be incompatible with their concept of human nature. Many institutionalist social economists, however, accept the doctrine of cultural determinism and hold that individual persons cannot influence history appreciably. These institutionalists accept the doctrine of free will only to the extent that it can be reconciled with cultural determinism. Clarence Ayres, a leading institutionalist, always argued that free will and cultural determinism are not contradictory because they apply to different levels of generalization: free will pertains to the individual level of generalization; cultural determinism is relevant to the social level of generalization. In other words, Ayres believed that a person could enjoy free will with respect to his own individual actions, but that these individual actions would have no appreciable influence on the course of history, which is fully determined by broad cultural forces.

The philosophical foundations of Catholic social economics include two principles which were developed by Heinrich Pesch: the principle of solidarity and the principle of subsidiarity. According to the principle of solidarity, the oneness of man in the workplace should be expressed through the organization of voluntary associations from the lowest level up through the supra-firm level. According to the principle of subsidiarity, problems should be solved through these voluntary associations at the lowest possible level within the hierarchy. These principles imply that problems should be referred to the governmental level of compulsory public control only as a last resort. Institutionalist social economists view voluntary associations pragmatically; institutionalists would accept and advocate voluntary associations enthusiastically to the extent that they facilitate the solving of practical problems. Most institutionalists, however, are somewhat skeptical about the effectiveness of voluntary associations because of the problems posed by free riders and cheaters. Free riders are nonmembers who benefit from the activities of the association without bearing the costs of membership; cheaters are members who enhance their self-interest by violating the policies of the association. These institutionalists believe that the activities of voluntary associations should be supplemented by governmental intervention to impose compulsory public control.

Catholic social economics is based on the principle that private property is either a natural or a sacred right; therefore, a basic incompatibility seems to exist between Catholic social economics and socialism. Institutionalist social economists, however, view private property as just another human institution to be evaluated pragmatically and to be accepted, modified, or rejected according to the outcome of the evaluation. Institutionalist social economics, therefore, is compatible with socialism.

Catholic and institutionalist social economists have much in common. There is a basic compatibility between these alternative approaches with respect to methodology and objectives. There are, however, some differences in emphasis. Catholic social economists emphasize religion and metaphysical considerations, ultimate goals, free will, and voluntary associations. This approach to social economics appears to be inconsistent with socialism. Institutionalist social economists emphasize secular and naturalistic considerations, pragmatic and instrumentalist methods, cultural determinism, and governmental intervention to impose compulsory public control over the economy. This approach to social economics is consistent with socialism.

Reference

Dugger, W. M. 1977. "Social economics: one perspective," *Review of Social Economy* 35 (December), 299-310.

4

THE INSTITUTIONALIST APPROACH TO SOCIAL ECONOMICS

Lewis E. Hill

It is my conviction that the essence of social economics consists of the unique set of socioeconomic objectives and goals which are pursued by most social economists. If this conviction is true, then the objectives and goals of social economics may be compatible with any one of several philosophical approaches to the economic science. It was my purpose in a previous essay to argue that the philosophy and methodology of institutional economics are thoroughly consistent with the objectives and goals of social economics (Hill, 1978). Indeed, it continues to be my firm position that institutional economics can provide the most valid philosophical foundation and the most useful methodology for social economics. It is the purpose of this article to explicate this position and to extend and elaborate the arguments from my previous essay.

My approach will be historical, with the arguments being drawn from the history of philosophy and the history of economic thought. The first section will define social economics, describe the goals and objectives which most social economists accept, and specify the characteristics which identify social economics and differentiate it from the marginal analysis of the dominant neoclassical school of economic thought. The second section will trace the historical development of philosophical empiricism, pragmatism, and instrumentalism, which provide the philosophical basis of institutionalism. The third section will summarize the historical evolution of institutional economics, with an emphasis on the pragmatic and instrumental methodology that characterizes institutionalism. The fourth section will attempt to reconcile the institutionalist philosophy and methodology with social economics and to develop a synthesis of institutional and social economics.

SOCIAL ECONOMICS

Social economics may be defined as the socioeconomic analysis of human behavior within a broad social and political context for the purpose of improving the quality of life and enhancing human welfare. Social economists have always expressed and demonstrated a very special concern for the economically deprived people who comprise the have-nots of our society. Most social economists accept the humanistic values of the Judeo-Christian tradition and base their commitment to human welfare on metaphysical preconceptions. All social economists are dedicated to the quest to achieve social justice. Social economics is an applied policy science that is intended to solve the problems of social injustice and economic privation (Hill, 1978). Professor William M. Dugger has specified the five identifying characteristics of social economics in the following quotation.

> In brief, five related characteristics make social economics a unique and significant discipline within social science: (1) It is a *value-directed* approach to solving the problems of the disadvantaged. (2) *Amelioration* rather than preservation or revolution is its aim. (3) Social economists are impelled to be *activists*, within the limitations of their own life-situations. (4) Understanding is sought through a *holistic* rather than a reductionistic

approach. (5) Society, the fabric within which the strands of problems are woven, is viewed as an *organic* whole. These five characteristics form the backbone of social economics and clearly differentiate it from the classical-neoclassical school of economics. This is not to say that social economists object to the dominant neoclassical school, but it is to say that social economy is different from neoclassical economy in several important respects (Dugger, 1977, p. 300).

Dugger's first identifying characteristic holds that social economics is value-directed. This proposition implies several corollaries. First of all, it is implied that social economists accept the epistemological validity of normative value judgments. Social economists insist that a value-free economic science is probably impossible and certainly undesirable: impossible, because most economic concepts are saturated with implicit value premises, undesirable, because normative value judgments are necessary intellectual tools for any social scientist who aspires to be both empirically relevant and socially responsible. It is also implied that the normative preconceptions of social economics are ultimately based on the Judeo-Christian tradition of Western civilization. Social economists infer their value premises from this tradition and use these premises as the driving force in their socioeconomic analysis. Glenn L. Johnson has indicated that both positive and normative knowledge are essential in problem-solving research (Johnson, 1986). Social economists use normative value judgments as intellectual tools for the purpose of solving socioeconomic and politicoeconomic problems. In this value-directed effort to solve problems, the highest priority is accorded to solving the problems of the people who are economically and socially disadvantaged (Dugger, 1977, pp. 300-302).

Another of Dugger's identifying characteristics is that social economics tends to be ameliorative, rather than conservative or revolutionary. The mainstream of orthodox economics is always conservative in the sense that it is dedicated to the preservation of the current socioeconomic structure and organization. Conservative economics provides an apologetic rationalization for the status quo which justifies the indiscriminate preservation of the bad features along with the good features of the existing system. The radical underground of economics is always revolutionary in the sense that it is dedicated to the total destruction of the contemporary socioeconomic system in the hope that it will be replaced by an ideal system. Revolutionary economics advocates an open attack on the status quo which justifies the destruction of the good aspects along with the bad aspects of the current system. Social economists seek to avoid the alternative errors of preserving the bad or destroying the good. Their purpose is to preserve and perpetuate goodness and justice, but to eliminate and eradicate evil and injustice. Their method is to reform the socioeconomic system by alleviating conditions of social injustice and economic privation and by solving the problems of the people who are socially or economically disadvantaged (Dugger, 1977, pp. 302-305).

The third identifying characteristic is that social economists tend to be activists, rather than to pursue a more passive role with respect to socioeconomic theory and policy. Many economists from the mainstream of the economic science retreat to their ivy-clad offices and classrooms whence they manipulate their abstract and irrelevant models. But social economists are different; most of them practice the same ameliorative brand of social economics that they preach and seek to implement the humanitarian actions which are implied by their socioeconomic theories. Social economists tend to become personally and actively involved in the quest to enhance human welfare and to improve the quality of life for all of the people, with special emphasis on achieving social justice for people who are economically deprived. All social economists, however, do not have equal opportunities to practice their activism. The extent to which social economists participate in socioeconomic and politicoeconomic activism, therefore, is conditioned and limited by their life situations (Dugger, 1977, pp. 305-306).

Dugger's fourth identifying characteristic is that an understanding of social economics is sought through a holistic approach, rather than a reductionist approach. In sharp contrast to the social economist, the orthodox economists of the mainstream are very much inclined to use partial equilibrium analysis to abstract individual cause-and-effect relationships from the whole matrix of socioeconomic action and reaction. Social economists consider the economy at the level of awareness that Micahel Polanyi has designated "focal awareness," which comprehends the whole, rather than at the level of subsidiary awareness, which concentrates on the parts (Polanyi, 1964, pp. 55-59). The parts are considered only in their relationship with the whole; they are never abstracted from the whole phenomenon, because the the process of abstraction confuses the meaning and obscures the significance of the partial phenomena. The holistic approach is required of any economic scientist who seeks to solve practical problems. In order to solve a problem successfully, it is necessary to consider the entire problematic situation as a whole, and to analyze it through the use of a very broad socioeconomic and politicoeconomic approach. The holistic approach, therefore, is necessary to achieve the purpose of social economists to solve the problems of the people who are socially disadvantaged and economically impoverished (Dugger, 1977, pp. 306-308).

The final identifying characteristic is that society is viewed as an organic whole, rather than as a sum of its mechanical parts. Orthodox economists frequently use a model to explain economic causation. First, they select the dependent variable and the independent variable; next, these variables are abstracted from reality through the use of extremely restrictive counterfactual assumptions in order to derive a first approximation of the conclusion. Then, additional dependent variables are added in sequence as the counterfactual assumptions are relaxed in order to achieve a closer approximation to reality. Social economists reject these models of the economy because they are mechanical and additive; they believe that socioeconomic models should be organic and cumulative. Social economics is based on the presumption that the economy is an extremely complex matrix of interactive behavioral variables. A system of such complexity should be conceived only as an organic whole and analyzed only at the social level of generalization. It should not be concluded, however, that social economists are unconcerned with the individual. Entirely to the contrary, the welfare of the individual human being is the primary concern of social economists; they are interested in the relationship between the society and the individual and the affirmative or negative impact of social action on the individual. The purpose of social economists is to eliminate the negative impact of social action which causes problems and to replace it with the affirmative impact of social action which constitutes solutions for problems. Social economists use their concept of society as an organic whole as an intellectual tool for the purpose of solving socioeconomic and politicoeconomic problems (Dugger, 1977, pp. 308-309).

In brief, social economics is the socioeconomic analysis of human behavior within a broad social and political context for the purpose of improving the quality of life and enhancing human welfare. It is value-directed rather than value-free, ameliorative rather than conservative or revolutionary, and activistic rather than oriented toward a passive reaction to socioeconomic problems. Moreover, social economists utilize a holistic rather than a reductionist approach to the analysis of the economy as an organic whole.

PRAGMATISM AND INSTRUMENTALISM

The philosophical basis of the institutionalist school of economic thought is pragmatism and instrumentalism. Pragmatism is a term that Charles Sanders Peirce invented to designate the philosophy which is based on the presumption that all reality has practical consequences and that, therefore, the best way to know and to understand reality is through the consideration of practical consequences. Peirce believed that the meaning of a proposition, concept, or idea can be properly defined only in terms of the practical consequences which it implies for the conduct of life (Peirce, 1958, pp. 180-202). He summarized the fundamental doctrine of pragmatism in the following imperative:

> consider what effects, which might conceivably have practical bearings, we conceive the object of our conception to have. Then, our conception of these effects is the whole of our conception of the object (Peirce, 1958, p. 124).

The purpose of the pragmatic epistemology is to integrate thought with action in order to solve practical problems. According to Peirce, doubt motivates inquiry, and the sole purpose of inquiry is to produce beliefs, which will alleviate doubt. Whenever a person encounters a problematical situation, he is stimulated to thought, and his thoughts create ideas. Each person should use the pragmatic imperative to clarify his ideas to the highest possible degree (Peirce, 1958, pp. 118-124). Ideas can be transformed into beliefs through the process of fixation. The best method of fixing a belief is through scientific inquiry. The belief becomes a rule of action which is intended to resolve the problematical situation and to alleviate the doubt. If the rule of action proves to be effective, then the belief is continued to become a habit (Peirce, 1958, pp. 91-112). What, then, is truth? Peirce has defined truth in the following quotation:

> This great law is embodied in the conception of truth and reality. The opinion which is fated to be ultimately agreed to by all who investigate is what we mean by the truth, and the object represented by this opinion is the real (Peirce, 1958, p. 133).

Peirce believed that the positive philosophy of science is contradictory to religious or metaphysical thought (Peirce, 1958, pp. 137-141), but he insisted that there can be no contradiction between science and religion within the pragmatic philosophy of science. According to Peirce, science can be defined in any one of three ways: first, science is systematized knowledge; second, science is a methodology which is intended to produce systematized knowledge; and third, science is the "scientific spirit" which establishes the goal of acquiring systematized knowledge. Science is progressive and oriented to the future because every scientific discovery is a progression toward the truth (Peirce, 1958, pp. 350-351).

Peirce defines religion as a sentiment, perception, or recognition of First Cause and Final Cause and of "a relation to that Absolute of the individual's self, as a relative being" (Peirce, 1958, pp. 350-351). Theologians, however, demonstrate a strong tendency to define religious doctrines in terms which are not only static, but also extremely narrow. Religious doctrines, therefore, tend to be static and oriented to the past religious experience of the theologians who have promulgated the doctrines. Consequently, there is constant tension and controversy between scientists and theologians concerning the purpose of science and the meaning of religious doctrines. But religion cannot be defined as a set of doctrinal beliefs. "Religion is a life, and can be identified with a belief only provided that belief be a living belief--a thing to be lived rather than said or thought" (Peirce, 1958, p. 354). Science and religion treat different and therefore contradictory subject matters: science deals with efficient causes; religion deals with teleological considerations. Science asks the question: "How?" Religion asks the question: "Why?" Because science involves the quest for truth, there can be no contradiction between science and any true religion (Peirce, 1958, pp. 350-353).

According to Peirce's philosophy of religion, Christianity is differentiated from the other religions by the Doctrine of the Two Ways. The Way of Life symbolizes love and the other creative propensities of the human personality. The Way of Death symbolizes hatred and the other destructive propensities of the human personality. Peirce based his theory of normative value on the Doctrine of the Two Ways. The Way of Life motivates the creative and benevolent behavior that is compatible with bad normative disvalues (Peirce, 1958, pp. 353-357). Like social economics, Peirce's pragmatism is directed by values drawn from the Judeo-Christian tradition.

William James, who elaborated and popularized pragmatism, developed a functional epistemology which proved to be more psychological than logical. According to this epistemology, an idea should be evaluated as true or false according to what it does, rather than what it is. True ideas help us to distinguish the useful aspects from the harmful aspects of reality and to achieve a harmonious relationship with reality. Moreover, true ideas fulfill our expectations and facilitate the achievement of our objectives, but false ideas deceive and mislead us into wrong courses of action and cause failure in our efforts to achieve our objectives. All true ideas are useful, and conversely, all useful ideas are true. The truth of an idea is a prediction of its usefulness; the usefulness of an idea is the verification of its truth (James, 1908, pp. 197-238). According to James, "'The true,' to put it briefly, is only the expedient in the way of our thinking, just as 'the right' is only the expedient in the way of our behaving" (James, 1908, p. 222).

Like the social economists, James accepted and advocated a melioristic social philosophy, which implies that pragmatists should pursue an activistic program of socioeconomic and politicoeconomic reform. The doctrine of meliorism lies between the optimism of most idealists and the pessism of many realists. James believed that socioeconomic progress is neither inevitable nor impossible. He contended that each individual has a personal responsibility for the amelioration of the dangerous and drastic conditions of the universe. In this manner, he alleged the existence of a cause-and-effect relationship between the individual activistic reformer and socioeconomic progress (James, 1908, pp. 273-301).

"On pragmatic principles," James wrote, "we cannot reject any hypothesis if consequences useful to life flow from it" (James, 1908, p. 273). Clearly, religious beliefs produce useful consequences in the lives of many people; therefore, these religious beliefs must be regarded as true for these people. They are the "tender-minded" people who need to believe in an Absolute in order to find meaning for their own lives. Other people are tough-minded; they feel no need to believe in God. Because religious beliefs serve no useful purpose for these people, these beliefs should not be regarded as true for them (James, 1908, pp. 273-301). James concludes his discussion of religion with the following quotation:

> But if you are neither tough nor tender in an extreme and radical sense, but mixes as most of us are, it may seem to you that the type of pluralistic and moralistic religion that I have offered is as good a religious synthesis as you are likely to find. Between the two extremes of crude naturalism on the one hand and

transcendental absolution on the other, you may find that what I take the liberty of calling the pragmatistic or melioristic type of theism is exactly what you require (James, 1908, p. 301).

The last of the founding fathers of pragmatism was John Dewey, who developed his own particular brand of pragmatism, which he called instrumentalism. The distinguishing feature of instrumentalism is a very heavy emphasis on the use of logical or scientific inquiry for the purpose of solving practical problems. According to Dewey, a problem is a disequilibrium between a man and his environment in which actions produce unintended and undesirable consequences, instead of intended and desirable "ends-in-view." The instrumental process of solving problems involves five steps. The first step is to define the problem as a set of undesirable consequences which are likely to occur in reality. Also, it would be helpful to specify a set of desirable consequences, which would constitute a satisfactory solution. The second step is to analyze the problem through the perception of all of the relevant facts and the analysis of all of the cause-and-effect relationships that may be involved in the problem or the solution. The third step is to conceive a plan of action. Initially, a brainstorming process should be used to conceive ideas; then, the ideas should be evaluated and symbolized. The fourth step is to formulate a plan of action. The ideas are expanded into a plan of action, which is then carefully evaluated and revised. The fifth step is to implement the plan of action. If the plan of action effectively solves the problem, then the instrumental process has been verified. The instrumental process always begins with thought, which is motivated by the existence of a problem; it always ends with action, which is intended to solve the problem (Dewey, 1938, pp. 101-117).

Dewey's instrumental philosophy, like Peirce's pragmatism and social economics, is value-directed; it is based on an applied axiology which must be used to evaluate the desirability or undesirability of practical consequences, the validity or invalidity of cause-and-effect relationships, and the truth or falsity of ideas. Dewey always insisted that judgments of fact and judgments of value are identical both in methodology and in purpose. All judgments of both fact and value are induced empirically from previous experience for the purpose of making decisions and solving problems; all judgments of both fact and value are verified instrumentally by reference to subsequent experience. In other words, Dewey attributed to ordinary people the common sense or intelligence to learn how to induce judgments of fact and value from their past experience and how to verify their judgments from their subsequent experience (Dewey, 1929, pp. 254-286).

Instrumentalism implies a social interpretation of morality. According to Dewey, "Morals is connected with actualities of existence, not with ideals, ends and obligations independent of concrete actualities" (Dewey, 1922, p. 829). He believed that religion lost its true meaning of creatively integrating the individual with an infinite whole and had become nothing more than an institutionalization of mythical superstition, irrational dogmas, and liturgical ceremonies. The true basis of morality is to be found in scientific inquiry into the social aspects of human behavior. Morality involves the harmonizing of incompatibilities in the social environment and the solving of problems involving social relationships. Moral actions are expressions of the human awareness of the ties that bind each person to all humankind (Dewey, 1922, pp. 314-322).

In this manner, Peirce's logical pragmatism evolved through James' psychological pragmatism and into Dewey's instrumentalism. There was also an evolution of the pragmatic attitude toward religion. Peirce accepted metaphysical preconceptions and appears to have been a devout Christian (Peirce, 1958, pp. 353-357). James accepted the truth of religious beliefs for most people (James, 1908, pp. 273-301). Even the agnostic Dewey seems to have been more opposed to the institutional church than to the true spirit of Christianity (Dewey, 1922, pp. 314-332). Nevertheless, there is great continuity from Peirce through Dewey. All of the pragmatic philosophers based their epistemology on the analysis of practical consequences, and all of them accepted a relative concept of pragmatic truth. Moreover, all of the pragmatists placed a very heavy emphasis on solving practical problems. It is my belief that the differences between Peirce and Dewey are more a matter of emphasis than of substance. Clearly, Dewey's instrumentalism represents a secularization of Peirce's pragmatism, but it is my conviction that James and Dewey continued to accept the basic principles of pragmatism which Peirce had formulated in his early essays.

INSTITUTIONAL ECONOMICS

Institutional economics may be defined as a pragmatic theory of socioeconomic and politicoeconomic behavior, derived empirically through the application of inductive logic to qualitative and quantitative historical facts, and applied instrumentally to the solution of practical problems. The philosophical basis of institutionalism is pragmatism and instrumentalism. Institutional economics utilizes an empirical epistemology and an inductive logic; it emphasizes the historical methodology. The purpose of institutionalism is to solve practical socioeconomic and politicoeconomic problems. Institutional economics was originated by Thorstein Bunde Veblen, a radical social critic and economic philosopher. John Rogers Commons developed the historical dimension of institutionalism. Wesley Clair Mitchell advanced institutionalism in the direction of quantitative analysis, and Clarence Edwin Ayres became the greatest philosopher of the institutionalist school of economic thought (Hill, 1975).

Veblen was more forceful and effective in expressing his social criticism than in formulating and advocating the affirmative aspects of his socioeconomic theories. As an extremely articulate and sophisticated agrarian radical, Veblen lashed out at the business and financial interests who were exploiting and oppressing the producing classes within the capitalistic system (Veblen, 1904; Dorfman, 1972). He completely rejected conventonal economic analysis as being totally invalid and therefore completely false. The market-oriented economy was regarded as a set of inhibitory institutions and as an instrument for the oppression of the producing classes. Veblen rejected the assumption of the rational economic man as an artificial, irrelevant, and misleading abstraction. He alleged that most human behavior is economically irrational. Laissez-faire was considered to be a false and pernicious doctrine which provides a license for the strong to exploit the weak and for the forces of destructivity to triumph over the forces of creativity. In this manner, Veblen established an eradication tradition of complete rejection of the assumptions, analytical techniques, and conclusions of conventional economics (Veblen, 1919, pp. 56-251). Some institutionalists have followed this tradition of total rejection of orthodox microeconomic analysis, but this radical position is far from unanimous among contemporary scholars of institutionalism.

Affirmatively, Veblen accepted and advocated that the economy is an organic whole, which should always be conceived at the social level of generalization, and that, therefore, economics should be an evolutionary science. Man was conceived to be a social animal who is driven by opposing sets of instincts and propensities. The affirmative or benevolent instincts and propensities motivate behavior which is creative, productive, and useful; the negative or malevolent instincts and propensities motivate behavior which is destructive, exploitative, and wasteful (Veblen, 1899,

1904, 1914). This dichotomy became the basis for Veblen's theory of
normative value. Value consists of the good instincts and the creative
behavior that they motivate; disvalue consists of the bad instincts and the
destructive behavior that they motivate (Tool, 1977, pp. 824-828).

Veblen developed a methodology that consisted mostly of
historical empiricism. He used inductive logic to generalize from observations drawn from history. His methodology, however, was faulty. The
observations were casual and unsystematic, and the history was downright
haphazard. But Veblen compensated for the weakness in his methodology
with the flamboyance of his style and the brilliance of his rhetoric.
Veblen left all institutionalists a legacy of radical social criticism (Hill,
1975).   The task would remain for later institutional economists to
improve the methodology and to develop the affirmative and constructive
aspects of the theory of institutionalism.

John Rogers Commons upgraded the institutionalist methodology
by developing historical empiricism to a state of near-perfection. Most of
the conventional or mainstream economists who have been concerned with
human resources have simply applied deductive microeconomic theory to
the analysis of the conditions which are assumed to prevail in hypothetical
labor markets. But Commons established a different and infinitely better
approach to the analysis of labor problems. Commons organized a group
of his colleagues and graduate students to conduct the most comprehensive
research project ever undertaken into the history of labor in the United
States. Observations were then drawn from this historical record, and
inductive logic was used to generalize from observations. It was in this
manner that Commons induced his theory of the American labor movement empirically from his observations that were drawn from the history
of that movement (Commons, 1946, pp. 1-11). Finally, he applied inductive and empirical theory to the formulation of economic policy and to the
solving of socioeconomic and politicoeconomic problems. Commons not
only established historical empiricism as a powerful methodology for
institutional economists but he also revolutionized the field of labor
economics. His Wisconsin group of institutionalists became the academic
arm of Robert L. LaFollette's progress movement for socioeconomic and
politicoeconomic reform.   Commons and his associates provided the
intellectual tools which LaFollette and other reformers used in their effort
to meliorate the harsh conditions that prevailed in the American economy
during the early years of the twentieth century (Harter, 1962; Gruchy,
1967, pp. 135-246).

Wesley Clair Mitchell developed a valid and useful quantitatively oriented analytical science, which he contributed to the methodology of institutionalism. Mitchell had inherited from Veblen the determination to formulate inductive economic theory from the observation of human behavior, but he had also inherited from John Dewey the determination that his observation of human behavior would be rigorously scientific and quantitatively accurate. The result was that Mitchell's theories were as scientifically valid and precise as Veblen's theories had been casual and confused. Mitchell was certainly the greatest economic statistician of the first half of the twentieth century; he developed a set of extremely advanced statistical techniques and applied them to the analysis of economic conditions and the solution of socioeconomic and politico-economic problems (Mitchell, 1927; Gruchy, 1967, pp. 274-336).

Mitchell's special interest was business cycle theory. Most of the economists who have specialized in business cycle theory have applied the deductive and hypothetical analytical techniques of conventional or mainstream economics. These techniques involve the use of counterfactual assumptions, narrow and mechanistic analysis, and irrelevant conclusions; therefore, conventional business cycle theory has proven to be at best useless and at worst counterproductive in dealing with the practical economic problems of the business cycle. In sharp contrast to the conventional economists, Mitchell approached the business cycle with no preconceptions or assumptions and investigated this phenomenon with great care and extreme thoroughness. He then utilized his quantitatively oriented historical empiricism to derive an inductive theory of the business cycle. Mitchell's research into the business cycle has established a tradition of painstakingly accurate empirical research and has produced valuable insights into the problems associated with economic fluctuations (Mitchell, 1927; Gruchy, 1967, pp. 247-336).

Clarence Edwin Ayres, the last of the founders of the institutionalist school of economic thought, became the leading philosopher of institutionalism. He was a disciple of Veblen in his economics and a disciple of Dewey in his philosophy (Ayres, 1951). Ayres followed the intellectual leadership of Veblen into a total rejection of conventional economics. He absolutely denied the philosophical preconceptions, the assumptions, the methodology, and the conclusions of the microeconomic or marginal analysis of the market economy. He considered the concepts of the rational economic man and the automatically self-regulating market mechanism to be ridiculous fictions; therefore, he was unalterably opposed to laissez-faire, which he considered to be a wrong idea in theory and prescription for disaster in practice. As a result of vociferous criticism of conventional economics, Ayres joined Veblen as the intellectual progenitors of the radical institutionalists who totally reject microeconomic marginal analysis (Ayres, 1944, pp. 3-88).

Ayres formulated an evolutionary theory of economic progress, which treated the economy as an organic whole that should be analyzed from a holistic rather than a reductionistic approach. Any theory of economic progress consists of a theory of normative value and a theory of economic causation. The theory of normative value is necessary to distinguish progress from regress. The theory of economic causation is necessary to specify the causes of economic progress that should be sought and the causes of economic regress that should be avoided. Ayres found the cause of progress in the accumulation of technology, which he believed to be inherently dynamic; he found the cause of regress in the stagnating effects of socioeconomic institutions, which he believed to be inherently static and inhibitory (Ayres, 1944, pp. 89ff.).

Ayre's theory of normative value was a synthesis of the substantive aspects of Veblen's theory with the procedural aspects of Dewey's theory. Ayres accepted and utilized as the substance of his value theory the Veblenian dichotomy between the affirmative propensities of the human personality, which motivate creative, productive, and useful behavior, and the negative propensities, which motivate destructive, exploitative, and wasteful behavior. Ayres developed the concept of the life process to symbolize and to summarize the affirmative aspects of the Veblenian dichotomy. This life process became the standard of normative value in Ayres' instrumental-institutionalist theory. It is by reference to this standard of value that people judge the consequences of their actions to be good or bad and their conduct to be right or wrong (Ayres, 1944, pp. 205-230; Ayres, 1961; Tool, 1977, pp. 832-836).

Ayres also accepted Dewey's instrumental theory of normative value and used it to explain the procedure through which ordinary people can apply the life-process standard of value in the process of making decisions and solving problems. Ayres agreed with Dewey that all judgments of fact and value are induced empirically from past experience and utilized instrumentally as intellectual tools or instruments for making decisions and solving problems. Moreover, both Ayres and Dewey emphasized that judgments of fact and value are verified instrumentally by reference to subsequent experience. Ayres alleged that ordinary people are entirely competent to learn from experience how to interpret the life-process standard of value and how to apply this standard of value to the.

instrumental process of making decisions and solving problems (Ayres, 1961). It was in this manner that Ayres integrated the philosophical tradition of pragmatism and instrumentalism into the economic thought of institutionalism.

THE SYNTHESIS OF INSTITUTIONAL AND SOCIAL ECONOMICS

This brief survey has shown that institutional economics shares with social economics all five of the identifying characteristics which have been specified by William M. Dugger (Dugger, 1977). Like social economics, institutionalism is value-directed. The institutionalists inherited an emphasis on value and a sound theory of normative value from the pragmatists and instrumentalists. Peirce's pragmatic theory of value had its roots in the Judeo-Christian religious tradition; James and Dewey developed this theory in the direction of functionalism and instrumentalism. Institutional economists have always accepted the epistemological validity of normative value judgments. Institutionalists have incorporated value premises into their economic theory and have utilized value judgments as essential intellectual tools in the formulation of economic policy and in the solution of economic problems (Tool, 1977). Both institutional economic theory and institutional economic policy, therefore, must be regarded as being value-directed.

Like social economics, institutionalism is ameliorative and activistic. The institutional economists accepted and utilized the ameliorative social philosophy of Peirce, James, and Dewey. Veblen was radical, but the other founders of institutionalism were reformers who sought to meliorate the antisocial, exploitative, and wasteful conditions that prevail in capitalism. Commons applied his historical institutionalism in his effort to improve the working and living conditions of American laborers and their families; Mitchell used his quantitative institutionalism to define, analyze, and solve the problems of economic instability. Ayres' theory of economic progress implied a set of policies which were intended to reform the capitalistic economy and to improve human welfare. All of these founders of institutionalism were activists in their pursuits of socioeconomic reform. They established a tradition of socioeconomic and politicoeconomic activism which most institutionalists have followed (Hill, 1975). Activism in quest of ameliorative social reform has come to characterize institutional economics.

Like social economics, institutionalists utilitize holistic rather than reductionist techniques of analysis and conceive society as an organic whole rather than as a mechanical assemblage of separable parts. All of the originating scholars of institutionalism from Veblen through Ayres rejected Marshallian partial equilibrium analysis as artificial and irrelevant and refused to abstract a single isolated and simplistic causal relationship from the full complexity of reality. Institutionalists have always analyzed the economy at the social level of generalization as a whole gestalt; they have never attempted to reduce the whole to its parts or to abstract the parts from the integrated whole. Veblen was the first institutionalist to conceive the economy to be an organic whole, and virtually all institutionalists since his time have accepted the principle of organic unity as one of the fundamental preconceptions of institutionalism (Gambs, 1946, pp. 24-26). Institutionalists share with social economists the holistic approach to the analysis of the society and the concept of the society as an organic whole.

One important question remains: Are the secular values of the instrumental institutionalists compatible with the metaphysical values that are accepted by many social economists? This question has been clearly articulated by Mark A. Lutz in a recent interesting and provocative essay. Lutz has written:

> Our critical survey of the mutual compatibility of prag-
> matism and instrumental value theory, with the image of
> man underlying social economics, has pointed to what I
> consider to be irreconcilable differences. It appears to
> me that such incompatibility resides in the adherence of
> instrumental value theory to the same radical naturalism
> and relativism that is the sad hallmark of the modern
> secularized mind; a mind increasingly alienated from its
> own spiritual self and source of dignity (Lutz, 1985, p.
> 169).

It is my conviction, however, that the respective value systems of instrumental institutionalism and social economics are completely compatible.

There can be no doubt concerning the pragmatic value theory of Peirce; clearly, Peirce accepted metaphysical preconceptions and developed a theory of value with strong metaphysical implications. Peirce's concept of the Way of Life and the Way of Death are undoubtedly metaphysical. James initiated the process of secularizing the pragmatic philosophy by

introducing functionalism into the pragmatic theory of value; the secularization process was completed by Dewey and Ayres who treated normative
value as an instrument to be used in logical and scientific inquiry. It is,
nevertheless, my firm belief that the development of the pragmatic-
instrumental theory of normative value is continuous from Peirce through
Ayres, and that, therefore, Peirce's metaphysically oriented pragmatism is
thoroughly compatible with Ayres' secular instrumentalism. Ayres' use of
the Veblenian dichotomy is simply a secularization of Peirce's metaphysical
Doctrine of the Two Ways, and Ayres' instrumental life process is just the
secular equivalent of Peirce's metaphysical Way of Life.

In a previous essay, it was my position that Ayres' theory of
normative value implies a set of metaphysical preconceptions (Hill, 1979).
Ayres based his theory of normative value on his concept of the life
process. The value of the life process, however, presupposes that life is
worth living, but neither the value of the life process nor the worth of
life can be demonstrated or proven scientifically. Both of these preconceptions, therefore, must be accepted by faith as metaphysical principles, or
they must be rejected as not only unproven but also unprovable.
Moreover, the affirmative aspects of the Veblenian dichotomy imply the
metaphysical concept of the perfectibility of man; the negative aspects of
the dichotomy imply the metaphysical concept of original sin. The extent
to which Ayres' theories imply metaphysical preconceptions, however, is
not an essential issue in the question of the compatibility of instrumental
values with social economics.

The essential issue in the compatibility question is the similarity
of the practical policy actions which would result from the application of
the respective philosophies to the solution of socioeconomic and politicoeconomic problems. Peirce's metaphysical system of pragmatic values and
Ayres' instrumental-institutionalist theory of normative value would
motivate and justify identical policies that seek ameliorative socioeconomic
reform; these policies are accepted and advocated by most social economists. According to my most deliberate judgment, there are no contradictions between instrumental institutionalism and social economics. Entirely
to the contrary, it is my conviction that the institutionalist school of
economic thought is completely compatible with social economics.

The ultimate goal of most social economists is to improve the
quality of life and to enhance the socioeconomic welfare of all of the
people, with a special emphasis on improving the welfare of economically
disadvantaged people. This ultimate goal includes several immediate
objectives: full employment, price stability, economic efficiency, an

equitable distribution of income, and a set of programs to provide an adequate socioeconomic safety net for the people who fall through the gaps in the market economy, among others. Each of these immediate objectives can be stated negatively as a socioeconomic problem. The objective of full employment corresponds to the problem of unemployment; the objective of price stability corresponds to the problem of price inflation. The failure to achieve the objective of economic efficiency becomes the problem of economic inefficiency, and the failure to achieve an equitable distribution of income becomes the problem of distributional inequity and injustice. The failure to achieve the programs which would provide an adequate socioeconomic safety net becomes a syndrome of problems representing the various dimensions of alienation, privation, and suffering. These and other problems must be solved in order for social economists to be successful in achieving their immediate objectives and their ultimate goal. It is the thesis of this essay that instrumental institutionalism provides the most effective methodology through which social economists can solve their socioeconomic problems and achieve their objectives and goals.

SUMMARY AND CONCLUSION

The strength of institutional economics lies in its pragmatic and instrumental philosophy of science and scientific methodology. The strength of social economics lies in its objectives and goals which involve the quest to enhance human welfare and to improve the quality of life for all people, but especially for disadvantaged and impoverished people. If the philosophy and methodology of institutional economics could be utilized to achieve the objectives and goals of social economics, then the strengths of these two schools of economic thought could be combined in such a manner as to improve both institutionalism and social economics.

The major premise of this article holds that instrumental institutionalism provides the most effective methodology for social economics. The minor premise alleges that the normative value theory of instrumental institutionalism is thoroughly compatible with social economics. The conclusion logically follows that instrumental institutionalism constitutes the best approach to social economics.

References

Ayres, C. E. 1944. *The Theory of Economic Progress.* Chapel Hill, NC: The University of North Carolina Press.

_____. 1951. "The coordinates of institutionalism," *American Economic Review* 41 (May), 47-55.

_____. 1952. *The Industrial Economy.* Boston: Houghton Mifflin Company.

_____. 1961. *Toward a Reasonable Society.* Austin, TX: The University of Texas Press.

Commons, J. R. and Associates. 1946. *History of Labour in the United States*, Vol. I. New York: The Macmillan Company.

Dewey, J. 1922. *Human Nature and Conduct.* New York: Henry Holt and Company.

_____. 1929. *The Quest for Certainty.* New York: Minton, Balch and Company.

_____. 1938. *The Theory of Inquiry.* New York: Henry Holt and Company.

Dorfman, J. 1972. *Thorstein Veblen and His America.* Clifton, NJ: Augustus M. Kelley.

Dugger, W. M. 1977 "Social economics: one perspective," *Review of Social Economy* 35 (December), 299-310.

Gambs, J. S. 1946. *Beyond Supply and Demand.* New York: Columbia University Press.

Gruchy, A. G. 1967. *Modern Economic Thought.* New York: Augustus M. Kelley.

Harter, L. G. 1962. *John R. Commons: His Assault on Laissez-Faire.* Corvallis, OR: Oregon State University Press.

Hill, L. E. 1975. "Analysis of the history and methodology of institutional economics," *Proceedings of the International Congress of Economic History and the History of Economic Theories*, Piraeus, Greece, March 10-15, pp. 153-165.

_____. 1978. "Social and institutional economics: toward a creative synthesis," *Review of Social Economy* 26 (December), 311-323.

_____. 1979. "The metaphysical preconceptions of the economic science," *Review of Social Economy* 37 (October), 189-196.

James, W. 1908. *Pragmatism: A New Name for Some Old Ways of Thinking.* New York: Longmans, Green, and Co.

Johnson, G. M. 1986. *Research Methodology for Economists: Philosophy and Practice.* New York: Macmillan Publishing Company.

Lutz, M. A. 1985. "Pragmatism, instrumental value theory, and social economics," *Review of Social Economy* 43 (October), 140-172.

Mitchell, W. C. 1927. *Business Cycles: The Problem and Its Setting.* New York: The National Bureau of Economic Research.

Peirce, C. S. 1958. *Selected Writings: Values in a Universe of Change.* New York: Dover Publications, Inc.

Polanyi, M. 1964. *Personal Knowledge: Toward a Post-Critical Philosophy.* New York: Harper & Row.

Tool, M. R. 1977. "A social value theory in neoinstitutional economics," *Journal of Economics* 11 (December), 823-846.

Veblen, T. 1899. *The Theory of the Leisure Class.* New York: The Macmillan Company.

_____. 1904. *The Theory of Business Enterprise.* Charles Scribner's Sons.

_____. 1914. *The Instinct of Workmanship.* New York: B. W. Hueboch, Inc.

_____. 1919. *The Place of Science in Modern Civilization and Other Essays.* New York: The Viking Press.

THE INSTITUTIONALIST APPROACH TO SOCIAL ECONOMICS: COMMENT

Edward J. O'Boyle

Responding to Professor Hill's essay is more demanding than responding to Professor Hunt's essay in the sense that institutionalism is not a system like either Marxist socialism or solidarism and so we do not have a rough architectural sketch to compare. The absence of such a sketch, it seems, is a logical consequence of the pragmatism that serves as institutionalism's philosophical foundations. On the other hand, commenting on Professor Hill's essay is less demanding, at least for me, because historically institutionalists and Catholic social economists have not viewed one another as being entrenched in hostile ideological camps. Socialists and Catholic social economists, in contrast, have been known to confront one another in hostile if not downright warlike fashion.

My remarks on Professor Hill's contribution are organized and presented differently than in the case of Professor Hunt's contribution. In what follows, there are just two sections instead of three--areas of agreement and areas of disagreement. One or two questions are intertwined in these two sections.

AREAS OF AGREEMENT

With regard to intermediate ends at least, we are agreed that meeting man's material needs is paramount. Further, there is agreement among a large number of Catholic social economists that "the highest priority is accorded to solving the problems of the people who are economically and socially disadvantaged." Among Catholic social economists the equivalent expression is "the preferential option for the poor."[1] In a closely related matter, there is agreement that man is by nature a social being.

Other areas of convergence relate to a perception of social economics as anthropocentric and normative. In this regard, it seems that we agree that social economics is normative because it is anthropocentric. Further, the socioeconomic order is represented in similar terms, that is it is seen as operating organically rather than mechanically as with mainstream economics. However, it is not clear whether this convergence is a matter of substantive agreement as well. By organic does the institutionalist mean a social order in which certain institutions are established intermediate between the individual and the family on the one hand and the state on the other in order to protect the former from the oppression of the latter?

Professor Hill's definition of social economics--"an applied policy science that is intended to solve problems of social injustice and economic privation"--is especially helpful in a book such as this because by penetrating to the very core of social economics it provides a clearing for its various and distinct strands to come together. I applaud its economy and unifying simplicity.

More than 30 years ago, Bernard Dempsey chided his fellow Catholic social economists for their

> . . . preoccupation with capitalism as an abstract concept [which] has inhibited study . . . of institutions as they are . . . [yet] the relevant moral concepts must be studied as they can be applied to these institutions as they are. Enough good hard work on the economic and moral

aspects of these problems can combine with recent technological progress to produce a really "good society" (Dempsey 1958: pp. 162-163).

In this regard, I wish that Professor Hill had affirmed instrumental institutionalism as *a* most useful methodology rather than *the* most useful methodology. While clearly necessary to social economics, institutional economics is not methodologically sufficient to the many tasks that social economists have yet to tackle in order to "solve the problem of social injustice and economic privation."

AREAS OF DISAGREEMENT

I detect three main areas of disagreement. Pragmatism is not *the* most valid philosophical foundation for social economics largely because, by definition, pragmatism cannot fully probe the depths of the three central questions: Who is man? What is man? Whose is man? I would take the same strict position even if I judged the contribution of scholastic philosophy in these matters to be incomplete and insufficient because man is much more than what he does. Man's authentic reality is more than just the set of practical consequences that follow from whatever he does because man is more than mere material being. Man's spiritual side is not revealed satisfactorily through pragmatism because philosophy cannot be made to do the work of theology.

Important disagreements surface in the related matters of truth, science, and religion. In scholastic thought--the philosophical foundations of Catholic social economics--truth is seen as one, as absolute, as forever fixed in objective reality. Quite apart from its utility to man, truth simply is. In principle, two roads lead to truth: faith and reason. Strictly speaking, belief is the acceptance of truth on faith or, more precisely, on the authority of another. Knowledge is truth discovered through reason or through direct personal experience. To believe the truth of a thing is a matter of faith. To know the truth is a matter of reason.

The institutionalization of a set of beliefs is called a religion. The institutionalization of a specific body of knowledge discovered through the scientific method is called variously a discipline, a field, a specialty, or simply the science of, say, economics. The "how" or the "why" of a thing is not the exclusive domain of science or religion. Put differently, one sees signposts marked "how" and others marked "why" along both roads to the truth.

In principle, since truth is one, faith and reason, belief and knowledge cannot contradict one another. In practice, they can and often do as with Galileo and the Vatican some centuries ago and with creationists and evolutionists today. Such disagreements seem to indicate that truth is not one but several. What they really mean is that man's mind and heart perceive the one truth "through a glass, darkly." From time to time, religionists and economists alike may be either foolish or wise. What man believes or knows is neither foolish nor wise but either true or not true. It is man's business to sort out the difference.

Another area of disagreement relates to the holistic approach versus the reductionistic approach. Professor Hill asserts that the holistic approach is a requirement for social economics. For sure, the complete rejection of orthodox microeconomics by some institutionalists does not conform to Catholic social economics. The holistic approach versus the reductionistic approach is no more an either/or matter in social economics than is telescope versus microscope in (planetary and biological) science. Both approaches, it seems to me, are efficacious and necessary because some problems are so awesome and pressing that partial analysis is the only viable short-term approach. Since truth is one, whatever is learned through the reductionistic method, however tentative and risky, in principle cannot contradict what is discovered by the holistic method.

Too much should not be made about our differences. Social economics is like a rambling house with many rooms, each different, each with its own special purpose. A dining room is for eating, a bedroom for resting, a sitting room for sewing. Only a fool would tear down the interior, load-bearing walls in order to create one large room for all. There are more than enough rooms for socialists, institutionalists, Catholic social economists, and others in the house of social economics provided that each of us is ever mindful that we share common quarters for one reason: to build a society that rejects injustice and economic privation.

Notes

[1]Professor Hill uses "alleviate" to express the response of institutionalists to the plight of the disadvantaged. My preferred expression, which is not necessarily a widely held view and which is not a major issue in Catholic social economics, is "programs of aid to the needy" which would include some that are alleviative, some that are curative, and others that are preventive.

Reference

Dempsey, B. W. 1958. "There is no such thing as capitalism," reprinted in his *The Functional Economy*. Englewood Cliffs, NJ: Prentice-Hall.

THE INSTITUTIONALIST APPROACH TO SOCIAL ECONOMICS: COMMENT

E. K. Hunt

After reading the Lewis E. Hill article, I was struck by the similarities of vision and scope between my own conception of social economics and that of Hill. It would be extremely redundant to list all the points of agreement since I agree with, and indeed I embrace, nearly everything in his article. I have what may or may not be a major disagreement with Hill that I shall discuss below.

In the five part definition of social economics that Hill quotes from William Dugger, I fully accept and embrace all of the points except number two: "Amelioration rather than preservation or revolution is its [social economics'] aim." And from my reading of Dugger and Hill, as well as from conversations with each of them, I am not sure how much I differ on this point. Before discussing the differences, however, I would like to reaffirm some important agreements I have with them.

All social and economic theory must by its very nature be both explanatory or scientific on the one hand, and, simultaneously, normative on the other. Theorists who pretend their ideas are value-free are either fooling themselves or trying to fool others. Any economic theory that could properly be called social economics would have to examine society as an organic whole with a specific history and a probable future. It would have to be concerned with the relation between the individual and the social whole, and its value orientation would have to be directed toward improving the quality of life--particularly of the disadvantaged. On all of these points Dugger, Hill and I are in total accord.

What does it mean, however, to assert that social economics is ameliorative and not conservative or revolutionary in its aims? It seems to me that most of us see aspects of the status quo that we value and want to preserve and other aspects that we believe to be harmful and would like to change. I have never met a conservative who wants to change absolutely nothing. Nor have I ever met a socialist who wants to change everything. Moreover, all of us desire change that will ameliorate the evils of the system as we see them and want to protect the status quo when it effectively serves human welfare. The differences between the conservative and the socialist center on the nature, magnitude, and consequences of the desired changes.

Since, as Hill and I agree, the social economist sees various institutions as very significantly interconnected parts of an organic whole, it follows that the consequences, both direct and indirect, of many institutional changes will be pervasive and extensive. Does this mean that these very consequential changes are revolutionary and not ameliorative? Are the changes recommended by conservatives those whose impact is minor and inconsequential? Are the revolutionary changes pervasive and consequential? And are the social economists' ameliorative changes, as viewed by Dugger and Hill, simply "sort of" important and consequential but not too much so? Instead of deciding beforehand that one's social analysis will conduce toward this vague "middle ground," one should identify the causes of the economic, social, and political problems of the disadvantaged, recommend changes that would improve the situation, and see how pervasive and consequential these changes would be. Veblen, who is deeply admired by both Hill and myself, and whom Hill identifies as the founder of his approach, certainly favored changes that would be profoundly consequential. He seems quite revolutionary to me. For these reasons I am not sure just how much I differ from Dugger and Hill. I hasten to repeat that my vision of the world, of social economics, and of the proper philosophical foundations for social economics incorporates nearly every idea in Hill's excellent essay, and I consider nearly every idea there to be consistent with the ideas expressed in my own essay.

5

SOCIAL ECONOMICS: A SOCIALIST PERSPECTIVE

E. K. Hunt

Social economics, if it is anything, must be an approach to economic theory that recognizes and places importance on the sociality of all human economic activities *and* simultaneously explains and evaluates the meaning and significance of this sociality. Classical liberalism, including both classical economics and neoclassical economics, has given little or no importance to this sociality. The word "socialism" originated in England in the 1820s. It was coined to differentiate a particular view --the socialist view--of capitalism from the asocial, individualistic view of classical liberalism. Socialist economic theory can therefore lay claim to being one of the oldest and richest traditions within the history of social economics. In the following article I shall briefly sketch the outlines of one socialist perspective on social economics. It is, perhaps, unnecessary to say that there are differences among socialist economists on many of the issues I shall discuss.

Human beings, in common with most living creatures, must actively transform their environment to sustain their species. As with many species, such as beavers, ants, bees, and wolves, among others, human beings can only effect this transformation if each individual functions in very specific social relations as part of a collectivity of the species. There is, however, one profoundly important difference between the sociality of beavers, ants, bees, and wolves and the sociality of human beings. In the former, the specific nature of the social relations and hence the structure and manner of functioning of the entire collectivity is genetically built in to each individual. For any specific kind of ant, for example, the colony of which a given individual is part is nearly identical to all other colonies of the same kind of ant that one might find in other places or times. The social behavior of the ant, as well as the specific structure of the collectivity of the ants, is genetically determined and occurs automatically.

For human beings, however, neither social behavior nor the collectivity of which the individual is a part is genetically determined. On the contrary, human behavior and social structures exhibit significant variability from place to place and time to time. This variability is not unlimited, however. The behavioral patterns of any given individual vary only between genetically determined limits, some of which are common to the entire human species and some of which are peculiar to the individual.

The extent or degree of variability within the limits set by the genetic constitution of the species and the individual is rather large. Moreover, specific qualities and quantitative measures of human development almost never reflect (or expose) such genetic limits. This is because long before such limits become operative, the individual encounters and is shaped and affected by social limits to development. The individual human being, because he or she is an interdependent being, develops only within the context of very specific social relations which exert an extremely powerful influence on both the qualitative nature and the quantitative extent of the development of a whole range of human needs, powers, and capabilities.

It was, perhaps, one of the most powerful and important of all of Karl Marx's insights that human beings live and function within a specific society that has a clearly discernable structure. That social structure can be described as accurately as can the physical structure of any living organism. Moreover, the interconnections or social relations that comprise the social structure can be apprehended mentally and understood scientifically in much the same way that the relations among the parts and of the parts-to-the-whole of an animal organism can be understood.

Marx also saw that just as animal organisms fall into "natural" categories or species, social systems similarly fall into distinctive "types." If we wish to understand scientifically the functioning of a particular dog, for example, we must first study the essential nature and mode of functioning of the dog species. When we understand what features this particular animal shares with the entire dog species--or the essential nature of what it means to be a dog--we can then seek understanding of how these essential characteristics of the species function and hence how this particular dog, insofar as his behavior affects his species nature, functions. Only then would we look for peculiarities or idiosyncracies of this particular dog and attempt to determine how, if at all, these peculiarities alter this animal's general species-behavior.

Marx's insight that human societies, like animals, naturally fall into certain clearly discernable types or species is, indeed, a powerful insight. It shows that in order to understand any specific society, one must first understand the nature and functioning of the type or species of societies of which it is a member. Only after one has this understanding can one insightfully explore the significance of the peculiarities of the society in question.

The question of what constitutes the essential features of a given species of societies and what characteristics differentiate one species from another is, of course, of paramount importance. The answer, for Marx, was his famous designation, the "mode of production." Our society is an instance of the general species of societies whose nature derives from their capitalist modes of production. There were at least four other modes of production identified by Marx (although Marx definitely did not consider his list to be exhaustive) including the primitive, the Asiatic, the slave, and the feudal modes.

Discussion of these modes would go far beyond the scope of this article. It is also impossible to reiterate the detailed arguments that I have presented elsewhere (Hunt, 1984, 1986) that the commonly held opinion that Marx was a historical determinist is not only wrong but grotesquely so. For the remainder of this article I shall elaborate on two themes found in the writings of Marx and later Marxists--themes that I consider to be of utmost importance for social economics.

One of the most important issues facing social scientists is whether there are good reasons to accept a set of normative criteria with which to evaluate and compare various social systems or models of production together with the range of human development that tends to obtain within each of these modes. This is the second of my two themes, and I shall close this article with a discussion of this issue.

First, however, I wish to discuss what I believe to be one of the most profound contributions of Marx and the Marxist tradition generally to the study of social economics. Marx has an elaborate and insightful discussion of how the ordinary, normal functioning of capitalism veils and obscures the social nature of economic phenomena and systematically tends to shift the focus of the economic investigator away from social relations and social interactions, and toward the abstract relations among things and the abstract, impersonal, asocial functioning of the market. To understand Marx's argument we must examine the two most important defining features of a capitalist mode of production. Capitalism is an economic system in which resources are allocated by, and income distribution is determined within, the market. Marx called this a "commodity=producing society." In addition, capitalism is characterized by a particular class structure. I shall first discuss his views on the market allocation of resources and then on the class structure of capitalism. In both, I will focus on why capitalism creates a superficial impression that social relations and social activities are not social but merely social market relations.

The most conspicuous aspect of capitalism is the pervasive or ubiquitous functioning of the market. In any society human beings are interdependent, each depending upon and requiring innumerable things, services, and activities from many others. In capitalism, nearly all human social and economic interdependencies are mediated by the market. This means that in capitalism, every thing, service, or activity that I need from another I must buy in the market. Similarly, if I perform or act for others, it is only in response to their buying things, services, or activities from me in the market.

When one stops to consider any one of the thousands of things necessary to sustain daily life, one becomes aware of how extensive and complex human social interdependence is. For example, we may begin our day by eating a bowl of cereal. For that cereal we depend upon farm workers who plant and harvest the grain, transportation workers who take it to mills, production workers in mills who transform it into the cereal we eat, transportation workers who transport it to grocery stores, and clerks who sell it to us. But that is only the beginning. The farm workers (as well as all of the other workers in the process) use machinery and tools that must be constantly produced by thousands of other workers. These latter workers, in turn, require materials, partly finished goods, tools, and machinery produced by still other workers. From this example we see that even the simplest act of consumption or production involves interdependencies among tens or even hundreds of thousands of productive individuals. Thus, above all else, an act of consumption or an act of production is a social act. It is social because it requires the cooperation and social coordination of countless productive activities on the part of other people.

This merely reflects the fact that in all societies people must socially transform the natural environment in order to make it liveable. This social transformation of the environment is production. For Marx, three facts about production were true in every society.

First, production did, of course, require a natural environment to transform. Human beings could not exist in a vacuum.

Second, nature itself contributed nothing toward its own transformation--it simply was the "stuff" being transformed in production. Only human labor transformed nature. Marx's views contrast sharply with the orthodox neoclassical conception of capitalism, which claims that nature and tools both contribute to production and that landlords and capitalists are entitled to rewards commensurate with the contributions of nature and tools. For Marx, the fact that we exist in a natural environment that can be transformed in such a way that it fulfills our needs, however, had nothing whatsoever to do with the fact that landlords own the natural environment. Likewise, tools, which certainly must be used in production, were themselves in existence, he insisted, only because working people had produced them, and not because of the peculiarities of ownership. Thus labor was the only human cause or source of production.

Third, any individual laborer or producer was, Marx argued, very nearly helpless alone. Production was a social activity where the production of one laborer depended upon the simultaneous or previous production of many other laborers. These three facts were true in every socioeconomic system, including capitalism.

What distinguished capitalism was that productive activity was not directly or immediately social. An individual producer had no direct social relation to (and generally had no knowledge of) either the workers upon whom his own production depended or those who depended upon his production. He bought what he needed in the market and produced for sale in the market. Therefore, the labor of the workers upon whom he depended confronted him not as the activity of particular people but as the market prices of the commodities they had produced. Likewise, the people who depended upon his labor did not know him as an individual. They knew nothing of the peculiar characteristics of him as a person or of his labor. His labor existed for them only as the selling price of the commodity he had produced.

In capitalism, then, labor was not directly social. It became social only when it appeared as the price of a commodity that was exchanged. The prices of commodities and the buying and selling of commodities at these prices constituted the indirect social relations of interdependent laborers. Thus, in capitalism the social interdependence of workers appeared, in the form of commodity prices, to be a set of relations among things (commodities) rather than a set of relations among workers. In capitalism, Marx (1961, Vol. I, pp. 72-73) wrote:

> . . . articles of utility become commodities only because they are products of the labour of private individuals or groups of individuals who carry on their work independently of each other. The sum total of the labour of all these private individuals forms the aggregate labour of society. Since the producers do not come into social contact with each other until they exchange their products, the specific social character of each producer's labour does not show itself except in the act of exchange. In other words, the labour of the individual asserts itself as a part of the labour of society, only by means of the relations which the act of exchange establishes directly between the products, and indirectly, through them, between the producers. To the latter, therefore, the relations connecting the labour of one individual with that of the rest appear, not as direct social relations between individuals at work, but as . . . social relations between things.

The common belief that the exchange of commodities is merely a set of relations among things, rather than social relations among human individuals, makes a fetish of things, so Marx called this belief the "fetishism of commodities." Marxist economics focuses on the human relations directly involved in market exchange, as well as other social and productive relations that form the necessary economic foundation for the kind of exchange that characterizes capitalism.

The prices of commodities, for Marx, had no inherent relation to the physical characteristics of the commodities. Wheat, for example, had certain physical characteristics when it was produced for the use of the producer and those directly associated with him or her in a precapitalist society with no markets and no prices. Wheat had exactly the same physical characteristics when it was produced, in capitalism, only for sale at some price in the market where its users had no direct social relation with its producers. Since prices had no inherent connection to the physical characteristic or useful qualities of things, prices could only be mental abstractions that were socially attached to things in order to coordinate the interdependence of producers. The social coordination or allocation of productive labor, in capitalism, depended entirely on prices and buying and selling. Therefore, prices were abstractions whereby capitalism rendered private labor into social labor through market exchange. As such, prices represented this social labor. But they appeared to be attributes of commodities rather than attributes of people. These views were the foundation of Marx's labor theory of value, which, unfortunately, I do not have the space to discuss in this article.

Whether social labor is allocated to the production of food, shelter, clothing, and other necessities or to yachts, mansions, pornography, hydrogen bombs, or nerve gas depends upon whether sellers of commodities (who are generally capitalists) can find buyers who are able and willing to pay the price that makes production of those various commodities profitable. Marx and his disciples have put considerable stress on the fact that the search for profits, and not inherent human or social needs, allocates and directs labor in capitalism. No matter how useful or beneficial some particular productive activity may be, it will generally not be undertaken if it does not yield profit to a capitalist. Likewise, the most useless, or even socially harmful, activities will be undertaken if they yield a profit for a capitalist.

Already in our discussion of the market, however, we have found it necessary to introduce the other defining feature in Marx's conception of capitalism: the distinction between workers who produce and capitalists who, through their search for profit, direct and control (and hence socially allocate) productive workers.

Marx's first defining feature of capitalism was that the market coordinated and allocated social labor by mediating all productive relationships among workers in such a way that the social nature of labor appeared as the prices of commodities. This allocation was effected through the search for profits. To understand Marx's views on the nature and role of profits we must understand his second defining feature of capitalism, its peculiar class structure.

Marx believed that in every historical setting and within every cultural or national boundary in which capitalism had existed, four classes of people had existed: the class of capitalists, the class of small shop-keepers and independent craftsmen or professional people, the class of workers, and a poverty-stricken class that generally owned little or no property and whose members, for a variety of reasons, could not work. In some settings capitalism had had other classes as well. In the period of early capitalism, for example, by the side of these four classes were peasants and nobility, the remaining vestiges of the two main classes characteristic of feudalism. But the above-mentioned four classes were always characteristic of capitalism, and together they constituted its second defining feature. We shall briefly discuss Marx's view of each class.

Of the four, the working class and the capitalist class were by far the most important. In most capitalist settings, and always in well-developed capitalist economies, the working class constituted the absolute majority of the population and created or produced nearly all of the commodities. The capitalist class had the bulk of economic and political power in a capitalist society. We shall therefore discuss these two classes first.

A capitalist class could not exist without a class of wage laborers. Working for wages, or wage labor, characterized the working class in capitalism. Wage labor came into existence in the sixteenth to eighteenth centuries when large numbers of peasants were pushed off the land by landlords who took over the peasant's land and the formerly common lands. When that happened, the peasants were forced to go to the cities, where they found commercial market-oriented economy. The peasants could no longer sell the commodities they produced in order to acquire the commodities necessary to sustain their lives because they had no access to the land or to means of production.

But the worker in the city had to buy commodities in order to live. And he or she could not buy commodities without selling something first so as to acquire money for purchases. Such a worker had but one saleable thing--his or her body or capacity to produce. The worker could not sell his or her body once and for all, or we would have had a slave economy and not a capitalist economy. In capitalism, the worker recurringly sold control over his or her capacity to work, or labor power, for definite periods of time only. For example, he or she "hired out" by the hour, the day, or the week. The wage was the price the worker received for selling control of himself or herself for this period of time. Therefore, the defining characteristic of the working class of capitalism was that it was comprised of wage laborers who had to sell their labor power as a commodity in order to survive.

The class that owned the means of production, of course, was the capitalist class. Exactly the same historical forces that created the wage laborer created the capitalist. The enclosure movements and the other forms of what Marx called "the primitive accumulation of capital" deprived the working class of any access to the means of production while simultaneously putting these means into the hands of the capitalist class. Therefore, the creation of the wage labor class was also necessarily the creation of the capitalist class.

Because of their ownership, capitalists needed to do nothing productive. They were free to do almost anything they chose. A few of them might simply choose to engage in productive endeavors. But such endeavor had absolutely nothing to do with their role as capitalists. They could cease such endeavor at will and still remain capitalists. Thus, for example, the Rockefeller family has produced governors, bank presidents, a vice-president of the United States, and so forth. Any one of them was also free at any time, without jeopardizing the family's status as capitalists, to become a functionless playboy.

The capitalist class owned the materials necessary for production. They then bought labor power as a commodity on the market. They directed the laborers, whose labor power they had purchased, to produce. The laborers produced commodities having some given magnitude of value. These commodities were owned by the capitalists, of course, who then sold the commodities. The value that the laborers had produced was generally sufficient for the capitalists to pay the laborers their wage, to pay for raw materials used, to pay for the wear and tear of the machines and tools used, or to acquire new machines and tools, and to leave a surplus for the capitalist. The capitalist received the surplus purely as a result of his ownership of property.

Not all of this surplus, however, was profit. The capitalist might have borrowed funds to augment his capital, or he might have rented the land on which his factory was constructed. For the capitalist, the interest he paid on his debt and the rent he paid on the land were both expenses which he deducted, along with his other expenses, from the value his laborers had created in order to arrive at his profit. The persons who received this interest and rent were also, in Marx's view, receiving income purely from ownership. Thus, the surplus value created by workers, in excess of the value of their own wages and the materials and tools used up in production, went to profit, interest, and rent. All three of these latter

forms of income were derived from ownership. Therefore they were all
capitalist income. Ownership of money, land, or tools and machinery
could thus all become capital under the right circumstances, and the return
from owning capital could take the form of interest, rent, or profit.

The capitalist class was comprised of those people whose ownership was so significant that it brought them sufficient income to live in
luxury and to have great economic and political power without every
having to engage in any form of socially useful toil.

In every capitalist economy there was another social class that
stood between the capitalists and the wage laborers. This was the class of
small shopkeepers, independent craftsmen, and professionals or other
independent proprietors. This class had features resembling both capitalists and workers. They owned their own means of production and did
much (and sometimes all) of the work in creating or selling their commodities. Most frequently they themselves, like wage laborers, had to work,
but they also, like capitalists, hired wage laborers to assist them. Included
in this class would be most doctors, lawyers, independent accountants,
barbers, and many owners of such small businesses as hamburger stands,
dry cleaners, repair garages, small retail shops, and the like. This class has
always been much smaller than the working class and much larger than the
capitalist class. In some circumstances the interests of this class might be
very close to those of the capitalist class, whereas in other circumstances
their interests might be closer to those of the working class.

Finally, the last class in capitalism was the poorest class. It
included people who received little or no income from either owning or
working. Included in this class were two distinctly different groups. First,
there were those who could not work for a variety of reasons, such as
mental, physical, or emotional handicaps or problems; people who were
too young or old to work and had no one to support them; and people
such as single parents of very small children whose necessary activities left
no time for wage labor. The second group included people who were able
and willing to work but for whom capitalism did not provide enough jobs.
Throughout the history of capitalism there have always been millions of
such involuntarily unemployed people. They have generally performed two
very important economic functions. First, they have weakened the
bargaining power of employed laborers in their wage negotiations, since if
employed workers demanded too much, they could easily be replaced.
Second, capitalism has always been an unstable economy. It has experienced alternative periods of prosperity and depression. The involuntarily
unemployed have constituted a reserve of workers who could be used in

times of prosperity when the economy was growing and needed more workers and could be discarded when recession or depression set in and fewer workers were needed. Thus, the size of this lowest or poorest class in capitalism has always varied in accordance with general business conditions.

After examining the sources of income among all four classes, Marx concluded that interest, rent, and profit were not the only forms taken by the surplus created by the working class. Taxes also came from this surplus. Whether the taxes were collected from wage earners or from the recipients of interest, rent, and profits, they represented a claim on the product of labor and were hence a part of the surplus value created by but not received by workers. Thus we see that two of the classes in capitalism--the highest and the lowest--did not contribute to the production of commodities but lived off the surplus created by wage laborers.

Within the context of Marx's theory, it is interesting to note that whenever workers become angry or frustrated by their support of unproductive consumers, it is, of course, much more conducive to the peace and stability of capitalism if all of their anger and frustration is turned against those living in dire poverty--the unemployed and unemployable--rather than against those living in extravagant luxury--the capitalists. It is not surprising that conservatives generally protest the parasitic nature of the very poor and the powerless, while critics who have been influenced by Marx protest the parasitic nature of the wealthy and the powerful. In Marx's view, however, both classes were integral parts of capitalism and would continue to exist as long as capitalism existed.

Thus the market allocation of productive labor and natural resources, together with the four-level class structure of capitalism, constituted the main defining features of capitalism for Marx. In discussing this class structure however, we used the concepts of private property and capital, concepts which Marx understood somewhat differently than they are understood in conventional economic theory. We shall, therefore, discuss them at somewhat greater length.

It is difficult to find a general definition that will cover all property rights, in all societies, in all times. One thing, however, is clear. A property right is not simply or even primarily a relation between an isolated individual and a material thing. An isolated individual could use any material object in any way he or she chose, subject only to the laws of physics, chemistry, and human anatomy. He or she would have absolutely no need for, and no conception of, property rights. Property rights are essential social relations between people. But not all social relations are property rights.

An adequate general definition of property rights is, of necessity, fairly vague and complex. The best definition, in our opinion, is as follows: within a particular social or cultural setting (e.g., a modern nation-state) property rights represent a set of social relations that define privileges and corresponding sanctions. The privileges and sanctions are related to objects (whether material or not). The privileges and sanctions are coercively established and coercively maintained by an agency of coercion that is widely believed to "rightly" or "properly" use coercive force (such as the police).

For most of us, private property simply means private ownership of our personal means of consumption. We have the exclusive privilege of using and disposing of our own food, clothing, and assorted personal effects (though generally not of the dwelling in which we reside). Others cannot have this privilege with our personal effects. They face coercive sanctions. If they try to use or dispose of our personal effects, their action constitutes theft, and they face coercion from the police, one of our institutionalized agencies whose use of coercion (within defined limits) is generally deemed proper.

Private ownership of the means of consumption strikes most of us as a reasonable and useful social convention. It would seem difficult for a society to function if certain items, such as food and clothing, were not allocated in such a manner as to give particular individuals the right to use and dispose of particular means of consumption, at least where that consumption is primarily a private matter. Defenders of private property generally use the means of personal consumption to illustrate that private property is "natural," "inevitable," and "just." Marx's concern, however, was not so much with private ownership of the means of consumption as with private ownership of the means of production. Marx insisted that all production was social. But there were two different ways in which it was social. First, in handicraft production, a single or at most a few producers working together created a finished product. Even in the case of a single producer, there was an economic or productive dependence on other producers who had to provide the individual producer with materials on which to work as well as equipment, machines, and tools with which to work. Defenders of private ownership of the means of production have generally used examples of handicraft production to construct their defense. In such production, the individual's social dependence was similar to that involved in private consumption; that is, others produced both the necessary means of consumption and production. Thus, when handicraft production alone was considered, the same rationale would defend private ownership of both productive and consumptive goods.

Marx felt that it was ironic that handicraft production was frequently used as the basis for defending capitalist private ownership of the means of production. He argued that it was such historical processes as the enclosure movement and increased indebtedness, among other things, that had made independent handicraft production impossible for the vast majority of workers and, in so doing, had simultaneously created a supply of unemployed wage workers. In other words, the necessary condition for capitalism's historical creation was that the form of production that was used to defend capitalist ownership had to become inaccessible to most producers and therefore had to become relatively unimportant to the whole capitalist economy.

There were, of course, still a few independent handicraft producers in most capitalist economies of Marx's time (as there are today). They constituted a small part of the class of independent small shopkeepers, producers, and professionals that stood somewhere between the capitalist class and the working class. Obviously, this first form of productive interdependence, characteristic of handicraft production, was not the most important form nor was it the characteristic form in a capitalist economy.

The second form of productive interdependence, then, was the one most characteristic of capitalism. This interdependence reflected the form of social production that inevitably went with a capitalist economy and was, historically, the outcome of the Industrial Revolution. This form of productive interdependence was characteristic of factory and industrial production. In industrial production, no single worker or small group of workers produced a finished commodity. There was an elaborate division of labor in which each individual repetitiously performed a single or a few tasks and only the coordinated effort of hundreds (and even, in some cases, tens of thousands) of individuals resulted in the production of a particular commodity. Such industrial production generally involved massive factories or work places, as well as very expensive and elaborate machines and tools.

Thus, industrial production, which was the form social productive interdependencies generally took in a capitalist economy, made it utterly impossible for the vast majority of working people to individually own as private property the means necessary for them to produce. In capitalism most production was totally social. It was social in the same way that handicraft production was social; that is, workers in a factory depended upon other workers to produce the materials on which they worked and the tools with which they worked. But it is also social in a new way: namely, that any production process now involved the coordinated endeavors of hundreds or even thousands of workers working with complex, expensive machinery.

In this situation what then constituted the nature of private ownership of the means of production? Marx was aware that in the case of private ownership of the means of individual consumption--or private ownership of the means of individual, independent handicraft production --such ownership meant the privilege or right to use and dispose of the things owned. In industrial corporations, however, the ownership of stock (which constituted ownership of shares of the means of production) conferred this right to only a few of the biggest and most powerful owners. And even then, this right generally consisted only in naming powerful managers to oversee, direct, and control the use of these means of production by working people who did not own them. The common privilege of all ownership of stocks for every owner, from the smallest to the largest, was the right or privilege to take a proportionate share (depending on the amount of stock owned) of the surplus value created by workers. Ownership of the industrial means of production, in capitalism, thus had only one inherent or common privilege for all owners: to reap where they had not sown, to receive a part of the value of commodities produced without having to take any part whatsoever in the production of these commodities.   Thus Marx (1961, Vol. III, p. 427) argued that capitalism had resulted in a

> . . . transformation of the actually functioning capitalist into a mere manager, administrator of other peoples capital, and of the owner of capital into a mere owner, a mere money-capitalist. Even if the dividends which they receive include the interest and the profit of enterprise, i.e. the total profit (for the salary of the manager is, or should be, simply the wage of a specific type of skilled labour, whose price is regulated in the labour-market like that of any other labour), this total profit is henceforth received only in the form of interest, i.e. as mere compen- sation for owning capital that now is entirely divorced from its function in the actual process of reproduction just as this function in the person of the manager is divorced

from ownership of capital. Profit thus appears . . . as a
mere appropriation of the surplus-labour of others.

During Marx's time (and, indeed, right up to the present) the
dominant economic ideology of capitalism justified colossal incomes from
ownership as being the fruits of high moral character. In capitalism, the
ideologists argued, workers earned wages because of, or in payment for,
the strain of producing. On the other hand, because it has always been
extraordinarily difficult (very nearly impossible) for a noncapitalist to save
enough to become a capitalist, the ideologists argued that whenever
anyone did become a capitalist they must have undergone strain and
sacrifices that were much more severe than the mere strain of productively
creating things that were socially needed. Therefore, their profit, rent, and
interest were earned because of, or in payment for, the strains and
sacrifices of their abstinence.

There were many arguments by which Marx refuted the ideologists'
apologetic views on profit. Here I shall mention only three of them.

First, the abstinence and strain that were necessary for one to
become a capitalist involved no contribution to society. For example, if
a person saved all his life in order to buy a factory, he saved only for
himself. He had not, in so doing, done any of the work necessary to
construct the factory. All of the work had been done by working people.
Rather, the extent of his stress and strain merely reflected the fact that in
any class-divided society there had to be significant barriers to entrance
into the ruling class. If it had been relatively easy for anyone to become
a capitalist, then everyone would have become a capitalist; there would
have been no workers; nothing would have been produced, and everyone
would have starved. There had been in history, and were in Marx's time,
numerous socioeconomic systems that got along fine without the abstinence of capitalists--in fact, without capitalists at all. But there had never
been, and there never would be, a society without working people creating
needed products.

Second, if sacrifice and abstinence could justify capitalists' income,
then they could similarly justify the wealth, power, and income of any
ruling class in any society. For example, in the American South prior to
the Civil War, the economic system was one of commercial slavery. Slaves
were very expensive, and most Southern whites did not own slaves. Slave
owners, of course, enjoyed great wealth and lavish incomes from the surplus their slaves produced over the costs of their maintenance. For a non-
slave owner to become a slave owner was very difficult. It required

extreme strain and abstinence. It is therefore clear that according to this ideology the surplus that these owners extracted from the sweat and toil of their slaves was merely the just reward for the owners' strain and abstinence.

Third, the majority of capitalists inherited their ownership of capital. They not only did not strain and abstain, most of them lived lives of indolent luxury. And for those who had not inherited their wealth, most had become capitalists not because they had produced and abstained, but through some combination of ruthlessness, shrewdness, chicanery, and luck. Marx detailed the piracy, slave trading, and colonial plundering in the early process of building capitalist fortunes.

When confronted with these criticisms, defenders of capitalist ideology had two responses. The first response was that regardless of how a capitalist acquired his fortune, he abstained when he did not fritter the whole thing away. He could have consumed so incredibly profligately and luxuriously that he would soon have had none of his inherited fortune left. In fact, a few capitalists actually did this, and every capitalist constantly had the choice of, on the one hand, abstaining from such extreme profligacy and luxury in order that he or all of his descendants might live in ordinary profligacy and luxury or, on the other hand, recklessly throwing his entire fortune away. And, in fact, in order for a capitalist family to remain in the ruling class, generation after generation, the members of the family had to "abstain" to that degree just as they had to abstain from committing suicide before they had had any offspring to inherit their wealth. Such abstinence, in the ideology of capitalism, remained a moral justification for the large incomes of capitalists.

The second response to critics was that abstinence alone did not morally justify ruling-class income, but only abstinence that led to or perpetuated the ownership of nonhuman objects as capital. Thus the defenders of capitalism argued that abstinence in the acquiring of slaves did not justify property income because slave owning was inherently immoral, whereas the owner of capital did society a great service because capital was productive. The capitalist used his capital productively and thereby contributed to everyone's well being.

It is clear that we cannot understand all of Marx's critique of the ideology of capitalism until we understand his conception of the nature of capital. Therefore, I shall conclude my discussion of the nature and functioning of the capitalist mode of production with an analysis of the Marxian view of capitalism.

The standard ideology of capitalism, which one finds inextricably interwoven into all neoclassical economic theory, is based on the notion that capital is one of the three factors of production--land, labor, and capital--that are necessary for production in every society. These factors of production are said to account for all production. Above all, the ideology holds that the three are complementary and not alternatives or competitors. All production requires the cooperation of all three. Without labor, no production is possible; without land, no production is possible; and without capital, no production is possible. Ideologists conclude that all three factors need to cooperate peacefully and harmoniously.

But the ideology goes on to insist that all three factors of production are merely collections of three different kinds of commodities. Land, labor, and capital are names for three different sorts of commodities that are bought and sold in the market. Since commodities do not cooperate peacefully and harmoniously, it is obvious that the ideologists mean that the owners of the commodities must cooperate peacefully and harmoniously.

Next, the ideologists argue that entrepreneurs go into the market and buy certain quantities of each of the three commodity factors of production. The entrepreneur then combines these factors in a production process that yields output in the form of commodities having certain value. He sells these commodities on the market. If everything has functioned properly, then two very interesting "facts" can be observed to result from the process. First, one can ascertain precisely the productive contribution of each of the factors: land, labor, and capital. Second, the price that the entrepreneur pays for each of these commodities--wages being the price of labor, rent being the price of land, and profit (or interest) being the price of capital--turn out to be exactly equal to the value of the productive contribution of each factor; that is, each factor gets just what it contributes to production. Hence there cannot possibly be any economic exploitation. It is clear why the ideologists of capitalism hold that harmony and not conflict is the natural social state of capitalism. This conservative ideology can still be found in virtually all neoclassical economics textbooks on microeconomics theory.

Capital, in this ideology, is merely a commodity like the other factors of production. It produces for society and receives a reward based on its productivity. If one doubts the productivity of capital, argues the ideologist, then one should try making steel without a blast furnace, or digging a trench without a shovel, or tightening a screw without a screwdriver, or, in general producing without tools. Capital is identified as commodities that are tools (or other means of producing). And because tools are indispensable, they argue that capital is indispensable.

But Marx immediately saw several difficulties. Human beings had always used tools. Yet capitalism, capital, and profit were social categories that did not even exist as such in some societies. In fact, capitalism, capital, and profit had actually existed for only a few hundred years.

Obviously, land did not yield rent and tools did not yield profit simply because they entered into the production process. They had been used in societies that did not even have rent or profit. Clearly tools were not, per se, capital. Moreover, since one could own both land and tools and yet receive no rent or profit, it was equally clear that ownership of land or tools does not necessarily or automatically mean capitalistically owned land that yields rent or capital that yields profit. The problem of identifying the nature of capital remained unsolved within the context of capitalist ideology.

The key to solving the riddle in Marx's opinion was to realize that land, labor, and capital were not, in the same sense, factors of production. Moreover, tools and land, simply purchased as commodities, required other social conditions before they could become profit-yielding capital and rent-yielding land.

The production process, Marx insisted, presupposed that human beings lived in an environment they could transform. Production was this transformation of nature by human beings. Although land, as this environment, was certainly necessary, to say that nature "produced" something was to engage in a kind of confusion (Marx called it fetishism) where human qualities were attributed to nonhuman things. It was the equivalent of saying that nature transformed itself expressly for human use.

Just as saying that land, as an inanimate object, could produce anything by itself was a confusion (or a form of fetishism), so was the notion that tools produced anything by themselves. A tool undertook no activity. It was an object produced by human labor. The producer of the tool had in mind, of course, that the tool would be used in further production. But the tool, as such, did not produce anything. Only people produced things--usually by using tools.

The statement that tools were absolutely necessary for modern production was true. But it did not mean that tools engaged in production. It meant, rather, that production was social and that producers were interdependent. The carpenter, for example, depended upon the working people who produced hammers, nails, saws, and lumber. After the carpenter had built a house, the procapitalist ideologist would insist that a hammer, some nails, a saw, and some lumber--together with a carpenter --built the house. Contrary to this ideology, Marx argued that human beings had socially built the house by dividing the work in such a manner that some had produced the hammers, others nails, others saws, others lumber, and still others had brought all of these human exertions together by performing the last step (carpentering) in this social production process. In fact, capital was not simply a commodity that produced. Capital was a word that was attached to tools only when a very specific set of social relations existed. Capital, then, did not refer to tools per se, or to tools sold as commodities per se, but to tools sold as commodities and used in a specific way within the context of a specific set of social relations.

Capital existed when (1) tools were produced as commodities, (2) these commodities were owned by a social class other than the class that productively used them, and (3) the class that used the tools to produce received the permission to use them only on the condition that these producers did not receive ownership of the product they produced and that they accept instead a wage having less value than the value of the commodities they produced. The difference, or extra value, went to owners in the form of interest, rent, or profit.

Capital, then, was the capacity of capitalists to place themselves between every human productive interdependency and to extract a return for allowing this interdependent production process to proceed. Between the carpenter who had to use a hammer, a saw, nails, and lumber and the producers of these items he required stood several capitalists. The worker-producer. But the carpenter did not receive these items directly from the capitalists involved. A capitalist owning the construction company bought them from the other capitalists.

In all human productive interdependencies one laborer required the labor of others and others required his labor. In capitalism, however, laborers never dealt with each other. Every interdependency of labor found actual expression in, or actually took effect through, financial dealings among capitalists. The interdependence of labor became, in capitalism, an absolute dependence of any particular laborer on a capitalist. At every point where one worker needed another worker stood a capitalist who had to get his cut, in the form of profit, interest, or rent, or he would not permit the process to go on.

Thus capitalism was a society in which labor became social by taking the form of the price of a commodity and in which every social interdependency of labor took the form of commodities owned by nonlaborers who extracted a concession for allowing producers to produce. In such a society and only in such a society did tools become capital that yielded profit.

Thus, for Marx, the historically specific social relations whereby the owners of the means of production exploited workers within a capitalist system were totally obscured when the procapitalist ideologists argued that rent and profit simply resulted from the physical nature of land and tools, which rendered them indispensable to production. Marx argued that this was a "complete mystification of the capitalist mode of production." The capitalism of the ideologist was "an enchanted, perverted, topsy-turvy world in which Monsieur le Capital and Madame La Terre do their ghost-walking as social characters and at the same time directly as mere things" (Marx, 1960, Vol III, p. 809).

By contrast, Marx's definition of capital stressed its historical specificity:

> One thing . . . is clear--Nature does not produce on the one side owners of money or commodities (means of production), and on the other men possessing nothing but their own labour-power. This relation has no natural basis, neither is its social basis one that is common to all historical periods. It is clearly the result of a past historical development, the product of many economic revolutions, of the extinction of a whole series of older forms of social production (Marx, 1961, Vol III, p. 169).

> Capital is not a thing, but rather a definite social production relation, belonging to a definite historical formation of society, which is manifested in a thing and lends this thing a specific social character . . . . It is the means of production monopolized by a certain section of society, confronting living labour-power as products and working conditions rendered independent of this very labour-power (Marx, 1961, Vol III, pp. 794-795).

Capital was the social relation that defined the two most important classes of the capitalist mode of production. It did not exist on a significant scale prior to capitalism and it would not exist after capitalism had been overthrown. Marx's contribution to our understanding of this remains to this day at the center of the Marxian vision of social economics.

Having completed a survey of Marx's view on why capitalism's appearance generates the asocial economics of the neoclassical school, I shall finish this article with a brief statement of Marx's belief that the capitalist mode of production is ethically defective and should be transformed into some form of socialist mode of production. The implicit (but never explicitly discussed) ethical theory underlying Marx's views is a variant of the Aristotelian view that the ethically good situation is one in which human development reaches the maximum inherent in human genetic potential. A social system or mode of production, in this view, is ethically defective when the social limits to human development stunt or thwart that development long before individuals come close to their "species" or genetic potential. This development, in Marx's view, required that society adequately fulfill human needs and also create the types of social interaction necessary to develop all human capacities, potentials, and powers.

Capitalism simultaneously increased society's capacity to produce while systematically rendering this increased productive capacity less serviceable in fulfilling some of the most basic of human needs. More production certainly made possible a more adequate fulfillment of the basic needs for food, shelter, and clothing. Due to the extreme inequalities in the distribution of wealth and income, however, millions of workers in the capitalist system of Marx's time suffered from extreme material poverty and deprivation.

Most of the pre-Marxian socialists based their moral critique of capitalism on a condemnation of the misery caused by this widespread poverty and inequality. Many interpreters of Marx's ideas have erroneously asserted that this was also the primary basis of Marx's moral critique. And when Marx argued that the continued development of capitalism would only sharpen and increase the misery of workers, these interpreters have imagined him to have been arguing that the poverty and material deprivation of workers would grow worse. The fact that the purchasing power of workers' wages has generally risen during the century since Marx's death is therefore widely cited as a refutation of Marx's economic theory. The interpreters have, however, simply misunderstood the primary basis of Marx's moral critique of capitalism. Although Marx was appalled by the inequality of capitalism and the material deprivation and suffering of the working class, he was well aware that with the increasing productivity of the capitalist system it would become possible for workers to win

higher wages in their struggles with capitalists.   If they did win such
increases, Marx (1961, Vol. III, p. 618) wrote, then:

> a larger part of their own surplus . . . comes back to . . .
> [workers] in the shape of means of payment, so that they
> can extend the circle of their enjoyments; can make some
> additions to their consumption-fund of clothes, furniture,
> etc. and can lay by small reserve-funds of money. But just
> as little as better clothing, food, and treatment, and a
> larger peculium, do away with the exploitation of the
> slave, so little do they set aside that of the wage-workers.

The most fundamental evil of capitalism was not, Marx insisted,
the material deprivation of workers. Rather, it was to be found in the fact
that capitalism systematically prevented individuals from achieving their
potential as human beings. It diminished their capacity to give and receive
love, and it thwarted the development of their biological, emotional,
aesthetic, and intellectual potential. In other words, capitalism severely
crippled human beings by preventing their development.

This crippling effect could not, moreover, be overcome within a
capitalist system. The forces that increased social productivity could only
be utilized in capitalism through the very methods that degraded workers.
This was because the technological improvements were always introduced
for one and only one purpose: to increase profit. Profit was the source
of capitalists' wealth; profit could only be increased by extending and
solidifying the control of the capitalists over the work process. But it was
the control of capital over nearly all processes of human creativity that
was the source of the degradation of workers in capitalism. Marx (1961,
Vol. I, p. 645) concluded that the "accumulation of wealth at one pole is,
therefore, at the same time accumulation of misery, agony of toil, slavery,
ignorance, brutality, [and] mental degradation at the opposite pole."

The social nature of the work process was, for Marx, extremely
important. It was through social cooperation in transforming nature into
useful things that human beings achieved their sociality and developed
their potential as individuals. If that production were a cooperative
venture among social equals, it would develop bonds of affection, love, and
mutual affirmation among people. Moreover, such creative endeavor was
the source of human aesthetic development. It is significant that when
ancient people spoke of the "arts" they were referring to various productive skills. Moreover, the creation and use of tools have always been

involved in the advancement of human knowledge and scientific understanding.

The production process, however, had the exact opposite set of effects on workers in a capitalist system. In feudalism the exploitative class structure had severely limited human development. Yet because these exploitative social relations were also personal and paternalistic, not all of the human developmental potential of the work process was stunted or thwarted. Work in feudalism was more than merely a means of making a liveable wage for the worker while he created wealth for his overlord. This changed with capitalism, when, in Marx's opinion:

> the bourgeoisie, wherever it has got the upper hand, has put an end to all feudal patriarchal, idyllic relations. It has pitilessly torn asunder the motley feudal ties that bound man to his "natural superiors," and has left remaining no other nexus between man and man than naked self-interest, than callous "cash payment." It has drowned the most heavenly ecstasies of religious fervor, of chivalrous enthusiasm, of philistine sentimentalism, in the icy water of egotistical calculation. It has resolved personal worth into exchange value . . . (Marx and Engels, 1965, p. 15).

In a capitalist society the market separated and isolated "exchange value," or money price, from the qualities that shaped a person's relations with things as well as with other human beings. This was especially true in the work process. To the capitalist, wages were merely another expense of production to be added to the costs of raw materials and machinery in the profit calculation. Labor became a mere commodity to be bought if a profit could be made on the purchase. Whether the laborer could sell his or her labor power was completely beyond his or her control. It depended on the cold and totally impersonal conditions of the market. The product of this labor was likewise totally outside of the laborer's life, being the property of the capitalist.

Marx used the term alienation to describe the condition of individuals in this situation. They felt alienated or divorced from their work, from their institutional and cultural environment, and from their fellow humans. The conditions of work, the object produced, and indeed the very possibility of working were determined by the numerically small class of capitalists and their profit calculations, not by human need or aspirations. The effects of this alienation can best be summarized in Marx's own words.

> What, then, constitutes the alienation of labour? First, the fact that labour is external to the worker, i.e., it does not belong to his essential being; that in his work, therefore, he does not affirm himself but denies himself, does not feel content but unhappy, does not develop freely his physical and mental energy but mortifies his body and ruins his mind. The worker therefore only feels himself outside his work, and in his work feels outside himself. He is at home when he is not working, and when he is working he is not at home. His labour is therefore not voluntary but coerced; it is forced labour. It is therefore not the satisfaction of a need; it is merely a means to satisfy needs external to it. Its alien character emerges clearly in the fact that as soon as no physical or other compulsion exists, labour is shunned like the plague. External labour, labour in which man alienates himself, is a labour of self-sacrifice, or mortification. Lastly, the external character of labour for the worker appears in the fact that it is not his own, but someone else's, that it does not belong to him, that in it he belongs, not to himself, but to another . . . . As a result, therefore, man (the worker) no longer feels himself to be freely active in any but his animal functions--eating, drinking, procreating, or at most in his dwelling and in dressing up, etc.; and in his human functions he no longer feels himself to be anything but an animal. What is animal becomes human and what is human becomes animal (Marx, 1959, p. 69).

It was this degradation and total dehumanization of the working class, thwarting man's personal development and making an alien market commodity of man's life-sustaining activities, that Marx most thoroughly condemned in the capitalist system. It is my belief that Marx's analysis of why the superficial appearance of capitalism leads to the asocial economics of the neoclassical school has not been improved on to the present. Moreover, Marx's ethical critique of capitalism remains the most fundamental and convincing of all ethical critiques of capitalism. Were it not for the fact that Marx's ideas have been severely distorted by virtually all of his intellectual and political foes (and not infrequently by his self-professed followers as well), I believe that his profound significance for social economics would be acknowledged by all social economists.

References

Hunt, E. K. 1984. "The relation between theory and history in Marx's writing," *The Atlantic Economic Journal* 22:4 (December), 1-9.

_____. 1986. "The relation of philosophy and economic theory in the writing of Karl Marx," in *Marx, Keynes, and Schumpeter*, edited by S. Helburn. New York: M. E. Sharpe, pp. 95-121.

Marx, K. 1959. *Economic and Philosophic Manuscripts of 1844*. Moscow: Progress Publishers.

_____. 1961. *Capital*, Vols. I and III. Moscow: Foreign Language Publishing House.

Marx, K. and F. Engels. 1965. "The communist manifesto," in *Essential Works of Marxism*, edited by A. P. Mendel. New York: Bantam.

SOCIAL ECONOMICS: A SOCIALIST PERSPECTIVE: COMMENT

Edward J. O'Boyle

At the very beginning of his essay, Professor Hunt states that in regard to social economics his is not an orthodox Marxian perspective. Rather, it is a socialist perspective that draws importantly from the work of Marx. What follows reflects my own judgment as to the efficacy of Marxist thought. Even so, my comments are directed more toward social economics on grounds that this book is not an end in itself so much as it is a means to a deeper insight as to how we eventually might construct "the good society."

Our task is to "unpack" the meaning of social economics not for Marx's age but for our own and for our children's. My remarks, therefore, are organized along three main lines: areas of considerable agreement, areas of considerable disagreement, and questions of mutual concern. In this regard, the following is selective rather than comprehensive in the hope that being selective better serves our mutual objective--the good society, the social economy.

AREAS OF CONSIDERABLE AGREEMENT

Whereas conventional economics centers on things, social economics centers on persons. This difference in orientation has profound implications for social economics (making it a normative science as opposed to a positive science) and for the social economy (the good society necessarily is a just society). Agreement that social economics is anthropocentric understandably produces agreement in several related areas, some of which are discussed below. This agreement, I suggest, constitutes the strongest bond among social economists from the socialist perspective and others from the Catholic perspective.

A second area of agreement is that man's nature is social and that he has two principal material needs: the need for income that is sufficient for wellbeing and the need for work itself. Conventional economics asserts that individual self-interest is a sufficient means to material needs fulfillment. Social economists reject that view emphatically. Agreement that the need for work itself is part of the human condition gives social economics a greater workplace emphasis than is found in mainstream economics.

Social economists also are agreed that meeting man's material needs is the proper goal of the economy. This agreement flows from the logically prior accord to the effect that social economics is anthropocentric.

In addition to our agreement that man is social in nature, we are agreed that human behavior is variable from place to place and from time to time. Moreover, both perspectives share the view that the social order imposes limits on the behavior of human individuals. Professor Hunt's strong affirmation that the socialist perspective is not deterministic opens important opportunities for dialogue with Catholic social economists.

The two perspectives converge on the issue of alienation at least to the extent that it is understood to be a real workplace phenomenon. The significance of this alienation is to render man less a person and more nearly an object. Accord on this matter also flows from agreement that social economics is anthropocentric. In conventional economics, on the other hand, man the worker is likened to other economic resources rather than differentiated from those resources.

The last area of agreement that I would comment upon here is that property matters critically. More specifically, both perspectives share the view that property is linked to need fulfillment and that man's two material needs cannot be met adequately without some reform as to how property is owned and controlled under private enterprise.

AREAS OF CONSIDERABLE DISAGREEMENT

Catholic social economics affirms that man is not entirely social in nature. Man has an individual side to his nature. Every individual, even though he is conditioned by his environment, is truly unique, one of a kind. A central part of man's individuality is his free will which empowers him to change the limits that the social order imposes. This duality with regard to his nature creates in man a tension between self and other. This conflict as to his social obligations and rights is not resolved satisfactorily through the self-interest of individualism alone or the common good of collectivism alone. According to Catholic social economics the tension is managed through the practice of the two cardinal social virtues: justice and charity.

It follows that Catholic social economics would take exception to the assertion that any worker is very nearly helpless alone. An individual worker can make a difference if he is adequately empowered by the two social virtues of justice and charity. This empowerment is called socializing man to differentiate it from the collectivist's socializing the means of production.

Another area of considerable disagreement which relates to the one immediately preceding is the antagonism between workers and owners. The socialist perspective argues that this antagonism is built into the capitalist mode of production and is inevitable. Socializing the means of production as a solution is rejected by Catholic social economics because the antagonism derives not so much from the way in which production is organized as from the way men relate to one another in the workplace. Catholic social economists therefore encourage a moral rebirth whereby it is man and not the means of production that is socialized. In this regard, ownership and control of the means of production may take several different organizational forms in order to support the necessary moral rebirth. Just as form follows function in modern architecture, reorganization of the modern workplace follows the rebirth of man. Put differently, the problem is not with the owners of the means of production but with modern man himself. The solution, therefore, lies mainly in reforming man. Catholic social economics affirms that there are no dragons to be slain because, as some would argue, there are no dragons or, as others would say, we are all dragons.

Important differences exist between the socialist perspective and the Catholic perspective regarding property. Catholic social economics asserts that the right to private property extends beyond consumption to production and that the right derives from man's own nature. The argument in skeletal form is that material resources are the necessary means to meeting his material needs (income and work) and man cannot meet those needs adequately and thereby perfect his own nature without the stable and secure ownership of those resources including the means of production. Even so, only a system of private property that promotes the efficient utilization of material resources to produce goods and services and the efficient application of those goods and services to meet man's needs is morally defensible. In other words, the right to private property is not absolute. It is subordinate to the common good in the sense that the materials resources are intended for the common good, that is to serve the needs of all men, not just those with property rights. Catholic social economics argues that state intervention is not the only remedy for a system of private property that fails to serve the needs of men. Reforming or socializing man is another and frequently superior remedy.

QUESTIONS OF MUTUAL CONCERN

Can we reconcile our differences as to whether man's nature is social or individual or both? Specifically, can we agree on the answers to these three critical questions: Who is man? What is man? Whose is man? How do we best demonstrate man's social nature? Is Professor Hunt's analogy of dog to man a convincing demonstration? Would another analogy, such as bee/hive to man/workplace be more convincing? Or, is man's social nature so evident that no such demonstration is required?

In the matter of man and society, which is the more important, which is to be valued more highly? Does society have an essence and existence separate and apart from the human individual? Or, is society only an abstraction, a manner of speaking?

Which is the greater danger? A social order in which some acquire their wealth unjustly, some do not work yet have greater wealth than others who do work, some use their wealth foolishly? Or, a social order where private wealth is greatly reduced and made more nearly equal for all, the material needs of all are met adequately by the state, and the state appropriates the surplus, however large or small?

How are we to reconcile our differences as to property? Can we instructively pursue this question along lines that differentiate owning, exchanging, and using as they relate to consumption goods? Is it instructive to differentiate owning from controlling relative to the means of production? Or, control of the means of production that derives from owning versus control that derives from belonging? Can we further illuminate the rights and obligations of men as they relate to the means of production by postulating the workplace as an industrial commons?

Agreement on these questions, for certain, advances social economics and promotes the social economy more so than does disagreement. Even so, I am encouraged that even our disagreements are productive because they force us to work more diligently at understanding how we differ and whether those differences ultimately matter so that perhaps some day men of greater insight might accomplish a full reconciliation, thereby creating a more robust social economics.

SOCIAL ECONOMICS: A SOCIALIST PERSPECTIVE: COMMENT

Lewis E. Hill

Professor E. K. Hunt has written an exceptionally good critique of capitalism from the perspective of Marxian socialism. This critique is valid in substance and eloquent in style; it surely constitutes an extremely important contribution to that body of scholarship which has come to be known as social economics. The contribution, however, seems to me to be largely negative in the sense that Hunt is more concerned with demonstrating the asocial nature of capitalism than in developing the Marxian variety of social economics into a comprehensive system of economic thought. The purpose of this comment is to respond to Hunt's essay and to compare and contrast the socialist and the institutionalist approaches to social economics.

Professor William M. Dugger has specified five identifying characteristics of social economics, which are relevant to this discussion. According to Dugger, social economics is value-directed, ameliorative, activistic, holistic, and organic. Does the Marxian version of social economics meet these criteria? Clearly, Marxian social economics is activistic and holistic. Whether the Marxian variety of social economics is value-directed is questionable. Surely, Marxian social economists make normative value judgments, but it seems to me that these value judgments are not so fundamental as to direct the system of economic thought. Moreover, the Judeo-Christian tradition of normative value does not appear to be an essential preconception in the Marxian system. In a similar manner, it seems doubtful whether Marxian social economists conceive the society and the social economy as an organic whole or as a system of mechanical or mechanistic relationships. The one criterion that Marxism clearly violates calls for social economics to be ameliorative; obviously, Marxian social economics tends to be revolutionary rather than ameliorative.

Which is the better approach to human progress in the social economy: amelioration or revolution? It has always been my conviction that amelioration is generally more productive of human progress in the social economy than revolution, because ameliorative evolution is inherently creative, whereas radical revolution is inherently destructive. It is my belief that most of the improvement in human welfare in Western civilization generally, and in the United States particularly, has resulted from ameliorative evolution rather than from radical revolution. Because of its inherently destructive nature, therefore, radical revolution should be regarded as a last resort, only, among the means of seeking to improve human welfare.

This is not to say that revolution is never justified. It may well be that the *ancien regime* is so very bad that it must be destroyed in order to clear the way for human progress. This seems to have been the case of both the French Revolution and the Russian Revolution. In all probability, both the French and the Russian people enjoy a higher level of welfare than would have been the case without their respective revolutions. Nevertheless, one wonders if the French people would have been better off had their revolutions stopped short of the Reign of Terror, and if the Russian people would have been better off had the October Bolshevik Revolution never occurred. England and the United States are special cases. In England, the Puritan Revolution and the Glorious Revolution were more evolutionary than radical. With respect to the United States, Charles and Mary Beard contend that the American Revolutionary War was nothing more than a political struggle which fails to qualify as a true socioeconomic revolution. According to the Beards, the real American Revolution was the American Civil War, which destroyed the slavocracy of the Southern states. What about the Cuban and Nicaraguan revolutions? It is my belief that history has not yet recorded the final verdict. Clearly, the progress of these revolutions has been limited by the counterrevolutionary policies of the government of the United States.

Marxian social economics is similar to institutionalist social economics in some respects. Both Marxian and institutionalist social economics are basically materialistic in that they find the causation of the course of history in the naturalistic world where it is determined by materialistic considerations. The Marxian dialectic of the forces of production and the relations of production is approximately equivalent to the Veblenian dichotomy between technology and institutions. Both Marxian and institutionalist social economists seem to have the same problem with the conflict between free will and determinism because these philosophical concepts apply to different levels of generalization: free will applies to the individual level of generalization; determinism applies to the social level of generalization. Apparently, Ayres believed that free will governs individual actions, but that this freedom is so limited by the cultural environment that individual actions have no appreciable influence over the course of history. Hunt seems to reverse this argument by denying that Marx was a historical determinist, while he is insisting that the nature of the human species is determined by the mode of production. Neither Ayres' nor Hunt's explanation is entirely satisfactory to me. It is my belief that further research will be necessary to answer the question concerning the relationship between free will and determinism.

There are also differences between the Marxian and institutionalist social economists. Most institutionalists do not conceive of the society as being divided into clearly distinguishable socioeconomic classes. Technology is seen as an integrative process--not as a divisive element. Within any classification, therefore, the culture which is brought into being by the machine technology tends to distribute people along an infinitely varied spectrum ranging continuously and indistinguishably from the capitalistic class, through the class of professionals, managers, technicians, and supervisors; into the working class, and the working class varies continuously and indistinguishably from skilled, through semi-skilled, and into unskilled labor.

Moreover, most institutionalists see production as a continuous and integrated process that should not be artificially divided or segregated. It is, therefore, arbitrary and meaningless to impute specific productivity to individual factors of production, such as capital, labor, and land, or to specific functional economic classes, such as the working class, capitalists, land owners, and entrepreneurs. This discussion implies that institutionalists would deny that the "abstinence" of the capitalists justifies or legitimizes the income that they receive from their property. Institutionalists would also deny that the private ownership of property is a natural right; rather, they would insist that property ownership is just another human institution which is not necessarily any better or any worse than any other human institution. Institutionalists regard the distinction between handicraft production and the factory system as a difference of degree, only, and not of kind. The manner in which each system of production should be treated as law is conceived to be an instrumental matter, rather than a matter of principle.

All institutionalists would affirm and approve the implicit Marxian objective of human development to the highest possible extent, because this objective is thoroughly compatible with the life process, which is the basis of the institutionalist theory of normative value. Moreover, institutionalists would join Hunt in denouncing the alienation that Marx found in the capitalistic system. Institutionalists would insist that the alienation is not inherent in technology, but is caused by inhibitory institutions.

Marxian socialism and institutionalism are separate systems of economic thought. They come from distinct intellectual roots, are based on diverse philosophical preconceptions, and utilize different epistemologies and methodologies. Marxian socialism is a logical extension of the classical economics of Adam Smith and David Ricardo. Institutionalism is a uniquely American system of economic thought that is based on the radical economics of Thorstein Veblen, John Commons, and Wesley Mitchell and on the pragmatic philosophy of Charles Sanders Peirce, William James, and John Dewey. Marxism and institutionalism, therefore, represent different approaches to social economics. Nevertheless, a broad compatibility appears to exist among institutionalism, Marxian socialism, and social economics. All reject the narrow and irrelevant methodologies of orthodox positive economics, and all advocate broad socioeconomic and politicoeconomic policies which are intended to improve social justice, to increase human welfare, and to enhance the quality of life.

References

Beard, C. A. and M. R. Beard. 1934. *The Rise of American Civilization.* New edition, two volumes in one, revised and enlarged. New York: The Macmillan Company.

Dugger, W. M. 1977. "Social economics: one perspective," *Review of Social Economy* 35 (December), 299-310.

6

TOWARD A DEONTOLOGICAL SOCIOECONOMICS*

Amitai Etzioni

Few deny that the origins of neoclassical economics lie in a particular social philosophy and ethics, namely hedonistic utilitarianism. Contemporary economists often ignore these roots and treat their concepts as if they were value-neutral and "scientific." In effect, the focus on profit, self-interest, and the individual's desires continues to reflect the origins of this approach.

The main ethical alternative to utilitarianism is deontology, an ethic that sees human beings as subject to "binding duties" (*deon* is Greek). The result is a continuous struggle between a nobler and a more debased self, between moral commitments and urges. Kant is the leading deontologist; we draw here on some of his positions to indicate the ethical basis for a new economics and, more generally, a new social science.

---

*This article draws on the author's *The Moral Dimension* (New York: The Free Press, 1988) and more directly on his "Toward a Kantian Socio-Economics," *Review of Social Economics,* XLV (April 1987) 37-47.

At issue is the status of individual rights and of moral tenets. Utilitarians base their moral position on the general welfare. The government should not impose a moral tenet on individuals because such interventions reduce the total sum of human happiness, and because each person is the best judge of his or her preferences. (This position is part and parcel of the core assumptions of the neoclassical paradigm which underlies much of mainstream Western economics but also important parts of political science, psychology, sociology, and law.) Kantians challenge the position that all human desires have an equal standing, that none can be judged by overarching criteria as more worthy than others. They also question whether utilitarianism provides a sound defense of individual rights. As Michael J. Sandel put it: "If enough cheering Romans pack the Coliseum to watch the lions devour the Christians, the collective pleasure of the Romans will surely outweigh the pain of the Christians, intense though it may be." In contrast, Kantians emphasize that each person is endowed with basic rights, founded on justice, an inviolate moral imperative which cannot be traded off for the sake of enhancing the total welfare. To make this point, Kantians draw on a distinct realm of rights and obligations, of moral values, set apart from that of satisfactions and goods, the foci of utilitarianism and the neoclassical concept of utility.

All this leads to a critical difference in the view of self: by the utilitarians, the person is a unified bundle of desires, of preferences; by Kantians, the self is divided, one part standing over the other, judging it and deciding whether or not to yield to any particular desire. Indeed, this ability of self is viewed as an essential quality that distinguishes humans from animals. Also, while judgments might be based on many values (for example, aesthetic ones), at issue here is the significant role of moral values in human judgment.

Kant took numerous other positions, and those cited here are intertwined in his work with extensive metaphysical assumptions. Many of those are either irrelevant to the issue at hand or may be rejected without losing the important observations we draw upon. In the following discussion, reference to Kant is strictly limited to questions of the human ability to judge and the role of moral values in such judgments.

TOWARD A BI-UTILITY CONCEPTION

Paralleling the renewed interest in Kant is a movement, encompassing some economists and some members of other social sciences who study economic behavior, which questions one of the cornerstones of neoclassical economics--the assumption that individuals seek but one ultimate utility to which all specific desires can be reduced. Everyday observations and empirical evidence have led many scholars to question the empirical validity of the assumption that actors seek to maximize one utility, the person's desires. One line of response to such challenges has been to stretch the concept of utility and of satisfaction to include living up to one's moral obligations, such as benevolent acts and services to the community. Margolis (1982, p. 11), after observing that "in recent years efforts to incorporate altruistic preferences within the conventional framework have become fairly common," adds:

> We have no more need to distinguish between the bread
> Smith buys to give to the poor and that which he buys
> for his own consumption, than to distinguish his neigh-
> bor's demand for sugar to make cookies from his demand
> for sugar to make gin in the cellar.

This approach ignores the crucial difference between acting and judging an act, and the deep substantive differences between satisfaction resulting out of pleasure and out of living up to a moral obligation. (The question has been raised if discharging one's moral obligations ought to be considered a source of satisfaction, of feeling, or whether this constitutes too much of a concession to the utilitarian psychology. I side with those who assume that obligations do require a psychic force or "handle" to be effective, however, one that is radically different in nature from satisfying a desire. The distinction is completely familiar from elementary introspection. On the other hand, I agree that references to moral values as a second source of utility stretch the term; it might be better to refer to two ultimate sources of valuation rather than to utility.)

The difference is most evident in the numerous situations in which the two sources of satisfaction conflict rather than in the relatively few situations in which the two are compatible, in which the person's desires are also ways of discharging the moral obligations of the same person. Thus, if one is keen on the money in the till but refrains from pocketing it when chances seem favorable that the money will not be missed because one feels that it is not right to steal, the resulting satisfaction is quite different from that generated when one does pocket the cash.

Conceptually stretching the concept of utility to encompass self-love and love for others destroys the central thesis of Adam Smith, at least the Adam Smith of *The Wealth of Nations*, that economic relations thrive on self-interest. If there is no difference in principle between love for self and love for others, there is no need for an invisible hand, and the difference between market and family relations pales; indeed, so does the distinction between profit and loss. After all, one man's loss is another man's gain.

Similar signs of theoretical strain in the mono-utility conception appear in discussions of preferences, the elements of which jointly make up the utility. Thomas Schelling (1984) provides a long list of examples that trouble the economist's assumption of uni-vocal, unencumbered preferences. One example will have to stand for the many: a guest asks his host to keep his car keys if he becomes intoxicated. Puzzle: What is the guest's preference? To have his keys? Then why ask the host to refuse? To be prevented from driving while under the influence? Then why ask for the keys?

What ties the Kantian recognition of the distinct standing and special significance of the human capacity to render judgment to the car keys of a prospective drunk? A major reason the preferences of people are encumbered is their moral judgments. Schelling's potential drunk, for example, experiences simultaneously the urge to drink and a moral commitment not to endanger the lives of others.

Economists have responded to these observations in several ways. Some continue to seek to establish that there are no moral factors, merely moral pretenses (see below). Others have increasingly recognized that there is a second set (a side basket) of preferences that affect behavior, preferences that reflect concern for others and the community or a commitment to moral values. Of those, John Harsanyi (1955), Howard Margolis (1982), and Richard Thaler and H. M. Shefrin (1981) have attempted to show that this second set of preferences can be accommodated within neoclassical economics by assuming a supra-preference that ties moral and nonmoral preferences into one utility.

Others have come closer to making the break. They recognize, in varying degrees, the power of moral obligations. Sen (1977) goes part of the way in explicating the concept of commitment, although he does not see it as necessarily concerning moral obligations. Goodin (1980) sees a close association between the notion of a commitment and the sense of setting aside an important realm as a "sacred" one, to use Durkheim's term. People treat moral principles as important and do so by setting them aside as a *differentiated* set of considerations. Okun (1975, p. 100) refers to these areas as "the domain of rights." Walzer (1983, p. 7) lists 14 major areas of "blocked exchanges," including basic freedoms (one has a claim on them without paying for them), marriage (licenses for polygamy are not sold), and divine grace.

One characteristic of such considerations, Goodin suggests, is to repudiate the instrumental rationality of considerations of costs and benefits. A person feels obligated to save a life, make a donation, and so on, without such calculations. *Only after these commitments are violated* do people enter into a second realm of decisions in which moral considerations are weighed against others and calculations enter. This, by the way, explains why people *sometimes* calculate how much to give or, if they give X, what it will do for their reputation. This should not be used, however, to argue that they do not have *other*, "sacred," nonnegotiable, moral commitments. In short, morality affects their choices twice.

Hirschman (1984, pp. 12-14) uses the terms *preferences* and *meta-preferences* to conceptualize the judgment involved. He adds that if these two levels of preferences always coincided, the meta-preferences would be merely shadows of the preferences and would have no significance. The same would hold if they always conflicted, because this would suggest the meta-preferences are powerless. As Hirschman put it, they would not only be dismissed as wholly ineffectual but doubt would arise as to whether they existed at all. The fruitfulness of the assumption lies in the frequently observed behavior of either choices that are blocked by moral judgments or of choices followed that lead to regret, guilt, and so on, that have behavioral consequences (Etzioni, 1986).

All this points to a new philosophical and ethical base for a different paradigm for the study of economic behavior, for a socioeconomics that recognizes at least two utilities, the traditional one and that of living up to one's moral values. Each provides inherent and different satisfactions, fundamentally divergent sources of value. Probably the most promising starting point for such an endeavor is to explore what lies behind the preferences.

OPENING THE PREFERENCES

Neoclassical economics holds that preferences not only reflect one overarching utility but that they are given. "Given" is interpreted to mean that they are studied by other disciplines, such as psychology and sociology. However, if all that was at issue was a matter of division of labor, then in order to understand economic behavior one would have to take from these other disciplines their findings on the factors that shape preferences and incorporate them into joint models. This is, in effect, what many applied economists do, on an ad hoc basis, in defiance of orthodoxy (McKean and Keller, 1983). This practice indicates the merit of a conceptual adaptation.

Other economists imply that the forces that shape preferences are irrational and hence are not subject to scientific study. Stigler and Becker (1977) go a step further and assert that all such explanations are "not illuminating," and thus preferences should be assumed to be constant and explanations for variations in behavior should be sought within neoclassical economics, in differences in income and in constraints. Sociologists and psychologists, however, have known for many decades that behavior which is considered irrational from the viewpoint of the observer is not random, not exempt from scientific laws. Stigler and Becker's attempts to conceptualize behavior such as music appreciation and drug addiction (in which one changes his preferences as he gets into the act) as constituting an investment of scarce capital rather than as changing preferences require numerous far-fetched assumptions (Blaug, 1976) and are but one more indication of how strained the mono-utility theory has become.

Beyond attempts to shore up the paradigm of a discipline lies an ethical issue. Neoclassical economists' objections to opening up preferences to an empirical study of their dynamics and the factors that shape them are rooted in utilitarian individualism. If preferences are individually set and fixed, general welfare can, at least in principle, be calculated. However, once one recognizes that choices by individuals are deeply influenced by social processes, power holders, and persuasive advertising, one must develop a conception of who guides the social processes, who is in power, and whose values advertising promotes. Otherwise, the factors that affected preferences, and through them economic behavior, are not accounted for.

Neoclassical economics often seems, in effect, to argue that by not admitting that preferences are malleable in their theory they protect the individual's rights in reality. This is simply a case of a misplaced level of analysis: the theory will not change reality; it merely refuses to take in on the conceptual level what there is.[1] Indeed, one may go a step further and suggest that by refusing to deal with the forces that affect individual preferences one also neglects the study of the factors that shore up individual liberties, factors that are themselves to a significant extent social, political, moral, and not intraindividual. Liberty is best protected when individuals are linked to one another in communities and voluntary associations rather than in an atomized mess, the picture of free-standing individuals so much at the center of the neoclassical political philosophy. Socioeconomics encompasses the study of these factors. The decisions of criminals, for example, are viewed as *both* influenced by considerations of costs and benefits (as economists have stressed in recent years) *and* as affected by the extent of their moral upbringing and the values promoted by the peer groups they join (Wilson, 1985).

DE-COLONIZATION IS NOT ENOUGH

Economists may suggest that part of the difficulty their discipline has run into along the lines indicated so far is the result of the application of neoclassical economics in recent decades to noneconomic behavior such as decisions to have children (treated as "durable consumer goods"), religious commitments (viewed as a quest for "after-life consumption"), and the intrapersonal development of music appreciation and drug addiction. These analyses share one feature: the application of neoclassical economics to areas in which exchange relations do not exist, and hence prices must be imputed. These raise very difficult technical problems that need not concern us here other than to raise the question: How far can one stretch the assumptions, the interpretation of the data, and the regression analyses without violating not merely the validity of the conclusions but also the ethics of science? That economists are concerned about these matters is reflected in articles such as "Let's Take the *Con* out of Econometrics" (Leamer, 1983, italic provided; Black, 1982).

Beyond the ethical issues raised by the methodology are the questions raised by the assumptions. We saw that people set aside certain areas of their lives as having a special claim, as "sacred," and that one of the main ways these are characterized is by objecting to calculating costs and benefits in these matters. To assume that people will normally trade those is more than technical error. ("Prices" here would be much higher than is imputed from areas in which trade is normal precisely because taboos are violated.) To introduce cost/benefit analysis into our "temples" is to diminish their values, to violate their taboos (Kelman, 1981). For example, the notion that it is inefficient to prevent hijacking (Landes, 1978) or that it is efficient to form a market for babies available for adoption (Posner, 1977) disregards the effects such markets have on sanctity of life, on the treatment of the aged and the handicapped, and on parenthood. The same holds true for the argument that duels are an efficient way to settle conflicts (Schwartz et al, 1984).

In private conversations, many neoclassical economists admit that these analyses, often referred to as imperialistic intrusions into other disciplines, "go too far" or "are a bit silly" and suggest that economists should stick to the study of economic behavior. Behind these statements is an assumption that the social world is compartmentalized into some divisions that are governed by market mechanisms and some that are not. However, we suggest that nonmarket factors strongly affect *economic* behavior. For instance, relations among employers and employees, incentive schemes, labor markets and productivity cannot be adequately conceptualized without taking into account the intrinsic value of work for the identity of many workers (those who internalize certain values), the role of work ethics, the effects of team spirit, the value put on cooperation, and so on.

The same holds for relations among businesses. Neoclassical economic models treat the market as if it were self-sustaining. Lists of the conditions for perfect competition vary, but the following elements are often included: the largest firm in any given industry is to make no more than a small fraction of the industry's sales (or purchases); the firms are to act independently of one another; actors have complete knowledge of offers to buy or sell; the commodity (sold or bought in the market) is divisible; and the resouces are movable among users (Stigler, 1968, pp. 181-182).[2] This is but a more formal conceptualization of the notion that self-interests are automatically compatible with one another and require no external factors to advance their harmonization or limit their conflicts. Markets, however, are embedded in societies that provide both the rules which competition requires and the institutional framework without which it cannot be sustained.

Moral factors are but one step removed. The rules, and the institutions that embody them, such as the courts, the Securities and Exchange Commission, and corporate charters, are not the result of deliberate rational negotiations, but are the product of historical, societal, and cultural evolution. Part and parcel of these evolutions are the sets of general and particular values, embodied in behavioral rules and in institutions.

While it has been stated numerous times (Hirsch, 1976), and the evidence is abundant, it seems one still must repeat the basic observation that rules and institutions cannot rest on deterrence because there are not enough policemen, inspectors, and auditors for it to be effective, and the guardians themselves need guarding. Rules and institutions hence must rely, to a significant extent, on internalized moral commitments. Deterrence functions as a secondary mechanism that deals with those who violate these commitments, and thus backs up but cannot replace moral commitments.

Hence, a theory of *economic* behavior, of markets, must account for the factors that enhance rather than weaken the rules of the game, that affect the strength and reach of the relevant moral commitments. For instance, private property and limited liability, two cornerstones of capitalism, are nothing but two moral concepts defining the rights and obligations of owners. While economists tend to treat these concepts as given and as static, they are in flux in the sense that their legitimating power changes over time. For example, the extensive introduction of social regulation in the sixties and early seventies in effect constituted a diminution in the power of these concepts because the government increasingly limited the autonomous use of private assets and incorporated capital, and specified the ways they had to be employed. The forces that led to the rise of social regulation (and later to its decline) include economic, technological, and political developments (Tolchin and Tolchin, 1983). However, among them, changes in the moral conceptions of a society play an important role. For instance, the question of whether employers are free to hire, fire, and promote as they see fit or whether they must favor minorities and women is in part a moral issue. Moral issues also loom in statements such as "the business of business is business," or that businesses should shoulder certain responsibilities: for example, not to invest in South Africa.

The role of ethical factors is also evident in the attitudes toward fraud in transactions. Most business transactions are conducted by word of mouth. To write down all agreements, to have them reviewed by lawyers, and to rely on enforcement by courts would bring the economy to a near standstill. Mutual trust is essential. True, in part trust is based on self-interest; those who violate it are likely to lose future business. However, in many situations in which the relations are transient, a major factor that sustains trust is the internalization of values by those involved, who feel that violating one's commitment is highly immoral (Phelps, 1975).

Similarly, moral attitudes affect the level of savings and personal as well as public debt. Until the 1950s, Americans considered being in debt a serious moral transgression and most of them did not violate the taboo. Personal debt rose significantly only after these attitudes changed (Longman, 1985; Maital, 1982). Simultaneously, until the public grew relatively more tolerant of deficits, legislators did not run up the public debt (Buchanan, forthcoming). More than half the people entitled to welfare do not avail themselves of the opportunity, in part because of the stigma attached (Moffitt, 1983).

The notion that people will free ride and hence need both "side" payments (Olson, 1965) and close supervision (Ehrenberg and Smith, 1982; Williamson, 1975) in order to carry their share of the load rather than to "shirk" is not backed up by the evidence for collective action (in service of public goods such as voting) or in studies of work in private settings. Experiment after experiment has shown that most people, given a chance, will not free ride (Marwell and Ames, 1981). Indeed, this finding is so widely supported that designers of experiments found it dull and focused on a subsidiary question: whether or not the contributions to the group that are made match the *size* of the contributions economists calculated are the proper contributions. Studies of voting were unable to sustain the notion that self-interest propels citizens to exert themselves. (The studies seek to understand why people vote if there is nothing in it for them, personally, directly, and specifically.) Researchers found two reasons to account for voting: the act is expressive in that the effort itself is satisfying (Barry, 1978), and the act discharges a moral obligation. These findings significantly improve the predictive power of the models. Following the interdependent utility notion, some neoclassical economists and political scientists see in these expressive and moral acts nothing but self-interest but, as indicated above, this approach blurs the issue that needs clarifying. Other evidence strongly suggests that *close* supervision, especially of work that requires initiative, responsibility, or attention to quality, is counterproductive, while, in many situations, involving the workers in the work process enhances productivity.

In short, it is not enough for neoclassical economics to give up its imperialism, its attempts to understand noneconomic behavior in rationalist, egotist terms. The role of moral commitments and the factors that shape them must be taken into account in studying economic behavior, including subjects such as saving, incentives to work, behavior of markets, and productivity. An integrated paradigm of social factors (among which only moral ones were explored here) and economic factors is to be tested by the same criteria by which neoclassical economics is judged: the ability to predict and to explain, parsimony, and the ethical implications of the paradigms for those who view the world through its framework.

A POSITIVE OR A NORMATIVE SCIENCE?

We suggest that a deontological economics will not only provide a sounder basis for predictions (by encompassing major facets of human behavior that neoclassists ignore) and a more explanatory theory (e.g., by dealing with the factors that shape and reshape preferences) but also a more defensible ethical basis. The question has been raised whether this makes our economics into a "value-driven" one, a normative theory, or-- do we maintain the claim for a positive social science?

As I see it, there is no value-neutral social science, all have normative implications. The very decision, entailed in any paradigm, to focus on some factors--and by implication not on others--has normative implications, whether intended or not. Thus, neoclassical tendency to ignore cooperation and altruism entails a value judgment, as does its tendency to play down the role of power, especially the political power of major economic actors. On the other hand, our decision to include these concepts makes our paradigm more critical of the world-as-it-is, less accepting.

However, we accept that statements made ought to be modified if empirical evidence, and logical interpretations of the evidence, suggest that the statements are incorrect. Social science differs (or *ought* to differ) from ideology in that social sciences should not focus on depicting the world as it ought to be, but as what it is and how it might be. We seek to help members of society recognize and live their values, not preach or impose ours.

Notes

[1] I am indebted to Mike McPherson for this point.

[2] For a formal discussion of the Walrasian model and related points, see Malinvaud (1972, pp. 138-143) and Bohm (1972, pp. 128-142).

References

Barry, B. 1978. *Sociologists, Economists and Democracy*. Chicago, IL: University of Chicago Press.

Black, F. 1982. "The trouble with econometric models," *Financial Analysts Journal* 35, 3-11.

Blaug, M. 1976. "The empirical status of human capital theory: a slightly jaundiced survey," *Journal of Economic Literature* 14 (September), 837-855.

Bohm, P. 1972. "Estimating demands for a public good: an experiment," *European Economic Review* 3, 111-130.

Buchanan, J. M. *Liberty, Market and State: Political Economy in the 1980s*. Wheatsheaf Press, forthcoming.

Ehrenberg, R. G. and R. S. Smith. 1982. *Modern Labor Economics: Theory and Public Policy*. Glenview, IL: Scott, Foresman & Co.

Etzioni, A. 1986. "The case for a multiple utility conception," *Economics and Philosophy* 2, 159-183.

Goodin, R. E. 1980. "Making moral incentives pay," *Policy Sciences* 12 (August), 131-145.

Harsanyi, J. C. 1955. "Cardinal welfare, individualistic ethics, and international comparisons of utility," *Journal of Political Economy* 63, 309-321.

Hirsch, F. 1976. *Social Limits to Growth*. Cambridge, MA: Harvard University Press.

Hirschman, A. O. 1984. "Against parsimony: three easy ways of complicating some categories of economic discourse," *Bulletin: The American Academy of Arts and Sciences* 37:8 (May), 11-28.

Kelman, S. 1981. "Cost-benefit analysis: an ethical critique," *Regulation* (January/February), 33-40.

Landes, W. 1978. "An economic study of U.S. aircraft hijacking, 1961-1976," *The Journal of Law and Economics* 21, 1-31.

Leamer, E. E. 1983. "Let's take the 'con' out of econometrics," *American Economic Review* 73:1 (March/April), 3-11.

Longman, P. 1985. "The fall of the idea of thrift: how the economists came to label virtue a vice," *The Washington Monthly* (January).

Maital, S. 1982. *Minds, Markets, and Money*. New York: Basic Books, Inc.

Malinvaud, E. 1982. *Lectures on Microeconomic Theory*. Amsterdam: Elsevier Science Publishing Co.

Margolis, H. 1982. *Selfishness, Altruism and Rationality: A Theory of Social Choice.* Cambridge, MA: University of Chicago Press.

Marwell, G. and R. E. Ames. 1981. "Economists free ride, does anyone else?" *Journal of Public Economics* 13, 295-310.

McKean, J. R. and R. R. Keller. 1983. "The shaping of tastes, Pareto efficiency and economic policy," *Journal of Behavioral Economics* 12 (Summer), 23-41.

Moffitt, R. 1983. "An economic model of welfare stigma," *American Economic Review* 73, 1023-1035.

Okun, A. 1975. *Equality and Efficiency: The Big Tradeoff.* Washington, DC: Brookings Institution.

Olson, M. 1965. *The Logic of Collective Action.* Cambridge, MA: Harvard University Press.

Phelps, E. S. 1985. "Introduction," in *Altruism, Morality, and Economic Theory.* New York: Russell Sage Foundation, pp. 1-9.

Posner, R. A. 1977. *Economic Analysis of Law.* 2nd ed. Boston: Little, Brown & Co.

Schelling, T. C. 1984. "Self-command in practice, in policy, and in a theory of rational choice," *American Economic Review* 74:2 (May), 1-11.

Schwartz, W., K. Baxter and D. Ryan. 1984. "The duel: can these gentlemen be acting efficiently?" *The Journal of Legal Studies* 13, 321-355.

Sen, A. 1977. "Rational Fools," *Philosophy and Public Affairs* 6, 317-344.

Smith, A. 1937. *The Wealth of Nations.* New York: Modern Library, Inc.

Stigler, G. J. 1968. "Competition," in the *International Encyclopedia of Social Sciences* 3, New York, pp. 181-182.

Stigler, G. J. and G. S. Becker. 1977. "De gustibus non est disputandum," *American Economic Review* 67:2 (March), 76-90.

Thaler, R. and H. M. Shefrin. 1981. "An economic theory of self control," *Journal of Political Economy* 89, 392-406.

Tolchin, S. and M. Tolchin. 1983. *Dismantling America: The Rush to Deregulate.* Boston: Oxford University Press.

Walzer, Michael. 1983. *Spheres of Justice.* New York: Basic Books, Inc.

Williamson, O. E. 1975. *Markets and Hierarchies: Analysis and Antitrust Implications.* New York: Free Press.

Wilson, James Q. 1985. *Thinking about Crime.* New York: Random House, Inc.

7

SOCIAL ECONOMICS IN THE HUMANISTIC TRADITION

Mark A. Lutz

INTRODUCTION

The purpose of this article is to introduce the student interested in social economics to a venerable tradition that goes back even further in history than do the other perspectives rooted in Thorstein Veblen, Karl Marx, or the late nineteenth century encyclical of Pope Leo XIII. It started with the Swiss Count Jean Charles Leonard Simonde de Sismondi publishing his *New Principles of Political Economy* in 1819, and has continued through Thomas Carlyle, John Ruskin, John Atkinson Hobson, and Richard H. Tawney into contemporary times.

It has always been an economics of human welfare informed by an ethics grounded in a human image stipulating certain basic material and nonmaterial human needs. Equipped with this "human standard," the economic thinkers have been critically examining socioeconomic systems, even cultures such as an "aquisitive society" or "consumerism," from the point of view of human values. Their writings reveal a strong conviction that deep down there is in every context an ultimately right set of economic institutions, a best and humanly most appropriate way to organize an economy. That right or best way might be fully shared in the majority opinion of a free democracy, but for various reasons it need not always be so. For example, the fact that a majority of Southerners in pre-Civil War America saw nothing wrong with slavery did not at all make that particular socioeconomic institution right. Rather, what is right, just, and true can never be derived from what happens to be popular or sanctioned by the powerful, neither is it simply the result of some abstractly conceived social agreement as in the so-called Contractarian doctrines.

It may very well be due to this lack of respect for the merely pleasant, socially successful, and expedient, that most of the practitioners in this school of thought have always been outspoken critics of conventional economic science and the establishment, and have opted to do so even at the risk of their own careers and social reputations. As a direct consequence, neither Sismondi nor Ruskin or Hobson held a university chair in political economy; instead they had to carry their case directly to the public at large. John Hobson, for example, spent his life in writing almost 50 books, many of them best-sellers.

The relative isolation from academia, however, had an unexpected benefical side effect: their writings could take shape in the harsh realities of everyday life, allowing the authors to address newly perceived social problems in a concrete and common sense manner readily understandable to the layman and general public. Perhaps for this reason alone, their impact in the public policy arena compares rather favorably with that of their more conventional academic counterparts.

In what follows, we hope to bring out the underlying unity of their economic thought and to demonstrate that social economics has much to gain in further developing their basic insights in the context of the pressing social problems of today. In the process we will have to limit ourselves to the problems of the advanced industrial economies, an unfortunate limitation since the problems of the developing Third World are far more serious and have been preoccupying modern humanistic thinkers and activists. We encourage the interested reader to read more about this omitted topic elsewhere (see Lutz and Lux, 1988, ch. 13).

THE HUMAN-CENTERED SOCIAL ECONOMICS IN HISTORICAL PERSPECTIVE

In the first decade of the nineteenth century, Count Sismondi (1773-1842) already had a reputation as a history scholar. At the same time, he was also known as an early follower of the economic doctrines of Adam Smith. But when studying the industrial progress in England during the ensuing years, he became more and more disturbed by the increasing suffering and hardship that followed the Napoleonic Wars, particularly the new phenomena of recurring business cycles that had choked the British economy in 1815 and 1818-1819, only to hit again in 1825. These events led to a reconsideration of his economic thinking that produced the first book in humanistic economics, his *New Principles of Political Economy* first published in 1819 and republished slightly revised in 1827. In it, he aimed to put economics upon a new basis: instead of teaching how to increase national wealth, or the "wealth of nations," he sought to increase human *well-being* of all. In the process he called for state intervention to regulate several aspects of commerce, industry, and income distribution. These reforms included the regulation of working hours, child labor, the right of workers to form trade unions, and greater worker protection through mandatory employer-financed sickness, old age, and accident insurance schemes. He also favored government action that would help maintain small proprietorships in agriculture and business in order to slow the spread of factory production which he blamed for the recurring slumps and the increasing proletarization of the economy.

In short, Sismondi established a brand new and comprehensive vision that was to form the very bedrock of all the subsequent thinking in humanistic economics. To him, economics was not only a science but, more importantly, an art in which ethical considerations must play a crucially important part. As the ultimate goal of his new economics he replaced maximum production of wealth with the utmost "development of Man, and of all men." Not surprisingly, he was one of the very first economists to throw himself full force against the increasingly entrenched doctrine of laissez-faire.

The trail from Sismondi to John Ruskin, another great pillar in the development of economic ideas more congruent with human values, runs through Thomas Carlyle (1795-1881), who as a student was given the task of translating an article by Sismondi on (the new) political economy from French into English. The article had been commissioned by Dr. Brewster in Edinburgh for his reputed Encyclopedia (Sismondi [1815],

1966). Very likely, that job had some influence on the 20-year-old Carlyle and may account for his subsequent hatred for all the practitioners of the "pig philosophy" and "dismal science," terms he coined to describe the orthodox economics of his day. With Carlyle later becoming Ruskin's mentor, we can establish a direct intellectual channel from Sismondi to Ruskin.

John Ruskin (1819-1900) was initially interested in art history. Through extensive lecturing and writing he had hoped to mold and cultivate the tastes of the English working class toward a greater appreciation of the fine arts. When it became increasingly obvious that all his efforts in this respect were painfully in vain, he placed all the blame on the economic aspects of their lives, particularly the influence of demeaning work in dulling their senses. From there on it was only natural that he devoted most of the rest of his life to criticizing with much eloquence and emotional energy the inhumanities of the industrial system together with its spokesmen: the economists.

This brief introductory paragraph already points to Ruskin's most essential contribution toward a humanistic social economics: he not only accepted Sismondi's reorientation of economics toward human welfare for all but also stressed that well-being or welfare cannot be confined to material welfare alone. Rather, if economic institutions and economic activity interfere with the aesthetic and moral development of people, then these human costs have to be somehow internalized into any meaningful economic thought capable of serving as a worthwhile guide for social policy. One of the main reasons why he chose ceaselessly to attack economists was their preconception that "an advantageous code of social action may be determined irrespective of the influence of social affection." In this way, "Political Economy ends up denying the motive power of the Soul," a fatal error since "the force of this very peculiar agent, as an unknown quality, enters into all the political economist's equations, without his knowledge, and falsifies every one of their results" (Ruskin, 1866).

As a result, all the policy prescriptions (the "advantageous code of social action") of political economy were "a lie," in the sense of being dangerously misleading by corroding the human, social, and moral element in society. What was badly needed, according to Ruskin, was a policy-making science no longer confined to the assumption of "soulless atoms" in self-interested social interaction, but one that took instead the whole person as its fundamental assumption and starting point.

Perhaps the most important new element coming out of Ruskin's new social economics was the central focus he gave to the quality of work. His concern about worker alienation rivaled that of the young Marx two decades earlier. Ever since, it has been much more difficult for any concerned social economist to gloss over the (social) problem of uncreative, routine, and meaningless jobs held by the typical factory worker.

More generally, Ruskin reconceptualized the notion of social welfare in redefining "wealth" from exchange value and subjective utility to "life," the objective life-sustaining property intrinsic to goods and services, and with it, ethical value instead of pecuniary value became the touchstone of his social economics.

Unfortunately, Ruskin lacked the necessary intellectual background to understand fully the real nature of the orthodox political economy he was so fond of targeting for contempt. As a result, he was often unfair toward John Stuart Mill and the many others who spoke out against excessive laissez-faire and against the wage-fund doctrine. Therefore, his critical reflections on the superstructure of ordinary political economy simply lacked the sophistication of his more constructive insights pertaining to its philosophical and methodological foundation (Fain, 1956). Not surprisingly, his innovative pronouncements on economics would have been totally ignored were it not for two disciples who, in the decades to come, managed to imbue them with new life. One was the Indian, Mohandes K. Gandhi, who applied the same basic principles to the problem of Third World development, the other was John A. Hobson who attempted to rearticulate the very essence of Ruskin's philosophy within the framework and language of the prevailing economic thought.[1] It is to this second thinker, perhaps the most sophisticated and profound and certainly the most prolific writer of the humanistic tradition, that we now turn.

John Atkinson Hobson (1858-1940) studied classical literature at Oxford, where John Ruskin also taught. At the age of 29 he became a University Extension Lecturer in Literature and Economics, but soon had to quit this job due to the orthodox uproar that followed the publication of his first book, *The Physiology of Industry*, in 1889. That work challenged Say's Law of Markets by arguing that too much saving and investment, far from promoting prosperity, would bring recession or depression instead.

Hobson continued to develop and refine that underconsumptionist perspective in many subsequent books, one of which was his celebrated *Imperialism: A Study* (1902).[2] But in the meantime, he got busy with constructing his economics of social reform following the blueprint of John Ruskin whom he called "the greatest social teacher." In a book titled

John Ruskin, Social Reformer (1898) he summarized succinctly his teacher's
contribution:

> [One] great reform in Mr. Ruskin's method has reference
> to the term 'Political'. Although the first great English
> treatise on Political Economy bore the title 'Wealth of
> Nations', the science in the hands of Adam Smith's
> successors had never taken a true 'social' or 'national'
> standard even for the computation of commercial wealth.
> The *laissez-faire* assumption that each individual, in
> seeking to get the most for himself, must take that course
> by which he would contribute most to the general well-
> being, *implied a complete failure to comprehend the organic
> structure of society*. A nation was conceived as a mere
> aggregate of its constituent members: the good of the
> whole as the added good of all the parts. . . . Economic
> laws were merely generalisations of the discreet action of
> individual businessmen . . . 'writ large' and called political
> . . . .

And he added the following highly pertinent observation relating social
economics to a conception of the self:

> In passing from Mercantile Economy to Mr. Ruskin's
> science and art of Social Economics, we do not abandon
> the self-seeking motives . . . [but] we enlarge the scope
> and expand the nature . . . [of] the 'self' which is seeking
> satisfaction . . . by imposing sacrifices of the narrower self
> in favour of a wider self *which grows as we identify our
> good with that of others* (quoted in Allett, 1981, pp. 18-
> 19).

Hobson's emphasis on wholism and a more whole (or 'enlarged')
self that underlies Ruskin and his own social economics also characterizes
much of the subsequent work within the humanistic economic paradigm.
We now take a closer look at some of the most important features of
Hobson's pioneering reconstruction.

To begin with, Hobson strongly rejects the view underlying
methodological individualism according to which it is 'a mere superstitition
to look upon society as anything other than the members who compose it.'

He observes: "This declaration sounds final and yet its very language carries its refutation. 'Compose it.' Composition implies an orderly relation of parts . . . . If society is a composition it must have a unity consisting of the relations of its members." And he adds: "The maintenance and activity of these relations can be shown to be a source of value" (Hobson, 1901, p. 146).

This relatively straightforward Gestalt-type realization becomes the bedrock of his social economics. It makes for the foundation of a hierarchy of values attributing to Man a higher nature enabled by an innate common sense understood as a 'sense of the common' or *sensus communus*. Through such a sense we can be motivated by some social instinct, eminent general will or Reason, each aiming at the good of the whole, or the common good. It's an interest going beyond one's narrow self and manifests itself in so-called "disinterested conduct" and altruistic behavior. Moreover, the social context transforms individual nature and "enriches the human personality through the largest measure of sociality" (Hobson, 1929a, p. 73). Again, Hobson was not so much concerned "with a society in which completeness of the individual life is the sole end, but with a society in which the desires, purposes and welfare of the individuals are comprised in the achievement of a common life" (Hobson, 1914, p. 160). Although authentic personality and genuine community are both ultimate ends in Hobson's social thought, he realized that they both entail each other. This kind of axiology may have been strongly influenced by the liberal idealist philosopher T. H. Green at Oxford, particularly in his (social) interpretation of self-realization.[3] We should also point out that to Hobson, the hierarchy of values underlying his social reform theory were meant to be both objectively and interculturally valid. He grounded the lower values in human physical needs (food, clothing, and shelter) and the higher values in the sustaining of society (social cooperation) and enrichment of human personality (self-respect).[4] Attainment of the latter was made possible by social equality and truly equal opportunity for all in both political and economic affairs.[5]

Armed with the hierarchy of human values, John Hobson redefines economics as: "an art . . . concerned with the contribution made to Welfare for the side of those activities concerned with the making and spending of income" (Hobson, 1926, p. 171). And he did so in spite of authoritative contentions that economics ought to be merely descriptive, positive, and value-free. Instead, by putting human purposefulness at the center of his social inquiry, he saw a way to transcend the fact-value distinction. He argues his case as follows:

Human conduct differs from every other known sort of organic conduct in that the operative units entertain, and are immediately influenced in their activities by advance images of 'the desirable' termed ideals. The drive or urge towards these ideals is an 'ought'. Seeing that these and this feeling of ought . . . are more and more potent factors in the economic conduct of today, the disposition to deny the term 'normative' to economic science, or to draw tight limits to its application, is an obstructive procedure which hampers progress of a social science.

> The 'ought' is not something separable and distinct from the 'is'; on the contrary, an 'ought' is everywhere the highest aspect or relation of an 'is'. If a 'fact' has a moral import that moral import is part of the nature of the fact, and the fact cannot be fully known as a fact without taking it into consideration. We may of course, institute an inquiry which ignores the 'ought'. . . . it may often be convenient to pursue this course, but do not let us deceive ourselves into believing that we are investigating all the facts and excluding something which is not a fact. This is only another instance of the protean fallacy of individualism, which feigns the existence of separate individuals by abstracting and neglecting the social relations which belong to them and make them what they are. To abstract from any fact those relations of cause and consequence which give it moral significance is to make it less of a fact than it is . . . . Ethics do not 'intrude' into economic facts; the same facts are ethical and economic (Hobson, 1901, pp. 66-69).

Recognizing that utility is not, as Bentham taught, a homogenous quantity, but a matter of qualitative differences, Hobson lost faith in regarding economics as a quantitative science of values measured in market prices to him pregnant with distortions and imperfections. Instead, a more meaningful economics must become qualitative and be animated more by sound ethical considerations than by following the imperative of market demand.

Hobson's social value of 'organic welfare' allows him to engage in a new kind of human welfare--economics centered on a human standard.

Equipped with this standard, he proceeds to analyze production, primarily work, to see whether it satisfies or frustrates our constructive and creative propensities. Similarly, it looks at consumption from the perspective of the "higher standards of life" and so distinguishes the desirable from the desired. But most important, in recognizing an organic unity between worker and consumer, Hobson studied the interaction between social institutions, particularly those pertaining to the quality of work with personal character, preferences, and patterns of consumption. In this context, he spent much time investigating "the reactions of economic processes upon the group feelings which promote or hinder willing intelligent co-operation in the service of a widening common good" (Hobson, 1926, p. 173). On this basis he also rejected much of Arthur Pigou's economic welfare economics (Hobson, 1926, pp. 98-104).

In studying these interactions of social institutions and individual preferences and behavior, John Hobson greatly enriched the social economic thought pioneered in by Sismondi and Ruskin, specifically by stressing the effect of economic security on "steadiness of character" and moral development. He observed that "irregularity of employment is the most destructive agency to the character, the standard of comfort, the health and sanity of wage earners, [since] it takes out of a man that confidence in the fundamental rationality of life which is essential to the soundness of character." And he concludes that "religion, ethics, education, can have little hold upon workers exposed to such powerful illustrations of unreason and injustice of industry and society" (Hobson, 1914, p. 199). The same theme is echoed with even greater eloquence two decades later:

> When moralists talk of altering human nature they are often misunderstood to mean that instincts and desires deeply implanted in our inherited animal outfit can be eradicated and others grafted on. Now no such miracles are possible or needed. But substantial changes in our environment or in our social institutions can apply different stimuli to human nature and evoke different physical responses. For example, by alterations in the organization and government of businesses and industries, so as to give security of employment and livelihood to workers, and some increased 'voice' to them in the conditions of work, it seems reasonably possible to modify the conscious stress on personal gain-seeking and to

educate a clearer sense of social solidarity and service. . . .
Security is, therefore, the first essential in any shift of the
relative appeal to personal and social motives (Hobson,
1929a, p. 234).

Similarly, the insecurity of the competitive economy tends to
inhibit feelings of social responsibility of businessmen: "Just in proportion
as the competitive activities assume prominence is he compelled to sink
this social feeling, . . . to cultivate those arts of sweating, adulteration and
deceit which seem necessary to enable him to sell goods at a profit"
(Hobson, 1929a, p. 234).

Besides security, Hobson also stressed, following Ruskin, the effect
of meaningful work on creative and constructive human development. The
prevailing "conditions of labor" he saw as an invasion and degradation of
the worker's humanity, "offering neither stimulus or opportunity for a man
to throw himself into his work, for the work only calls for a fragment of
that 'self' and always the same fragment. [As a result] not only is the
labor divided but the laborer." And he concludes, "a man who is not
interested in his work and does not recognize in it either beauty or utility,
is degraded by that work, whether he knows it or not" (Hobson, 1914, p.
88).

Finally, he emphasized the feedback process of an unjust social
institution on individual behavior. Above all, he singled out the problem
of unearned income in modern capitalism. "So long as property appears
to come miraculously or capriciously, irrespective of efforts or requirements, and as long as it is withheld irrationally, it is idle to preach 'the
dignity of labor' or to inculcate sentiments of individual self-help"
(Hobson, 1914, p. 298). A new rationality of the economic order was to
him a most important prerequisite to raise the "moral efficiency" and so
capable of spilling over into all departments of life, including religion,
family, and civic ethics.

In addition to further completing the research program started by
John Ruskin 50 years earlier, to build a new economics centered on a
whole person with an inborn capacity for self-fulfillment, a social economics that would reckon with the economic as well as the "non-economic" costs and benefits of alternative economic institutions and policies,
John A. Hobson was also a lifelong activist pushing for legislative
implementation of his ideas. As a member of the Independent Labour
Party he led government commissions recommending the establishment of
a national "living (minimum) wage," as well as works committees designed

to increase workers' participation in decisionmaking in various industries. Earlier, as a member of the liberal party, he was a vocal and highly influential spokesman for new legislation aiming at nationalizing monopolies and a graduated income tax. All things considered, he can be said to have had a preeminent role in preparing the way for the emergence of the welfare state in England.[6]

In any account of social economics, Hobson must figure as a towering figure inspiring countless followers at home and abroad. We honor him here with a relatively extensive coverage not only as an interesting and somewhat neglected social economist but also because his work still stands as an absolute high water mark of the humanistic tradition in modern economic thought. Contemporary debates in social economics can only gain by being more aware of his thought and work.

Our historical sketch would not be adequately complete without drawing attention to two other eminent British social economists: Richard Tawney (1880-1962) and E. F. Schumacher (1911-1977). One was more interested in the historical rise of capitalism, the other in the effect of technology transfers on the traditional sector of Third World economies. But both criticized the acquisitive consumerist society of their times, and both used a normative framework grounded in basic human needs. Similarly, both advocated an environment in which economic activity would be reimbedded in a larger social context free of excessive materialism and greed. Both of them showed a somewhat greater sensitivity to the spiritual dimension than did Hobson. Although their overall theoretical framework seems to lack the penetrating logic and the comprehensiveness that lives on in the bookshelves and minds filled with Hobson's work, they nevertheless may have significantly advanced social economics with their direct plea for full economic democracy in the form of worker ownership or worker self-management. With this, they certainly did anticipate one of the distinguishing characteristics of the contemporary humanistic perspective.

Such has been the history of this oldest type of social economics, the human-centered approach. There has been much development of some basic ideas since Sismondi's *New Principles* was published in 1819. Yet, the fundamental elements have not changed: an economics centered on human values seen as universal and therefore as objectively valid, the substitution of health or life for wealth, a strongly normative approach that does not ignore "non-economic" effects of industrial and commercial institution and policies, and with it a certain contempt for a too narrow and overspecialized economics. The latter is well expressed in yet another quote by Hobson: "Every bit of knowledge needs to be assayed by submission to the touchstone of the Universal before its value can be ascertained. . . . The over-specialist has let slip the standard of knowledge, and is at the mercy of all sorts of private superstitions and illusions. . . . Man is the measure of all things, and the specialist who has made himself less than a man can measure nothing" (Hobson, 1901, pp. 233-234).

We are now ready to inquire to what extent some of the more recently articulated ideas have succeeded to develop and solidify this vision further. In the process we will take a look at three different problems: the essential humanistic critique of modern economic theory, the basic principles of a humanistic welfare economics and their implications for institutional reform and social policy, and we will end with some brief comments on how this type of social economics fits with the other contemporary perspectives in social economics.

TOWARDS A HUMANISTIC CRITIQUE OF MODERN ECONOMICS

As already mentioned, the economics that Sismondi and Hobson had critized is no longer the same as the economics of today. John Maynard Keynes's new macroeconomics and the work done by the contemporary Post-Keynesian school have been advancing the science in the direction long advocated by Sismondi and Hobson. Similarly, to the extent that economics has been relying more on empirical methods, such as econometrics, in order to better test and hopefully improve its descriptive quality, it is not at all at odds with the humanistic perspective. But there are two major analytical developments, perhaps we should say "fundamental innovations," that do go very much against the grain of the human point of view. We will confine our comments here only to those two problematic aspects: the new formalistic "Rational Economic Man" and the so-called "New Welfare Economics."

The Human Limitation of Rational Economic Man

The perception that any meaningful social theory needs to presuppose an appropriately meaningful human image has long been a distinguishing characteristic of any human-centered perspective. More recently, this perception has been sharpened to imply that an appropriate image of the person has to somehow bring out the *essentially human*, the distinctly human traits of the person. It was for this very reason that the psychologist Abraham Maslow sought to reconstruct psychology by deemphasizing both the study of animal behavior and the (Freudian) preoccupation with human pathology, and by focusing on the essential elements of a *healthy* human personality instead. His new "humanistic psychology" produced the famous "hierarchy of basic human needs," ranging from the natural survival needs of food and shelter to the distinctly human needs of genuine self-esteem and self-actualization (Maslow, 1954, ch. 1). In his later works Maslow tended to prefer to discuss human nature in terms of a simple (but often tension-ridden) duality: *deficiency needs* of the organism which are purely natural and *growth needs* of the self, the former being more natural than human, the latter more human than natural (see, above all, Maslow, 1968). To some extent, this view of a twofold nature of Man, endowed with higher (god-like) and lower (creature-like) needs and ambitions, came to Maslow from the European existentialist tradition. He believed that American psychologists interested in the concept of "human identity" could learn much from the existentialist's treatment of the human predicament "presented by the gap between human aspirations and human limitations, between what the human being *is*, and what he would *like* to be, and what he *could* be" (Maslow, 1968, p. 10). In the same context he also writes:

> From the European writers, we can and should pick up their greater emphasis on what they call 'philosophical anthropology', that is, the attempt to define man, and the difference between man and any other species, between man and objects, and between man and robots. What are his unique and defining characteristics? What is so essential to man that without it he would no longer be defined as a man (Maslow, 1968, p. 12)?

In short, Maslow allowed himself to be quite strongly influenced by this philosophical perspective distinguishing authentic being from actual being. It implies a difference between an actual self and an authentic or "real" self. Similarly, the term "self-actualization" refers now to the authentic or "higher" self rather than to the satisfaction of actual desires as experienced by the "lower" ego-self. Neither is it an actualization of certain isolated traits of the human organism, but a Gestalt of traits, an essence that is distinctly human. As Walter Weisskopf puts it so well: "striving for self-realization can be interpreted as the striving for the realization of human essence" (in Maslow, 1959, p. 221). To realize oneself now also means the realization of specifically those innate capacities that give us *dignity* as human beings.

Leaving Maslow and psychology aside and turning to philosophy and the German Immanuel Kant, we find a rich framework ready to accommodate a truly multidimensional view of human nature and human action (see Kant, 1785). This view and its applications to social economics is quite succinctly described in the previous article on deontological economics by Amitai Etzioni and needs no repeating here. It is our conviction that a multiple utility view based on Kantian philosophy, more than anything else, helps set the very foundation of a more humane economic science.[7] It introduces as self-evident the phenomenon of ethical behavior and helps reveal the tragic divorce between modern economics and genuine human nature. Let us take a closer look at these two aspects, starting with the self-evidence of ethical behavior.

Moral and ethical behavior is directly rooted, of course, in the distinctly human nature of self-consciousness or self-awareness. We have the ability to reflect on our desires, to have so-called "second-order" desires or "higher order" preferences. Examples of such preferences about preferences include statements such as: I wish I would be smoking less, I wish I would not watch TV all day long, I'd like to save more or to be reading better books, I wish I would not lie and cheat as often as I do, etc. All these are clearly statements that are an intrinsic and important part of our experience of everyday life. Neither are they just statements that express mere wishful thinking, but they are often powerful "inner voices" whose council we follow. The above sample of statements tend to get coined precisely when we fail to muster sufficient inner strength or moral integrity to do what we consider to be "right," "moral," or "ethical." In brief, we can now see that ethical behavior is simply action that is compatible with our values, with behavior motivated by *desirable* desires or *preferable* preferences. Or, otherwise put, it is action responding to our "higher," "more integrated," "more ideal" self.

All this sets the background for better seeing the essential limitation of modern Rational Man. According to this picture everybody has a preference structure endowed with certain properties such as transitivity, completeness, etc. Rational action consists in maximizing the satisfaction of these preferences in an optimal manner, i.e., without violating certain constraints relating to income, wealth, or time. It's a problem of (constrained) maximization, where reason is employed only instrumentally, to reach one's objectives determined by one's preferences. There is no consideration of relying on one's reason to determine or "control" these preferences in the first place.

As a result, economics cannot recognize the distinctly human higher order preferences and the notion of a higher self that this implies. There is no place for actions motivated by commitment to individual values, such as fairness. There is a blind spot with respect to self-motivation and its causes. There is no room for the notion of personal integrity or trust, the latter relating to the integrity of others, *not* to their self-interest.[8]

In a pioneering article published more than 10 years ago under the title of "Rational Fools," Amartya Sen has demonstrated that the very notion of commitment *cannot* be fitted into the one-dimensional picture of constrained maximization, regardless how much we may want to stretch that term. Neither can we simply assume a more complex notion of a two-stage maximization process where we first engage in an "overarching utility" maximization process and thereafter maximize the expected behavioral consequences of a chosen preference function (see A. Sen, 1977, 1985, 1987; Sen and Williams, 1982; Lutz and Lux, 1988, ch. 6). One way to see the basic problem of the overarching utility 'solution' can be demonstrated in the following manner. Let us postulate that agents choose on the basis of some criteria of choice, and those criteria are supplied by our preferences which assign "utility" to the outcomes of alternative selections. Accepting this, how can we then choose alternative preference orderings? If the "overarching choice" consists in us having to decide whether we want to behave selfishly or morally, we need to have some criteria on the basis of which to make this choice. Are these criteria and preferences to be taken from our moral self or from our selfish 'narrow' self? In other words, we cannot simply choose our orders of preference (or our criterion of choice) without already being committed to a prechoice criteria of choice. Here is a good example of the intrinsic limitation and incompleteness of a "science of choice," and with it, an argument that deep down economics is part of philosophy.

In conclusion, Rational Man is an all-out maximizer assumed to follow his own self-interest, as the assumption made on theoretical grounds of the rationality of free riding easily demonstrates. In contrast, the humanistic person is a 'restrained maximizer' where the restraining is urged and often accomplished by considerations of moral obligation and commitment in response to the ideals and values of a higher or more authentic self. Whether we see that higher self as a "social self" or a "spiritual self" is another matter. But what is important is to realize that such "social ideals" cannot be explained in a contractarian way since it cannot explain how members of a social contract agree to agree in the first place. Rather, we have to assume on a priori grounds that everybody counts equally.[9] In other words, morality and ethics have to be grounded in something that transcends the social domain. Being more than merely a nominalist construction, it points to a philosophy of the kind of nonnaturalistic realism we have in the deontological framework of Kant.

The relevance of all this anthropology to social economics now becomes quite transparent. There is no big problem in attempting to explain and predict economic behavior in terms of Rational Man. Most businessmen do behave that way and so do we as consumers. But it is a great and dangerous fallacy to take the truncated picture of one-dimensional rational man, an individual who lacks the human qualities of self-awareness and a social consciousness, as the very basis for recommending socioeconomic policy. The result would be a social economy that would best accommodate the interaction of atomistic rational men while potentially discouraging social institutions that enable, even encourage, reasonable and responsible actions as well as meaningful human relations. In brief, in doing so we can fully expect to produce a blueprint for an increasingly dehumanized, inhuman economic system where the social fabric wears increasingly thin. Tragically, this is exactly what the "new" welfare economics, the second target of our critique, ends up doing.

The Inhuman Nature of the New Welfare Economics

We have already alluded to the "old" welfare economics of Arthur Pigou in light of Hobson's human welfare economics. Nevertheless, in spite of those limitations, this old welfare school of the orthodoxy was doing something right: it assumed, and quite reasonably so, that the material need satisfaction of different individuals could be observed, measured, and compared. In other words, the economist as scientist could say that a starving person would get more satisfaction out of a loaf of old bread than a well-to-do millionaire looking forward to feeding the birds. Similarly, it was held to be rather uncontroversial that poor relief financed by a moderate luxury tax was the kind of social policy that could reasonably be expected to increase overall material well-being in society. The basis for such claims was the conviction that people as people are more alike than they are different, at least when it came to their physical makeup.

All this changed when Lionel Robbins switched the discourse from material welfare to psychological satisfaction, or utility (see Cooter and Rappaport, 1984). Now it was the job of the economist to measure what was going on inside people's skulls--an impossible task. How could we really scientifically measure and compare the satisfactions that bread would generate for the starving versus the ecstatic and noble exaltation sure to be experienced by the loving bird feeder? Since different people were likely to differ in their capacity to enjoy life, we really could not tell which of them would gain more and who would gain less. It followed that the economist, as scientific economist, could say absolutely nothing about any welfare impact of redistributional measures. This new twist was known, of course, as the argument denying the possibility of interpersonal comparisons of utility.

It was not long, however, until Roy Harrod, another distinguished British economist, pointed out something very disturbing: if we accept Robbins' reasoning, then economists could not make any policy pronouncements whatsoever (Harrod, 1938). How do we really know if a monopolist, particularly a highly sensitive one, loses less than millions of consumers would gain by means of an antimonopoly policy? By the same token, we would also be led to suddenly question the alleged benefits of free trade, another favored policy point long held by economists. All this debating took place in the second half of the 1930s. Needless to say, it put economics for a short time in some sort of disarray.

But the impasse was broken with the discovery of the so-called Kaldor/Hicks criterion (Kaldor, 1939; Hicks, 1939). It can be illustrated as follows: imagine a policy that would hurt the poor and benefit the rich. If the rich can "compensate" the poor and still have something left over after such compensation, then we can say unambiguously and scientifically that such a policy would enhance overall social well-being. So far, so good. It was an ingenious move that had some merit and appeal, at least in theory, though it had to be granted that in practice it would not be easy to properly determine the amount of compensation necessary to pay every loser.

The next step was the deadly one: if we can determine that a policy move would indeed be preferable according to this compensation criterion, then there is not really a need to actually pay the compensation. All we need to ascertain is the possibility of "potential compensation." Ever since, modern economics has been busy in happily applying this new rule to all sorts of policy questions, primarily under the guise of cost-benefit studies. The Kaldor/Hicks criterion won out quickly and easily in spite of the voiced misgivings of another distinguished economist, the American William Baumol (1946-1947). Early on he had pointed out the implicit assumption underlying the popular Kaldor/Hicks potential compensation criterion: that the marginal utility of money is the same for all people, regardless of whether they are rich or poor. In other words, when it comes to money we *can* compare interpersonal utilities. To see this, imagine a policy that benefits the rich exactly to the extent that it would hurt the poor--let us say, both groups are affected to the tune of a million dollars. According to the Kaldor/Hicks criterion, such a policy would be neither good nor bad, the economist would have to be neutral in this case. Yet, such a stance logically implies the assumption that a million dollars is producing the same utility for the rich as it does for the poor.

The circle is now complete: after denying, in the name of science, interpersonal comparisons and therefore redistribution policies, the economist proceeds to scientifically recommend policy on other matters by assuming that the marginal utility of income or money is a constant and the same for everybody. Regardless of whether this is good ideology or just poor science, it certainly is awful common sense and hardly an advance over the methods of the old material welfare school in economics.[10]

Once we become more fully aware of the intrinsic weakness of the "new" welfare economics, the way is cleared for devoting one's energies toward developing a replacement, a *human* welfare economics, a social justice oriented human welfare economics. Let us now articulate some of the most basic principles of such a social economics, bearing in mind not only some principles of humanistic psychology but also the philosophic anthropology of Immanuel Kant.

THE NORMATIVE FOUNDATIONS OF HUMAN ECONOMY

We begin by articulating the straightforward organizing principle underlying our humanistic vision of social economics: social and economic institutions and policies should be constructed to enable *for all* as much material and social need satisfaction and human dignity as available resources will permit. This norm is believed to be objectively true and valid, but open to critical discussion and falsification attempts. This normative principle is grounded in a human personality seen as being essentially moral and social in nature. Moreover, these basic values are not affected by conflicting manifestations of these values between different cultures. They transcend both culture and social agreement and are grounded in humanity, and are therefore universal. Using a terminology suggested by Jean Maurice Clark, they are values *to* society rather than just (observed) values *in* society.

Specification of material needs is a rather uncontroversial undertaking, since survival and health of the organism does dictate an appropriate amount of food and shelter. Although specific identification of the social needs is more controversial, it is commonly accepted that man *is* a social being and cannot enjoy mental health in complete isolation. It was, however, one of Abraham Maslow's greatest contributions to identify material *insecurity* as something that tends to inhibit the realization of our social nature. With his findings, he marvelously confirmed the earlier insights of Hobson and others on this very important point. It's also an explanation why competitive Economic Man behaves in an atomistic manner with little consideration for the social and moral aspects of his actions, and therefore an argument for relegating his egoism to a pathological special case within a greater and more whole panorama of human nature.

Turning now to the specific nature of the social needs, we feel that plain common sense supports Maslow's two basic needs of belongingness and social esteem, but still, there are no reasons for precluding consideration of other reasonable suggestions by others.

We are now ready to tackle the value of human dignity. Of course, there is a 'sense of dignity' which tends to go hand in hand with an individual sense of self-respect, Maslow's (and Hobson's) gateway to self-realization. In this context, we have to once again respect the basic assumption that the only way to gain genuine self-respect is through realization of our *social* nature, and not by satisfaction of our individual material needs and wants driven by greed or lust for pleasure and power.

But our case need not rest on any psychological evidence since the feeling of dignity merely reflects the ontological existence of the dignity intrinsic to human nature. We claim that dignity is reserved for human beings and derives from Man's special consciousness and self-awareness, from our twofold being, both "nature like" and "God-like." The foundation for such a conception has long been laid by the moral philosopher Immanuel Kant (1785) and needs no further elaboration here. Quite obviously, the concept of intrinsic dignity so understood cannot be fitted within a naturalistic framework that deifies empirical science and discounts any domain above the sensory world of material and social phenomena. It is through taking human dignity seriously, by trying to grasp its meaning fully, that social economics is bound to be given a nonnaturalistic, spiritual bent.[11]

Through Kant we are not only given an objective ontological foundation for dignity but we are also told how its claim manifests itself in the concrete world of social intercourse: to treat a fellow human being as an end, a nonutilitarian value, and never merely as a means, as a commodity or a "thing" to be used, exploited, and enjoyed. (Once again, the arrogant and essentially nonhuman, better *in*-human, nature of modern economics readily shows in its insistence that *all* behavior can be expressed within the framework of an objective function to be maximized. To the extent that fellow human beings enter into this calculus, they enter, of course, as means, as mere objects on the same level as the other factors. No room for dignity here.) From this follows the implication that the value of nonexploitation is directly derivable from the goal of "dignity for all," but we can say a bit more, as we will demonstrate below.

Turning now from the normative principles to the institutions that they recommend, it should come as no surprise that what is implied here, first and foremost, is the need for a *genuine welfare state*. More generally, an economy needs an institutional framework that enables an effective social control of the market economy in order to bring its outcomes more into harmony with the (objective) values *to* society discussed above. In this context we need, above all, to provide jobs to all who want one; in other words, the ideal of a *full employment* economy. Considerations of the social needs would recommend democratic participation by all in the political as well as the economic domain. It would also demand institutional measures that discourage excessive competitiveness and encourage more *social cooperation* instead. Similarly, there is the desideratum of supporting to a maximum possible extent meaningful human relationships in the family and beyond. But, as Ruskin and Hobson had so clearly recognized, the really crucial elements here are structures promoting *meaningful work*. We ought to do so by legislatively discouraging certain technologies only compatible with inordinate fragmentation and alienation of the worker.

The importance of work not only relates to questions of material welfare and social need gratification but to the goal of dignity as well. Not only should workers not be exploited on the job but they should also not be treated as mere "instruments of labor" or "things" to be rented for a wage in order to accumulate more profits. As David Ellerman (1986, 1988, and in this volume) has so succinctly argued, the *only* work structures that are compatible with a respect for a Kantian type human dignity are *worker cooperatives* or "democratic enterprises" where the wage system-- so prevailing in both capitalism and socialism--is abolished. Workers now hire capital instead of the other way around. It appears that such a normative principle in favor of worker self-management is unique to the modern humanistic perspective in social economics and should therefore also be seen as one of its most distinguishing characteristics.

At the same time, it raises the important question of operational significance. Why have worker cooperatives done so poorly in the history of capitalism, and why are they having so much trouble in Yugoslavia today? Is it really reasonable to suppose that a modern industrial state could effectively operate within such an institutional framework, or has industrial progress long outgrown this "utopian" ideal? Questions such as these have long troubled economists of the humanistic tradition. Today, in light of the basic lesson from the Spanish Mondragon cooperatives and together with the theoretical breakthroughs in cooperative economics, particularly the work of Benjamin Ward, Jaroslav Vanek, and David Ellerman, all these questions and more can now be newly reexamined in the light of new data and an atmosphere of heightened relevance and optimism. In any case, the social economics of economic democracy are likely to remain a major element on the research agenda of the humanistic perspective.

We now have all the necessary elements on the political economic agenda for a human economy, but they are still not sufficient. There is a most essential additional consideration without which the goals of economic security, full employment, and economic democracy may be simply unattainable. The problem resides in the ability of society to actually control the economy and its economic destiny. What is missing is the realization that true social control of economic activity implies respect for a crucially important *principle of correspondence* between the political and the economic domains. A serious problem arises if the economic marketplace stretches beyond (typically national) political jurisdictions. Such is the case, of course, when national economies compete in an integrated global economy. The nation that tries to regulate its markets by setting standards of minimum welfare provisions, working conditions or worker protection, environmental protection, resource conservation, etc., may find itself undersold by foreign producers and/or their own industries moving abroad in order to circumvent the

costly regulations. As John Culbertson (1984, p. 21) puts it: "World economic integration would enforce a lowest-common-denominator competition. Low standards undercut high standards. Low standards are thus
enforced on all." He describes it as a process of "general regression
toward economic barbarism" and therefore bound to be of greatest concern
to economists. "From a human point of view, or in relation to the
achievement of civilized patterns of human life, the raising of such
standards may seem to be what economics, and economies, are all about"
(Culbertson, 1984, pp. 90-91). Add to this Culbertson's more controversial
point that due to population growth factors, unregulated free trade and
foreign investment will eventually pull down our wages and our standard
of living to levels that are competitive with South Korea, India, and China.
If true, it is by no means clear that even worker cooperatives will remain
viable, although they could certainly be expected to help ease the pressure
for essentially two reasons: first, wage reductions could be accomplished
with less industrial strife and antagonism, and second, capital flight or
investment abroad would no longer be a major threat accelerating the
erosion of living standards. Nevertheless, from a humanistic perspective
we can put no more faith in unregulated free trade than we can in the
libertarian doctrine of laissez-faire. Here, once again, a humanistic social
economics emerges as a most radical and unconventional strand not likely
to appeal to the timid or intimidated.

There seem to be only two remedies for the current predicament
resulting from the lack of correspondence: either we follow Hobson in
staking our hopes and devoting our energies toward establishing a new
world government, or else, and more realistically, we seek to cope with the
situation by reintegrating social control of the economy to the national
level. The latter implies, of course, regulated, not free, international trade.
We may label this policy "protectionism" if it is understood that what we
seek to protect are the human aspects of our economic system. It's a
"protection" of the public interest, not of some private interests, as popular
rhetoric would have us believe.

Our intellectual commitment to the correspondence principle can
be seen to reveal a break with orthodox ideology. One scholar, Immanuel
Wallerstein (1976, p. 348), interested in the evolution of the present world
economic system, has argued:

> . . . that capitalism as an economic mode is based on the
> fact that the economic factors operate with an arena larger
> than that which any political entity can totally control.

> This gives capitalists a freedom of maneuver that is struc-
> turally based. It has made possible the constant expansion
> of the world-system, albeit a very skewed distribution of
> its rewards. The only alternative world-system that could
> maintain a high level of productivity and change the
> system of distribution would involve the reintegration of
> the levels of political and economic decision-making.

If Wallerstein is correct, an effective enforcement of a correspondence principle may be tantamount to mortally wounding the very heart of capitalism. Moreover, a system based on democratic worker cooperatives abolishes not only the absentee ownership that comes with the selling of stock certificates but with it also the very hallmark of capitalism, the stock market.

Let us be clear, however, that letting go of capitalism should not be interpreted as advocating a brand of socialism that closely identifies with historical materialism, materialist determinism, centralized control of economic activity, and limited civil liberties regarding free speech and the pursuit of religion. Rather, it would be a communitarian "socialism" that conquers the wage system and promotes the highest possible degree of decentralized community decisionmaking in both economic and political affairs. Obviously, there is at present no such system, no such human economy, except in the lofty domain of cherished ideals. One day it may very well emerge as a point of a transcendent-type convergence of present-day dichotomy between left and right, between socialism and capitalism. In light of our social economics, a more meaningful dichotomy now becomes "up" versus "down" as measured by the "human standard." The up signifies a move toward an economic system where human beings are free to live authentic lives and follow spiritual goals that allow them to better escape the "structures of sin" recently denounced by the Pope. Short of arrival at that historical point, we can expect many more Ruskins and Hobsons raising their voices, even if they are greeted by orthodox silence rather than applause.

COMPARING HUMANISTIC WITH CONVENTIONAL SOCIAL ECONOMICS

Quite obviously, not all thinkers that have been discussed here always spoke with one voice on all matters. Nevertheless, they all insisted on some sort of "human standard" as a normative foundation to their economics; in the process they all focused on a type of human personality that allowed for lower and higher dimensions. This alone, perhaps more than anything else, already points to a deep and penetrating differentiation relative to two major strands in contemporary social economics: instrumentalist institutionalism and Marxian socialism. Let us first turn to each of those two perspectives before focusing on the traditional mainstream in American social economics: the Catholic strand.

Instrumentalist Strand in Humanistic Perspective

The basic problem making for dissonance here is one of "worldview." Humanistic thinkers, for more than a century, have been uncomfortable with "naturalism," a philosophical perspective greatly enhanced by Darwinian evolution and which seeks to understand man and social ethics from an essentially *biological* point of view, while neglecting or discounting a meaningful spiritual domain.

An outspoken willingness to approach the world in such naturalistic light characterizes much of the work of Clarence Ayres, an acknowledged champion of contemporary instrumentalist thought in social economics. All "reason" is confined to *instrumental* reason, there is no recognition of "ends-in-themselves" and no appreciation of "distinterested" motives. Even John Hobson, perhaps the humanist most sympathetic to naturalism, believed that a full view of human personality has to come to grips with the notion of a "higher life" seeking "spiritual goods" devoid of "biological utility." The spiritual domain beyond biology is one inhabited by Reason which must not only serve as an instrument for the gratification of Maslow's deficiency needs but must reckon with Maslow's growth needs in exercising "control over the whole fund of activities in the interest of personality and mankind" (Hobson, 1926, pp. 19-20). This noninstrumental Reason manifests itself in disinterested action, grounded in our distinctly human capacity of free will, and it is apprehended primarily by an enlightened common sense understood as a "sense of the common."

It is also the denial of genuine human free will that tends to induce instrumentalists to rely too heavily on biological metaphors for their evolutionary way of thinking. As Hobson already observed, this tends to imply an excessive emphasis on efficient causation and gradual change in presenting "a figure of human nature too clumsy for any work of transferring human institutions in ways that are at once quick, safe, and economical" (Hobson, 1926, p. 29).

Similarly, it discourages the description of social ideals, institutions, and policies based on Reason and instead promotes a naturalistic account grounded in observable desires and social preferences. Not surprisingly, most modern instrumentalists tend to be overly accepting of modern corporate capitalism, consumerist materialism, and the prevailing wage system. For the same basic reason so many of them seem too intrinsically incapacitated to even grant the possibility of serious limits to science and technology, however broadly these terms are defined.

Probably the greatest casualty of the instrumentalist-naturalist perspective is the concept of human dignity, so central to the humanistic point of view.[12]   In contrast, a humanistic economist can recognize something that confuses his instrumentalist cousin: that there may be at times a conflict between human dignity and technology.   Similarly, a naturalistic account of human nature carried on in terms of science only, is likely to offend the essential dignity of Man.

Implicit to instrumentalism as a social philosophy is also an a priori type inclination to deny the very possibility of absolute truths, or of an ethics that is ontologically rather than socially grounded. Logically, on the heels of this denial tends to follow a predisposition to cultural relativism believed to be preferable to the only alternative conceivable: "cultural absolutism" understood as a "cultural imperialism" where any one culture imposes its values on all others. If there is any yardstick at all to meaningfully evaluate cultures, we are told to find it in science and technology.

If relativistic instrumentalist social economists see it as their task to pragmatically *make* truth while humanistic thinkers, in adhering to an epistemology of critical absolutism, seek to *discover* what is true, it becomes clear that the gulf between the two perspectives is rather deep. A similar gulf exists, albeit for somewhat different reasons, vis-a-vis the Marxian point of view.

The Marxian Socialist Strand in Humanistic Perspective

The relationship between Human Economy and Marxian political economy is both complex and still not entirely resolved. For one, there is less of a friction here than with the instrumentalists simply because most Marxist social economics attempts to be scientific and "value-free" rather than normative. Seen from this angle, humanistic economics appears somewhat more complementary and less conflicting. In addition, both perspectives have been sharing a strong interest in studying factors behind capitalist economic crisis, an interest motivated by a general distrust and disenchantment with the capitalist economic system. So much could readily be admitted by Hobson when lecturing: "Though I have never been a full blooded Marxist, I desire to acknowledge the great services he rendered by tracing trade depressions and unemployment to vices inherent in the profiteering system" (quoted in Allett, 1981, p. 13).

More generally it should be clear that from its very beginning and until 1848, socialism was primarily a moral economy, a normative humanistic body of criticism of the emerging capitalist industrial order. Even the writings of the young Karl Marx continued in this spirit by heavily relying on such humanistic concepts as alienation and by criticizing commodity-type human relationships.

The real problem between humanistic and Marxist economics lies in the more mature inclination of Marx to rely on his scientific socialism --with its assumptions and conclusions--as a basis for social policy. In this way, he and his followers ended up, willingly or unwillingly, fostering the kind of class antagonism that promotes a *revolutionary* uprising of the oppressed and exploited working classes. At the same time, it has often worked to discourage any forces that aim at *reforming* capitalism from within, particularly through the establishment of ("utopian" or "bourgeois socialist") worker cooperatives, the increasingly central goal of the humanistic vision. Similarly, the Marxian image of the human person has never been sensitive to claims of the uniqueness of the individual, and therefore has been driven to overestimate the collective nature of their "New Man." Not surprisingly, postrevolutionary socialism has primarily been highly centralized and bureaucratic.

Finally, it has been alleged that there is no such thing as human nature in Marx.[13] To the extent that there is, we believe it still is overly materialistic, perhaps even deterministic. Accordingly, the sharp rejection of historical materialism by Hobson and other humanistic thinkers should not come as a surprise.[14] Yet such rejection left little in Marxian social philosophy to serve as a source of inspiration. Add to this the strong humanistic reservations about the validity of the labor theory of value and it becomes readily apparent just why the initial equation between humanism and socialism no longer holds.[15]

Going beyond both, the naturalism of instrumentalism and the materialism of Marxism, brings us to the traditional mainstream in social economics: the Catholic strand.

Catholic Social Economics in Humanistic Perspective

Catholic intellectuals have never been able to find a meaningful home in the secular economics rooted in Adam Smith or Karl Marx. This is one of the prime reasons why we have the social encyclicals of the Popes and the birth of a separate Association of Catholic Economics which later became the Association for Social Economics. Neither can they be expected to feel comfortable with the naturalistic social philosophy of John Dewey and his ardent follower Clarence Ayres. What was needed was a social perspective built on a view of the person more fully compatible with the essentially spiritual nature of Man, as well as an ethics grounded in the spiritual domain.

It is for these basic reasons that there is a rather close correspondence between the humanistic economists and their Catholic cousins. At the same time, humanists ever since Pico della Mirandola have been uneasy with many aspects of Catholic dogma and the supposed authority of an institutionalized Church. Nevertheless, almost all of them did not reject some sort of Christianity, and just about all felt the need for a strong spiritual foundation for their socioeconomic creed. This is perhaps most noticable in the writings of a Richard Tawney or an E. F. Schumacher.[16] Like Jean Maurice Clark (1957, p. 57), they would readily admit that "Man's radical heritage includes in his unconscious a cosmic force, a bit of eternity." Going even farther, most of them believed in a reality that eludes science, a reality which according to Clark (1957, p. 57) represents "a power in which man lives and which lives in man, and does for him many of the things that received religion expresses, in its own way, in countless scriptural texts." Even John Hobson (1910, pp. 249-250), certainly the most secular representative of the humanistic tradition discussed here, was only opposed to a "religion being put back into the traditional Protestant groove of personal piety" and called for the "active cooperation of churches in the reconstruction of social institutions, so as to furnish a worthy tenement for the social soul."

More generally, humanistic social economics has always accepted a legitimate sphere of religion, in the words of Hobson (1910, p. 250), "The spirit [of which] must transcend humanity, seeking a One which is higher and holier." Such a spirituality has little in common with self-interested religious aspirations grounded in a utilitarian calculus of heaven and hell. Rather, it's a spirituality of social service designed to help the poor directly, as well as by means of dismantling the "structures of sin" inherent in both capitalism and Marxian socialism. In the process, its general focus naturally blends with the recent Popes' emphasis on the right to work and the dignity of labor. Similarly, it is incompatible with both the collectivist centralization of economic decisionmaking and the chaos of atomistic laissez-faire.

Accordingly, it should not come as a big surprise that there has been some significant cross-fertilization as was the case with Ruskin and the Christian socialist Ludlow. More significantly, Erwin Nemmers (1972, p. 2) quotes John A. Ryan, one of the founding fathers of modern Catholic social economics, as writing in his autobiography:

> More than twenty-five years ago, I drafted a dedication which I thought of using . . . for my book, *Distributive Justice*. It reads as follows: "To John A. Hobson, whose illuminating analysis of the economics of production and distribution, has greatly facilitated the author's attempt to determine the morality of these processes."

Nevertheless, there is a major difference with the Catholic perspective relating to the foundation of its ethics: the normative elements are seen to be based on an innate moral sense founded in Reason instead of revelation grounded in a particular scriptural text, or by virtue of certain papal pronouncements considered infallible.[17] In other words, most thinkers in the humanistic camp would feel compelled to reject any revelation that conflicts with Reason, provided, of course, that Reason is understood metaphysically rather than scientifically. Without these major differences, the Catholic and the modern humanistic strand of social economics would collapse to essentially the same perspective.

CONCLUSION

The primary purpose of this essay was to draw attention to a relatively neglected strand in contemporary American social economics. To some extent this neglect may be accounted for by the fact that unlike its instrumentalist cousin its pedigree does not feature any American economists, although some institutionalist economists such as Richard T. Ely, Rexford Tugwell, and Jean Maurice Clark had, to some extent, been influenced by John Ruskin or John Hobson. Today, however, we can witness an American revival, particularly in the form of the contemporary Human Economy movement which followed on the heels of E. F. Schumacher's best-selling *Small is Beautiful* (1973). It has been further reinforced by a recent interest in 'appropriate technology' in the context of development economics.

We have also attempted to demonstrate that this type of social economics not only features a rich and coherent tradition but also that it has much to offer by casting new light on contemporary socioeconomic problems. Among other things, it offers a penetrating critique of modern mainstream economics, particularly its normative branch fed to students under the label of the "New welfare economics." In its place it puts a more *human* welfare economics that recognizes the higher nature of human beings and fully respects human dignity. Moreover, with its modern stress on the Reasonable Person rather than Rational Man it is in tune with the recent developments rediscovering deontological human action, a development that seemingly has swept through practical philosophy and has now even started to invade economic theory.[18]

Finally, we have argued that this version of social economics is unique in the sense that it cannot be reduced to any of the other contemporary social economics strands. So, for example, it may very well be the only perspective that by its own inner logic makes the case for economic democracy in the form of employee self-management. At the same time, its strong democratic faith, deeply anchored in a long tradition, refrains from advocating authoritarian imposition of its values on a public that for various reasons may lack, for the time being, the willingness to pursue that goal. Instead, it offers its principles and normative conclusions to intellectual debate and open-minded criticism. We feel that American social economists have little to lose and much to gain by being more familiar with its uniquely different approach to the common concerns of a meaningful social economy.

Notes

[1]Others confessing to be strongly influenced by Ruskin were R. H. Tawney ([1919], 1966) and R. T. Ely (1901).

[2]Hobson's underconsumption theory is discussed in Nemmers (1972) and in the relevant chapters of Bleaney (1976) and Allett (1981).

[3]To Green, self-realization was to be understood as the development of moral excellence in common fellowship with other members of society (see Allett, 1981, pp. 188-89).

[4]Hobson's stress on self-respect may be indicated by the following quotation:

> It is only the self-respecting man who respects his fellows; it is only he who feels he gets his due that is solicitous and exact in seeing that others get their due. Such a man alone has educated in him a sense of social justice unembittered by personal grievance and extended by sympathy towards others . . . (quoted in Allett, 1981, p. 226).

[5]Hobson observes: "A man living with self-respect in a society of his equals, . . . equal opportunities in industry and education, his social instincts no longer maimed by the selfish struggle between individual and individual, . . . would for the first time be free to express his social sympathies. . . . Until such conditions are ripe for such a life the ideal personality cannot be born" (quoted in Allett, 1981, p. 226).

[6]For an excellent account of Hobson's political activism, see chapters 7 and 8 in Allett (1981).

[7]Other attempts include Lutz and Lux (1982, 1988).

[8]For a more comprehensive treatment of this point, particularly the issues of motivation and trust, see Lutz (1985a, pp. 112-115).

[9]This point is also made in a recent review by Harsany (1987) of a new book by David Gauthier (1986).

[10]For a recent critique of the new welfare economics along the lines followed here, see Cooter and Rappaport (1984) and the following exchange between Little (1986) and Cooter and Rappaport (1984).

[11]See on this issue Lutz (1985b) and the following exchange Hill (1986)-Lutz (1986).

[12]This issue has been discussed elsewhere; see Lutz (1985b) and Lutz (1986).

[13]The issue has been discussed by Geras (1982).

[14]See Hobson (1929, p. 44 and chapter on Proletarian Economics). The rejection of Marx by Gandhi also hinges on this very point. See, for example, Iyer (1973, pp. 101-105).

[15]For a critique of the labor theory of value by Hobson, see, for example, (1937, pp. 73-74) or Ellerman (1985).

[16]See, for example, Schumacher ([1974], 1980).

[17]This, however, also indicates a rather close identification with contributions of solidarists aiming to ground their doctrines in what they call "natural law."

18See Etzioni's contribution in this book and Sen (1987).

References

Allett, J. 1981. *New Liberalism, The Political Economy of J. A. Hobson.* Toronto: University of Toronto Press.

Ayres, C. 1944. *The Theory of Economic Progress.* Chapel Hill, NC: University of North Carolina Press.

Baumol, W. 1946-47. "Community indifference," *Review of Economic Studies* 14:1, 44-48.

Bleaney, M. 1976. *Underconsumption Theories.* New York: International Publ., ch. 8.

Clark, J. M. 1936. *Preface to Social Economics.* New York: Farrar and Rhinehart, Inc.

_____. 1957. *Economic Institutions and Human Welfare.* New York: Alfred A. Knopf.

Cooter, R. and P. Rappaport. 1984. "Were the ordinalists wrong about welfare economics?" *Journal of Economic Literature* 22, 507-530.

Culbertson, J. M. 1984. *International Trade and the Future of the West.* Madison, WI: 21st Century Press.

Ellerman, D. 1985. "On the labor theory of property," *Philosophical Forum* XVI:4 (Summer) 293-326.

_____. 1986. "The employment contract and liberal thought," *Review of Social Economy* 44:1 (April), 293-326.

_____. 1988. "A Kantian approach to normative economics," *Journal of Economic Issues,* forthcoming.

Ely, R. T. 1901. "Introduction" in his new edition of Ruskin's *Unto This Last.* London: George Allen.

Fain, J. T. 1956. *Ruskin and the Economists.* Nashville: Vanderbilt University Press.

Gauthier, D. 1986. *Morals by Agreement.* Oxford: Calendron Press.

Geras, N. 1982. *Marx and Human Nature: Refutation of a Legend.* London: N.L.R. Verso Editions.

Harrod, R. 1938. "Scope and method of economics," *Economic Journal* 48, 390-397.

Harsany, J. C. 1987. "Review of Gauthier's Morals by Agreement," *Economics and Philosophy* 3, 339-351.

Hicks, J. R. 1939. "The foundations of welfare economics," *Economic Journal* 49 (December), 696-700, 711-712.

Hill, L. 1986. "Pragmatism, instrumental value theory and social economics: comment," *Review of Social Economy* 44:2 (October), 193-196.

Hobson, J. A. 1889. *The Physiology of Industry* (with A. F. Mummery). London: Murray.

_____. 1898. *John Ruskin, Social Reformer*. London: Nisbet.

_____. 1901. *The Social Problem*. London: Nisbet.

_____. 1902. *Imperialism: A Study*. London: Nisbet.

_____. 1910. *A Modern Outlook*. London: Herbert and Daniel.

_____. 1914. *Work and Wealth*. London: Macmillan.

_____. 1926. *Free Thought on the Social Sciences*. London: George Allen & Unwin Ltd.

_____. 1929a. *Economics and Ethics*. London: D. C. Heath & Co.

_____. 1929b. *Work and Life*. London: Macmillan.

_____. 1937. *Property and Impropery*. London: Gollancz.

Iyer, R. 1973. *The Moral and Political Thought of Mahatma Gandhi*. New York: Oxford University Press.

Kaldor, N. 1939. "Welfare propositions of economics and interpersonal comparisons of utility," *Economic Journal* 49 (September), 549-552.

Kant, I. 1785. *Grounding the Metaphysics of Morals*. Translated by J. Ellington in his ed., I. Kant, *Ethical Philosophy*. Indianapolis: Hackett Publ. Co.

Little, I. M. D. 1985. "Reply to P. Cooter and R. Rappaport," *Journal of Economic Literature* 23 (September), 1186-1188.

Lutz, M. A. 1985a. "Beyond economic man: humanistic economics," in *Economics and Philosophy*, edited by P. Koslowski. Tuebingen (Germany): J.C.B. Mohr, pp. 91-120.

_____. 1985b. "Pragmatism, instrumental value theory and social economics," *Review of Social Economy* 42 (October), 140-172.

_____. 1986. "A rejoinder to Lewis Hill," *Review of Social Economy* 44:2 (October), 196-200.

_____. 1989. "The normative foundations of human economy" in *Alternative Development Experiments*, edited by P. Kisanga and O. Nudler. London: Zed Publ., forthcoming.

Lutz, M. A. and K. Lux. 1984. "New directions in humanistic economics," *The Forum for Social Economics* (Fall), 51-54.

_____. 1988. *Humanistic Economics: The New Challenge*. New York: Bootstrap Press.

Maslow, A. 1954. *Motivation and Personality*. New York: Harper & Row Publ. Inc.

_____, ed. 1959. *New Knowledge in Human Values*. South Bend, IN: Regenry/Gateway, Inc.

_____. 1968. *Toward a Psychology of Being*. New York: Van Nostrand Reinhold Co.

Nemmers, E. E. 1972. *Hobson and Underconsumption*. Clifton, NJ: Augustus M. Kelley Publ.

Ruskin, J. 1866. *Unto This Last*. New York: John Wiley & Sons.

Schumacher, E. F. 1973. *Small Is Beautiful*. New York: Harper & Row.

_____. 1980. "The age of plenty: a Christian view," [1974] reprinted in *Economics, Ecology, Ethics: Essays towards a Steady State Economy*, edited by H. Daly. San Francisco: W. H. Freeman.

Sen, A. 1977. "Rational fools: a critique of the behavioral foundations of economic theory," *Philosophy and Public Affairs* 6, 317-344.

_____. 1985. "Goals, commitment and identity," *Journal of Law, Economics, and Organization* 1:2, 341-355.

_____. 1987. *On Ethics and Economics*. New York: Basil Blackwell.

Sen, A and B. Williams. 1982. *Utilitarianism and Beyond*. New York: Cambridge University Press.

Sismondi, J.C.L.S. de. 1819. *New Principles of Political Economy*. Paris: Chez Delauney.

_____. 1966. *Political Economy*. [1815] New York: Augustus M. Kelley.

Tawney, R. H. 1920. *The Acquisitive Society*. London: Harcourt, Brace & World, Inc.

_____. 1966. "John Ruskin," *Observer*, February 19, 1919, reprinted in *The Radical Tradition*, edited by R. Hinton. London, 42-46.

Wallerstein, I. 1976. *The Making of the Modern World System*. New York: Academic Press.

8

FOUR STRANDS OF SOCIAL ECONOMICS:
A COMPARATIVE INTERPRETATION

Warren J. Samuels

This chapter interprets the four strands of social economics presented in the preceding chapters. It attempts neither to present the final
word on what separates or unites the four strands nor to argue that any
one of them is right or wrong, but to indicate something of their limits
and their relationships to each other, and to do so from a particular
complex explicit perspective. In the process I shall identify what I think
is the distinctive core of social economics, emphasizing that it may be
pursued in various ways.

Part I identifies the perspective from which this interpretation is
made. Part II examines the three traditional strands presented by
Professors O'Boyle, Hill, and Hunt. Part III considers the fourth strand
presented by Professors Etzioni and Lutz. Part IV expands upon certain
themes previously identified and also examines some additional points, as

suggested by the cross-critiques which the authors have given each other's contributions. Part V states certain conclusions.

INTERPRETIVE PERSPECTIVE

The perspective which I bring to this interpretation has several elements, the most important of which are as follows.

1. I take an eclectic, open-ended "matrix" approach to the study of schools and strands of thought. Each strand of social economic thought can be understood both on its own terms and from the perspective of its rivals. There is strand A's view of itself but also B's and C's views of A. Each will be different because A views itself on its own terms whereas B and C view A from their own respective perspectives; likewise with the view of each of B and C, respectively. Social economics overall can be comprehended as the more or less amorphous matrix representing the combination of all its strands, including the elements which they hold in common and the tensions which derive from their differences.

It is not necessary to accord a privileged position to any particular view of any school or any strand. There is no reason conclusively to presume that the only "correct" view of a school of thought is that held by the adherents of that position or of one strand thereof. To establish a particular privileged position requires a solution to the problem of the hermeneutic circle, whereby one can choose between such strands only on a premise which takes one of them as given, which thereby constitutes the adoption of the position chosen, so that the choice of position is tautological with and gives effect to the adoption of the premise. There is no conclusive reason why one cannot select the premise of one's choice, but whether one recognizes it or not that premise comprises one's particular faith presupposition, defining "faith" broadly.

Although I will not be directly utilizing the matrix approach in interpreting the four strands of social economics, it ultimately underlies my view of them. Having necessarily to adopt my interpretive position does not require that I attribute to it any privileged, exclusivist status.

2. Values are both relevant and important. Both the meaning and the critique of things--actions, phenomena, policies, and so on-- typically are addressed in terms of values which may or may not be explicit. There is a profound social valuation process in which values are identified, juxtaposed to each other, tested in various ways, and, again in various ways, chosen, as well as reformulated, reevaluated, and rechosen.

This valuation process encompasses the market but also much more than the market and more than prices of commodities. Values also relate to the structure of power, the conditions of access to power, and the use of power; to the understanding of the nature of man, of virtue, and of what constitutes an authentic human being and the good society. It is very difficult to separate the normative (valuational) from the positive (descriptive and/or explanatory) elements of statements.

Recognition of the foregoing raises questions concerning the sources and the specific content of values as well as the relationships between and among values, these latter including interdependence, conflict (and thus tradeoffs), and mutual reenforcement. A further question concerns the variability of the application of a general value in particular, concrete cases, and the exercise of judgment and choice necessarily involved therein (even when it is noncognitive). General valuational (and other) concepts are given selective perception and application.

3. There is a fundamental problem of order: the necessity to continually resolve conflicts of freedom with control, continuity with change, and hierarchy with equality. Order may be defined in terms of selective substance adduced to any one of these terms, but that is not the sense intended here. The problem of order involves the process of working out these inexorable conflicts. A corollary is that there is always social control: freedom is always freedom in terms of the pattern of control which gives rise to it. To speak of freedom is to speak of the correlative facilitative control. It is also to speak of the interests exposed to the exercise of that freedom and of the unintended consequences thereof.

4. One characteristic of the material addressed in the three foregoing points is the relevant *process*: In each case, something has to be worked out. It is not given once for all time and all places: the substance and meaning of a school or strand of thought as understood by its advocates and rivals; the content, interrelationships, and applications of values; the substance (and the critiques) of the resolution of the several conflicts comprising the problem of order. This means that each is necessarily futuristic. Each pertains to something which in reality or in practice has to be worked out. One's particular specification (for example, of values) must be understood as contingent and problematic. To affirm the reality of values, for example, is neither to establish the content of values or the conditions of applicability of any particular value nor to deny that people's values (however much subject to further selective perception and application) are very much a matter of custom and habit.

One example of the last point may be useful. Consider the conflict between what I shall call practical idealism (which may take the form of theological idealism, and which resembles philosophical realism) and practical realism. The idealist generally believes that there is only one best solution to a problem, one best reconciliation of conflicting values, and that this best solution exists independent of man; man can elect it or not but it exists. The realist believes that solutions are generated by real-world decisional processes; that different decisionmaking structures reach different solutions; and that one can only talk of solutions derived from and specific to the underlying power (value weighting) structure; --such that the "best" or "right" solution is the one which is actually chosen, given the decisional structure (that is weighting by power[1]), there being no other relevant operative basis of choice.

The idealist thus emphasizes the one best, ideal solution; the realist, the necessity of choice and the one actually chosen. My present points are that the two are not mutually exclusive and that there is a necessity of choice in each case. Assume that everyone is a practical idealist and believes that there is only one best solution to a problem. But assume also (as is more than likely the case) that each practical idealist has a different candidate for what constitutes that one best solution. Choice would still have to be exercised as to which candidate is in fact the one best solution. Alternatively, assume that everyone is a practical realist and believes that the correct solution is the one that emerges from the decisionmaking process--but that each has a different candidate for what constitutes that one correct solution or for the desirable decisionmaking structure or the one necessary to produce the correct solution. Choice would still have to be made as to which candidate is in fact the one to be chosen. In both cases, there must be choice and the resolution of the problem at hand must be worked out. In that choosing and working-out process both the mode of discourse and the basis of individual and collective judgment will be comprised of values.[2]

The following also can be said: first, if there are in fact absolute, preexistent fundamental values, then presumably they should in time impose themselves upon all people. Second, for the person who does not believe that objective reality and absolute, preexistent fundamental values exist, this nonbelief is of no fundamental consequence for either personal actions or public policy, for choice at this level is required whether or not one believes in an objective reality and absolute, preexistent fundamental values. For the believer, man is necessarily imperfect and cannot discern perfectly the will of God, and hence there are differing views of what God expects; choice has to be exercised. For the nonbeliever, it makes no difference; for he or she, too, choice has to be exercised. Third, it is presumptuous to assume that, since there are absolute, preexistent fundamental values and they have not been accepted by all people, there is something deficient if not malicious about some persons' capacity to reason or for moral judgment.

Another way of making the point is that whether one believes that values are made or discovered by man, man is involved in the serious business of articulating values. Choosing is not the same thing as making, but significant differences in understanding the functioning and perform-ance of the social economy derive from, and in turn influence, the values that one articulates, and it is these understandings that form the basis of individual and collective action. Whether one believes that values are made or discovered by man, human life is an exploration as to the meaning of values.

Perhaps the key lesson is that the fact of the problem of the conflict between practical idealism and practical realism tells us more about the psychology than the nature of moral values. By this I mean the need by some for a sense of confidence that there is a transcendental ground for policy, and the propensity of others to tolerate a sense of uncertainty or ambiguity.

5. There are certain relevant important, perhaps fundamental, antinomies (though each can have varying denotations): absolutism versus relativism, idealism versus realism, realism versus nominalism, rationalism versus empiricism, and so on. One can approach them as matters on which one has to find the "correct" answer, or as conundrums whose very nature both complicates and enlightens human understanding and to which the matrix approach discussed above has special relevance: meaningful-nesss flows not necessarily from any one position on an antinomy but from the matrix formed by the totality of positions.

6. The practitioners of any inquiring discipline, such as econom-ics, have both the necessity and the opportunity to define their field of inquiry. The operative definition of the central problem and scope of economics may well be the most important thing that one can say of the field, its most significant feature, its most fundamental possession. The central problem and scope of social economics are broader than the corresponding features of mainstream neoclassical economics (although these vary among its practitioners). That does not preclude an understand-ing of the marginalist analysis of markets from making potentially valuable contributions to both the understanding and the operation of the total

valuational process applicable to the resolution of the problem of order, including resource allocation, contributions to be understood on both their own terms and the terms of other schools, including the several strands of social economics.

7. The four strands of social economics--which I shall designate as theological idealism, pragmatism-instrumentalism, materialism, and moral humanism--constitute viable analytical frameworks within which to analyze the human condition, the social economy, and socioeconomic policy. Each of these positions has both its strengths and limitations jointly derived from its nature, such that each yields a distinctive tone or orientation to discussion and is at the same time incomplete vis-à-vis each other. Practitioners of each tend to take a position on the various antinomies noted above and to finesse the analytical and substantive problems consequent to doing so (a situation necessarily characteristic of the approach taken in this chapter).

The forte of theological idealism is its emphases on transcendental values, on authenticity in life and relationships, and on pursuing the relationship of man to what is fundamental and universal in reality.

The forte of pragmatism-instrumentalism is its focus on consequential human meaningfulness rather than truth in the sense of correspondence with a given, preexistent transcendent reality.

There is an idealist or valuational element in pragmatism, insofar as meaning in the sense of consequences requires consideration of values. There is a consequentialist element in theological idealism--in addition to an intuitive yearning--insofar as values are understood in terms of their consequences for man, even within a religious mode of discourse.

The forte of materialism, especially in the conditionistic (nondeterministic) form advocated by Hunt, is its emphasis that the circumstances of production and the social relations associated therewith are important to how human beings live and associate with each other, how value problems arise, how values arise, how the social valuational process operates, and how consequences must be understood systemically.

The forte of moral humanism is a combination of the features of theological idealism and pragmatism. In the case of both theological idealism and moral humanism, and perhaps even pragmatism, there are interesting, if often subtle, combinations of absolutism and relativism.

For present purposes, and without any intent to denigrate, we may consider varieties of religious experience, varying forms of theological teleology, as functional with regard to persuasion and motivation, if not also psychic balm. Theological teleology may be comprehended as either theological idealism or philosophical realism. The present point is the necessity of choice that must be exercised with regard to the substantive content of religious doctrine and its application to socioeconomic policy. Theological teleology, or theological idealism, constitutes for present purposes a source of value premises, a culturally most important source. But it is a heterogeneous source when it comes to specific content and its specific applications to issues of socioeconomic policy. Generalized affirmation of values within the rubric of a particular religion, for example, will not suffice when specific policy decisions have to be made. It may be that the generalized values are operative only on one level of abstraction. Belief in the Thomist best alone is simply not unequivocally dispositive of specific problems of policy.

Such belief, however, may be significant for the degree of pluralism and toleration to be found in a society or, what may amount to the same thing, for the nature and degree of realization of the "whole person" when metaphysical doctrines are applied to problems of socioeconomic policy. No less celebrated a writer than Adam Smith was concerned about the excesses of superstition and the dangers of religious zeal (Smith 1937, pp. 754, 745, and passim). Social economists must be concerned about belief in absolutes, or the pretense of belief in absolutes, and its consequences for man and society. One must distinguish the policy analysis of values from the compulsion to reach and to affirm absolute values, whether the latter is advanced by a theological or a secular priest.

8. In discussions of values in a discipline like economics, including social economics, there tends to be a conflict between metaphysics and science. Both of these terms have been given variable meaning. For present purposes let us understand metaphysics as dealing with the absolute and ultimate, with that which cannot be rendered objective (depending, of course, on the criteria of what is "objective"), with the subjective and normative. Metaphysics is comprised of ontology, theology, ethics, aesthetics, and values. Science deals with the objective and the confirmable, and comprises the disciplines which attempt to combine strict logic with careful empiricism. We now have a deep appreciation that both metaphysics and science constitute different efforts at persuasion.[3] But the points that I want to emphasize are these: that while metaphysics and science can be so defined as to be mutually exclusive, in practice all disciplines are combinations of the two; that even if one can agree that there are areas of analysis which are distinctively amenable to the study of the objective and the confirmable, which is questionable in any absolute sense, there are other, important areas of human interest which are not so

designatable and which must be and are in fact made the subject of metaphysical inquiry.

9. It is desirable that I state my own theological position, as it must inevitably influence what I have to say. It is agnosticism, apropos of which I want to make three points: First, I do not believe that my agnosticism prevents me from appreciating either the nature or the operative implications of theological idealism. Second, theological idealism is particularly important for present purposes as a source of motivation and moral strength. And third, given my view that even if all social economists were theological idealists (even of the same religion) one would still have to choose between them as to substance, the practical significance of my agnosticism is minimal. Thus I accept metaphysics as an important mode or subject of inquiry, while I am ambivalent toward organized religion as social control, in a manner comparable to my ambivalence toward the state, especially its authoritarian, antipluralist tendencies or uses.

I am, of course, aware that for Christian (and *mutatis mutandis* for other) theological idealists the essential message of their religious belief system is otherworldly and concerned with salvation, and that their preeminent mission in this world is to spread the gospel of the salvation of the soul and is in those regards pan-political. The role of social economics (insofar as it is concerned with secular matters) in such a thought scheme is thus rather minimal.[4] Insofar as it has a place, however, then the present discussion applies. I intend to neither belittle nor ignore the theological message or belief system of the religious but such seems not overwhelmingly pertinent here, for the reason given.

I am also aware that the origins of social economics in the United States are manifestly Catholic: the present Association for Social Economics was initially the Catholic Economic Assocation. One has to be sensitive to the feelings of the founders and long-time members, but one also has to take the field as one currently finds it.

I am further aware that much of the foregoing emphasizes practical consequences and thus a preoccupation with the relative and a seeming denial of the absolute, that it reflects what is to some a skeptical view of the world, that it is consonant with an emphasis on power, that it comports with the view of God treated as illusion functioning as psychic balm and social control, and that it seems to give short shrift to Christian (and other religious) ideals qua ideals and perhaps even to ideals in general. Some of these perceptions are accurate, but I am certainly not affirming that a religious social economics is wrong, nor am I denigrating

--rather I am emphasizing--the ideational valuational process in society. As an agnostic, my pragmatism is functional rather than ontological and emphasizes the necessity of both selective perception and choice consequent to substantive differences in the specification and application of values. The discussion is consistant, pro tanto, with whatever degree of theological determinism one wants to combine with it. The discussion is not intended to be contrived in a manner prejudicial to the idealist but to emphasize the relevant necessity of choice. Nor is the discussion intended to glorify power, but to emphasize that where there is choice there is the weighting of preferences or of views, and that the weighting is by power (defined nonpejoratively as participation in decisionmaking and the bases thereof).

In these connections, I ought also to declare my view of the high-priest function, which I take to mean manifest function: the administration of belief and other duties on the basis of knowledge other than that which is pretended. One finds this both advocated and practiced in the world of affairs, by both sacerdotal and secular persons. On the one hand, I am uncomfortable with it; on the other, I think that its performance may possibly be inexorable.

10. It is also desirable that I state my own position as to school of thought. I am an eclectic who has a manifestly strong component of institutional economics, particularly of the Wisconsin-John R. Commons variety. This too must influence my evaluation.

The reader will have little difficulty in identifying the impact of the foregoing on what I have to say below.

THE THREE TRADITIONAL STRANDS

The chapters by O'Boyle, Hill, and Hunt represent theological idealism, pragmatism-instrumentalism, and materialism, respectively. Each of these positions can be stated in absolutist, mutually exclusive terms. If this were done, the protagonists of the three positions can only talk past one another. Although there are significant differences between the three, it is not my intention to stress these differences, but to see them as in part complementary, in part coinciding, and in part giving effect to each other.

O'Boyle stresses that social economics is economic science instructed by moral discipline. He affirms the role of the Papal Encyclicals in the process of moral discipline. He stresses the role of Heinrich Pesch in working out the modern conception of Catholic social economics.

Central to all of these is the role of values concerning human life and
welfare. O'Boyle concentrates on a solidarist conception of the errors
made by individualism and socialism with regard to the nature of man and
presents correlative diagnoses of the central problems and abuses
associated, respectively, with capitalism and socialism. In the second half
of his article, O'Boyle presents the solidarist conception of community
organization and ends.

Let me make the following comments with regard to O'Boyle's
article. First, it is a recognition, indeed a manifestation, of the service of
Catholic social economics--theological idealism--as social control. There
is no question but that he is correct. It is my own view that *all* of
economics serves as social control[5] and that, while one can juxtapose social
to neoclassical economics in the manner done by our several authors,
neoclassical economics is itself a form of economic science instructed by
moral discipline, that of utilitarian calculation combined with the values
of more goods are better than fewer goods, status emulation and justice
as resident in the notion of Pareto optimality given existing entitlements.
These three values are incomplete, but they are in fact forms of moral
discipline. Furthermore, it seems to me that both Marxist materialism, a
la Hunt, and institutionalist pragmatism-instrumentalism, a la Hill, also
represent modes of moral discipline involving values. All strands of social
economics are enlisted in the service of social control. All schools of
economics, including all strands of social economics, are participants in the
social valuational process and function as social control. All schools of
economic thought, certainly from Adam Smith on, recognize the necessity
of moral rules and of what I shall call institutionalized processes for their
development and application to practical problems.

Second, the solidarist approach to the conflict between individualism and socialism is a valuable source of correction. But, given the
aforementioned complexities of the problem of order, there are innumerable ways in which solidarist thinkers can resolve the conflicts
between freedom and control, continuity and change, and hierarchy and
equality. The solidarist offers an approach but not a conclusive detailed
solution to the problem of order, for example, the conflict between so-
called individualism and socialism. There are multiple interpretations and
thus multiple potential applications of the various Papal Encyclicals.
Catholic moral values often appear absolute but are flexible with regard
to other values and to time and place, at least on the level of application.
Its malleability is one of its strengths, even though to some the point will

appear to be dangerously relativistic. But especially is it a contributor to, and a participant in, the total social valuational process.

Third, O'Boyle agrees, with Pesch, that man's higher end is twofold: his individual perfection in union with God, and his social perfection by means of a cooperative effort with other men in order to promote the welfare of the entire human community. Let it be understood that neoclassical, Marxian, and institutional economists also believe that theirs are modes of achieving cooperative efforts in order to promote the welfare of the entire human community. I do not want to diminish social economics by making such a statement, but rather to show one way in which these other schools may be understood (in the same manner as comprehending them as contributing to social control) and to suggest that the notion "promote the welfare of the entire human community" can be understood, even within social economics alone, in different ways. One of the social-control functions of religion is to form and channel aspiration to the end of personal and social "improvement," a term which I encapsulate in quotes to emphasize that improvement, and the aspirations functional to its realization, are at least in part both system-specific and flexible (relative), the determination of which is what social control is in part all about.

My main point, however, has to do with O'Boyle's affirmation that in Catholic social economic thought both man's end and the goal of the economy are to provide for man's material needs as well as for the development of man's character. He says that there are two distinct aspects of those needs: the need for income sufficient for human well-being and the need for work. It seems to me that among the key values shared by social economics, Marxism, and institutionalism are these: that work is central to the creation and realization of human identity, not something merely to be reckoned negatively as disutility; that the foregoing requires participation in decisionmaking in the workplace and in matters pertaining to it, that is, participatory economic democracy; and that opportunity to work is the principal means by which, in the modern economy, the great mass of people are able to acquire the means required for human well-being, even aside from work as central to human identity (see Samuels et al., 1984). Lutz's humanistic social economics is in full agreement with these ideas.

This means that every economic system must be understood and evaluated in terms that transcend (but which do not exclude) considerations of both production and distribution: provision of employment as a means to income. (That this remains controversial suggests the limited

impact of the Keynesian revolution.) The irony that juxtaposed to what
O'Boyle calls moral discipline is what many economists call the discipline
of the reward and incentive system of any economy, should not obscure
this arguably more transcendent (but not independent) consideration.
Perhaps the point is that the provision of employment as a means to
income, through the operation of the wage system, need not be contemplated solely in terms of capitalist businessmen or socialist commissars.

If all of our authors agree on the general importance of values and
the valuational process, provision of employment as a means to income
and identity is one key specific value on which they seem to all agree. But
notice two things: that each might propose different means to its achievement, means which are so distinguished by other values as to appear if
not actually to be in conflict; and that this particular value needs somehow
to be related to and balanced with other values. The social valuational
process is not so simple as to permit the unabashed affirmation of one
such value. On the other hand, it seems true that all modern socioeconomic systems have seriously neglected the value of the provision of
employment as a means to income and to identity. Alas.

Fourth, there seems to exist within social economics--and in all
ideologies and within all schools of economic thought--a tension between
emphases on *order* and on *liberty*, a tension which can be stated in other
ways as well, for example, between closure and openness, between those
who, wanting to impose or to seek correct values, find them in the status
quo and those who find only wrong, or primarily wrong, values in the
status quo. Order in practice tends to be identified in terms of one or
another specification of the status quo (thus the need to choose between
idealizations of the status quo). Liberty, when it is not understood solely
or principally in terms of the status quo's pattern of freedom and control,
tends to be identified as the ability to differentiate oneself from or to
change the status quo. This is very complicated and subject to kalei-
doscopic formulations which cannot be comprehensively surveyed here, due
to the vast complexities of the overriding problem of order described
above. But some social economists emphasize order, at least their conception of order, and others liberty, at least their conception of liberty. This
is the case notwithstanding that liberty is always a function of control and
that the system of order always gives rise to some pattern of liberty.

The point here is that any particular system or situation of moral
discipline can be seen, depending hermeneutically on one's initial
premise(s), affirmatively or negatively, as political absolutism or tyranny,
or as the social control necessary for the achievement of a certain

understanding of freedom and moral values. Individualism, socialism, and nationalism, to mention but three, are ideologies that have been used to sustain the moral advance but also the moral degradation of man, depending upon one's point of view or values, and both can be explicated in terms of different conceptions of order and of liberty. Moral discipline under the aegis of theological idealism has a mixed record, to put the matter gently.

The further point arises that because, as O'Boyle says, "man is one and not several, there is a need to reconcile any differences in views held about man not only within a given domain but also across domains and to work out any implications for theory and applications in each of the affected sciences." This need for reconciliation is key, and the point is that social economists, like all other human beings, must confront the question: reconciliation on which or whose terms? There is no escaping this inexorable necessity of choice. The seeming attractiveness of any status quo is that it provides a ready-made answer, one which will continue absent a decision to the contrary, absent the agony of having to choose what is to be changed or, more accurately, will change depending upon the operation of its particular mode of change. This is the great strength of any status quo and the significance of its privileged position. But it is also its great weakness, because accepting the status quo on its own terms begs the underlying problem. If the reader declines to accept that statement with regard to the society in which he or she lives, then the reader ought to ask if it applies to some society which he or she finds disagreeable.

In these regards, the genius of Marxism is to emphasize the relevance, indeed the importance, of the mode of production and its accompanying social relations, therefore of the structure of social power, for understanding the existential meaning and conditions of applicability of values. And it is the genius of the pragmatic-instrumentalist institutionalist to stress the relevance, indeed the importance, within given circumstances, of the consequences of values, especially those pertaining to power structure. Both Marxism and pragmatism-instrumentalism stress the limits of considering values in a vacuum. Both, it seems to me, stress the relevance--as an empirical matter and not as a conservative principle of policy--of the fact of unintended and unforeseen consequences in the pursuit and realization of values.

Thus, one of the things that has to be worked out is the substance to be adduced to what O'Boyle calls "man's authentic nature" or the "vision of man as a co-creator of the universe" and what Hunt calls "unalienated" man. One facet of this is the role of moral principles, as developed, for example, in Papal Encyclicals, as a check on concentrated private and state power. Another facet is working out what is to be meant, in particular circumstances, by "overly centralized" and "overly decentralized" decision-making, or by "excessive individualism" and "excessive collectivism," especially in a world of hierarchy and externalities. These matters arise whether or not one takes a theological idealist position. These terms are incomplete and lack specificity, and require normative judgment in their application.

Still another facet is working out that which, both in general and in detail, is attributed to God and to man. Another is working out what will be accepted as "productive" and the mode of its substantive determination. Still another is working out the substantive content of rights, including but not limited to property rights, in circumstances in which it is felt that they should be considered "inviolate," involving conflicts of interests and of rights in a world of hierarchy and externalities. Yet another is the working out of the details constituting the "individual" and the "social" in a world in which both are aspects of personhood. Finally, inter alia, there is the working out of conflicts between values, between moral rules, and between social control institutions in a world of plural values, plural moral rules, and plural social control institutions. I advance these considerations as generic matters; in practical cases they are always given selective, subjective content, depending upon how the hermeneutic circle is breached.

I have stressed above, using the language of O'Boyle and Hunt, the value of the development of authentic, unalienated man and of the society in which the welfare of the entire human community can be promoted. Marc Tool (1986, p. 10), the institutionalist, using the language of Fagg Foster, has affirmed a particular principle of value, to wit: "Act or judge in a manner to 'provide for the continuity of human life and noninvidious re-creation of community through the instrumental use of knowledge,'" a formulation which permits, among other things, both continuity and change. Also to be stressed is the more specific but still general value of access to employment as a means of income, participation in decisionmaking, and identity. Apropos of both values I want, without intending to compromise them in any fundamental way, to state the following argument: First, those two values have a degree of specificity relative to other values but remain sufficiently general as to require considerable specific implementation and thus reference to other values. How does one specifically promote access to employment in a manner conducive to the acquisition of income, participation in decisionmaking, and identity, say, in the form of noninvidious recreation of community? The values themselves go only so far in leading us to means and to the utilization of other complementary or supplementary values.[6]

The several strands of social economics, notwithstanding the fact that they seem to coincide in affirming the two values, constitute only frameworks within which the values themselves must be analyzed and worked out; that is, they are, and are part of the larger, social valuation processes, not statements of complete and unequivocal final values and means. In partial contrast, neoclassical economics, with its quest for determinate, unique, optimal solutions, and with its focus on price per se, both narrows and trivializes valuation and social decisionmaking and ends up either with empty formal solutions or substantive solutions that give effect to implicit antecedent normative premises--premises which social economists typically demand to have made explicit and to have examined critically rather than bury and take for granted. I said in partial contrast, because neoclassical economics does help explicate how markets work, the process of reaching commutative equivalence, and the mechanics of choice, among other things. I said help explicate how markets work, because in both the Marxist and (especially) the institutionalist view of the economy, the market is more than an abstract mechanism. It is a set of institutions that give rise to, structure, and operate through demand-and-supply relationships. So neoclassical economics tends to give effect to the desire of many social economists for specific, determinate solutions to problems, but can do so only on the basis of limiting assumptions to which the derived solutions are essentially tautological. At best, in the case of all schools, and of all strands forming a school, we have a mode of discourse, a framework, within which to work out solutions--and which must interact with other modes of discourse and other frameworks in the total social valuational, decisionmaking process.

Hunt's socialist perspective stresses the importance of existential material conditions and the social structure accompanying those conditions. Values, in this view, cannot be contemplated in the abstract alone. Aquinas argued that when reason comes to particular cases reason requires more than general principles; it also requires particular principles. In a comparable manner, the operative meaning of a value is at least in part in terms of the social situation in which it is contemplated. Thus, for example, the value "freedom" (or individual autonomy within society) is always a matter of the specific social system, the particular structure of freedom and control. The same is true of justice and welfare (see Gordon, 1980). One must understand and reckon with the total structure of power as well as the complex belief system of the society. One must be able to view a socioeconomic system at arm's length, independent of its own terms, for every system will project an ideology which, by accepting the terms of the system, will function to persuade one of its nobility.

As Hunt argues, capitalism creates the impression that social relations and social activities are not important and that capitalism can best be understood in terms of prices or market relations, that is, capitalism obfuscates the phenomena of power. Capitalism is not unique in this; this obfuscatory function is performed in all societies. This is particularly important when it comes to the reification of a function and its identification with a social class (whether understood in Marxian terms or not), perhaps with the further attribution of its "productivity." Such attributions are system-specific and normative rather than positive; they are derivative and legitimizing of institutionalized claims to income--in the case of capital, for example, it is a matter less of a technical economic category (plant and equipment) and more of a social category (representative of the highest hierarchical positions in a particular system).

But stressing the importance of material conditions and power structure does not prevent Hunt from centering on reaching the maximum human development inherent, as he puts it, in human genetic potential. This is the view which is so much akin to Catholic and institutionalist value principles. Of course, there still needs to be worked out in detail both what is meant by human potential and the proper means thereto, as well as the meaning of alienation.

Hill adds that while we must keep our valuational sights high we also should keep our practical feet on the ground and be concerned with consequences. Not unlike Hunt, Hill stresses holism and evolutionism, but his stress is on pragmatism and instrumentalism. From my point of view, these are not so much, if at all, theories of truth (certainly not Truth) but of meaning, especially human meaning (and it is at this point wherein pragmatism and theological idealism may conflict, but wherein one still has to choose between the various formulations of theological idealism). Moreover, the fact that something "works" means that we are applying not only deductive and inductive reasoning but also normative or valuational understanding, that is, values.

As Hill puts it, pragmatism and instrumentalism are value-directed, based on an applied axiology which must be used to evaluate the desirability or undesirability of practical consequences. As he also argues, following Peirce, metaphysical and theological values, so far from being merely mythical superstition or irrational dogmas or liturgical ceremonies, can have instrumental value. The key is what promotes the life process of man. But this concept is not self-defining: the details as to what it means and what promotes it have to be worked out--and, says Hill, they are worked out in a pragmatic manner of which the social valuational process is an important part. While all of our authors seem to agree that practical policies lauded by social economics are to constitute ameliorative socioeconomic reform and promote an improved quality of life for all people, but especially for the presently disadvantaged and impoverished, it is also true that the details of all this have to be worked out. The key, it seems to me, is that the people whose interests are at risk should to the greatest extent possible be involved in working this out. But that is easier said than done in a world of huge populations, enormous multipoint sources of cumulative externalities, uneven educational achievement, and differential economic and political power--though to recognize this predicament is not ipso facto to conclude a policy.

Perhaps the most proximate question found in Hill's essay is that raised by Lutz in the quote to which Hill responds. The question seems to concern what Lutz considers irreconcilable differences between secularism and spiritualism--the problem marking this essay as well. Lutz finds pragmatism and instrumental value theory possessed of "the same radical naturalism and relativism that is the sad hallmark of the modern secularized mind; a mind increasingly alienated from its own spiritual self and source of dignity." Lutz may well be correct here: our secularism prevents us from going beyond the image of man resident in pragmatism and relativism, even from fully comprehending his point.

But even if we all assume that there is an absolute practical or theological idealism, or a transcendent spiritualism, we still need to determine which version is the correct one; just as, if we assume practical realism, we still need to determine what the actual policy is to be. In both cases we cannot avoid the burden of human choice. Neither holy scripture nor human authority is monolithic; different perspectives with varying policy implications are found in and/or attributed to each. Among those who trust the word of God, there are profound differences as to just what that word signifies for human affairs in concrete instances. It may well be that O'Boyle's notion of man as co-creator of the universe encompasses the substance of working out resolutions of those differences, though certainly not all persons will accept the idea of co-creation (though the argument may be as to level of meaning of "co-creation"). Hill's response, that the respective value systems of instrumental institutionalism and social economics are completely compatible, affirms both the importance of values to each and the significance of theological idealism as a viable part of the total valuational process. Neither his nor my response, let it be observed, denigrates religion as a way of life or, for that matter, as social control or psychic balm. It is a major source and/or embodiment of values--however much it is also true that those values are subject to selective application.

That all this "working out" is complicated and problematic, as well as emotionally anxiety-creating, is nicely illustrated by one of Hill's quotations from Peirce, wherein it is argued that "The opinion which is fated to be ultimately agreed to by all who investigate is what we mean by the truth, and the object represented by this opinion is the real." Now there is a great deal of truth to this view of truth (and of the real): the conventionalist, or consensus, view of truth is highly descriptively accurate in economics. But what does one have when one has consensus, even unanimity? Only, I suggest, consensus and unanimity, nothing necessarily beyond. Why? First, it is hubris to claim more for consensus than the fact of consensus itself. Second, the consensus may change. Third, the consensus may be driven by something external to the discussion, for example, the dominant ideology, power structure, culture or mode of production, or some combination thereof. Fourth, even given consensus as to general doctrine it is unlikely that consensus extends to all the details thereof. I would have the foregoing remarks apply equally to a world in which the consensus was neoclassicist, institutionalist, or Marxist. I am not prepared to equate orthodoxy, of any kind, with truth (Truth). Again, pragmatism and instrumentalism are much more a theory of meaning than of truth (Truth), especially insofar as the latter refers to the definition of reality subject to an epistemological correspondence test. And, of course, even if one is concerned with truth, one has to choose between claimants.

Several other matters can be noted at this point. One is that social economics needs to be concerned both with the values which constitute "virtue" and the institutions (including belief systems) which help define the "social." Focus on individual virtue is important, but it can be used to avoid consideration and reform of institutions and systems; focus on institutions and systems, including their reform, are important, but ought not be used to distract consideration of personal behavior. The reader will by now not be surprised to have me say that the specific details of what constitutes virtue and the evaluation of institutions need to be worked out.

The second is implicit in the foregoing: The record of human history, including the present, is what comprises the data of the social sciences, including economics. Data, of course, is theory or ideology laden; it is a social product. But it is especially a matter of the past. Human values and decisionmaking, in contrast, are futuristic: they relate to the world of the future, the human history as yet unwritten because not yet created. They relate to and indeed are instrumental in the creation of the mankind and society, the history, of the future. Perhaps the deepest message common to all strands of social economics is that mankind cannot forego the burden of action, that in endeavoring through systematic inquiry to apprehend the future of man and society, or to know what God has in mind for man, both man and society in the future are in that process at least to some extent created. This message counts even if one believes in the transcendental--unless one leaves everything to God and nothing to man, which I do not see being done in any strand of social economics. Even if one believes in absolutes, experience suggests that we still have to work out the details.

By way of preliminary conclusion, it tells me something instructive about the compatibility of the strands of social economics to read of Heinrich Pesch that "he did not argue on the level of most ethical discussions, which up to now have taken place in an illusory world of speculative possibilities and moral rigour rather than in a world constrained by fact and of explanatory hypotheses. Furthermore, Pesch avoided postulating the *absolute* observance of ethical norms by the imperfect man in his natural and imperfect surroundings" (Recktenwald, 1987, p. 852). We not only need discussions constrained by fact and of explanatory hypotheses but also speculation as to what might constitute the better world in the making. The conceptualization of such possibilities has been the historic glory of theological idealism.

Another way of making the point is to affirm what may be called the Zen Buddhist limitation of utopist theological idealism: that one ought to be cautious in passing judgment, especially "final judgment." One can and must be observant, interpretive, speculative, and understanding (at least in the sense of *verstehen* and possibly in the sense of what Adam Smith called sympathy), all in search of enlightenment, rather than the myopic affirmation of a particularistic and exclusivist creed. Such a view would make the antinomies of absolutism-relativism, philosophical realism-idealism, and so on, much less fearsome.

THE FOURTH STRAND

In certain respects Etzioni's deontological socioeconomics is close to the theological idealism of O'Boyle, though perhaps it is better denominated as moral idealism; while in certain other respects it is rather close to Hill's pragmatism and instrumentalism.

Etzioni, through the medium of a critique of the neoclassical treatment of preferences, affirms two things: the importance to human beings of binding moral rules or duties, and the critical role of social economics in studying the formation of both ordinary preferences and moral commitments. It is unequivocal that moral rules are important to the organization, operation, and performance of the socioeconomy. Etzioni is correct in affirming the dependence of market (as well as all other) economies on a facilitative set of moral rules, and in acknowledging the tendency of market economies to undermine the very institutions (legal and moral) which both render them possible and structure them. No matter how one phrases the matter, the mono-utility construction (including its various defensive realignments, as Etzioni notes) blurs important distinctions and begs serious questions--a statement which undoubtedly can be applied to the interpretation given in this article as well.

But one has to be cautious here. Affirming the importance of moral values, as Etzioni surely is aware, does not exhaust the relevant body of social analysis. First, moral rules represent both social control and individual protection. Moral rules inexorably function as social control, especially as they become internalized. The protection of individual, human values against perceived debasement by utilitarian considerations is itself social control. Let us not evade the point: religion and morality constitute social control. That they may be understood in terms of protecting a nobler from a more debased self does not vitiate this situation.

Second, there is the inexorable necessity of choice in choosing between moral rules when they come in conflict and in determining the structure of society, especially the distributions of power, responsibility, and duties among individuals or groups of individuals. This, too, is social control and it encompasses the necessity of choice.

Third, there is the inexorable necessity of having to balance continuity with change with regard to both the substance and the application of moral rules. There is no need for me to consider what some may deem the critical matter, the identification of absolute, unchanging moral rules. For even if we assume that there are absolute, unchanging moral rules, we still have to choose among various offerings and suggestions as to what they are, possible resolutions of conflicts between moral rules, and suggested changes in those resolutions. Even those who believe in absolute, unchanging moral rules typically do not pursue lives of passive resignation; the religious fundamentalist is often as activist in the secular world as the nonbeliever.

Fourth, even if, indeed especially because, one questions the utilitarian, instrumental rationality of considerations of costs and benefits, because costs and benefits must themselves be made subject to moral considerations, it nonetheless remains true that moral rules themselves must be and are made subject to consequentialist evaluation. It is true that, as Etzioni argues, to "introduce cost/benefit analysis into our 'temples' is to diminish their values, to violate their taboos." But this is only one side of the matter. Values themselves are in fact made subject to an evaluative process, with regard to them considered both independent of other values and in juxtaposition to other values.[7] (This is especially important in regard to the role of values in comprehending "consequences" --which like "facts" are also theory- and/or value-dependent.) The necessity of choice consequent even to belief in absolute values, as above, inexorably opens the door to consequentialist--and thereby "cost" and "benefit"--considerations. Pragmatism or instrumentalism is inexorable, whether we like it, or like to recognize it, or not.[8] But so is valuation-- and that is the distinctive message of social economics.

There are two different contextual senses of the term "moral." One refers to the generic idea of the category "moral," quite independent of the substance of what is deemed to constitute morality. The other refers to the more or less precise specification of what constitutes morality --which may be society- or culture-specific.

Because of what the sociologist and psychologist calls internalization of social control, and for other reasons, including the exercise of deliberative choice as to what values one will claim one's own, people, as Etzioni stresses, do attempt to live up to their moral values. But this must not obscure the individual and social processes that operate to determine the limited range of moral values within which individuals are enabled to choose what will be their moral values. Nor, as Etzioni also insists, must it obscure either the wider range of forces governing preferences of all kinds or the role of power therein.

Etzioni chastises mainstream economics for its ostensible neglect, actually its obfuscated introduction, of values in the imagery of a value-free economics. There is no value-free social or policy science; at least this is a safer presumption than the opposite. The task of economists and other social scientists is not to impose, especially surreptitiously, their own values but rather to facilitate the valuational process, in part by making values explicit and by helping both recognize and analyze values--which in part must include the evaluation of various values in terms of consequences and tradeoffs. This fourth strand of social economics, then, as portrayed by Etzioni, manifests some of the same problems as do the first three strands: the absolutist versus relativist nature of moral rules; whether the individual is a given or a social product; the conflict between practical idealism and practical realism; the complexity of the elements comprising the problem of order; and *inter alia* the consequences of the inexorable fact of the process through which moral values and rules are worked out. In so many of these respects the existence of the problem is testimony more of the psychology than of the nature of moral values-- though this should not be taken as a denial of metaphysics.

We come now to Lutz's rendition of humanistic social economics.[9] It too stresses the higher nature of human beings and human dignity.

It would appear that Lutz's "humanistic" social economics is a complex and subtle blend of theological idealism and human-centered ("secular"?) thought. He does not want to completely discard the theological, but he wants to have a larger place for mankind's working out its own destiny than theological absolutism or determinism seems traditionally to have allowed. This is, of course, a venerable problem: the greater the role permitted for man, perhaps the less allowed to God. Again we are in a context of co-creationism. Perhaps man is fulfilling God's will, but such requires selective perception as to all things done by man, some morally offensive--which raises the question whether God permits all that is done by man, including the morally offensive.

Lutz's approach is humanistic but, although it has an apparent Thomist aspect to it, it represents a more or less substantial departure from scholasticism.

Consider Lutz's classic statement of what I consider the Thomist approach to policy analysis: the "strong conviction that deep down there is in every context an ultimately right set of economic institutions, a best and humanly most appropriate way to organize an economy." My first point is that not much of what follows is manifestly particularly either derivative or reflective of this position.

Second, it seems to me that what is the "ultimately right set of economic institutions" and what is the "best and humanly most appropriate way to organize an economy" will be interpreted differently by different people, and that therefore these things remain to be worked out.

Third, notice that Lutz writes of human needs and human values. There may be a latent implantation of these needs and values in man by God, but the emphasis here seems to be on the human rather than the divine, at least in contrast with medieval scholasticism (and perhaps modern fundamentalism).

Fourth, although he writes of human needs, much of the subsequent discussion is of human values in the sense of goals, something arguably less absolute or predetermined.

Fifth, at several points Lutz affirms the objective and intercultural validity of values. He does this in summarizing Hobson (for whom he also notes that the lower values are grounded in human physical needs and the higher in the sustaining of society and enrichment of human personality or self-respect); in arguing that basic values are not affected by conflicting manifestations of them between different cultures; in arguing that Kant's concept of the intrinsic dignity of man "cannot be fitted within a naturalistic framework that deifies empirical science and discounts any domain above the sensory world of material and social phenomena" such that "social economics is bound to be given a non-naturalistic, spiritual bent"; in affirming a Kantian "objective ontological foundation for dignity" and "an economics centered on human values taken as objectively valid"; and in arguing that humanistic social economists see their task not as pragmatically making truth but seeking to discover what is true.

But Lutz also rejects as having a truncated picture of one-dimensional men any approach that contemplates the "best" accommodations of the interactions of atomistic rational men; faults what he considers the instrumentalist denial of genuine human free will; faults the Marxian conception of human nature as too materialistic and overly deterministic; and notes that because of "its strong democratic faith deeply anchored in a long tradition," humanistic economics "refrains from advocating authoritarian imposition of its values on a public that for various reasons may presently lack for the time being the willingness to pursue that goal."

Lutz needs to work out the relationships between his theological idealism and his human-centered corpus of values, and, inter alia, the relationship between his belief in a set of Thomist best-policy solutions and his democratic faith with its implication of the necessity for a free and viable process of reaching workable collective decisions--though perhaps this calls for more synthesis than the subject permits (which, if true, is itself important).

So much for my first concern, the relationship between theological idealism and humanistic social economics. Second, it seems to me that for all of Lutz's discussion of values--typically values with which I concur--there remains the necessity for social processes within which substantive content is to be adduced or worked out or attributed to these values. For example: Lutz writes of Sismondi becoming "more and more disturbed by the increasing suffering and hardship" which accompanied the laissez-faire post-Napoleonic economy. But surely we understand that one of the fundamental questions facing any society is that of the identification of injury and of evidence of injury. Every society comprises a structure of sacrifice, and most if not all critical issues of socioeconomic policy have to do with the distribution of sacrifice. Society has to work out which injuries it will accept as potential or actual objects of corrective action and which it will ignore, which it will consider the inescapable costs of progress.

Other examples of things that must be worked out include: Whether and when production and work satisfies or frustrates our constructive and creative propensities. When materialism and greed are "excessive." What constitutes the human qualities of self-awareness and social consciousness. What is meant by "realization of our *social* nature" as distinct from "individual material needs and wants driven by greed or lust for pleasure and power." When competitiveness is "excessive." When work is meaningful and when inordinately fragmented and worker alienating. When one has achieved "the highest possible degree of decentralized community decision-making in both economic and political affairs." In every case, the invocation of a value is accompanied by the operation of selective perception and application. One can agree with the goal of increasing human well-being and enabling the utmost development of *all men*, but this value, as important as it is, does not unequivocally point to "the ultimately right set of institutions" or the best practices of economic policy. Further means-end amplification must be made. Unless one makes careful provision in both theory and practice for the processes of working these things out, social economics will appear to be either so much wishful thinking, moral absolutism, or simply incomplete.

I think that Lutz would not disagree: He articulates as "the straightforward organizing principle underlying our humanistic vision of social economics: social and economic institutions and policies should be constructed to enable *for all* as much material and social need satisfaction and human dignity as available resources will permit." He goes on immediately to say that "This norm is believed to be objectively true and valid, but open to critical discussion and falsification attempts. This normative principle is grounded in a human personality seen as essentially moral and social in nature. Moreover, these basic values are not affected by conflicting manifestations of these values between different cultures. They transcend both culture and social agreement and are grounded in humanity, and are therefore universal."

One can agree with his valuational sentiments while questioning the idealistic universalist claims and also agreeing that critical discussion and something like falsification is involved in working out the normative principle.[10] He uses the term falsification, I think, because he believes that the "norm is objectively true and valid," that is, it is a matter of a claim of it being true in reality; whereas I would apply a more pragmatic test, with pragmatism not directed toward truth in an epistemological sense but the normative (really normative cum positive) category of workability. One can distinguish between his ontological approach, his social economics considered as (an approach to) policy analysis, and the real-world need to work these things out through interpersonal and interinstitutional interaction.

Third, humanistic social economics, whether or not defined to include medieval scholastic socioeconomic thought, is not alone in seeking the superimposition of values on economic life. Both classical and neoclassical, as well as Marxian, economics represent systems of values. Indeed, the historic significance of these schools consists to no small degree of the revolutions which they helped contribute to the human, social valuational process. One may not fully like the values that they promote, but they are values nonetheless. The problem of values is not resolved by invoking the category of values or specific values; the problem of values must be worked out. The question is not about the presence or absence of values per se but which values, the tradeoffs among values, and the process of formulating and choosing them, including working out, on the basis of experience and normative evaluation thereof, complex and problematic means-ends relations--for example, the relations of capitalism and the Industrial Revolution to capital accumulation and the welfare "of all." Here, too, I think that Lutz would not disagree. But again the matter (having to work things out) needs to be made explicit. The belief in or pretense of theological realism or determinism is no more persuasive than that of scientific realism or determinism when it comes to practical socioeconomic policy.

Thus one can affirm the critical role of "considerations of moral obligation and commitment in response to the ideals and values of a higher or more authentic self," one possessed of self-awareness and social consciousness, and that "Whether we see that higher self as a 'social self' or a 'spiritual self' is another matter." But precise meaning has to be given to all these terms: moral obligation, commitment, ideals and values of a higher or more authentic self; and these meanings remain to be worked out.

Elsewhere in his chapter, however, we have glimpses of a firmer theological idealism, for example, in Lutz's statements that "social economics is bound to be given a non-naturalistic, spiritual bent" and that "humanistic thinkers, for more than a century, have been uncomfortable with 'naturalism', a philosophical perspective greatly enhanced by Darwinian evolution and which seeks to understand Man and social ethics from an essentially *biological* point of view, while neglecting or discounting a meaningful spiritual domain." One can sympathize with his dismay over what sometimes appears as a biological determinism. But the key question involves the relative roles of divine teleology, nonteleological natural selection and human discretion.

Must we assume that "morality and ethics have to be grounded in something that transcends the social domain?" Do we need something "more than merely a nominalist construction . . . a philosophy of the kind of non-naturalistic realism we have in the deontological framework of Kant"? While for a (Christian) theological idealist values are presumably grounded in this manner, this view is not dispositive of the issues to which it is addressed. One still has to choose between alternative substantive contents adduced to theological idealism. Theological idealism may be True or it may instrumentally function as psychic balm and legitimation, but as a source of persuasive values one still has to pick and choose among both contestants and their applications.

Let me make my position unequivocally (though, of course, neither very comfortably nor uncontroversially) clear: first, even if all social economists believed that a spiritualistic (supernaturalistic) bent had to be given to social economics, such social economists very likely would disagree as to the analyses and policies they envisioned as flowing from that spiritualistic approach. Theological idealism is a legitimate point of view, but it actually comprises legitimate *points* of view. One need only acknowledge the conflict between Social Gospel and Social Darwinist, or conservative fundamentalist, movements within Christianity to understand the point I am making.[11] The Christian message (not to neglect the

Hebrew, Moslem, and other messages) has been interpreted as both con-firming-reinforcing and challenging-sabotaging existing arrangements, including structural inequalities. Some believe that capitalism is fully consistent with the message of Christ, whereas others believe that the two are inconsistent, the ethic of capitalism understood to be egoism and the ethic of Christianity to be love.

Second, theological idealism is in fact one of the means through which social economics is informed. Even for believers it is much more a discursive framework within which descriptive and policy analysis is worked out than a body of settled values, analyses, or conclusions.

Third, social economics is not, or not necessarily, limited to theological idealism; the latter is only one source of social economics. Not all discussion of values requires the invocation of the spiritual, though invocation of the spiritual need not and ought not be excluded, so long as it is willing to participate in an open-ended valuational process. There is unquestionably a strong place for spiritualistic (theological idealist) approaches to social economics, but those approaches do not comprise all of social economics. This does not mean that the believer must com-promise or disregard his or her values or ontology to be a social economist.

Fourth, utilization of a theological mode of discourse does not unequivocally add to the putative standing of a value.

Fifth, the relation of religion to man involves more than a possible exogenously originating source of transcendent values. Religion may involve projection by mankind of certain hopes and fears. Different types of godliness envision and use different social values as support systems. Various concepts of religion and of God become useful adjuncts to varying modes of the advancement and suppression of particular values and practices.[12]

Sixth, social economics must be self-critical. It should not exist to either represent or blindly accept some supernatural or metaphysical system--though saying so neither denies nor denigrates the possibility of such beliefs.[13]

At least some of the foregoing is implicit if not explicit in Lutz's discussion of Catholic social economics in humanistic perspective. He notes the unease which many humanists have had with "many aspects of Catholic dogmas and the authority of the Church." In his acknowledge-ment that "Nevertheless, almost all of them did not reject some sort of Christianity . . ." he seems implicitly to acknowledge the problem of having to choose between forms of Christianity[14] and of Christian messages applicable to issues of socioeconomic policy. That "just about all felt the need for a strong spiritual foundation for their socioeconomic creed" is not dispositive of the question whether a strong spiritual foundation is uniquely dispositive of issues of socioeconomic policy--quite aside from other questions, such as the status of Christianity relative to other religions.

At the same point where Lutz notes the importance of considerations of moral obligation and commitment he also says that the reason why "morality and ethics have to be grounded in something that transcends the social domain" is that we cannot otherwise explain how members of a society "agree to agree in the first place." But one need only follow the argument of Adam Smith's *Theory of Moral Sentiments* that through the operation of the principles of approbation and disapprobation people work out and continually revise judgments of the propriety of the actions of oneself and of others whence issue moral rules. (Also note one of the arguments of his *Lectures on Jurisprudence* that moral rules can also be imposed coercively by hierarchically dominant groups or rulers.) One can resort to a nonspiritual explanation (say, a spontaneous order explanation) of the formation of moral rules and of social cooperation--though admittedly this may still not be satisfactory for some persons precisely because it does not encompass the transcendental.[15]

I must applaud Lutz's emphasis on political and economic democracy. Social economics, tendencies for religious or theological absolutism aside, seems unequivocally to stand for greater economic pluralism, for wider participation in both economy and polity for all people, in all countries--though the precise form of participation remains to be worked out. On the one hand, social economists seem to perceive this as the tendency of much of the history of the last several centuries; on the other, they lament the continued and/or new concentrations and abuses of power which they observe.

But I am not sure that we have advanced to the point where it can be unequivocally said, or even as strongly affirmed as Lutz seems to want to be read, that worker cooperatives embody "the increasingly central goals of the humanistic vision" and that social economics is "the only perspective that by its own inner logic makes the case for economic democracy in the form of employee self-management." Whether a particular institutional configuration, itself subject to variegated constructions, can so readily be deemed to constitute the "best and humanly most appropriate way to organize an economy" seems highly question-begging, however felicitous the sentiments advanced to support it. The institution of the worker cooperative does not have the capacity to resolve unequivocally all of the multiplicity of problems that focus on work, work group versus work group relations, work group versus consumer relations, and externality and public goods issues--all of which are ubiquitous and important issues of inter-dependence. Affirmation of worker self-managed firms as anything more than a viable experimental institution is inconclusive if not dubious. It seems to me that the complex meaning of economic democracy in practice is something that has to be worked out, if only because arrangements intended to diffuse power in one direction may concentrate power in another, and arrangements understood in terms of freedom in one respect may also be comprehended in terms of control (coercion) in another. Economic democracy is not so simple that it can be achieved by one overriding institutional innovation.

There are two dangers: one involves actual or perceived confusion of positive and normative social economics, the other involves the actual or seeming restriction of both positive and normative social economics to making the case for worker cooperatives or other worker-managed organizations.[16] The distinctive genius of social economics is its insistence, first, on the importance of values and the total valuational process and, second, that both values and the valuational process be made both explicit and the object of inquiry. It may or may not involve an identification with particular values but it certainly is not an identification with specific institutional arrangements which problematically promote certain values.

There are several further specific matters in Lutz's chapter that warrant comment. First, his defense of protectionism is very subject to abuse, as are all protectionist lines of reasoning. Internationalization of the labor market has involved threats to the living standards of workers in the developed countries and both opportunity and danger for workers in the developing countries. Systematic targeting by some countries of industries in other countries coupled with policies to promote huge balance of payments surpluses have made a mockery of "free trade." But protectionism is no fundamental solution to the problems so generated. On the other hand, given systematic manipulation of foreign trade by some countries, there is no conclusive reason why a country cannot seek to bring about freer access to the others' markets.

Second, while institutionalism is pragmatic and instrumentalist, Lutz's dismissive attitude is at least in part misplaced.

1. He writes that for Ayres "All 'reason' is confined to *instrumental* reason, there is no recognition of 'ends-in-themselves' and no appreciation of 'disinterested' motives." Given what I have had to say about the

necessity for choice even if one adopts a theological idealist or practical idealist position, and that such choice must and will inevitably involve instrumental considerations, this criticism is too strong if not simply wrong.

2. Lutz interprets institutionalist instrumentalism as denying genuine human free will. Two points: first, here he is on slippery ground, inasmuch as the theological idealist has to confront the problem of theological determinism, or the relative roles of God and man. Second, although there is a strong technological determinism in the Veblen-Ayres strand of institutionalism, there is almost none in the Wisconsin-Commons strand, and even in the former strand this seems (to this writer at least) to involve much more conditionism than determinism (see Samuels, 1977).

3. Lutz laments the tendency of instrumentalism "to deny the very possibility of absolute truths, or of an ethics that is ontologically rather than socially grounded." While this is undoubtedly so, the practical consequence of this does not, so far as I can see, distinguish the cultural relativism of institutionalist instrumentalism from the kind of ontological absolutism seemingly preferred by Lutz. This is because even if all social economists accepted ontological absolutism there would still have to be the exercise of choice to determine just what that absolute truth or ethics comprised. The difference is largely one of metaphysical or psychological tone (which, I agree, is important to many people). Even if one believed that truth is discovered rather than made, as Lutz does, we still have to choose between alternative formulations as to what precisely is the truth that we are discovering.

4. I am not certain how Lutz intends to reconcile his emphases on "genuine human free will" and "absolute truths, or . . . an ethics that is ontologically rather than socially grounded."

THE CROSS CRITIQUES

O'Boyle and Hill: First, for both writers social economics comprises a blend of positive and normative work, a blend of description and activist reform.

Second, the critical difference between them centers on the question of determinism, but the difference is not what one might expect. O'Boyle affirms the view that "truth is seen as one, as absolute, as forever fixed in objective reality. Quite apart from its utility to man, truth simply is." He also argues that "truth is one." Hill argues that "Catholic social economists place a heavy emphasis upon the free will with which God has endowed the human species. They see free will as a reflection of the image of God in which man was created" and "reject the interpretation which holds that human history is fully determined by the inexorable movement of broad cultural forces which are beyond human control." In his view, however, "Many institutionalist social economists . . . accept the doctrine of cultural determinism and hold that individual persons cannot influence history appreciably." Hill affirms the Ayresian notion that "free will and determinism are not contradictory because they apply to different levels of generalization," the individual can enjoy free will in his own individual sphere but not in the social, which is "fully determined by broad cultural forces."

O'Boyle and Hill seem to me to represent interesting blends of positions. O'Boyle combines a belief in unitary, fixed truth with a divinely ordained free will for men. Hill combines cultural determinism with pragmatism. In my view O'Boyle's position is subject to the necessity of having to determine what is the truth that is one and absolute; and Hill's, to the necessity to work out the interrelationships between the consequences of individual free will within broad cultural forces and the impacts of those broad cultural forces. In other words, both writers, if narrowly or strictly interpreted, seem to me to foreclose consideration of that which human beings must work out in practice; both manifest strong deterministic elements. But it is more than likely that, differences of metaphysical belief and discursive system (semantics) aside, both thinkers are sufficiently flexible and broad-ranging as to what is involved that such foreclosure is by no means complete.

Third, although there are deterministic aspects in each's official position (Hill rejects the presence of the religiously metaphysical and teleological, and O'Boyle rejects pragmatism "because philosophy cannot be made to do the work of theology"), it seems to me, in what may well be a minority position within social economics, that both pragmatism and theology function as modes of generating meaning, even though the particular substantive content is often clothed in deterministic garb.

Fourth, it also seems to me that neither position precludes the necessity to make further choices or to work matters out. This is true of pragmatism both per se and in contemplation of Hill's cultural determinism: not all believers in cultural determinism will agree as to what is substantively involved or what precisely is determined "beyond human control." So Hill's pragmatism at the practical level is in the same situation as O'Boyle's theological idealism. Whether one believes in pragmatism, in what works, or that truth is a unity, one still has to determine what that belief is dispositive of; solutions to questions and problems still have to be worked out. For example, even if Catholic social economics believes that private property is a natural or sacred right, that view does not unequivocally dispose of the question of what constitutes private property and how private property is to change. The result is necessarily in practice close to, if not identical with, the position of institutionalist social economics which argues that private property is a human institution which must be and is evaluated pragmatically and be accepted, modified, or rejected according to the outcome of the evaluation--a view which seems to demote the power of cultural (or technological) determinism.

Fifth, I agree with O'Boyle's remonstrations against those institutionalists who would completely reject orthodox microeconomics. Not all institutionalists believe that institutionalism and neoclassical economics are mutually exclusive. There are those who see institutionalism, neoclassicism, and social economics as complementary rather than in irreconcilable conflict.

Sixth, both authors are laudably concerned with redressing the grievances deriving from social injustice, rather than in avoiding such issues by retreating to a conservative, power-structure reinforcing notion of Pareto optimality.

Hill and Hunt: Hill argues that although it is not the case that revolution is never justified, amelioration is generally more productive of human progress than revolution. This seems a sufficiently sensible view for a pragmatist. What is absent, however, is any strong reliance on cultural determinism such as he invokes against O'Boyle. He does note that both Marxian and institutionalist social economics are basically materialistic, with the mode of production for the former and technology for the latter having a deterministic role. And he says that both Marxian and institutionalist social economists seem to have the same problem with the conflict between free will and determinism, and that further research is necessary to answer the question of the relationship between free will and determinism. Four points: first, if that is the case, then discussions of the justification of revolution must await disposition of the question of their efficacy. Second, it seems to me that a sensible position which does not prematurely foreclose analysis is the approach of pluralistic conditionism rather than monistic determinism. Third, all such reliances upon ostensibly transcendental, deterministic causes or processes, not unlike the neo-Austrian emphasis on spontaneous order processes, must have a place for individual human action in the formation and operation of whatever is the deterministic cause (the mode of production or technology or interindividual aggregation) and also be self-referential, that is, be applied to the theory and its application itself. Otherwise social economic analysis will tend to seriously misapprehend the characteristics of social processes that distinguish them from molecular and astronomical physics. Fourth, I seriously question whether research will conclusively resolve the conflict between free will and determinism: both are paradigmatic concepts, not readily if ever subject to refutation, and certainly not without arbitrarily breaking the hermeneutic circle.

For his part, Hunt, in his treatment of revolution (vis-à-vis amelioration) centers on the question of the nature, magnitude, and consequences of desired change, and suggests that the very consequential changes on which institutionalist and Marxist might agree would constitute revolutionary rather than ameliorative change, such that, for example, Veblen seems "quite revolutionary" to him. It is difficult to reach a conclusive answer on this. One needs to talk in more detailed terms about the contemplated changes. Surely using the model of the Bolshevik revolution is not dispositive of the issue. Surely, too, there is a wide spectrum of opinion within both schools of thought on the matter. And any determinism must be subject to the test of self-reference.

Hunt and O'Boyle: Not surprisingly, the most dramatic conflict or tension is between these two social economists.

Hunt rejects any supernatural source of knowledge. He affirms that within the Catholic church there are both conservative and liberal (including liberation) formulations each ostensibly applying the Christian gospel or message, but each taking a different position on how to deal with existing structural inequalities. He believes that to say that property is natural is to be obscurantist, raising fundamental questions about the particular substantive content of actual property rights and about both the variety thereof and changes therein, suggesting that if all manifestations are "natural" then naturalness is dispositive of no issues. Hunt interprets the Papal Catholic mainstream as affirming private property, capitalism, and the institutional status quo, while seeing "most problems as arising from individual moral failure."

Some of Hunt's positions are those made by the institutionalists, of whom I am one, such as I make in the present chapter. A central problem with Hunt's position derives from his recognition of diversity within Catholic social economics: the fact that the Papal encyclicals support reform--for example, the imposition of checks on concentrated power--of *both* capitalist and socialist systems. Property (or the interests protected as property) is considered natural but so also the interests of the nonpropertied. On balance, the Papacy seems to stand for amelioration in such matters, though liberation theology stands for major revolution and perhaps, if necessary, violent revolution in order to bring it about. I recur, then, to Professor Hunt's treatment of the definition of revolution in relation to institutionalist amelioration.

For his part, O'Boyle finds more to agree with in socialist social economics as characterized by Hunt than Hunt finds in Catholic social economics as characterized by O'Boyle. As to differences, O'Boyle first stresses the relevance of the individual side of man's nature--though this may be only a matter of emphasis. Next he believes that the antagonism between workers and owners derives not from the capitalist mode of organizing production but from "the way men relate to one another in the workplace." Here again is the conflict between focusing on individual virtue and institutional reform.[17]

Interesting here is the juxtaposition of O'Boyle's emphasis on relationships in the workplace, rather than larger structural organizational matters, to Lutz's emphasis, also in the name of a religiously informed social economics, on worker cooperatives. It would appear that theological idealism has more than one position. Whereas Lutz desires (what he considers to be) fundamental structural change in the organization of production, O'Boyle seeks the "moral rebirth" of individual man--noting that "ownership and control of the means of production may take several different organizational forms in order to support the necessary moral rebirth." But, he insists, "the problem is not with the owners of the means of production but with modern man himself." Either there are no dragons or we are all dragons. Hunt is therefore not erroneous in his emphasis that O'Boyle focuses on individual moral failure, though he may be so insofar as he fails to recognize that O'Boyle desires institutional changes to "serve the needs of all men, not just those with property rights." Still Hunt may well be correct in insinuating that O'Boyle tends to reify existing property rights and thereby severely limits the force of his potential reforms, although even here one must consider the radical implications of his proposal to postulate "the workplace as an industrial commons." But surely we need not treat either nature and nurture or institutions and man, respectively, as mutually exclusive categories.

But what of the quiet, positive, scholarly ambitions of social economics? Do these remonstrances against the type of social economics advocated by O'Boyle have any implications for the conduct of social economics as a mode of inquiry rather than of revolution or reform? Or are such matters irrelevant, our task being not to study society but to change it? The task is both positive and normative, though differently so among social economists, and is part of the valuational process and thereby part of the process of social change.

CONCLUSION

Social economics, no less than mainstream neoclassical economics as well as institutional economics and Marxian economics considered as separate schools, participates self-consciously and normatively in the larger social valuational process which is part of the inexorable process of reconstructing society. This task is not entirely a matter of human choice (by which I mean at least that there are such things as physical resource constraints) and insofar as it is a matter of human choice it is not entirely a deliberative matter. Society is nonetheless something that is constructed, and man is at the center of the process from which it emanates. This is a distinctly secular, rather than theological, view, and for the theological it can be taken only pro tanto. But this is the social valuational process and social economics is part of it. I know of no theological idealist, or religious, social economist who denies the importance of the human valuational process.

Social economics, no less than any other school of thought, is therefore part of the Platonic, utopist tradition. People working within social economics may be said to derive from their understanding of and experience within the existing socioeconomic system certain conceptions as to what an idealized alternative to it would look like, and on this basis they attempt to reform the system. Parallel to this is an Aristotelian sense as to what values really involve, or as to *real* values.

But this process is both subjective-normative-valuational and positive. It is the former in that selective perception, varying theories and models, and varying normative positions are employed in perceiving and understanding the status quo and in deriving some notion of an ideal from it. It is the latter in that at least to some degree efforts are made to understand and explain the existing system independent of subjective, normative, and idealistic notions, although this too is subject to selective perception. Both are difficult undertakings and, it seems to me, the most sensible position is to assume that one's economic "science" most likely has normative elements. Facts are theory-laden and theories are ideol-

ogy-laden--at least this is a safe presumption with which to enable one to
be constructively critical of oneself and of others.

What distinguishes social economics is at first glance its breadth
and deliberatively conspicuous and indeed central normative preoccupa-
tions. But fundamentally this means that social economists are concerned
with values; with the economy as a valuational process within the total
social valuational process (which includes the market but goes far beyond
the market); with the process by which values are formed, compared,
evaluated, reformed, and chosen; and with the consequences of values.
Social economists study these facets of value and, like other types of
economists, participate in the valuational process. This also means that
while social economists can, do, and should make use of mechanistic
models they should not pursue a mechanistic research program which
obscures the total processes of valuation by which economic problems,
economic conflicts, and all the detailed issues of economic decisionmaking
are worked out.

One historic function of social economics is to have insisted, not
only on the presence and importance of the total valuational process but
on the presence and importance of ontological assumptions in economics.
These assumptions include but go beyond scarcity, or comprehend scarcity
to be deeper and more complex and subtle than appears with regard solely
to the allocation of resources: scarcity in the sense of our inability to
pursue simultaneously and attain fully all values (not merely our demands
for commodities). This is also to say that social economics has served to
underscore the presence and importance of the metaphysical element in
economics, a metaphysical element which may include the theological. But
to say all this does not ipso facto establish the necessary or true substantive content of the ontology, the metaphysics, or the theology--for all three
in practice are fundamentally diverse.[18]

I suggest that the foregoing is useful even for the religious or
theological idealist among social economists. The question whether values
are transcendent and thus to be discovered and ever more closely
approximated, or are created by man in an explorative and emergent quest,
as important as it is, need not prevent analysis and interpretation of the
actual human valuational process. Christian (or other religious) economics
is one form of the exegesis of values, an attempt to interpret what God is
saying through the Bible--and, while preeminently interested in God,
contributing to the valuational process. There are obviously other modes
of pursuing the meaning of values.

One way of looking at all this involves a rather commonplace economics diagram: the combination of a social production possibility curve with a social welfare function. The point I want to make is that conventional practice typically makes assumptions about things which in practice must be worked out, things which typically involve values.[19] Specifically I want to argue that underlying this diagram are the operation and results of four processes at work in the economy. First is the process by which is determined which values (goods or goals) are to be represented on the axes, the values between which choice has to be made. This is not given by nature; it is worked out through markets, private and group choice, and politics. Second is the process by which the shape and location of the production possibility curve, which governs the tradeoffs that have to be made, is ascertained. (Economists have not studied this very much. But consider the production possibility curve relating price stability and employment levels. Whatever governs the empirical Phillips-curve tradeoffs will help govern the slope and location of this production possibility curve.) Third and fourth, inasmuch as the actual social welfare function is the product of individual preferences weighted by power structure, are the processes by which individual preferences and power structure are formed. In order to reach determinate and so-called optimal solutions, economists must and do make assumptions as to how these processes--and the values ensconced within them--work out. Either the results are empty formalism or a matter of presumption. Social economists, it seems to me, have assumed the terribly difficult task of studying these processes, the very processes that are mechanistically finessed by their more orthodox colleagues. Social economists should be studying how these processes work. If they want to make their own assumptions as to either how they should work or their performance results, they will be in these respects doing pretty much the same thing as their orthodox colleagues, but at least they will be, one hopes, concentrating on the processes and making their values clear, as well as pursuing a careful analysis of just what the values are and what they signify, and not merely take fine-sounding words and symbols for granted.

Penultimately I must consider an objection that appeals to many persons and not solely to the theological idealist: the argument that the position generally advanced in this chapter constitutes foundationless relativism, or nihilism. My response is as follows:

1. The alternative to the position advanced here, and the frequent consequence of accepting the nihilism objection, tends to attribute privileged status to the status quo, selectively perceived.

2.   Pointing this out in scholarly study is not tantamount to advocating wholesale destruction of existing arrangements.

3.   Opposition is generally (but not always) high priest advocacy or pretense.

4.   I prefer to face reality rather than hide from or obfuscate it: human arrangements are in fact a matter of choice and design, and the deepest processes of social choice involve the making and remaking of institutions, including language, notwithstanding selective pretensions or perceptions of determinacy. As I have urged throughout this chapter, even if all of us were absolutists (as opposed to relativists) we would still have to choose between those things we each accept as absolutes, for they are by no means identical. Thus I am not opposed to calling a spade a spade and letting it go at that: the psychic balm and status-quo legitimation functions can and ought to be identified and analyzed wherever they arise. Yes, these responses are predicated upon values and a definition of reality and are themselves part of the valuational process which, shall we say, is part of the process by which we confront and, in some combination, discover, make, and articulate reality. And I do not intend to be disengenuous when I say that it is within the realm of conjecture that such is what God intends: it is not at all clear that God does not want mankind to have knowledge of these and other matters.

Finally, it should be obvious that the present article would more than likely have been very different if it had been written by another social economist. Its construction by me must inevitably reflect my Wisconsin-Commons institutionalism and all the other matters discussed in Part I. But surely all possible authors of such an essay would agree that each reader has to work out his or her own position on the various conflicts and tensions between the four strands of social economics, just as, it seems to me, mankind in the aggregate must do so--or at least that is the position that I have advanced here.

Notes

[1]It should be noted that I use power in a strictly neutral and nonpejorative sense, as participation in decisionmaking and the bases thereof. The emphasis in the text on process, thereby on working things out, necessarily involves decision, choice, and power.

[2]This is to say that active decisionmakers, by making and acting upon the assumptions underlying their choices, both resolve and beg the problem of the hermeneutic circle.

[3]This is of course a modernist view of rhetoric--which, to a different type of rhetorician, is mere didactics rather than the presentation of truth.

[4]Indeed, the view has been expressed to me that Christianity has *no* distinctive program for social economics, that it is not even a systematic framework for social economics, though the same person, agreeing that there is an inexorable necessity of choice (which does not disturb him, though it does disturb others), also argues that Christianity can serve as a framework within which that choice can occur, and presumably somehow be guided.

[5]See Robinson (1962), chapter 1.

[6]If one attributes an ontological character to values, then such a purely instrumentalist (or social engineering) treatment may be objectionable. Of course, the argument here is that even if all agree as to the ontological character of values, there is likely disagreement as to what they are; and even if all agree as to what they are, there is likely disagreement as to both their application to particular cases and whether the convolutions of rationalization constitute casuistry in the pejorative sense.

[7]The matter is of course complex: for example, insofar as "consequences" and "data" are value-laden, then it may be objected that values are used to evaluate values. And how does one evaluate values? The point is that there is a valuational process in which values are exploratory, emergent, and juxtaposed to other values, whether or not one considers them as ontologically a priori. Throughout this chapter the agnostic position is taken which does not categorically deny ontological status but works with values as variables in the processes of human action. The risk is that such a view may impoverish the reality of values. See also the following note.

[8]For those who believe in the ontological nature of values and moral rules, choosing pragmatism or consequences as one's standard is not the same thing as choosing a value. In this view, values or moral rules are not made subject to an evaluative process; insofar as one considers them only in a secular, nonspiritualist context, one is depriving them of their ontological status, even denying them that status. Thus one can believe that nominalism produces doubt which produces fragmentation, not the other way around; that the processes of society are the outworking of antecedent values, not the formation of values worked out by social processes.

One can believe that the fact that there are differing concepts of absolute moral values does not mean that the conception we choose to be generative in our theory or our society should be the subject of cost-benefit analysis. My point is that in using the particular value we are implicitly attributing to it a particular privileged net-benefit status.

[9]Lutz traces humanistic social economics to Sismondi and then considers Ruskin, Hobson, Tawney, and Schumacher, concentrating on Sismondi and Hobson. But what about the medieval scholastic tradition, the principal source of Catholic social economic thought? It is Catholic social economics which Lutz later identifies as the mainstream of social economics. Scholastic socioeconomic teaching represented the same thing as modern papal encyclicals: the superimposition of a theologically based system of ethics or morals on economic life-- religion as social control.

[10]One can wonder as to how one knows that a "solution" has been worked out; what constitutes "worked out"; what about the role of power, the status of consensus or of majority rule; and the length of time working out must endure. The position taken here affirms that all this is open-ended, never ending and, yes, to be worked out, while recognizing that such may be inadequate if the theological idealist's ontological absolutism and determinism is correct.

[11]One may believe that the Social Gospel movement-message is a departure from theological determinism because it accepted pragmatic arguments from unChristian sources. Others may feel the same way about Social Darwinism.

[12]This is intended to say neither that all persons use religion for base motives nor that the use of religion for such motives is an important element of people's beliefs. Functionalism need constitute neither criticism nor apologia.

[13]As already noted, the roots of social economics are in the Catholic tradition and conceivably could have remained in that tradition, allowing those heterodox economists whose beliefs do not comport with the religious element to join a more secularly oriented association. But the Catholic Economics Association did become the Association for Social Economics and thereby broadened its base. Nonetheless, the argument does not turn on institutional or organizational features. Contemporary social economics *is* diverse, as is evidenced in the foregoing chapters. The only course, other than acceptance of pluralism, for the social economist who believes that he or she has the "right" answer is to read the others out of the school, pretty much as some neoclassicists read non-neoclassicists out of economics.

[14]For example, Lutz argues that a religious humanist social economics, in which "The spirit must transcend humanity, seeking a One which is higher and holier . . . has little in common with self-interested religious aspirations grounded in a utilitarian calculus of heaven and hell." Lutz also affirms "a major difference with the Catholic perspective relating to the foundation of its ethics: the normative elements are seen to be based on an innate moral sense founded in Reason instead of revelation grounded in a particular text, or by virtue of certain paper pronouncements considered infallible. In other words, most thinkers in the humanistic camp would feel compelled to reject any revelation that conflicts with Reason, provided, of course, that 'Reason' is understood metaphysically rather than scientifically. Without this major difference, the Catholic and the humanistic strand[s] of social economics would collapse to essentially the same perspective." Lutz's social economics clearly differs from medieval scholasticism.

[15]Although the text presents an empirical or utilitarian interpretation of Smith's analysis, some scholars hold a theological interpretation. Smith's writings manifest supernatural, natural, and utilitarian-empirical modes of discourse.

[16]Thus Lutz says, "Through Kant we are not only given an objective ontological foundation for dignity, but we are also told how its claim manifests itself in the concrete world of social intercourse." And "Turning now from the normative principles to the institutions that they recommend," he asserts the centrality of worker cooperatives in the manner already quoted earlier in the text.

[17]Insofar as the operative conception of individual virtue is institutional-system specific, one ultimately must confront the question of institutional reform, for otherwise one merely accepts status quo institutional arrangements and the conception of individual virtue correlative therewith.

[18]Linda Colley (1988, pp. 6, 7) thus queries, "Can we indeed believe that Victorian England possessed a consensual value-system, and that all sectors interpreted these values in the same way? Did self-reliance mean the same thing to a seamstress, a Chartist, a servant, a banker, and a landowner?" and concludes that "Victorian men and women often cherished deeply-held values, but there is little firm evidence that they consistently agreed upon what those values should be."

[19]This, again, is not to say that everything can be worked out, e.g., resource constraints. Still, "resource" is not a natural phenomenon; it is a product of physical existence and properties coupled with social usage. (In the absence, for example, of the internal combustion engine and the chemistry of plastics, oil was a bother, not a valuable economic asset.) This is representative of a larger question concerning whether the meaning of "nature" is derivative of nature itself or is derived, so far as humans are concerned, from (the choice of) human attribution.

References

Colley, L. 1988. "Sire of the poor," *London Review of Books* (March 17), 6-7.

Gordon, S. 1980. *Welfare, Justice, and Freedom*. New York: Columbia University Press.

Recktenwald, H. C. 1987. "Heinrich Pesch," *The New Palgrave: A Dictionary of Economics*. Vol. 3. London: Macmillan, 852.

Robinson, J. 1962. *Economic Philosophy*. Chicago: Aldine.

Samuels, W. J. "Technology vis-à-vis institutions in the JEI: a suggested interpretation," *Journal of Economic Issues* 11 (December), 871-895.

Samuels, W. J. and A. A. Schmid, J. D. Shaffer, R. A. Solo and S. A. Woodbury. 1984. "Technology, labor interests, and the law: some fundamental points and problems," *Nova Law Journal* 8 (Spring), 487-513.

Smith, A. 1937. *The Wealth of Nations*. New York: Modern Library.

_____. 1976. *The Theory of Moral Sentiments*. Oxford: Oxford University Press.

_____. 1978. *Lectures on Jurisprudence*. Oxford: Oxford University Press.

Tool, M. 1986. *Essays in Social Value Theory*. Armonk: M. E. Sharpe.

PART III:
BASIC APPLICATIONS OF SOCIAL ECONOMICS

9

UNDERSTANDING THE WELFARE STATE: THE SIGNIFICANCE OF SOCIAL ECONOMICS

J. Ron Stanfield

Over the last decade or so it has become commonplace that the welfare state and the corporate economy which is part of its fundamental structure are in crisis. Also commonplace is the notion that conventional economics is in crisis. In this chapter I will address primarily the crisis of the corporate-welfare state, but the problems that have led to crisis in conventional economics will also arise in several places. My procedure will be, first, to sketch the nature of social economics in contrast to formal or mainstream economic theory. Second, I will use one example of social economics, that of Karl Polanyi, to discuss the nature of the welfare state in terms of its origination from nineteenth century market capitalism. I shall then discuss the unresolved problems which account for the current crisis of the welfare state, and Polanyi's ideas are suggestive and useful in this regard as well. I conclude by noting the importance of the social economics perspective in coming to grips with the underlying problems of the corporate-welfare state and by suggesting that social economics itself needs to sharpen its focus on the psychocultural aspects of the current socioeconomic crisis.

SOCIAL ECONOMICS

My purpose in this first section is to sketch social economics. In doing so it is useful to contrast social economics with formal economic theory. Social economics can be defined as the study of the interaction of economy and society. In other words, social economics is interested in the social, political, and cultural spheres as they influence economic institutions and behavior as well as the impact of economic institutions and behavior on the social, political, and cultural realms.

Formal economics concentrates on rational acts of choice, articulated through the exchange process. This is tantamount to treating the economy as a self-contained subsystem with its own logic and structural laws. This logic is self-interested bargaining for maximum advantage, and the structural discipline is seen as being provided by the force of price competition.

Social economics is more concerned with historical analysis of the interaction between the economy and society. It has much in common with the functional method of sociology and anthropology--that is, it focuses on the role of the given institution in the social totality. The method of comparative institutional analysis is also important to social economics because of the latter's historical bent (Stanfield, 1986, ch. 3).

Social economics views the economy as an instituted process of provisioning social reproduction. *Institutedness* refers to the motivations and repeated practices that vest economic behavior with meaning and stability. The focus is on economic activity as *learned* behavior. There is no natural economic behavior. Individuals do not naturally reduce the quantity demanded of a product in response to a rise in its price. Whatever the basis of the desire for the product (which is largely learned), there is no necessary relationship between the desire and price. Instead, individuals in a market society are taught to make this response, and they could be taught to respond otherwise in an economy that is instituted and integrated differently. The economy is instituted through a system of communication and sanction. People are informed as to their expected behavior (and that of others) in given situations, and also as to the penalties and rewards which will be forthcoming for violating or fulfilling these expectations.

Provisioning refers to the basic material function of the economic aspect: contributing the material requirements for society to continue to exist and to grow and develop along the lines of its basic values. The economy is a differentiated subsystem which has this material provisioning function as its basic characteristic. This does not reduce the economy to its engineering aspect because social integration is also involved. To meet one's requirements it is not enough that an individual know what can be expected from the natural environment in relation to his or her other needs. The individual must also know what to expect from other people and how to induce from them the behavior which is necessary to meet his or her other requirements.

Several methodological contrasts between social and orthodox economics emerge. Whereas the formal approach focuses on the production and distribution of output and income, the social approach focuses on social reproduction, which includes, but is not limited to, production and distribution. In order to continue to exist as a going concern, any society must reproduce itself. This is no mere matter of physiological sustenance. It involves as well the acculturation of new generations with respect to the instrumental skills (e.g., balancing a checkbook), aesthetic appreciation (e.g., the nuances of football or cinema), and ethical awareness (e.g., the work ethic) necessary to participate in socioeconomic life. Nor is the matter solely one of intergenerational reproduction. The social economy as an instituted process is dynamic and interdependent. The skills, attitudes, and aspirations which are required and molded by the operation of the social process undergo incessant development. The economic system requires continuous reinstitutionalization.

Whereas formal economics is based on rationalistic psychology, taking the individuals as a datum, social economics is more behavioristic in its psychological reach and focuses on the *formation* of individuals. The societal approach begins the analysis with people and works from there to the level of the individual. This is a profound departure of social economics from the conventional approach to the economic system. The individual in the view of the societal approach is not a datum. The formation and change of individual preferences, valuations, capacities, and limitations are seen as constituting a critical part of the social economist's research program. For example, the conventional postulate of the rationality of "economic man" is challenged by social economists with respect to its appropriateness for research into comparative economics. It prejudges some very important empirical and institutional questions concerning the actual psychological motivations and integrative frameworks of social organization.

Moreover, the social economist is concerned with the psychological welfare of individuals insofar as it is linked to economic institutions and behavior. This concern goes beyond behaviorism to humanistic or self-psychology with the insistence that the individual experience joy in the conduct of his or her everyday life (Lutz and Lux, 1979). The social economist is particularly interested in the possibility that economic institutions pose obstacles to the individual's self-authentic development.

The formation of individual characters is therefore an important matter of concern for the social economist. The fundamental product of the four social subsystems is *people*, and the fundamental concern of all social analysis should be human character--the needs, aspirations, limitations, capacities, and follies of the human personality. This concern for the relation of economy to human character has yet to be accorded the systematic attention it warrants, but it does crop up in the literature from time to time (Swaney, 1983). A part of Aristotle's defense of private property was that without property to dispose of, people could not practice virtue in its disposition. The practices of charity, self-reliance, and social responsibility require that the individual be empowered to dispose of material means. Thomas Jefferson's agrarian ideal was based on agri*culture* as a way of life. The rootedness of the yeoman farmer in ecology was very important to Jefferson, as was the politically independent character of the self-sufficient farmer (Berry, 1978). Adam Smith celebrated the growth of efficiency generated by intensified division of labor but was concerned about the concomitant effects on the intellectual development of the worker (Smith, 1937, Bk. V, Ch. II, Art. II, pp. 734-735). The great English neoclassicist, Alfred Marshall, identified the study of economy and character as more important than the study of want satisfaction. Marshall observed that poverty degrades character and defended free enterprise because of the qualities of character it encouraged (Marshall, 1949, Bk. I, Ch. I). The concern of Marxists and others about work and character provides additional examples (O'Toole et al., 1973).

Another basic contrast lies in the areas of power and social relations. Confining its interest to the relations in the exchange process, formal economics neglects a wide range of social relations which are relevant to the economy in the material sense. Power in the orthodox view is solely market power, the ability to affect the prices at which products are exchanged or to exclude rivals from the market. The social approach insists upon inclusion of a wider range of relations and a broader concept of power. Class relations, authority, hierarchy, and media influence fall within the scope of the social economist's concept of power. Social relations are reproduced. Power consists of the ability to influence the reproductive process. The social economist insists upon a broader view of power and legitimacy since (s)he views economic institutions not in isolation but in terms of their relation to the social whole.

The social perspective is of necessity historical and evolutionary since the process of social reproduction is ongoing and evolving. Social change is incessant, even if now subtle, then dramatic. In this evolution, institutions evolve, change their functions and their relations to the overall social process. In contrast, the orthodox approach is essentially static, a-historical, and a-institutional. The most significant example now current is the modern corporation. To the orthodox economist, the large corporation is merely a firm with market power. From an evolutionary perspective, the modern corporation is a profound institutional mutation, quite distinct from the nineteenth century firm in its internal organization, scope, and relations to society at large.

The social perspective is inherently holistic whereas the formal perspective is reductionist because it treats the economy as a self-contained phenomenal matrix. The social economist insists upon the study of the twofold interaction of the economy and society. Economic phenomena influence and are influenced by political factors, the cultural realm of expressive symbolism, and the social relations of family and social life.

THE DISEMBEDDED ECONOMY AND THE DEVELOPMENT OF THE CORPORATE-WELFARE STATE

Karl Polanyi's analysis of market capitalism provides a firm foundation for interpreting the origin and development of the corporate-welfare state. Polanyi's most profound insight in this regard is the distinction between embedded and disembedded economies. He argued, generally speaking, that precapitalist societies had no separate economic sphere with a distinct and explicit set of motives and functions. His reading of the facts points instead to economic activity being motivated by the individual's general social location and interest.

> The outstanding discovery of recent historical and anthropological research is that man's economy as a rule, is submerged in his social relationships. He does not act so as to safeguard his individual interest in the possession of material goods; he acts so as to safeguard his social standing, his social claims, his social assets. He values material goods only in so far as they serve this end. Neither the process of production nor that of distribution is linked to specific economic interests attached to the possession of goods; but every single step in that process is geared to a number of social interests which eventually ensure that the required steps be taken (Dalton, 1968, p. 46).

This is not to say, however, that the motive of gain is absent in earlier societies, nor that people were intrinsically any less selfish or more altruistic in precapitalistic social economies. It is to say only that the motive of self-gain was but one thread in the social fabric such that no whole cloth was made from it. It was constrained and held in check by its interwovenness with religious, familial, and political motivations. That economic interests in modern society appear distinct is evidence that they have come to predominance in the determination of an individual's social location and interest. Gain has been promoted to a pillar institution. For Polanyi, the peculiarity of the social economy which came to maturity in the nineteenth century

> . . . was precisely that it rested on economic foundations. Other societies and other civilizations, too, were limited by the material conditions of their existence . . . . All types of societies are limited by economic factors. Nineteenth century civilization alone was economic in a different and distinctive sense, for it chose to base itself on a motive only rarely acknowledged as valid in the history of human societies, and certainly never before raised to the level of a justification of action and behavior in everyday life, namely, gain. The self-regulating market system was uniquely derived from this principle (Polanyi, 1957, p. 30).

The motive of gain and the institutional complex of the sup-ply-demand-price system came to be viewed as comprising an autonomous sphere of human activity, "the economic system, governed by economic motives, and subject to the economic principle of formal rationality (i.e., economizing)" (Dalton, 1968, p. 132). The "sociological situations which make individuals partake in economic life" were created by "specifically economic institutions." These institutions "are activated by economic motives and governed by laws that are specifically economic." The economy is conceived to be "working without the conscious intervention of human authority" (Dalton, 1968, p. 82). This is the disembedded economy: an autonomous sphere of human activity, self-motivated by greed or the threat of hunger and self-governed through a system of price-making markets.

The relationship between this disembedded economy and main-stream, formal economics is one of mutual reinforcement. Mainstream economics is the theoretical expression and ideological justification of the self-regulating market economy (Stanfield, 1979, chs. 2-5; Eichner, 1984, pp. 235-239). Without this expression, indeed this seventeenth century cultural revolution (Appleby, 1978), it is inconceivable that the body politic would have turned over to competitive markets the vital task of social provisioning (Stanfield, 1986, ch. 4).

For Polanyi, this is an unrealistic concept because it rests upon the fictitious commodities and leads to the neglect of the primacy of society. This in turn leaves social life open to disruption by the distur-bances of an uncontrolled market process. Provisioning is an integral part of social reproduction, providing the material wherewithal for the contin-uation of society as a going concern. The inherent instability and insecurity of the self-regulating market threatens social reproduction. The market mentality also generates character traits that undermine social cohesion. The bargaining mentality of securing maximum advantage for oneself is fundamental to the operation of a market economy. Socializa-tion and acculturation must create and legitimate this selfishness if the market economy is to operate upon a set of rational relative prices. Yet this mentality cannot fail to erode social bonds and generate pessimism, distrust, and cynicism.

Clearly, the market mentality and its glorification of gain produce a perverse tendency for economic considerations to dominate social, cultural, and political life. These other aspects become mere adjuncts of the economy. "Society [becomes] embedded in the economic system, rather than vice versa" (Dalton, 1968, p. 131). The result is the economic control of social activity. Here as elsewhere, the great champion of entrepreneurial capitalism, Joseph Schumpeter, provides candid instruction as to the nature of capitalist society.

> Bourgeois society has been cast in a purely economic mold: its foundations, beams and beacons are all made of economic material. The building faces toward the economic side of life. Prizes and penalties are measured in pecuniary terms. Going up and down means making and losing money . . . . The promises of wealth and the threats of destitution that it holds out, it redeems with ruthless promptitude (Schumpeter, 1962, p. 73).

Clearly, capitalism is an *econocentric* culture; its denizens find in matters economic the central locus of meanings that structure their existence.

Polanyi coined the expression the *fictitious commodities* in order to elaborate upon the tendency for economic motivation and expectations to dominate social and political life. He defined commodities "as objects produced for sale on the market" (Polanyi, 1957, p. 72).   Articles produced for direct use or ceremonial gift-giving are not commodities. This is the same distinction that Marx made and Polanyi, like Marx, was concerned about the implications of a social organization which instituted the essential function of provisioning on the basis of producing articles for sale in a system of price-making markets. Polanyi sought to emphasize the utopian character of such an organization with the concept of fictitious commodities.

> But labor, land, and money are obviously *not* commodities . . . . None of them is produced for sale. The commodity description of labor, land, and money is entirely fictitious (Polanyi, 1957, p. 72).

Polanyi was not denying that land, labor, and money were in fact exchanged like commodities. Organized markets for exchanging them certainly existed, and, indeed, had to exist in order for a market economy to exist. The commodity fictions supply "a vital organizing principle" for such an economy. Polanyi's point was no mere semantic trifle. It was central to his argument that the commodity fictions had to exist for a market economy to exist. The fictional, or mystified, bases of the market economy indicated the mythical character of the self-regulating market economy.

An image of the economy founded on fictional premises is not a realistic conception of social organization.

Polanyi went on to examine the implications of the commodity fictions. That is, what would be the result of a social organization that treats land, labor, and money as if they were commodities?

> To allow the market mechanism to be the sole director of the fate of human beings and their natural environment, indeed, even of the amount and use of purchasing power, would result in the demolition of society . . . . Undoubtedly, labor, land, and money markets *are* essential to a market economy. But no society could stand the effects of such a system of crude fictions . . . unless its human and natural substance as well as its business organization was protected against the ravages of this satanic mill.
>
> The extreme artificiality of market economy is rooted in the fact that the process of production itself is here organized in the form of buying and selling (Polanyi, 1957, p. 73).

Polanyi's answer is loud and clear. The commoditization of land, labor, and money, if unchecked, would destroy society. The impossibility of a self-regulating market economy is shown in the inconsistency of such an arrangement with the continuation of a functioning social order. To subject the provisioning of society to an unfettered market would destroy social organization.

Schumpeter's powerful concept of *creative destruction* provides excellent elaboration of Polanyi's message. "The essential fact about capitalism," for Schumpeter, is that it "is by nature a form or method of economic change," that it "incessantly revolutionizes the economic structure *from within*, incessantly destroying the old one, incessantly creating a new one" (Schumpeter, 1962, pp. 82-83). Innovations that create new products, new production techniques, or new market areas just as surely destroy old products, techniques, and market areas. It is but a short step to Polanyi's message. The destruction of existing economic ways and means necessarily disrupts and displaces existing political, social, and cultural ways and means. The friendships, family ties, and civic roots of the working class are no match for the necessity of relocation to secure employment or career advance. Naturally or historically significant sites or human emotional attachments cannot stand in the way of pecuniary success and progress. The incessant change in the means of earning a livelihood uproots and degrades the lives to be lived. This is no happenstance or incidental byproduct but rather an integral ingredient of market capitalism, a system of livelihood by competitive markets unfettered by conscious direction.

What was the result of the nineteenth century effort to establish a market economy? In answering this question, Polanyi's analysis demonstrates its considerable strength. Polanyi argued that the effort to establish a self-regulating market economy was necessarily accompanied by a contrary effort to protect society from the disruption which otherwise would have occurred. The market imperative toward extending commoditization generated a protective imperative to safeguard social organization from the effects of commoditization. "Human society would have been annihilated but for protective countermoves which blunted the action of this self-destructive mechanism" (Polanyi, 1957, p. 76). The protective countermoves are many and diverse. Governments intervened to protect labor with legislation regulating child and women labor, working conditions, workday lengths, and subsequent income maintenance programs. Legislation was enacted on land use planning, resource conservation, pollution control, and modern comprehensive environmental protection. The case for the other fictitious commodity, money or purchasing power, is less obvious but no less strong for it. Polanyi's reference was to money as the medium by which the division of labor is integrated. To allow the money markets free play would subject the organization of provisioning to catastrophic instability. The governmental response has been central banking, capital market regulations, and aggregate demand management.

It is important to note two additional points. First, it is not valid to present the protective state interventions as resulting from a leftward ideological shift or the increasing political power of labor. There is no universal ideological stance or economic interest which can encompass the breadth of intervention involved. Very often the programs were enacted by those quite enamored with a pro-market ideology. The comprehensive feature is not ideology or political power group, but the necessity of countering the disruptions of the market process.

The second additional point reinforces the first. The protective response is by no means limited to action through the state apparata. Trade unions and other voluntary associations such as trade associations, civic organizations, historical preservation societies, and naturalist societies play a major role. Even the modern corporation, the central economic institution of modern capitalism, can be viewed as part of the protective response. The principal animus behind the corporate revolution is the urge to stabilize and control the exigencies of the corporate environment, and these exigencies are largely the uncertainties concomitant to the operation of the market mechanism. Eventually, economic and business historians will likely view the modern corporation in this light, and corporate officials will likely follow suit, notwithstanding the free enterprise ideology which remains strong to this time. After all, the image of the corporation as an institution intent upon ensuring the orderly operation of the vital provisioning function is not only more correct but also far more complimentary than the traditional typification of the corporation as a profit-mongering monopolist.

Polanyi's double movement is now clearly in view. The market imperative begets the protective imperative.

> Social history in the nineteenth century was thus the result of a double movement . . . . While on the one hand markets spread all over the face of the globe and the amount of goods involved grew to unbelievable proportions, on the other hand a network of measures and policies was integrated into powerful institutions designed to check the action of the market relative to labor, land, and money . . . . Society protected itself against the perils inherent in a self-regulating market system--this was the one comprehensive feature in the history of the age (Polanyi, 1957, p. 76).

The double movement and the fictitious commodities provide specific instruction. Market capitalist economy incessantly extends the realm of commodity production, and each such extension creates anew the necessity of a protective response. As more food is prepared commercially, the need arises for new sanitation laws, consumer testing services, and labeling requirements. As child care or care for the elderly become commoditized, new laws are necessary for licensing and regulating such care centers. Here again the state is only the most visible and, perhaps, the most important arena for protective responses. The wider and more complex and uncertain the reach of business activity, the greater is the need for corporate and union protection. As consumers face a wider and more complex range of commodities in their market baskets, their need for collective action widens, e.g., consumer testing and reporting agencies.

There is no reason to limit the protective response in the future to these institutions. There is ample space for the operation of rejuvenated voluntary associations. Citizen and professional groups could be, and are in some cases, very important in maintaining standards in day care centers and nursing homes, controlling land use, protecting the environment, preserving neighborhood integrity and historical sites, and so on for a host of other areas in which local action is needed to complement the controls over the economy exercised by the state, corporations, and unions. There is growing need for such local action to mediate the relations between individual families and the megainstitutions of Big Government, Big Business, and Big Labor.

The lesson of the protective response concept is that the developmental tendency is toward an *administered economy* in which economic decisions are made and implemented through organizations of various kinds. This involves a political and bargaining mode of decisionmaking in place of the forces of the impersonal market. The protective response is collective action, though it need not be state-based. Such decisions are likely to be implemented via market prices, but that does not make the market the integrative mechanism.

> Exchange in order to serve as a form of integration
> requires the support of a system of price-making markets
> . . . . Insofar as exchange at a set rate is in question, the
> economy is integrated by the factors which fix that rate,
> not by the market mechanism (Dalton, 1968, p. 154).

That organized groups use the market forces to implement their power is the upshot of much of Galbraith's analysis, and his primary implication is precisely the predominance of administration over market competition (Papandreou, 1972, pp. 78-80).

This brings up another element of social economics, the insistence that economic science place pivotal emphasis upon the analysis of *power* and *value*. The market vision of the social economy, with its givens in regard to individual preferences and capacities and its subjective theory of socioeconomic behavior, denies the primacy of society and obscures the crucial relationship between power and economic value (Polanyi, 1957, p. 258). Polanyi noted the obscurity surrounding power and economic value and located it in the peculiar conception of freedom in the market economy.

> But power and economic value are a paradigm of social
> reality . . . . The function of power is to ensure that
> measure of conformity which is needed for the survival of
> the group . . . . Economic value ensures the usefulness
> of the goods produced . . . (Polanyi, 1957, p. 258).

Power, then, is the institutedness of the productive process. The vestiture of the discretionary authority to make and execute decisions is a power process as is the legitimation of this discretion. Value is an expression of the power process: economic values are sociological entities. Taking the individual as a datum, in the fashion of formal economics, obscures this pivotal fact because it ignores the socialization process which precedes and molds economic values. There is, of course, a technical component of values--production functions, physical transformation functions, and the like. But this cause-and-effect, manipulative knowledge derives its significance by its institutedness--social relations, customs, and power. Knowledge plus institutional context yields value judgments.

In sum, Polanyi's view of the economy focuses on social reproduction. The reality of the economic process is to reproduce society, with some degree of change and expansion. Power and value, hand-in-hand, manifest the reality of society and the necessity of reproducing society. The economy involves not merely the production of goods and services, its real significance lies in the reproduction of society. Social reproduction involves the material reproduction of the species acculturated to the ways and means of social existence, including functional competence, ethical awareness, and aesthetic appreciation.

Viewed in this light, in terms of social reproduction, power and economic value take on new meaning. They are the key categories of *social control*. This is of considerable importance because social control enters the discussion at level one in that there is no question of its being absent. The only relevant questions concern the form and content of this control and whether or not they are functional and legitimate (Stanfield, 1979, ch. 3). *Social reform* is equally comfortable in this focus since it is a conscious reconstruction of the form and content of social control in order to remedy some deficiency of function or legitimacy.

This sharply contrasts with the orthodox economists' departure from the isolated individual. In that view, the question of social control, and by extension, social reform, enter the analysis in terms of *whether* rather than how. This neglect of the primacy of society inevitably embodies a distortion of social control and social reform, and, all too often, a predisposition of suspicion toward them. Social control and social reform are thereby reduced to political intervention into the affairs of already extant individuals. This distortion of the social existence of human life exerts an important and pernicious influence on the conventional approach to social policy. As Adolph Lowe has observed:

> It is the essence of the [controls of the conventional approach to economic policy] that they take the behavior of the micro-units for granted . . . . In contrast, Control as here understood refers to a public policy that concerns itself with the shaping of the behavioral patterns themselves . . . (Lowe, 1977, p. 131).

By taking society as their methodological point of departure, Polanyi and the other social economists emphasize the ever present reality of social control and social reform (Stanfield, 1979, ch. 7).

THE CRISIS AND UNRESOLVED PROBLEMS OF THE CORPORATE-WELFARE STATE

Given Polanyi's stress on the spontaneous character of the emergence of the corporate-welfare state, one would expect this institutional configuration to lack a well-articulated theory of itself and its goals. This corollary hypothesis, then, would suggest that a fundamental problem would exist in that this social order lacks a coherent theory or ideology of itself. This is indeed a major theme of the literature on the corporate-welfare state (Stanfield, 1979, pp. 99-105). John Maurice Clark long ago spoke of the need for a new sense of individual responsibility to replace the self-help ideology of nineteenth century capitalism (Clark, 1967, p. 83). Richard Titmus has also developed the theme of irresponsibility in his work on the British welfare state (Titmus, 1969, pp. 215-243) as has William Robson in his book dealing with the need to have a welfare society to structure the operation of the welfare state (Robson, 1976). In the U.S. case, Daniel Bell has written about the need for *civitas* to enable effective operation of the public household (Bell, 1976, pp. 25 and 245). Norman Furniss and Timothy Tilton have also emphasized the absence of a positive theory or conception of the welfare state (Furniss and Tilton, 1977, pp. x and 23). Clarence Ayres argued that although the welfare state is a fundamentally sound institutional adjustment, it lacks an ideology or culture of achievement and tends to be overly oriented to consumption (Ayres, 1967).

The corporate-welfare state tends to be viewed negatively and not positively. Socialists argue that it is not socialism because it retains too much of capitalist inequality and alienation. Conservatives argue that it embodies too much creeping socialism to be capitalism. All in all, there is very little discussion of the corporate-welfare state in terms of what it is. Therefore, it lacks a central cultural edifice to lead people's lives and to provide them integration into the wider social economy.

As foreshadowed by Polanyi's designation of labor as a fictitious commodity, a persistent problem area of the corporate-welfare state lies in labor markets and industrial relations. The ideology and structure of capitalist society treats paid labor, especially manual labor, as activity which is performed solely out of necessity. The tendency is to deny or neglect the existence of intrinsic satisfaction in the work process. Even the Protestant or Puritan work ethic, which enjoins the theological duty of work, emphasizes its *external* necessity or usefulness rather than its inherent satisfaction. Culturally, not only in capitalist society but in all stratified societies historically, useful work is denigrated and held to be less worthy or honorific than leisure or activities such as war, politics, or sports. Accordingly, although there is nothing intrinsically distasteful in manual labor, it is culturally defined as irksome (Veblen, 1953, ch. 1).

The structure of the work process in capitalist society causes work to be alien or estranged activity. Alienated labor is coerced labor: labor necessitated by an external power within human society. In order to gain a livelihood in a wage economy, the individual must work for wages on terms which are satisfactory to the owner of the wage fund. Hence the concept of alienation expresses the endemic problem of capitalism, namely, the antagonism between capital and labor over the intensity, conditions, and wages of the work process. For the capitalist, profitability is the predominant concern. For the laborer, however, the need to work involves many vital functions in addition to earning an income, such as self-esteem, sociality, and the need to perform productive activities (O'Toole et al., 1973). The capitalist perspective, emphasizing productivity, neglects these wider dimensions of the work process and degrades it in the interest of productivity and profit (Marx, 1967, ch. 7; Braverman, 1974).

The activity of work is then undertaken with an eye to external necessity or reward. This institutional fact comes into conflict with the welfare state's effort to provide income and employment security. Policies that protect workers from cyclical or arbitrary unemployment and provide income to those unemployed tend to remove the threat of deprivation upon which the employers' discipline of the work force depends. Policies that strengthen labor union representation and bargaining over work rules and employment practices have the same effect. In other words, capitalist labor markets *require* the threat of unemployment and income deprivation to maintain acceptable wage levels and labor *intensity* (Marx, 1967, ch. 25). Recent analyses of capitalist accumulation crises have indicated the important role played by labor intensity and the related problem of overhead cost for supervisory personnel (O'Connor, 1984; Bowles, Gordon, and Weisskopf, 1983). The above is not meant to suggest that wage labor and income security are ineluctably inconsistent. Social democratic ideology maintains that industrial reform is possible in this regard and points to job enrichment, co-determination, and solidaristic wage strategies as ways to overcome the contradiction between capitalist labor markets and welfare state income and employment security. The point is that progress in this regard requires a new consciousness regarding the practice of industrial relations as well as significant structural reformation.

As also indicated by Polanyi's discussion of the fictitious commodities, capital markets represent another unresolved problem area of the corporate-welfare state. Private enterprise investment means that individuals and organizations have discretion over the deployment of their capital funds. Inevitably, state policy designed to stabilize the macroeconomy or regulate the microeconomy affects the spatial or temporal relative profitability of investments. The private sector responds by reallocating investment to reflect relative price changes--the time-honored function of markets. However, this also restructures capital and recomposes labor in ways that often conflict with policy objectives that already may be inconsistent in and of themselves. Full employment fiscal and monetary policies that strengthen labor's hand in a particular country may cause capital flight abroad. Interregional capital flight within the country may occur if the policy effects are differentially distributed because of industrial relations differences. Environmental, occupational, or other social regulatory programs tend to have similar differential effects on profitability among regions, nations, or economic sectors. Entrepreneurial investment decisions respond according to relative profitability, and the objectives of policy initiatives may well be frustrated in the process because the overall volume of investment and its location cannot help but influence the outcome of the political economic process. These and similar issues have been involved in the recent debate on the so-called "deindustrialization of America" (Bluestone and Harrison, 1982). Here again progress within the corporate-welfare state would appear to require a new image of investment and of the benefit-cost calculus that controls it.

As noted above, Polanyi's notion of protective response was not limited to nominal government forums. It includes nongovernment collective action such as the modern corporation and industrial union. The growth of private organizational power that results raises the issue of an obscure private government, especially in the case of the corporation (Mason, 1966, chs. 4, 5, and 11). This corporate cultural hegemony (Stanfield, 1979, ch. 3; Dugger, 1984, ch. 4) is interrelated with the ideological and structural problems discussed above. The absence of a positive ideology or theory of the corporate-welfare state has made it impossible to address this outcome of the spontaneous protective response. The corporate interest is apparently served by having concentrated power obscured by continuation of the competitive market ideology (Galbraith, 1973). The ideology of consumerism and invidious distinction serves one aspect of the corporate interest by its tendency to create income-earning, income-spending automatons (Stanfield and Stanfield, 1980; Galbraith, 1973). This consumeristic, invidious mentality is costly in terms of individual psychological health and social solidarity. It also conflicts with the social responsibility required for a well-functioning welfare state (Robson, 1976; Bell, 1976). As a result of the lack of trust and social responsibility, programs are more costly and have performance of their service missions eroded by the red tape necessary to combat fraud and diversion of funds to those who do not qualify within the program's guidelines (Kaufman, 1977).

This consumeristic mentality also tends to conflict with the macroeconomic performance needed to make the welfare state work on a financial level. Consumers driven to borrow and buy in the service of invidious narcissism and governments starved for tax revenues by tax revolts and tax-avoiding lobbies compete in financial markets with corporate borrowers with adverse consequences for corporate investment and the accumulation process of capitalism (O'Connor, 1984). Of course, the corporate spending thus "crowded out" is not immune to invidious waste and narcissistic excess in its own right (Stanfield, 1983, pp. 599-604). Here again there is a need to review the corporation as an entity with influence that extends far beyond mere economic power narrowly conceived. Its mission needs to be redefined and its accounting and accountability restructured (Estes, 1976). It is especially necessary for society to have some control over corporate cultural power, i.e., the power to shape consciousness.

A further unresolved problem is the international setting. Patriotism and the tradition of national autonomy persist despite the growing technological interdependence of national economies. Significant intervention exists, but the spontaneous protective response is even less a matter of conscious design in the global setting than the national one. Notwithstanding visionaries who have foreseen the need for a world New Deal (Ayres, 1962, pp. 280-330; Markowitz, 1973, ch. 2) or welfare world (Myrdahl, 1967), the basic problem remains of replacing the ideology of free trade with a doctrine that recognizes that domestic intervention by the corporate-welfare state necessitates concomitant international intervention and policy coordination. In other words, there is a need in Polanyi's terminology to reimbed the international economy in the social and political process (McClintock, 1988). Managed market economies cannot work if subjected to unregulated international markets. The degree of adjustment and social dislocation that would result from allowing free international trade would prove intolerable to the denizens of mature industrial society. The conclusion being reached by leading experts in international economics concerning the necessary balance in the international trade system is the same as that reached concerning domestic economic balances in the 1930s but forgotten in the neoclassical synthesis after World War II (Stanfield, 1979, ch. 2). As Ozawa has observed,

> The freedom of the marketplace alone is inadequate to cope with the problems of interdependence. Some form of government measures . . . is a desideratum if technological leadership in mature economies . . . is to be rejuvenated. The conventional aggregate demand management alone will not work . . . . It is time to recognize another basic deficiency of the marketplace, its inability to rejuvenate the industrial structure of a mature deindustrializing economy through innovation fast enough to maintain complementary interdependence with the newly industrializing countries (Ozawa, 1987, p. 59).

In other words, the market system plus aggregate demand policy is insufficient; some form of structural policy or *direct adjustment mechanism* is required. Here again a fundamental shift in consciousness is necessary. The Keynesian Revolution carried political economic philosophy to the point of recognizing governmental responsibility for macroeconomic stability, but limited its tool kit in the pursuit of macroeconomic goals to indirect aggregate demand policy (fiscal or monetary policy). It now seems necessary to add to these aggregate demand instruments some mechanism for direct control over wages, prices, and investment, i.e., some form of incomes and industrial policy.

CONCLUSION

The corporate-welfare state is a social structural transformation awaiting for its full realization a cultural reconstruction. In the critical areas discussed above, and others, progress requires a new mentality appropriate to the new reality. A *re-viewing* of the past and present is essential to the *imagining* of a more desirable future (Stanfield, 1986, pp. 47-53). This new mentality is resisted by powerful vested interests who have prestigious niches in the current social order. Of course, they also sincerely believe in the validity of the market mentality that is being challenged herein (Veblen, 1953, ch. 8).

Mainstream, formal economics is a large part of this ideological inertia. The "imagery of choice" and atomistic competition that it retains serve to obscure the reality of concentrated economic power (Galbraith, 1973, chs. 1, 2; Stanfield, 1979, chs. 3, 4). Moreover, if Polanyi's argument concerning the *socially* protective response is correct, then the twentieth century drift to various types of socialism and corporate-welfare states cannot be understood by a perspective that treats the economy in isolation from the rest of society. The protective response concept suggests that the interaction of social and economic phenomena account for the dominant institutional trends of the twentieth century. Accordingly, socialism and the corporate-welfare state can only be understood by a social economics perspective that focuses on this interaction between society and economy.

Clearly, then, the crisis of the age is cultural (Benton, 1983; Diedrich, 1983). This is not meant to deny the structural, accumulation crisis of late capitalism (O'Connor, 1984; Bowles, Gordon, and Weisskopf, 1983). It is only to say that progress requires a new consciousness, a new culture or integrated set of meanings to guide popular life. The crisis is therefore experienced psychologically in a deeply rooted sense of frustration and anxiety. This leads to a final conclusion concerning the contribution of social economics to the understanding of the corporate-welfare state. Social economics itself must become much more focused on the psychocultural aspects of the corporate-welfare state. If the economy is to be subordinated to the pursuit of human joy, social economists must develop an economics of joy. The challenge and promise of social economics is therefore very great indeed.

References

Appleby, J. O. 1978. *Economic Thought and Ideology in Seventeenth Century England.* Princeton: Princeton University Press.

Ayres, C. E. 1962. *The Theory of Economic Progress.* New York: Schocken Books.

_____. 1967. "Ideological responsibility," *Journal of Economic Issues* 1 (June), 3-11.

Bell, D. 1976. *The Cultural Contradictions of Capitalism.* New York: Basic Books.

Benton, Jr. R. 1983. "Economics as a cultural system and the loss of meaning," Ph.D. dissertation, Colorado State University, Fort Collins, CO.

Berry, W. 1978. *The Unsettling of America: Culture and Agriculture.* New York: Avon Books.

Bluestone, B. and B. Harrison. 1982. *The Deindustrialization of America.* New York: Basic Books.

Bowles, S., D. Gordon and T. Weisskopf. 1983. *Beyond the Wasteland.* New York: Doubleday.

Braverman, H. 1974. *Labor and Monopoly Capital.* New York: Monthly Review Press.

Clark, J. M. 1967. *Preface to Social Economics.* New York: A. M. Kelley.

Dalton, G., ed. 1968. *Primitive, Archaic, and Modern Economies: Essays of Karl Polanyi.* Garden City, NJ: Doubleday.

Diedrich, E. 1983. "Human welfare and econocentrism: the pathology of modern economic growth," Ph.D. dissertation, Colorado State University, Fort Collins, CO.

Dugger, W. M. 1984. *An Alternative to Economic Retrenchment.* New York: Petrocelli.

Eichner, A. S. 1984. *Why Economics Is Not Yet a Science.* White Plains, NY: M. E. Sharpe.

Estes, R. 1976. *Corporate Social Accounting.* New York: John Wiley.

Furniss, N. and T. Tilton. 1977. *The Case for the Welfare State*. Bloomington: Indiana University Press.

Galbraith, J. K. 1973. *Economics and the Public Purpose*. Boston: Houghton-Mifflin.

Kaufman, H. 1977. *Red Tape*. Washington, DC: Brookings Institution.

Lowe, A. 1977. *On Economic Knowledge*, enlarged edition. White Plains, NY: M. E. Sharpe.

Lutz, M. A. and K. Lux. 1979. *The Challenge of Humanistic Economics*. Menlo Park, CA: Benjamin/Cummings.

Markowitz, N. D. 1973. *The Rise and Fall of the People's Century*. New York: Free Press.

Marshall, A. 1949. *Principles of Economics*, 8th ed. New York: MacMillan.

Marx, K. 1967. *Capital*, Vol. I. New York: International.

Mason, E. S., ed. 1966. *The Corporation in Modern Society*. New York: Atheneum.

McClintock, B. T. 1988. "Managed trade: the case for socially-protective trade," unpublished manuscript.

Myrdahl, G. 1967. *Beyond the Welfare State*. New York: Bantam Books.

O'Connor, J. 1984. *Accumulation Crisis*. New York: Basil Blackwell.

O'Toole, J. et al. 1973. *Work in America*. Cambridge: MIT Press.

Ozawa, T. 1987. "Can the market alone manage structural upgrading? A challenge posed by economic interdependence," in *Structural Change, Economic Interdependence, and World Development*, edited by J. H. Dunning and M. Usui. London: MacMillan Press.

Papandreou, A. 1972. *Paternalistic Capitalism*. Minneapolis: University of Minnesota Press.

Polanyi, K. 1957. *The Great Transformation*. Boston: Beacon Press.

Robson, W. A. 1976. *Welfare State and Welfare Society*. London: George Allen and Unwin.

Schumpeter, J. A. 1962. *Capitalism, Socialism and Democracy*, 3rd edition. New York: Harper and Row.

Smith, A. 1937. *An Inquiry into the Nature and Causes of the Wealth of Nations*. New York: The Modern Library.

Stanfield, J.R. 1979. *Economic Thought and Social Change*. Carbondale: Southern Illinois University Press.

_____. 1983. "*The affluent society* after twenty-five years," *Journal of Economic Issues* 17 (September), 589-607.

_____. 1986. *The Economic Thought of Karl Polanyi: Lives and Liveli-hood*. London: MacMillan Press, and New York: St. Martin's Press.

Stanfield J. R. and J. B. Stanfield. 1980. "Consumption in contemporary capitalism: the backward art of living," *Journal of Economic Issues* 14 (June), 437-451.

Swaney, J.A. 1983. "Rival and missing interpretations of market society: a comment on Hirschman," *Journal of Economic Literature* 21 (December), 1489-1493.

Titmus, R.M. 1969. *Essays on the Welfare State*. Boston: Beacon Press.

Veblen, T. B. 1953. *Theory of the Leisure Class*. New York: New American Library.

10

PROBLEMS OF THE WELFARE STATE[*]

William M. Dugger

INTRODUCTION

The Welfare State in Historical Perspective

At the very outset, the welfare state must be put in historical perspective. European feudalism, Roman imperialism, and the Greek city--none of them developed a welfare state. Instead, they developed charitable orders and extended families. The welfare state is a very recent development; its origins go back not much more than a century or two. It is the nation state's response to the insecurities of industrial capitalism. Its varied programs are attempts to provide security and sufficiency, for all,

[*] In memory of Harold Washington, Reform Mayor of Chicago. Mark A. Lutz was helpful, as was Brother Leo V. Ryan, C.S.V., Dean of DePaul University's College of Commerce. My college generously provided release time and support for this project. The views expressed herein are not necessarily those of my colleagues or college. This chapter was presented on April 26, 1988, as the Kendall P. Cochran and Mona Hersh first Annual Lecture on Social Economics to North Texas State University and Texas Women's University.

in the wake of the insecurity and insufficiency, for many, that accompanied capitalism and the industrial revolution. The welfare state is also a concerted attempt to protect the weak and to make whole the dispossessed. Being an activity conducted by the state rather than the church or the family, it is far more effective and powerful than traditional charity. It is more effective, because it draws on the vast financial resources of the nation state. It is more powerful because it relies on the force of law. It is also of broader scope than traditional charity, stretching far beyond the local relations of the neighborhood and village and far beyond the personal relations of the congregation and parish to the political relations of the nation. The welfare state is not of the white neighborhood, the fundamentalist church, nor the patriarchical family, but of the democratic nation.

The welfare state, being in its infancy, faces a large number of ongoing problems and institutional resistances. Some of the most emotional resistance to the expansion of the welfare state comes from those whose power, income, and status are rooted in the neighborhood, the church, or the family. While it has been corporate capitalism that has continued to eat away at all three of these old institutions, much misplaced resentment is directed at the new welfare state (Block, Cloward, Ehrenreich, and Piven, 1987).

Being desperately needed by those it serves, the welfare state has survived even the harshness of the 1980s retrenchment. The welfare state has been wounded by the mean-spirited years, but the problems it faces are not insurmountable. Rather, they are growing pains; difficulties that can be met, tasks that can be performed. The welfare state has many challenges to grow by and many promises to keep. And the welfare state or its successor can rise to meet them. This claim is not optimistic, but realistic. It is based on the historical evidence; on the observed evolution of humans from small-scale tribalism to large-scale globalism and on the movement from primitive subsistence economies with no surpluses to advanced industrial economies with vast surpluses. From the stone age to the space age, progress toward affluence and security has been spotty, but real nonetheless. The record of human affairs on this planet is drenched with blood and inequity, but it *does* show progress. It is only realistic to expect progress to continue, and to expect the welfare state--progeny of the democratic nation--to play an important role in that progress.

My discussion and my realistic faith in resumed progress has been formed and tested by the recent U.S. experience, by the worst times of the worst welfare state. The Reagan administration's retrenchment has viciously distorted public priorities, but has not destroyed the welfare state.

The depravity of the Reagan years is hard to appreciate. But the Children's Defense Fund, a private, child advocacy group, tries to drive home the sheer meanness:

> President Reagan proposed an additional $3 million cut in the childhood immunization program for FY 1982 which would eliminate immunizations for 75,000 children at risk. In FY 1983 he plans to cut $2 million more. The Defense Department spends $1.4 million on shots and other veterinary services for the pets of military personnel. Additional millions are spent on the transportation of military pets when personnel are transferred. If the veterinary benefits for military pets were eliminated, 35,000 low income children could be immunized instead (Children's Defense Fund, 1982, p. 17).

Even at this low tide of the progressive spirit, and even in the worst welfare state of developed nations, hope exists. Pessimism seems to predominate at this particular historical juncture because of the lurch to the right in the United States caused by the cataclysmic war in southeast Asia. The United States never lost anything before, so we never learned how to be a good loser. Hence, the loss knocked us off our moorings. The war was perceived as a national defeat, as a loss of manhood. Particularly in the American right, marked by a traditionally paranoid style to begin with, the losing war in southeast Asia caused a mean-spirited desire to get even, a generalized reactionary distemper. And to make the distemper far worse, at the same time we were hopelessly bogged down in southeast Asia, blacks, women, gays, and youths rose up almost in unison against imperialism, racism, sexism, homophobia, and the bourgeois conformity that have plagued American life. International defeat and domestic unrest led to a massive backlash, a reactionary tidal wave that began with George Wallace's presidential campaign in 1968, during which Mr. Wallace ran against black people, women, students, federal judges, and government bureaucrats. The reactionary tidal wave finally peaked when it allowed a Hollywood cowboy to ride its crest into the White House in 1981 and to stay there for a second term, in spite of the worst recession since 1929. The mean-spirited era destroyed our innocent youth, but not our realistic hope. It even turned "welfare" into a racist code word.

Nevertheless, the reactionary wave will pass, may already be passing. And when it finally does, the problems identified in the following pages will become the promises of a reconstructed welfare state. Three broad problems must be addressed: (1) the welfare state needs a philosophical foundation, a legitimate reason for being; (2) the welfare state needs to improve its provision of goods (aid in kind) and of incomes (aid in cash); and (3) the welfare state must become a tool of the democratic process.

PROBLEM I: PHILOSOPHICAL FOUNDATION

Raison D'Être

Foremost among the problems of the welfare state is the fact that the welfare state lacks a philosophical foundation. The welfare state needs to belong, to be accepted as a legitimate institution. It needs a reason for being which is applicable to the age of the nation state and to the problems of mature industrial capitalism. The welfare states of the twentieth century require a far broader philosophical base than the charities of earlier times. The theology of religious orders, the personalism of tight communities, the ethnicity of immigrant neighborhoods, the patriarchy of extended families are all too narrow, and have largely disappeared anyway. Religious belief, face-to-face friendship, shared ethnic background, and patriarchical authority must give way to instrumental reasoning as the philosophical foundation for the modern welfare state. A broader, stronger mooring is required. The reconstructed welfare state must be built on a mooring that can withstand the inevitable reactionary backlashes, the waves of distemper bound to sweep across the social landscape from time to time. Furthermore, the welfare state is not a conspiracy. It is not the product of the greed and lust for power of a new class. In spite of the paranoid and resentful ramblings of the far right in the United States, the welfare state cannot be explained in terms of a new devil theory. Evil federal bureaucrats did not create the welfare state to serve their own selfish ends. Federal bureaucrats serve their own self-interest, as we all do. But their self-interest has not been the driving force behind the uneven growth of the welfare state. Instead, widespread need in the face of industrial abundance has been the driving force. The welfare state is more than the result of empire-building by power-hungry, welfare bureaucrats. The welfare state is more than the result of knee-jerk responses to the pleas of special interests. Its origins in the United States are in the New Deal, the democratic response to the widespread, grassroots demand for reform. The welfare state is integral to the spread of modern affluence. It is a response to the urgent needs of millions. And yet, in spite of everything, at the center of the contemporary American distemper is the profound belief that the welfare state has grown because of the empire-building machinations of government bureaucrats and their deviously self-serving supporters among liberal intellectuals and student radicals. These groups constitute the so-called "new class," the scapegoat of the ideology espoused by the new right. Barbara Ehrenreich explains:

> By hypothesizing a corrupt and powerful new class, the right has been able to resolve the contradictions inherent in an ideology that is both populist in tone and aggressively procapitalist in spirit. In the New Right's synthesis, nothing is wrong with the free market except that it has been hampered by regulations and policies imposed by the liberal new class. Thus the moral breakdown perceived everywhere by the New Right is not a product of *laissez-faire* capitalism and the amoral individualism it inevitably fosters, but of the new class's attempts to abridge *laissez-faire* through various forms of government intervention in the economy. It follows that the appropriate target for resentment is not big business but big government, and not the corporate elite but the "educated elite." Capitalism itself is moral, even "Christian," and works in the interest of the average "middle American." It is the attempts to interfere with it--from affirmative action to social welfare programs--which lead to trouble (Ehrenreich in Block, Cloward, Ehrenreich, and Piven, 1987, pp. 163-164).

As he rode the reactionary wave into the White House, Ronnie Reagan referred to members of the "new class" as "welfarists." In one of his frequent radio broadcast attacks on the welfare state, Mr. Reagan asserted, "We aren't salvaging people; we are making them permanent clients of a professional group of welfarists whose careers depend on the preservation of poverty" (quoted in R. Dugger, 1983, p. 497). After years of this reactionary buncombe from the highest level of American society, the welfare state is not viewed as a legitimate institution, but as a pathological one. Ronnie Reagan gave vent to this attitude toward "welfare" in a 1978 radio broadcast: "Welfare," Reagan announced, "is a dangerous drug destroying the spirit of people once proudly independent. Our mission should be to help people kick that particular drug habit" (quoted in R. Dugger, 1983, p. 497). It is not viewed as integral to the good life. It is not viewed as instrumental. Instead, the welfare state is viewed as dysfunctional, as an interference and obstruction, as a hindrance to the smooth operation of the market system. And so, in a curious twist of meaning, "welfare" is considered a cost rather than a benefit, a debilitating addiction and a pathological growth rather than a healthy function and a necessary organ (see Gilder, 1981; Murray, 1984; and Silver, 1980). David Hamilton explains:

> If we view the welfare state as a monstrous growth, as more or less an economic cancer that has grown on an otherwise well-articulated system, then we most certainly must view it as a cost. But if we view it as a means of resolving the inherent problems of a system flawed by an inability to distribute income in a manner that will sustain income and employment, then we must consider it a strategy to balance an unbalanced system (Hamilton, 1984, pp. 149-150).

Instrumentalism: Equity and Efficiency

Hamilton understands the welfare state as instrumental to the modern economy, as a necessary means of providing security and sufficiency. The welfare state, according to Hamilton and other instrumentalists, has a perfectly sound philosophical foundation--it is useful (Hamilton, 1967, 1970, 1971, 1984; Ayres, 1961, pp. 187-227; Cochran, 1969; W. Dugger, 1981). Its redistribution of income helps provide the continually rising effective demand essential to steady growth of output and to ongoing development of new goods and services. For example, sunbelt retirement communities and the myriad of new manufacturing and service establishments that have sprung up to meet the needs of older Americans would not exist if the New Deal had not founded the Social Security System. Furthermore, the welfare state's health and education programs help provide the quality work force essential to a high-tech economy. High-tech cannot exist without equally high-quality workers.

The welfare state is universal among highly industrialized economies, because the need for it is universal. Of course, the privileged seem universally to condemn the welfare state, arguing that it impairs the morality and blunts the initiative of the underprivileged. As instrumentalist Clarence Ayres put it,

> Quite commonly the people who are most fearful of the effect social security may have in eroding the initiative of its recipients are themselves the beneficiaries of a much older form of social security--that of property (Ayres, 1961, p. 225).

Some welfare states serve better (Sweden) than others (United States), but in all cases, the welfare state serves the values of equity and efficiency. The equity dimension of the welfare state is more widely understood than the efficiency dimension. In fact, an extensive technical literature has been accumulated on the subjects of equity and justice. The most influential work in the recent literature is that of John Rawls, and the most important Rawlsian principle is the "difference principle." Simply stated, the principle reminds us that any policy that benefits the rich and powerful is just, only if it also helps the poor and the powerless. "The intuitive idea is that the social order is not to establish and secure the more attractive prospects of those better off unless doing so is to the advantage of those less fortunate" (Rawls, 1971, p. 75). So the equity goal of the welfare state has received at least a backhanded seal of approval from Rawls and his followers.

The welfare state not only serves equity but efficiency as well. The welfare state insures against deep recession with an array of automatic stabilizers. Unemployment benefits and a whole series of income-based aid programs pump income into the economy when the private flow of income declines. In-kind programs of aid also expand when the private economy contracts. Both kinds of programs act as automatic stabilizers that replace income lost in the private sector, keeping the economy operating closer to its production possibility frontier than it would have operated in their absence. Progressive taxes serve the same efficiency purpose--when the private economy contracts, the progressive tax take contracts even faster, cushioning the decline of after-tax private incomes during recessions and keeping the economy closer to its production possibility frontier than it would have been in the absence of a progressive tax system. The efficiency effects of the welfare state are ignored by most orthodox economists. They fail to take note of its instrumental effects, particularly in mature industrial economies with tendencies toward secular underconsumption and cyclical instability. In such capitalist economies, the welfare state not only helps stabilize the fluctuations of the business cycle but also helps finance the formation of so-called human capital and helps underwrite the additional consumption needed to stave off secular stagnation.

Furthermore, the welfare state serves what Philip A. Klein describes as a "higher efficiency," an efficiency that goes beyond the perfect market's static, individualistic efficiency to an actual society's dynamic, collective efficiency. The higher efficiency is too broad to be found in the microeconomic relations between socially isolated individuals and perfectly competitive firms.   Instead, the higher efficiency has to do with the institutional structures and decisionmaking processes studied by institutional economists (Klein, 1984). The institutional structures of significance to the higher efficiency include a family institution capable of providing nurturing for children and caring for adults, a school institution capable of providing adequate education to all, a workplace capable of providing meaningful, participatory employment to all, and a political system capable of providing meaningful civil values and participatory political structures to hold us all together.   Significant decisionmaking processes in the government and in the economy must be open to criticism, flexible in the face of change, and democratically responsive to the concerns of participants and constituents. Otherwise, rigidity and stagnation set in, both in the government and in the economy, crippling the higher efficiency. The higher efficiency also has to do with the broader macroeconomic relations explored by the Keynesians and post-Keynesians and with the basic collective issues of humaneness and compassion that give ongoing coherence and value to nations and societies. Broad macroeconomic relations include the need to keep the pool of jobs growing in step with the labor force, the need to keep the rate of inflation under control, the need to roughly balance exports with imports, and the need to balance growth in gross national product (GNP) with quality of life. The higher efficiency is to be found in the institutional framework, in the philosophical foundation, and in the social values and meanings within which individual behavior takes place, not in the individual behavior itself. The welfare state is one of the central frameworks of the higher efficiency, a part of the essential infrastructure that makes the good life possible and meaningful for a continually broader range of human beings. Without it, neither a higher (social) nor a lower (individual) efficiency would make any sense.

Nevertheless, most economists fail to understand the efficiency dimensions of the welfare state. The supply-side economists who provided the theoretical justification for ill-fated Reaganomics in the United States and for ill-fated Thatcherism in the United Kingdom are the worst failures (Wanniski, 1978; Hailstones, 1982; Bartlett and Roth, 1983). Lester Thurow refers to them as economic fundamentalists (Thurow, 1983, pp. 126-131). The fundamentalists argue that the welfare state with its progressive taxes and income maintenance programs has robbed the industrial economies of their dynamism. But recent experience has been most unkind to the supply-siders. The Reagan administration in the United States and the Thatcher government in the United Kingdom tried to put the supply-side principles into practice with massive tax cuts for the rich, drastic cuts in welfare programs for the poor, and deregulation of powerful corporations. Progressivity of the tax system was largely destroyed, knocking one of the automatic stabilizers out from under the mature economy, thereby increasing its fragility, its tendency toward cyclical instability and secular stagnation. The economies in both nations have suffered severely as a result. The higher efficiency of each declined. A very sharp recession ushered in the 1980s decade and the rest of the decade has witnessed an agonizingly slow recovery from the self-inflicted recession. The weakness of the slow recovery has been punctuated by the stock market collapse in the autumn of 1987 and by the ongoing corruption and degradation of business practices in the United States (Brodeur, 1985; Clinard and Yeager, 1980; Etzioni, 1984).

Lacking an adequate philosophical foundation for the welfare state, most orthodox social analysts have ignored the higher efficiency it serves. And so, they were unprepared for the reactionary age of the 1970s and 1980s. They could not mount an effective defense of the welfare state against what Walt Rostow has called "the barbaric counter-revolution," because they failed to understand the instrumental foundation of the welfare state (Rostow, 1983). Unfortunately, ignoring the efficiency dimensions of the welfare state has been very costly, especially for the poor and the working class who suffer disproportionately from cutbacks in aid programs and from increases in unemployment. With the October 1987 stock market collapse in the United States, even the rich have suffered, at least on paper. (Further discussion is in Levitan, 1980; Schwarz, 1983; and Harrington, 1986.)

The welfare state serves equity; on this, most serious economists agree. But the agreement proved insufficient to save the welfare state from reactionary attack. Building a stronger foundation, one based on instrumental efficiency as well as social equity, remains the major problem faced by the welfare state. (For new directions see Ayres, 1961; Lutz and Lux, 1979; and Tool, 1986.)

PROBLEM II: PROVISION OF GOODS (AID IN KIND)

General Considerations

The next problem to be identified is actually a whole series of problems encountered when the needy are provided aid in the form of goods. The needy can be provided aid in kind or in cash. From the point of view of the needy, aid generally is best when provided in money instead of in kind, because money can be used as the needy recipients themselves see fit. Aid in kind, on the other hand, can only be used in the form of the good provided to the recipient. Aid in kind comes with strings attached. That is, aid in kind carries with it a degree of social control over the recipient. So recipients generally prefer aid in cash to aid in kind. Providers, however, frequently prefer aid in kind because of the social control over the recipient aid in kind gives to the provider. For example, a black family living in the streets of Chicago could be provided with either enough income to rent themselves an apartment, or they could be provided with a free apartment in Cabrini Green--a Chicago Housing Authority project. On one hand, if they were given the income, they might try to live in Cicero, an all-white ethnic area. On the other hand, if they are given the apartment, they will live in an essentially all-black area. Aid in kind imposes a form of social control on the recipient. In this case, it enforces racial segregation by concentrating poor black people into large public housing projects. Combined with strictly enforced open housing laws, aid in the form of cash might not result in segregated housing. So if aid provision in Chicago is controlled by white ethnics, aid in kind will be used to control the activities of black aid recipients. In particular, it will be used to maintain the segregated neighborhoods for which Chicago has become famous.

In addition to this extremely negative attribute, aid in kind also has a number of positive attributes. Obviously, aid in kind reduces the power of private providers. Several examples from contemporary life immediately come to mind: the Chicago Housing Authority (when not corrupted by slum landlords being appointed to run it) reduces the market power of slum landlords by expanding the supply of low-cost housing. The

Chicago Transit Authority likewise reduces the power of auto makers and auto dealers by providing a transportation alternative to the privately owned auto or cab. Public schools in the United States provide an alternative to church and proprietary schools. Yellowstone National Park provides an alternative to Disneyland. The National Health Service provides an alternative to fee for service health care in the United Kingdom. The Indian Health Service provides an alternative to private health care for reservation Indians in the United States. Free school meals provide an alternative to privately provided foods. All of these aid in kind programs provide public alternatives to private goods.

In addition to providing a needed alternative to private suppliers, aid in kind and some kinds of payment schemes also can rectify information inadequacies and transaction cost problems. By providing a good directly to the person who needs it, the problems the person may encounter in choosing the appropriate good for themselves can be reduced. The command of information that the individual consumer needs to make an informed, timely choice is extremely difficult to come by in questions of medical care and medical insurance. The same is true for the student trying to choose the right school. Providing aid in kind can help overcome these information problems. Furthermore, external costs and external benefits bestowed on others can be taken into consideration by aid in kind programs. The severity of the information and transaction cost problems to be rectified depends on the nature of the good provided. Generally, four kinds of goods are provided in kind, sometimes in direct competition with actual or potential private providers: (1) health care, (2) education, (3) housing, and (4) food.

Health Care

In the absence of a national health service, the United States has developed a fee-for-service delivery system coupled with a patchwork third party payment mechanism to serve the health care needs of most Americans. Health care providers, mainly hospitals and physicians, serve the health care needs of patients and charge a fee for each service provided. Most of the fees are then paid by a private insurer or by Medicare or Medicaid. Medicare and Medicaid were created by the Social Security Amendment of 1965. Medicare covers retired or disabled people receiving Social Security benefits. It also covers patients with kidney failure. Medicare is a federal program with uniform benefits across the nation.

But Medicaid is a state-federal program with benefit levels that vary by state. Medicare covers primarily the aged and disabled, while Medicaid covers primarily the indigent. Private insurance companies cover those who individually purchase a policy and those whose employers purchase a group policy covering employees. Unfortunately, loss of employment usually means loss of coverage. Those who are not covered must pay for their own care, or possibly go without it.

In 1970, total payments to health care deliverers were $65 billion. Third party payors accounted for $39 billion, or 60 percent. Out of the $39 billion in third party payments, government payments accounted for $22 billion, or 57 percent; private insurors accounted for $15 billion, or 39 percent; and philanthropy and industry accounted for $1 billion, or 3 percent. In 1984, personal health care payments to deliverers totaled $342 billion, up dramatically from 1970. Third party payors spent $246 billion of it, or 72 percent--their proportion of the total rose significantly. Out of the $246 billion in third party payments, government payments (primarily Medicare and Medicaid) were $135 billion, or 55 percent; private insurance payments were $107 billion, or 43 percent; and payments by philanthropy and industry were $4 billion, or 2 percent. The government share in 1984 was down slightly from 1970, while the private insurance share was up slightly (U.S. Health Care Financing Administration, 1988, p. 89).

The fee for service and third party payment features of the U.S. health system result in cost maximization. Fees are too high and/or too many services are performed. The patient does not know enough about the services provided and does not have to pay for all of them, so the patient does not keep costs down. Nor can the physician or hospital be expected to minimize costs because the costs are income to the physician and the hospital. So the third party payor is left holding the bag, overstuffed because those with the power and the knowledge to make decisions about health care services are the ones who receive payment for the services. The covered patient exerts little cost minimization pressure. They want the best that a third party payor can buy. But those not covered by a third party payor often suffer from inadequate provision of health care. In 1983, about 35 million people, 15 percent of the population, were not covered by a third party payor. An astonishing 10 million children under 16 years of age were not covered. This was 18 percent of all American children (U.S. Bureau of the Census, 1986, p. 101). In sum, it is not unreasonable to conclude that the existing U.S. system of health care results in either too much (payment), or too little (provision) (Barr, 1987, pp. 283-315).

When the third party payor is a private insurer rather than a government agency, additional information problems are encountered. Individual health insurance buyers seldom have perfect information about the policies available, their costs, and the relative values of the different benefit schedules offered. Group health insurance provided by employers is often purchased by sophisticated corporate officials, overcoming the information complexities. But, the group health insurance buyer serves the interest of the employer, which may or may not coincide with the interest of the employee being insured. As a result of these problems, regulation of insurance companies has become extensive. Appropriate regulation can mitigate the information problems of buying health insurance, but not the problems inherent to the fee for service, third party payment system which haphazardly developed in the United States.

In a more optimistic vein, a new institution is rapidly emerging in the U.S. health care system, an institution with great promise for overcoming some of the shortcomings of the current system. The new institution is the "health maintenance organization," the HMO. An individual joins an HMO by paying a standard fee. The HMO then provides the individual with the health care they require, either with no fee for service rendered or with only a nominal fee. The HMO either employs physicians and owns hospitals, or works out an arrangement with them, as needed. The HMO eliminates the fee for service and third party payment features which encourage cost maximization, making the HMO a more efficient delivery system. To the extent that the HMO tries to maximize its own profits at the expense of its own patient-members, however, it will tend toward delivering minimal services. But to the extent that the HMO evolves into a service organization rather than a proprietary firm, it will tend toward becoming a mini-national health service. Public policy favoring the latter course seems highly promising. The specific motivational processes and institutional structures that evolve within the HMO will make a big difference. But even a progressive HMO cannot solve the problems of uncovered individuals, those who are not covered by private insurance, Medicare, or Medicaid. Reforms of existing programs must take account of the need for universal coverage, particularly of children (Rodgers, 1982, pp. 90-100; Levitan, 1980, pp. 60-68). If complete reconstruction rather than reform is on the agenda for the future, then a comprehensive national health service is highly desirable. It eliminates the problems encountered in insurance payment systems and in fee-for-service delivery systems.

Education

The welfare state should insure that the next generation of citizens, parents, and workers are not only properly trained for the roles they have to play in society but that they also are sufficiently enlightened to perform those continually changing roles with wisdom and kindness. Clearly, the externalities of education are pervasive. Unfortunately, in the 1980s, the educational voucher scheme has moved to a high place on the reactionary agenda for America, crowding out far more important issues. Education in America used to rely on the three "Rs." Reading, writing, and 'rithmetic were central to public schools. But a new three Rs have entered the scene with the private school push for educational vouchers. The new three Rs relied on by private schools are the rich, the religious, and the racist. That is, private schools serve rich families, religious families, or white families who do not want their children attending school with blacks. The rise of the white academy in the South, in response to court-ordered school integration, is well known (the racist R). So, too, is the use of elite private schools by rich families (the rich R). But not so well known is a fundamental change in the condition of private Catholic schools (the religious R). The high point for Catholic education in the United States was reached around the mid-1960s. In 1965, about 5.5 million students were enrolled in about 13,000 elementary and secondary Catholic schools in the United States. They were instructed by 177,000 teachers; 64 percent of the teachers were religious and 36 percent lay. But by 1984, 27 percent of the teachers were religious and 73 percent lay. Religious teachers are members of different Catholic orders. They are primarily sisters and are terribly underpaid. The vast majority teach for very little more than room and board. Not surprisingly, the numbers of men and women joining religious teaching orders of the Catholic church have declined dramatically, so more and more lay teachers are being used in their place. However, lay teachers demand salaries more commensurate with teacher salaries in public schools. So the cost of Catholic elementary and secondary education, which used to be borne by the sacrifice of Catholic religious teachers, mainly women, is now increasingly borne by the families of the students. Educational vouchers for Catholic students have become crucial, as student enrollment in Catholic schools has steadily declined. In 1984 it had fallen to little more than half of the peak 1965 enrollment (U.S. Bureau of the Census, 1987, p. 132). Barring an exceptional rise in the numbers of men and women entering teaching orders, the decline in Catholic elementary and secondary education will continue--unless vouchers save the day. And so, a curious amalgam of forces have come together to put the educational voucher on the agenda for the 1980s. The amalgam is composed of radically dissimilar elements-- religious Catholic schools, elitist private schools, and racist white acade- mies. Those who wish to continue the dominance of public education in America need only wait for the curious amalgam to come apart. The breakup should not be long in coming, for the three Rs really have little but expedience to hold them together. The longer the line is held against vouchers, the more likely the three Rs will break up.

When progressive educational reform once again becomes possible, emphasis must be placed on helping the truly educationally disadvantaged. This means more support for preschool, elementary, and secondary education rather than for higher education, because it is in lower levels of the educational system that the disadvantaged are to be found in dispro- portionate numbers. The simple fact is, the disadvantaged drop out before they reach the higher levels. Absent vastly improved performance at the lower levels, aid to the higher levels of education is racially and economi- cally biased. Black and brown people and the poor need help getting through high school first. Only then will increased aid to higher education actually help the educationally deprived. (Further discussion is in Bowles and Gintis, 1976; and Katznelson and Weir, 1985.) The priorities of educational reconstruction must start at the lower levels with Head Start programs, proceed through the middle levels with programs aimed at the dropout problem, and only then move into the higher levels with need- based scholarships and guaranteed loans. After all, only a small fraction of black children now even attend college, let alone graduate. Black college attendance peaked in the late 1970s at about one-third of black high school graduates, only to fall toward about one-fourth of black high school graduates in the reactionary 1980s (U.S. Bureau of the Census, 1987, p. 137). So aid focused on higher education is unavoidably biased against black students, unless specifically designed with their needs in mind.

Housing

The information problems consumers encounter in renting or buying housing are far less severe than those encountered in buying medical care and education. Given the proper enforcement of construction codes and housing ordinances, and given ethical practices on the part of real estate intermediaries and credit suppliers, most affluent buyers and renters can more or less take care of themselves. Higher income eventually could solve the housing problems of many, if not most Americans. The residential construction industry is not monopolized, so higher income supporting higher demand eventually would bring forth a higher private supply in most cases. Hence, the need to provide housing aid in kind rather than in cash could be reduced significantly if adequate income support programs were in place. In an ideal world with sufficient income for everyone, with no forced condo conversions, and with rational rent controls that preserved the integrity of neighborhoods while allowing for the needed incentives to build new housing and renovate old, aid in kind would not be needed by most of us.

However, that ideal world does not exist, nor is it ever likely to exist. Furthermore, like medical care and education, consumer housing choices generate substantial externalities. Furthermore, racial discrimination in housing restricts minority housing choices to encircled, if not also embattled minority neighborhoods served by inadequate schools and municipal services and redlined by private lenders and insurers. Also, many of the newly homeless are so desperate that rational choice is difficult. As for those who have been homeless for an extended period, their lives on the cruel streets of large American cities have not exactly prepared them for optimal decisionmaking in the housing market, even if they had the income to finance their choices, which they do not. In New York City alone, over 25,000 homeless people are sheltered by the city each night, and more emergency shelter is needed. Those 25,000 or so include some 8,500 single men, 1,200 single women, and 17,600 family members (Barbanel, 1987). Homelessness has become a severe problem in many of America's large cities. Chicago is an excellent example, with which I am intimately acquainted. At night, after all the affluent white collar office workers have gone home to the suburbs or have locked themselves up securely in their fashionable high-rises, the street people reclaim the downtown area, giving the loop (the main business district of Chicago, formed by two overlapping loops made by north-south running "L" tracks) the macabre look of third world cities where thousands of single men and women and even families with children eat, sleep, and die in the street.

Housing programs should start at the bottom, where the needs are the greatest, and should aim at eliminating the oldest inequities the fastest. So when political conditions have changed enough to permit progress in housing to resume, the homelessness and segregation problems should be addressed first. Homelessness is related to a number of other problems, most of which have to do in some way with the breakdown of basic social institutions. The breakdown of mental health care in the United States has poured thousands of mentally disturbed people into the streets. We have closed most of our large state-run mental hospitals (warehouses for the mentally ill, little better than the old insane asylums or legalized shooting galleries where the habitués pop prescribed pills instead of shoot heroin) under the guise of providing decentralized, community-based care. In most states, the large, centralized hospitals were closed, but the community based facilities just never really got off the ground, at least not in the numbers required. So the former mental patients ended up in the streets. Family breakdown has poured thousands of separated men into whiskey bottles, needles, and alleys, while it has poured thousands of battered wives and frightened children into temporary shelters or the streets. Child abuse adds its toll of runaways. Industrial breakdown (unemployment) has added its thousands as well. And the breakdown of international law (U.S. backed war in Central America) adds the "illegals" to the legions of homeless Vietnam veterans, a fine legacy from another international breakdown. Nothing short of a federally funded and federally administered program of thousands of shelters for temporary housing in every city of the nation will suffice to solve the problem and salve our collective conscience. For the homeless are our scarlet letter, our mark of shame, a constant reminder of our own breakdown of public morality during the age of retrenchment.

The homeless are not our only stigmata. Cabrini Green in Chicago and the other large, segregated, high-rise public housing projects are also marks of shame on our urban landscape. Placing thousands of mothers with young children in huge high-rise apartment buildings insures the breakdown of parental supervision and equally insures the strengthening of gang violence. But it also insures that poor black people live in segregated housing that occupies a minimum of urban space. Scattered sight public housing, including suburban sites, should replace the giant housing projects, as quickly as the former can be built and the latter can be dynamited. Furthermore, the federal government should launch a nationwide law enforcement campaign on behalf of strict open housing laws. Instead of letting federal law enforcement officials snoop around into our private sex lives and compile lists of subversive "reds," our federal law enforcement resources should be made to enforce open housing law in all of our cities and suburbs. Cash bounties should be paid, at least at first, to black or maybe even white pioneers in formerly segregated areas, and maximum police protection should be provided families and individuals who exercise their right to live where they choose. Furthermore, unscrupulous real estate speculators and "blockbusters" who trade on fear and prejudice should be tightly controlled.

Food

Most people know how and what to eat, or they can learn with little effort. So from the point of view of pure economic theory, little reason exists to provide aid in kind in the form of food. Of course, in underdeveloped countries hit by drought, outside food aid is essential for survival. But third world people are not the only ones who are hungry in our world of agricultural surpluses. Low birth weight is a major cause of poor infant health among the urban poor in the United States, where agricultural surpluses are a perpetual problem. So, for many children and pregnant teenagers, nutritional aid in kind makes a big difference to their health and/or to the health of their unborn infants. Free school lunches also make a lot of sense, at least to those whose vision has not been clouded by an excessive faith in pure economic theory, or by large holdings of McDonald's corporate stock.

Be that as it may, the most important food aid in kind program in the United States has been the food stamp program. The food stamp program represents political pragmatism raised to a high art. Food stamps are a species of voucher which allow the recipient to spend them, but only on food. The food stamps are allocated on the basis of income, one of the very few aid programs in the United States to be so based. Most U.S. aid programs are categorical aid programs. They grant aid to recipients in specified categories--the aged, the blind, the disabled--rather than grant aid to people based on their income, more specifically, based on their lack thereof. But the food stamp program is a means-tested program. Food stamps are granted, on a sliding scale, to recipients according to their income. So the food stamp program reaches many of America's poor who are not covered or who are covered inadequately by other aid programs.

So the food stamp program, though a voucher program, has been a pragmatic success. The coalition supporting the food stamp program has also been a pragmatic success. Since food stamps are vouchers, they make the recipient spend them only on food. This aspect of the food stamp program maintains the support of agricultural and food interests. After all, it creates additional demand for their products. Such interests are not that supportive of other welfare programs. But they are of the food stamp program.

Although the food stamp program has been cut during the mean-spirited years of retrenchment, it has survived. When the time comes for progress to resume, the food stamp program should be a major vehicle for advancing aid to the needy. A voucher program may stigmatize the people using the voucher, and it may reduce their freedom of choice, so vouchers are less desirable to recipients than aid in cash, particularly under the current ideological conditions of contempt for welfare recipients. Such conditions make for a low rate of "take up." That is, the contempt for welfare recipients make even the desperate quite hesitant to apply for and use (take up) the benefits they qualify for. Paying with food stamps at the grocery store is demeaning, at least for now. This discourages people from using them.

But this particular voucher program has some very strong pragmatic reasons for supporting it and for enlarging it. Not only is the food stamp program supported by powerful agricultural and food interests, not only does it reach many of the poor who are not reached by categorical aid, but it also has a stronger appeal to the general American voter, who resents paying for just anything that the poor might want. But the resentment is reduced when the American voter thinks of paying for the food of hungry people. Perhaps the attitude is not rational; perhaps the attitude is not kind. It certainly is condescending; but the attitude is real and must be reckoned with if support for aid is to be expanded.

The same pragmatic political consideration is true, more or less, for the other aid in kind programs. Political support for subsidizing health care, education, and housing is generally greater than support for giving needy people money. So transforming aid in kind into cash grants, even though it increases the flexibility and discretion of the recipients, is inadvisable pragmatically because it erodes political support.

PROBLEM II, CONTINUED: PROVISION OF INCOME (AID IN CASH)

Nonwork Income

For most of us, our income is connected to our work. Particularly for the working class, if we do not work, we have no income. What is left over after we are paid is a kind of economic surplus, and it can be thought of as nonwork income. These are not trivial considerations, but are the conditions that define capitalism--wage labor receives income from work, and the rest is an economic surplus paid out in the form of nonwork income. In modern capitalism we consider the entrepreneur and the return to his entrepreneurial capital as a kind of income from work. The entrepreneur, or undertaker, creates a new business, takes a huge risk, and is rewarded for his "work" with entrepreneurial profits or losses, often in the form of capital gains, at least so our current mythology teaches us (Obrinsky, 1983). But two forms of income are not directly connected to work, not even in current mythology. These nonwork incomes are: (1) welfare payments, meaning the various cash grants to adults who are usually poor, sick, disabled, unemployed, or elderly, or to their children; and (2) rentier payments, meaning the dividend and interest receipts of persons. Welfare income is income of those who break with capitalism, with wage labor. But rentier income is the income of capitalists--rentier capitalists, not entrepreneurial capitalists. Naturally, recipients of the first form of nonwork income are despised; recipients of the second form of nonwork income are admired.

The absolute and relative sizes of these two forms of nonwork income are shown in table 10-1. The table shows a remarkable distributional event in the 1970s. In the 1970s the youth revolt, black revolt, women's liberation movement and, most importantly, the rise of the welfare rights movement had pushed welfare payments above rentier payments. For the first time in the nation's history, capitalists were not receiving the bulk of the economy's nonwork income. Instead, welfare nonwork income rose so high as to challenge and then surpass capitalist nonwork income. No wonder the capitalists objected to the interlopers into their vested interest in nonwork income. And no wonder a New Right rose up to voice their objections. By the 1980s they were able to counterattack against the usurpers quite effectively with Reaganomics, getting for themselves, once again, a larger share of nonwork income than the welfare usurpers. Nonetheless, as the table indicates, the counterattackers did not succeed by pushing the welfare share down, but succeeded

TABLE 10.1

Sources of Nonwork Income, 1940-1986
(billions of dollars)

Period	Personal Income	Welfare Payments	Rentier Payments	Welfare Share (Percent)	Rentier Share (Percent)
1929	84.3	1.5	12.7	2	15
1940-44	122.1	3.2	9.5	3	8
1945-49	190.7	10.6	13.4	6	7
1950-54	268.4	14.3	20.2	5	8
1955-59	353.1	22.4	29.9	6	8
1960-64	455.0	34.7	44.3	8	10
1965-69	655.5	55.9	69.8	9	11
1970-74	1,003.8	116.7	110.9	12	11
1975-79	1,643.7	229.4	201.6	14	12
1980-84	2,679.8	400.3	427.7	15	16
1985	1,314.5	487.1	552.6	15	17
1986	3,487.0	513.7	556.6	15	16

Note: Welfare payments include (1) OASDI, (2) unemployment
benefits, (3) veterans' benefits, (4) government employee
retirement benefits, (5) AFDC, and (6) other. The largest is OASDI--social security. The sixth category, "Other,"
includes all other transfer payments received by persons,
particularly important being various private sector pension
plans. These payments cannot be attributed directly to
welfare state programs, but are regulated and sometimes
underwritten by the welfare state.   Rentier payments
include personal dividend and interest income. Personal
interest income is the largest of the two.

Source: *Economic Report of the President* (Washington, DC: Government
Printing Office, 1987).

only by pushing their own share up. The rise in their share was due almost entirely to the dramatic rise in interest rates engineered by the monetarist takeover of the Federal Reserve Board with the appointment of Paul Volcker as its head in 1979. Perhaps rentier capital's gain in share came more at the expense of entrepreneurial capital than at the expense of welfare, as entrepreneurs were forced to pay higher interest rates for the finance capital they borrowed in order to create new businesses and undertake new risks. If so, the revenging capitalists succeeded mainly in shooting themselves in the foot. Unfortunately, this is not all of the story. Instead, an old Chinese proverb was demonstrated: "When you decide to seek revenge, begin by digging *two* graves." The economic retrenchment set in motion by the struggle over nonwork income not only injured entrepreneurial capital, but it also saw the poverty rate soar.

The poverty rate is that percent of the total population living below a certain level of income. The level is adjusted by family size and by changes in the cost of living. In 1985 that level of income was $10,989 for a family of four. In the five-year period 1975-1979, the poverty rate averaged 11.8 percent of the population. Retrenchment pushed it to 14.3 percent for the next half decade (1980-1984). Then, in 1985, the rate stood at an even 14.0 percent, still considerably above the rate immediately before the retrenchment began. The rising poverty rates in the first half of the 1980s meant that an average of eight million more people lived under the poverty line than in the last half of the 1970s (U.S. Bureau of the Census, 1987, p. 442). These were the kinds of heavy social costs of retrenchment I had warned about in an earlier work (W. Dugger, 1984).

Cash Grant Programs

Essentially, the U.S. welfare state provides four different kinds of cash aid other than old age, survivors, and disability (Social Security, proper).

1. Aid to Families with Dependent Children (AFDC) reached about 10.8 million people in 1985, up by about 300,000 over 1980. Total expenditures for AFDC that year were $16.8 billion; of that, about $9.0 billion was federal and $7.8 billion state-funded. Despite the evidence to the contrary, the New Right argues that AFDC breeds personal dependence, illegitimate children, and divorce. After extensive study of the available research and data, Frances Fox Piven and Richard A. Cloward state, "In conclusion, these data clearly undermine the main empirical

foundation of the attack on AFDC" (Block, Cloward, Ehrenreich, and Piven, 1987, p. 72).

2. Supplemental Security Income reached 4.3 million people with a total of $11.9 billion in aid, $9.6 billion of it federal. This program is administered by the Social Security Administration and paid out the princely sum of $226 per month per recipient in 1985.

3. General Assistance is a strictly state-level program that reached 1.3 million people with about $2.4 billion in aid in 1985. Benefits in this program vary wildly from state to state, with Southern states generally being the most miserly.

4. Unemployment insurance benefits totalled $14 billion in 1985. But an average of only 2.6 million people per week received benefits in that year while an average of 8.3 million people were out of work. Unemployment insurance programs are administered by the states and have become woefully inadequate.

People might be recipients of aid from several different programs. If they are very lucky in meeting the different eligibility requirements and if they are very diligent in applying for all the different benefits, they might be able to just get by. Clearly, the four programs need to be merged into one coordinated program, and the state administration of some programs needs to be replaced by a unified federal administration.

What most people call Social Security (OASDI) is under a unified federal administration. The program is funded in a pay-as-you-go fashion, not as an annuity or as a casualty insurance policy. This feature is not so much controversial as it is confusing. The current generation of employed workers and their employers pays for the benefits of the current genera-tion of retired and disabled workers and their survivors. To keep the system afloat on a current basis, the current payments into the common fund must be large enough to cover the current payments out of the common fund. Benefits are not limited by actuarial constraints, but by the willingness and ability of the current generation of workers to pay for the benefits of the current generation of retired and disabled workers and their survivors. Furthermore, nothing need prohibit the fund's administrators from borrowing to meet temporary shortfalls. And yet, in a 1978 radio broadcast, future President of the United States Ronnie Reagan declared that "Social Security is in effect, bankrupt" (quoted in R. Dugger, 1983, p. 43).

Needless to say, years after Ronnie Reagan declared it bankrupt, Social Security continues to provide billions in benefits. In 1985, it reached some 37 million beneficiaries, paying an average of $814 per month to a retired worker and spouse. Furthermore, it ended the year with reserves equal to 21 percent of all benefits paid and administrative expenses incurred during the year. (All cash benefit data are taken from the 1987 *Statistical Abstract*.) In sum, the U.S. Social Security system is sound and will remain that way.

No discussion of cash grant programs is complete without at least a note on the negative income tax. Reviewing the literature and the data, Nicholas Barr concludes that, for the United Kingdom at least, a negative income tax would have to increase the level of taxes significantly in order to avoid penalizing poor people who are moved off other kinds of aid programs and onto the negative income tax program alone (Barr, 1987, pp. 257-271). The negative income tax may be an idea whose time has come-- and gone.

PROBLEM III: TOOL OF DEMOCRACY (OR CAPITALISM?)

The problems encountered in the different kinds of aid programs, whether in kind or in cash, can be dealt with. But the welfare state must become more than a series of aid programs. It must become a tool of the democratic process, a way of enabling all of us to participate fully in the ongoing economic, political, cultural, and spiritual dimensions of social life. The welfare state must further the social agenda of a democratic nation. This must mean facing squarely the contradiction between the democratic polity and the capitalistic economy. The thrust of democracy is toward wider and fuller participation among the dispossessed. It is through the democratic polity that women's liberation, the civil rights movement, and other people's movements express their needs and demand their rights. The democratic polity's thrust is toward inclusion. However, the capitalist economy's thrust is toward exclusion. In particular, the thrust of capitalism is toward increased concentration of wealth and privilege (see Munkirs, 1985). The two thrusts are fundamentally contradictory. The welfare state, being of the democratic polity, is stuck in the middle of the contradiction.

Will the welfare state evolve merely to facilitate the functioning of the capitalist economy, by providing a safety net for the frightened middle class and a sop to the poor? Or will it come to transcend the bounds of wealth and privilege by providing the means to participate to the excluded? If the welfare state becomes a mere facilitator of capitalist expansion, can the democratic polity long endure? If the welfare state transcends the bounds of wealth and privilege, then can capitalism long endure? In transcending this fundamental contradiction in favor of democracy, a social agenda for democracy will be worked out. That agenda will include, at a minimum, fundamental changes in the mode of production and fundamental changes in our guns over butter priorities.

Changing the Mode of Production

Hierarchy in the workplace coexists very poorly with democracy and equality in the rest of society. Worker management and worker participation are more in line with the democratic way of life (W. Dugger, 1987). So the welfare state must eventually become involved with more than just the distribution of commodities and the redistribution of income. It must also become involved in the distribution of power and information in the production of commodities and in the sharing out of income. This does not necessarily mean that the welfare state should become involved in managing the means of production. But it does mean that the welfare state must encourage the transformation of hierarchy in the workplace into democracy in the workplace. Doing so means strengthening labor, making sure that the worker is able to participate in deciding how her work should be done, and how the results should be evaluated. Maintaining full employment will make it easier to push democracy into the workplace, as full employment puts backbone into the workforce. Fighting discrimination is also much easier when jobs are plentiful because it softens the harshness of competition between workers for good jobs. A significant increase in the mimimum wage rate would infuse some dignity into low wage jobs. Furthermore, plant closing legislation is clearly needed to at least give workers information about the status of their plants and their jobs (U. S. Congress, Office of Technology Assessment, 1986). Bringing democracy into the workplace could be speeded up with enabling federal legislation for worker-owned and worker-managed enterprises. Enabling legislation should include provisions for new financial institutions that cater to the worker-owned and -managed enterprise. Government purchasing and contracting procedures should also be changed to make room for the worker-owned and worker-managed enterprise. Furthermore, free technical assistance should be provided the fledgling co-op movement. In these ways, and probably others as yet unexplored, the mode of production can be transformed from hierarchy and minimum participation to cooperation and maximum participation.

Changing Priorities

The welfare state and the warfare state ultimately contradict each other, even though many of the welfare state's programs are justified in terms of the warfare state. The National Defense Education Act, for example, used military needs to justify extensive federal aid to education. Military needs can also justify socialized medicine, nationalization of the steel mills and the coal mines, and more. But, at bottom, warfare and welfare are incompatible. The incompatibility is a question of priorities-- do we want guns or butter, civilian workers or cannon fodder? In the United States, military spending has grown beyond all reason. As Seymour Melman has pointed out for years, military spending now absorbs much of the scientific and technical talent of the United States (Melman, 1974, 1983). President Eisenhower was one of the earliest mainstream politicians to recognize how strongly the military-industrial complex affected U.S. priorities. In his farewell address to the nation, Eisenhower stated,

> This conjunction of an immense military establishment and a large arms industry is new in the American experience . . . . We recognize the imperative need for this development. Yet we must not fail to comprehend its grave implications . . . . In the councils of government we must guard against the acquisition of unwarranted influence, whether sought or unsought, by the military-industrial complex. The potential for the disastrous rise of misplaced power exists and will persist (Eisenhower in Manchester, 1974, p. 877).

With Gorbachev and reform riding high in the Soviet Union, a historic opportunity for peace now exists. The barriers to disarmament treaties on the Soviet side have been weakened. Mutually beneficial disarmament could take place. At last, peace might break out. And when it does, the vast resources now wasted on Star Wars research, nuclear deterrence forces, and NATO could all be redirected to civilian use, to butter instead of guns. The resources needed by a reconstructed welfare state would be available. Poverty could be eliminated in the United States. Were peace to break out, the programs of a reconstructed welfare state could not only eliminate poverty but they could also revitalize the democratic process in the United States. The welfare state, to borrow a phrase from the Great Society's War on Poverty, has the potential to insure the "maximum feasible participation" of all citizens, in all dimensions of the life process. In a peaceful world, tremendous potential for progress exists. As the Students for a Democratic Society emphasized in their Port Huron Statement over a quarter of a century ago: "[W]e see little reason why men cannot meet with increasing skill the complexities and responsibilities of their situation, if society is organized not for minority, but for majority, participation in decision-making" (Miller, 1987, p. 332). This is the role of the welfare state: to reorganize society for full individual participation. It is also the goal of participatory democracy. The roles of the military-industrial complex and of capitalism itself in this welfare state vision of democracy and affluence remain to be seen. That is to say, the welfare state is more than a prop to the existing system, but a means to transform it.

CONCLUSION

As it now stands, the welfare state in the United States is little more than a disconnected series of stop-gap programs aimed at alleviating the worst symptoms of inequality. It has no legitimate reason for being, no permanent place in the social landscape. Aid in kind programs and aid in cash programs do a great deal of good, but numerous problems reduce their overall effectiveness. Existing welfare programs could be easily reformed, however. The welfare state could be reconstructed so as to insure that all Americans were able to participate fully in all dimensions of life. Aid in kind programs could be made to work far better than they do now: health care, education, nutrition, and housing could all be supplied in adequate amounts to all Americans. Aid in cash programs also could be made to work far better, insuring an adequate flow of income to all Americans. With adequate health care, education, food, and housing, and with adequate income, the only things still holding many of us back would be racism and sexism in social roles and authoritarianism in the workplace. Full employment and affirmative action would eat away the first two barriers to full participation. But authoritarianism in the workplace could require a more aggressive push of cooperation and democracy into the capitalist economy. Here is where the welfare state may find its reason for being, its social legitimacy. If the welfare state became more than just a prop to the existing economic system, if it became a tool of a participatory democracy, it would find its own legitimacy and justify its reason for being. So that is the direction of progress. That is the way forward for the welfare state. It must become an integral part of a revitalized democracy.

References

Ayres, C.E. 1961. *Toward a Reasonable Society: The Values of Industrial Civilization*. Austin: University of Texas Press.

Barbanel, J. 1987. "New York shifts debate on homeless problem," *New York Times* (November 23), 16.

Barr, N. 1987. *The Economics of the Welfare State*. Stanford: Stanford University Press.

Bartlett, B. and T. P. Roth. 1983. *The Supply-Side Solution*. Chatham, NJ: Chatham House Publishers.

Block, F., R. A. Cloward, B. Ehrenreich and F. F. Piven. 1987. *The Mean Season: The Attack on the Welfare State*. New York: Pantheon.

Bowles, S. and H. Gintis. 1976. *Schooling in Capitalist America*. New York: Basic Books.

Brodeur, P. 1985. *Outrageous Misconduct: The Asbestos Industry on Trial*. New York: Pantheon.

Children's Defense Fund. 1982. *A Children's Defense Budget*. Washington, DC: Children's Defense Fund.

Clinard, M. B. and P. C. Yeager. 1980. *Corporate Crime*. New York: The Free Press.

Cochran, K. P. 1969. "Tax implications," in *Committed Spending*, edited by R. Theobald. New York: Doubleday, pp. 81-113.

Dugger, R. 1983. *On Reagan: The Man and His Presidency*. New York: McGraw-Hill.

Dugger, W. M. 1981. "A note on institutionalism, straw men, and equality," *Journal of Economic Issues* 15 (September), 785-791.

_____. 1984. *An Alternative to Economic Retrenchment*. Princeton, NJ: Petrocelli Books.

_____. 1987. "Democratic economic planning and worker ownership," *Journal of Economic Issues* 21 (March), 87-99.

Etzioni, A. 1984. *Capital Corruption: The New Attack on American Democracy*. New York: Harcourt Brace Jovanovich.

Gilder, G. 1981. *Wealth and Poverty*. New York: Basic Books.

Hailstones, T. J. 1982. *A Guide to Supply-Side Economics*. Richmond, VA: Robert F. Dame.

Hamilton, D. 1967. "The political economy of poverty," *Journal of Economic Issues* 1 (December), 309-320.

_____. 1970. "Reciprocity, productivity and poverty," *Journal of Economic Issues* 4 (March), 35-42.

_____. 1971. "The paper war on poverty," *Journal of Economic Issues* 5 (September), 72-79.

_____. 1984. "Income maintenance and welfare," *Journal of Economic Issues* 18 (March), 143-158.

Harrington, M. 1971. *The Other America: Poverty in America*, rev. ed. Baltimore: Penguin.

_____. 1986. *The Next Left*. New York: Henry Holt.

Katznelson, I. and M. Weir. 1985. *Schooling for All*. New York: Basic Books.

Klein, P. A. 1984. "Institutionalist reflections on the role of the public sector," *Journal of Economic Issues* 18 (March), 45-68.

Levitan, S. A. 1980. *Programs in Aid of the Poor for the 1980s*, 4th ed. Baltimore: The Johns Hopkins University Press.

Lutz, M. A. and K. Lux. 1979. *The Challenge of Humanistic Economics*. Menlo Park, CA: The Benjamin/Cummings Publishing Company.

Manchester, W. 1974. *The Glory and the Dream*. Boston: Little, Brown, and Company.

Melman, S. 1974. *The Permanent War Economy*. New York: Simon and Schuster.

_____. 1983. *Profits Without Production*. New York: Alfred A. Knopf.

Miller, J. 1987. *Democracy Is in the Streets*. New York: Simon and Schuster.

Munkirs, J. R. 1985. *The Transformation of American Capitalism*. Armonk, NY: M.E. Sharpe.

Murray, C. 1984. *Losing Ground: American Social Policy 1950-1980*. New York: Basic Books.

Obrinsky, M. 1983. *Profit Theory and Capitalism*. Philadelphia: University of Pennsylvania Press.

Osberg, L. 1984. *Economic Inequality in the United States*. Armonk, NY: M. E. Sharpe.

Piven, F. F. and R. A. Cloward. 1971. *Regulating the Poor: The Functions of Public Welfare*. New York: Random House.

_____. 1982. *The New Class War: Reagan's Attack on the Welfare State and Its Consequences*. New York: Pantheon.

Rawls, J. 1971. *A Theory of Justice*. Cambridge: The Belknap Press of Harvard University Press.

Rodgers, H. R., Jr. 1982. *The Cost of Human Neglect: America's Welfare Failure*. Armonk, NY: M. E. Sharpe.

Rostow, W. W. 1983. *The Barbaric Counter-Revolution*. Austin: University of Texas Press.

Schwarz, J. E. 1983. *America's Hidden Success*. New York: W. W. Norton.

Sidel, R. 1986. *Women and Children Last: The Plight of Poor Women in Affluent America*. New York: Viking.

Silver, M. 1980. *Affluence, Altruism, and Atrophy: The Decline of Welfare States*. New York: New York University Press.

Thurow, L. C. 1983. *Dangerous Currents: The State of Economics*. New York: Random House.

Tool, M. R. 1986. *Essays in Social Value Theory*. Armonk, NY: M. E. Sharpe.

U.S. Bureau of the Census. 1986. *Statistical Abstract of the United States, 1986*. Washington, DC: Government Printing Office.

_____. 1987. *Statistical Abstract of the United States, 1987*. Washington, DC: Government Printing Office.

U.S. Congress, Office of Technology Assessment. 1986. *Plant Closing: Advance Notice and Special Response--Special Report*. Washington, DC: Government Printing Office, September.

U.S. Health Care Financing Administration. 1988. *Statistical Abstract of the United States, 1988*. Washington, DC: Government Printing Office.

Wanniski, J. 1978. *The Way the World Works*. New York: Simon and Schuster.

11

THE CORPORATION AS A DEMOCRATIC SOCIAL INSTITUTION

David P. Ellerman

INTRODUCTION

Our purpose is to apply the principles of democratic theory to the corporation (as, for example, in Dahl, 1985). The lack of democracy in a conventionally structured corporation is based on the employer-employee contract. The employment contract is analyzed as a limited economic Hobbesian *pactum subjectionis* for the workplace. Inalienable rights arguments, originally developed in the seventeenth and eighteenth century Enlightenment against nondemocratic thinkers such as Hobbes, are updated and applied against the employment contract. The abolition of that contract for the hiring or renting of human beings entails restructuring firms as democratic corporations where the membership/ownership rights are personal rights assigned to the functional role of working in the firm.

Then the corporation itself is transformed from a piece of property into a democratic social institution.

THE NON-DEMOCRATIC TRADITION OF LIBERAL THOUGHT

Is democracy the same as government based on the consent of the governed? No. There can be a nondemocratic government based on the consent of the governed as in a constitutional autocracy. Indeed, there is a whole liberal tradition of consent-based political thought that advocated nondemocratic forms of voluntary constitutional government (see Ellerman, 1986a). Thomas Hobbes is the best known representative of that tradition, and Hobbes' *pactum subjectionis*--

> *I authorize and give up my right of governing myself to this man, or to this assembly of men, on this condition, that you give up your right to him and authorize all his actions in like manner* (Hobbes, 1651, reprinted 1958, p. 142).

--is an example of an explicit (but hypothetical) voluntary political contract of subjugation. The ancient Roman *lex regia* given in the *Institutes* of Justinian (Lib. I Tit. II, 6)--

> Whatever has pleased the prince has the force of law, since the Roman people by the *lex regia* enacted concern- ing his *imperium*, have yielded up to him all their power and authority

--was a famous example of an implied contract of subjugation.

What, then, distinguishes a democratic constitution from a *pactum subjectionis*--if both are based on consent? That is the ancient distinction between an *alienation* or translation of power and a *delegation* of power.

> This dispute also reaches far back into the Middle Ages. It first took a strictly juristic form in the dispute . . . as to the legal nature of the ancient "*translatio imperii*" from the Roman people to the Princeps. One school explained this as a definitive and irrevocable alienation of power, the other as a mere concession of its use and exercise

> .... On the one hand from the people's abdication the
> most absolute sovereignty of the prince might be deduced
> .... On the other hand the assumption of a mere
> *"concessio imperii"* led to the doctrine of popular sover-
> eignty (Gierke, 1966, pp. 93-94).

Alienation or delegation, *translatio* or *concessio*? That is the question.

How can one tell the difference? Don't people often really give up their power in a formally democratic organization as it turns oligarchic? Indeed they do, but our purpose here is not to differentiate formally democratic organizations which have degenerated from those which have retained their democratic function. Our purpose is to distinguish voluntary organizations which are at least formally democratic from those which are not even formally democratic. That is relatively straightforward. If authority is only delegated, then (in theory) the governor rules in the name of and for the benefit of the governed. If power is alienated and transferred, then the ruler rules in his own name and for his own benefit. It is as if property has been transferred; there is no pretense the new owner uses the property in the name of or for the benefit of the old owner.

The property analogy was used in the nondemocratic liberal natural law tradition of Grotius, Puffendorf, and Hobbes.

> Puffendorf says that we may divest ourselves of our liberty
> in favour of other men, just as we transfer our property
> from one to another by contracts and agreements (Rous-
> seau, 1755, second part).

That tradition survives today in the libertarianism of one of America's leading moral philosophers, Professor Robert Nozick of Harvard University, who not only condones selling the right of self-government to a nondemocratic "dominant protective association" but applies the same principle to the whole person.

> The comparable question about an individual is whether
> a free system will allow him to sell himself into slavery.
> I believe that it would (Nozick, 1974, p. 331).

INALIENABLE RIGHTS THEORY IN LIBERAL DEMOCRATIC THOUGHT

The nondemocratic natural law tradition of liberal thought was based on the principle that basic natural rights were alienable or transferable with the knowing consent of the original bearers. Thus the tradition allowed both a collective *pactum subjectionis* and an individual self-enslavement contract.

Inalienable natural rights theory provided an answer to the tradition of alienable natural rights. Inalienable rights are rights which may not be transferred even with the knowledgable consent of the bearer. Inalienable rights theory did not simply "assert" that the basic right of self-determination was not transferable. The theory argued that a right is inalienable if the contract to alienate the right was in some manner inherently defective and invalid. A contract is inherently invalid if it puts a person in the legal role of a nonperson. A person by consent can in fact give up and alienate his or her possession and use of property. But the person cannot in fact voluntarily alienate or give up his or her status as a person. A voluntary contract to partly or wholly take on the legal role of a nonperson cannot be fulfilled; it is inherently invalid. A legal system that "validated" such a contract would be institutionalizing a fraud.

Systems of positive law have nevertheless declared such contracts as "valid." There is, of course, no expectation that a voluntary signer of such a contract will actually become a nonperson; the person only need behave in an "appropriate" manner to be "counted" as fulfilling the contract.

The self-enslavement contract was the classic example of a contract to take on the legal role of a nonperson. The voluntary contractual slave, like the involuntary slave, remained a person in fact; it was only in law that the slave was a nonperson. For the contractual slave, the appropriate behavior, such as complete obedience to the master, counted as fulfilling the contract to be a nonperson. The inherently contradictory and fraudulent nature of the slave's legal role was "obvious" when the slave behaved inappropriately, e.g., by committing a crime. The legal pretense of thinghood was then set aside; the slave suddenly became a person. As one abolitionist observed in 1853:

> The slave, who is but "*a chattel*" on all *other* occasions,
> with not one solitary attribute of personality accorded to

him, becomes "*a person*" whenever he is to be *punished* (Goodell, 1853, p. 309).

The "talking instrument" in work became the responsible person in crime.

A BRIEF HISTORY OF INALIENABLE RIGHTS THEORY: ANTISLAVERY THOUGHT

The roots of inalienable rights theory can be traced to the stoics. They expressed the contradiction in the slave's role in the doctrine that only the body of the slave was property; the soul was free and *sui juris*. Inalienable rights theory flowered in the French and Scottish Enlightenment. Rousseau argues that liberty cannot be alienated like property.

> For in the first place, the property I alienate becomes quite foreign to me, nor can I suffer from the abuse of it; but it very dearly concerns me that my liberty should not be abused, and I cannot without incurring the guilt of the crimes I may be compelled to commit, expose myself to become an instrument of crime . . . (Rousseau, 1755, second part).

In Diderot's *Encyclopedia*, the summa of the French Enlightenment, a particularly clear statement of the inalienable rights critique of slavery is cited in an article signed by Jaucourt.

> There is not, therefore, a single one of these unfortunate people regarded only as slaves who does not have the right to be declared free, since he has never lost his freedom, which he could not lose and which his prince, his father, and any person whatsoever in the world had not the power to dispose of. Consequently the sale that has been completed is invalid in itself. This Negro does not divest himself and can never divest himself of his natural right; he carries it everywhere with him, and he can demand everywhere that he be allowed to enjoy it (Diderot, 1967, p. 230).

The preeminent historian of anti-slavery thought, David Brion Davis, found that this was merely translated from the work of an obscure Scottish jurist, George Wallis (or Wallace), so the statement must be attributed to the Scottish Enlightenment (Davis, 1975). Frances Hutcheson, a major thinker in the Scottish Enlightenment, developed a theory of inalienable rights. Thomas Jefferson directly or indirectly drew on Hutcheson's work to frame the language about "certain unalienable rights" in the American Declaration of Independence (see Wills, 1979 [1978]).

The application of inalienable rights theory to slavery was relatively easy. Slavery law had the great advantage of explicitly stating that the slave had the role of a nonperson so social scientists and philosophers did not need to analyze such roles. They only needed to read the language of the law. For instance, an antebellum Alabama court asserted that slaves

> . . . are rational beings, they are capable of committing crimes; and in reference to acts which are crimes, are regarded as persons. Because they are slaves, they are . . . incapable of performing civil acts, and, in reference to all such, they are things, not persons (Catterall, 1926, p. 247).

The fraudulent nature of the slave's role was obvious to any antebellum social scientist willing to criticize the very foundations of the social system.

THE PACTUM SUBJECTIONIS AND OTHER ALIENATION CONTRACTS

The doctrine of inalienable rights, born of the fight against slavery, was also applied against the Hobbesian collective contract of subjugation.

> There is, at least, *one* right that cannot be ceded or abandoned: the right to personality. Arguing upon this principle the most influential writers on politics in the seventeenth century rejected the conclusions drawn by Hobbes. They charged the great logician with a contradiction in terms. If a man could give up his personality he would cease being a moral being. . . . This fundamental right, the right to personality, includes in a sense all the others. To maintain and to develop his personality is a

> universal right. It . . . cannot, therefore, be transferred
> from one individual to another. . . . There is no *pactum
> subjectionis*, no act of submission by which man can give
> up the state of a free agent and enslave himself (Cassirer,
> 1963, p. 175).

This application requires more analysis. How would a *pactum subjectionis* put people in the role of nonpersons (i.e., ceding "the right to personality") while a democratic constitution would not?

Things do not make decisions; they do not participate directly or indirectly in decisions made about their use. Persons make the decisions about how to use or employ things. When a person legally alienates and transfers decisionmaking power about his or her own activities, then the person is no longer a legal party to the decisions. The person has taken on an instrumental role; the person has the role of being solely a means rather than an end. The legal alienation of the decisions about a person's actions violates the (Kantian) autonomy of the person. However, when people delegate decisionmaking power, the people remain part (albeit sometimes a remote part) of the collective decisionmaking process. In theory, the agent or delegate decides in a manner so that the decision can be authorized, accepted, and ratified by the principals.

The old dichotomy of *translatio* versus *concessio* differentiates between contracts that place a person in the role of a decision-less instrument and contracts that vouchsafe a person's decisionmaking capacity. Here again, the analysis is de jure, not de facto. After a contract of subjugation, a person voluntarily obeying a command is in fact a co-decisionmaker; it is only in law that decisionmaking power has been alienated so the person is not legally part of the decision. It is the legal institution of the contract of alienation which fraudulently misrepresents an autonomous person as a being whose decisionmaking capacity can be alienated as property to another person.

Another contract which puts a person in a nonperson's role was the old coverture marriage contract which established the baron-femme relationship. By this contract, a woman became a *"femme covert"* brought under the wing of her "Lord and Baron," the husband. The contract denied an individual's autonomous personality by "identifying" the individual with another person. Lawyers called it the *identity fiction*: "The husband and wife are one person in law, and that one person is the husband." In this case, the misrepresentation involved in the legal contract was clearer since it was called a "fiction."

THE CORPORATION AS AN INSTITUTION OF GOVERNANCE

To apply inalienable rights theory to the corporation, we must consider the corporation as an institution of governance. Unless otherwise stated, I will take the corporation as the conventional "capitalist" corporation that hires in labor. The legal structure of a corporation might be construed in a rough analogy with representative government.

> The analogy between state and corporation has been congenial to American lawmakers, legislative and judicial. The shareholders were the electorate, the directors the legislature, enacting general policies and committing them to the officers for execution (Chayes, 1966, p. 39).

In the large corporations with publicly traded shares, there is a well-known separation of ownership and control (e.g., Berle and Means, 1932). The far-flung shareholders, as the citizens in a large public corporation, do not wield effective power over the managers--who typically own only a small portion of the shares. But let us, for the sake of the argument, waive these difficulties. Let us assume either a closely held corporation or a public corporation where the shareholders vigorously exercise their voting rights.

Does this theory of the corporation as a representative government mean that the corporation is a democracy? No, it lacks the most basic attribute of democracy, namely, self-government. The shareholders are not "the governed" in a corporation.

> Shareholder democracy, so-called, is misconceived because the shareholders are not the governed of the corporation whose consent must be sought (Chayes, 1966, p. 40).

If the people of Russia elect the government of Poland, that does not make Poland a democracy. The managers of a conventional corporation do "govern" the shareholders' property, but democracy is not a property management system; it is a system for the governance of people.

Who then are the people governed or managed in a corporation? There are a number of groups whose interests (e.g., property or persons) are affected by corporate activities, and they are often called the *stakeholders*: (1) employees (all who work in the corporation); (2) consumers; (3) shareholders; (4) suppliers, and; (5) local residents. But there are two quite different ways in which a person might be affected by corporate decisions: (1) the person is under the authority of and is given orders by corporate management; and (2) the person or property of the individual is affected by the corporate decisions, but the person is not under the authority of the corporate management. In the first case, the person is not only affected but governed by corporate decisions, and in the second case, the person is only affected.

There are also two types of control which a person or group of people might exert over corporate decisions: (1) direct or positive control which is the authority to make decisions; and (2) indirect or negative control which is the power to veto or otherwise constrain the decisions. In terms of choice theory in economics, indirect control is the right to determine certain constraints on the set of possible choices, and direct control is the right to make the choice out of the set of feasible choices allowed by the constraints.

There is a natural pairing between the two ways in which people may be affected and the two types of control. Suppose person A proposes an action that will affect person B. If the stakeholder B is only being affected by the decision--but is not being told what to do--then B should be able to protect his or her interests by the indirect control of being able to say "No." That leaves person A with an infinity of other options which may not even affect B at all. Thus the stakeholder who is only affected should not have the right to choose which of all those other options will be taken. This pairing between being (only) affected and indirect control can be expressed as the

AFFECTED INTERESTS PRINCIPLE. Everyone whose legitimate interests are affected by a decision should have a right of indirect control (e.g., a collective or perhaps individual veto) to constrain that decision.

The operation of this principle requires a voluntary interface between the acting party and the affected parties. That voluntary interface is usually the market. An effect outside that interface is an external effect or externality.

The other pairing of being governed (i.e., being told what to do) and direct control would realize the idea of self-government. This could be expressed as the

DEMOCRATIC PRINCIPLE. Everyone who is governed by a decision should have a direct control right (e.g., a vote) to participate in making that decision.

Returning to the list of interest groups or stakeholders affected by corporate decisions, it may be partitioned into two groups, those *governed* and those *(only) affected.*

Division of Stakeholders into:

(1) Governed Parties:
· employees,

(2) Affected Parties:
· consumers,
· shareholders,
· suppliers, and
· local residents.

Each party is listed according to its functional role. A given individual might play several functional roles. The consumers, shareholders, suppliers, and local residents are not under the authority of corporate management. They do not take commands from the managers. They are not "the governed." Only the employees, always in the inclusive sense of all who work in the firm, are the governed. Indeed, the command structure of the employment relation is its characteristic legal feature.

A capitalist corporation is not a democratic organization. The employees are the governed, but the shareholders have the franchise. A socialist firm is also undemocratic. Even assuming a political democracy as in democratic socialism, the employees in a government-run firm are an insignificant portion of the general electorate. The vast majority of the citizens are not governed by the corporate managers, even if the citizens are viewed as indirectly selecting the management in the political democratic process. Hence politically democratic socialism is undemocratic at the level of the firm.

A democratic firm would be a firm where those governed by the management would have the ultimate authority to make those decisions-- so the governance structure would embody self-government. The democratic firm, where the people managed are the people having the vote to select management, is variously called a *democratic worker-owned firm*, a *worker cooperative*, or a *labor-managed firm* (see Ellerman, 1983; or Ellerman and Pitegoff, 1983).

THE CONTRACTUAL STRUCTURE OF A CORPORATION

What is the contractual basis of the corporation, e.g., in the articles of incorporation and bylaws of a corporation? Do they form a "social contract" for the corporation? There is a portion of social contract thought which explicitly considers the corporation as a contractually based association in analogy with a constitutional government.

> To pursue the theory of a contract of society to its logical conclusions was necessarily also to arrive . . . at the idea that associations had a natural right to exist independently of state-creation. As a societas, each corporate body was the result of contract; and all such bodies derived their existence, exactly in the same way as the state, from the original rights of individuals which formed the basis of contract (Gierke, 1957, p. 169).

The contract considered as the basis for a corporation is the contract between the shareholders that is embodied in the articles of incorporation and the bylaws of the corporation. But as previously noted, the shareholders are not "the governed" of a corporation. Hence the articles-and-bylaws contract is not the contract between those who govern and the governed.

Social contract thought focuses on the contract between those who govern and the governed. In the capitalist corporation, that is the *employment contract*. There are, as noted above, two fundamentally different types of contracts of government: the contract of subjection of the alienable natural rights tradition, and the democratic constitution of the inalienable natural rights tradition. In the contract of subjection, the right to govern is alienated and transferred from the governed to their governors. It is not a delegation or *concessio*; it is an alienation or *translatio*. The governors are not the representatives of the governed; they rule in their own name.

A democratic constitution is just the opposite. It is erected to secure the right of self-government, not to alienate it. Any legitimate authority exercised by those who govern is delegated from the governed. The governors are the representatives of and rule in the name of the governed.

The employment contract is a limited contract of subjection in the workplace, a *pactum subjectionis* that is limited in duration (the term of the contract) and limited in scope (the scope of the employment). It is a legal alienation of the direct control rights over the employees (always within the scope of the employment), not a delegation. It is a *translatio*, not a *concessio*. The employer is not the representative or agent of the employees. The employer manages the employees in his own name, not in the name of the employees.

The capitalist firm is thus a peculiar institution. There is no clear analogue to this pair of contracts in political theory. It is as if the people in one country (the shareholders) joined together in a contractual association (the corporation) to elect a government (corporate management) to govern the people in another country (the corporate employees). The people in the second country (the employees) agree to another contract, a contract of subjection (the employment contract) to their governors. *That* would be the political analogue of a capitalist firm.

In a democratic worker-owned firm or worker cooperative, these two contracts are replaced by the one democratic constitution for the workplace. There are no absentee "owners" and no "employees." The worker-members of a democratic corporation agree in the articles and bylaws to the democratic procedures through which they will select management and thus self-manage their work.

INALIENABLE RIGHTS THEORY AND THE EMPLOYMENT CONTRACT

The contract to sell oneself into slavery is not only natural-law invalid: it is now recognized as being invalid in the system of positive law.

Since slavery was abolished, human earning power is forbidden by law to be capitalized. A man is not even

free to sell himself: he must rent himself at a wage
(Samuelson, 1976, p. 52).

Our present economic system of production is based on the voluntary
contract to rent or hire oneself out for a wage or salary, the employment
contract.

It may be readily admitted that a contract to sell oneself puts one
in the position of a nonperson. But analysis is required to show that the
contract to rent oneself out also puts one in the position of a nonperson,
an employed instrument, within the scope of the employment.

First consider the question of the legal responsibility for the
results of one's actions. The slave had none; all the legal responsibility for
the slave's actions was imputed back to the master as if the slave were an
instrument. But when the slave committed a crime, then the slave ceased
being an instrument in the eyes of the law and become a responsible
person.

The employee has a similar role within the scope of the employment. There are both negative and positive results of the workers' actions
(a.k.a. labor services). In economists' terms, the negative results are the
using up of the inputs to production, and the positive results are the
produced outputs. From the legal viewpoint, the corporation holds the
liabilities for the used-up inputs and has the legal ownership of the
produced outputs. If the workers are the members-owners of the corporation, then they have the positive and negative legal responsibility for the
results of their actions. But in a capitalist corporation, the workers are
"employed." The employees are not the members of the corporation so
they have no legal liability for the used-up inputs, and they have no legal
ownership of the produced outputs. The legal responsibility for the
positive and negative results of the employees' actions is imputed back
through them to their employer, the capitalist corporation, and thus indirectly to the member-owners of the corporation, the shareholders. Hence,
from the viewpoint of legal responsibility, the employees have the role of
instruments within the scope of their employment.

It is only in the employees' legal role that they are nonresponsible
instruments "employed" by their "employer." In fact, the workers remain
responsible agents in spite of the contract to rent themselves out as
"employees." Instead of matching the *de jure* instrumental role, the
employees are *de facto* responsible persons co-operating together with the
employer or the employer's agents. In spite of the employment contract
to legally "sell" labor services, human actions are in fact not transferable

as property. The whole artificiality of the employment contract is set aside when the employee or, in legal parlance, servant steps outside the legal purposes of the contract by committing a crime.

> All who participate in a crime with a guilty intent are liable to punishment. A master and servant who so participate in a crime are liable criminally, not because they are master and servant, but because they jointly carried out a criminal venture and are both criminous (Batt, 1967, p. 612).

The servant in work suddenly becomes the partner in crime.

The same conclusion--that the employee contracts into an instrumental role--also follows from an analysis of the governance and decisionmaking structure of the capitalist corporation. The employment contract is an alienation of decisionmaking authority, not a delegation. The employer is not a delegate or agent of the employees; the employer decides in his own name what the employees will do. From the legal point of view, the employees are not a part, directly or indirectly, of that decision. In the classic phrase, it is "none of their business." From the factual viewpoint, the "employees" remain autonomous persons who *de facto* participate in and "ratify" all decisions they voluntarily obey.

From the viewpoints of both decisionmaking and responsibility for actions, the employment contract is a contract to place an autonomous person into the legal role of an instrument, the "employee" role. Thus traditional inalienable rights theory must conclude that the employer-employee contract, the contract to rent human beings, is an inherently invalid contract. Decisionmaking rights and the responsibility for the results of one's action are inalienable. The only legal structure for work compatible with the Kantian autonomy of persons is the structure where participation implies membership. Then the people who produce the positive and negative results of production have that legal responsibility through their corporate embodiment, and they are legally a part of the decisionmaking structure since management is empowered by authority delegated from those who are managed. That is the legal structure of the democratic corporation, the corporation restructured as a democratic worker-owned firm.

THE CAPITALIST CORPORATION AND THE EMPLOYMENT CONTRACT

The capitalist corporation is a piece of property that may be bought and sold. But the property rights in the capitalist corporation are often misunderstood. It is commonly thought that it is the owners' capital right in the corporation--their "ownership of the means of production"-- that gives them the right to command the employees. In analogy with feudal times, it is as if rulership over the employees were part of capital ownership.

> It is not because he is a leader of industry that a man is a capitalist; on the contrary, he is a leader of industry because he is a capitalist. The leadership of industry is an attribute of capital, just as in feudal times the functions of general and judge were attributes of landed property (Marx, 1977, pp. 450-451).

But this is false. The legal right to command the employees is not an attribute of capital; it derives from the employment contract. The ownership of capital by itself only gives the capital owner the legal authority to make the worker a trespasser, not a servant. The capital owner only acquires the direct control right over the worker by virtue of the employment contract. The ownership of capital is only relevant indirectly as providing the bargaining power necessary to make the employment contract.

This appreciation of what is and what is not embodied in capital ownership forces a rethinking of the capitalist corporation. The conclusion is that it is employer-employee relationship, not the corporate ownership rights, which are crucial. The capitalist corporation is only the legal package for the employment relation.

This thesis will be illustrated by an analogy. Suppose that the slave plantation existed as a certain type of legal corporation--and further suppose that all slavery was based on lifetime labor contracts. Very likely the same confusion would arise. Corporate owners would think their rights over the slaves derived from their ownership of the slave corporations rather than from the slavery contracts. Calls for the abolition of slavery by invalidating the slavery contract--even with compensation for the unfulfilled portion of the contracts--would nevertheless bring forth protests that this was destroying their "property rights." But an appreciation of what is and what is not involved in corporate ownership would show this protest to be unfounded. The slavers would be losing not property rights, but contractual opportunities, the opportunity to benefit from an invalid and fraudulent contract.

What is a slave plantation-corporation if the master-slave relationship has been abolished? It is a corporate embodiment of various assets such as land, buildings, machines, and tools as well as some liabilities. All those would still be there after the abolition of the slave relationship. The point of this tale of the slave corporation is that such a company is really a creature of the master-slave relation. If that relationship was abolished, then the slave corporation collapses into an assemblage of assets unable to be used as a slave plantation.

The tale can be retold for the capitalist corporation and the employment contract. The abolition of the contract for renting human beings would not destroy any of the corporate owners' actual (as opposed to imagined) property rights. Through the corporation, the stockholders would still own the same land, buildings, machines, tools, and other assets as well as liabilities. The difference is that they would no longer be able to benefit from the contract to "employ" people to use those assets. Capital could only be remuneratively employed by being hired out or sold to labor, instead of labor being hired in by the capital-owners. Conventionally structured corporations would cease to be productive firms; they would simply be capital suppliers hiring out or selling their capital. Or corporations would cease to be conventionally structured by being restructured as democratic firms.

The capitalist corporation is a "wholly-owned subsidiary" of the employment relation. Without the employment relation, the capitalist corporation is an "empty" asset-holding shell. The problem is not the private property rights in a corporation any more than the problem in slavery was the private ownership of cotton farms. The whole capitalism/socialism debate has been misdirected. The problem is neither "private ownership of the means of production" (properly understood) nor markets. The problem is the employment relation, the market in human labor. The alternative is not the government-owned corporation where workers are "employed" for the "public good" rather than "private greed." The alternative is the democratic corporation where workers are not "employed" at all, where work implies membership, so the workers in each firm are jointly working for themselves.

We have argued that the capitalist corporation is a private nondemocratic Hobbesian government of the workplace. The *pactum sub-*

jectionis for this government is the employment contract. Inalienable rights do not suddenly evaporate as one moves from the public to the private sphere. When properly understood, the inalienable rights arguments hammered out in the Enlightenment against the Hobbesian contract apply as well against the employment contract. If and when this contract for the renting of human beings is recognized as being invalid, then the legal foundation and modus operandi of the conventional corporation will be removed. The capitalist corporation based on the employment relation would be replaced by the democratic corporation where all the people working in the firm are jointly working for themselves. Let us turn to consider the nature of the democratic corporation, the corporation as a democratic social institution.

PERSONAL RIGHTS VERSUS PROPERTY RIGHTS

The capitalist corporation is a piece of property. It is a common mistake to also think of the democratic firm as a piece of property owned by the workers who work in it. While such employee-owned corporations (e.g., conventional employee stock ownership plans or ESOPs) do exist, a democratic corporation is based on different principles. To elucidate the legal structure of a democratic corporation, we must consider the distinction between personal and property rights.

Economists occasionally consider rights which are quite different from property rights to goods and services and which are unsuitable for market allocation. Political voting rights are the principal examples. As James Tobin has noted:

> Any good second year graduate student in economics
> could write a short examination paper proving that
> voluntary transactions in votes would increase the welfare
> of the sellers as well as the buyers (1970, p. 269).

Yet, with a few exceptions, economists uniformly refrain from publicly advocating markets in political votes. The underlying reason is that political voting rights are personal rights rather than property rights. Personal rights are not allocated by markets; they are assigned by institutions to functional roles.

A *personal right* is a right assigned to the person of an individual because the individual qualifies for the right by having a certain functional role. Examples include:

- basic human rights, where the functional role is simply that of being human;
- voting rights in a municipality or township, where the functional role is that of residing within the town or city limits;
- union membership rights, where the functional role is that of working in the bargaining unit; and
- membership rights in a democratic firm, where the functional role is that of working in the firm.

In any democracy, political or industrial, the idea of self-government is institutionally implemented by treating the voting rights to elect the government as personal rights assigned to the functional role of being governed.

One acid test used to distinguish personal rights from property rights is the *inheritability test*. When a person dies, property rights (e.g., common voting shares in a corporation) pass to the heirs while all rights assigned to the person of the deceased individual (such as the four examples above) are extinguished.

A right which is to be assigned to a qualifying functional role is quite different from the marketable property rights to goods and services ordinarily considered in economics. Property rights are marketable so they can become highly concentrated in huge accumulations of wealth and power.   But people qualify for personal rights by having a certain functional role so those rights may not be "bought" or "sold." The would-be "buyer" might not qualify for the right, and if the person did qualify, there would be no need to "buy" the right. These rights are automatically distributed on a one-per-person basis (among those with the qualifying role).   The market mechanism of allocating rights does not apply to personal rights; their assignment is governed by other principles than allocative efficiency (e.g., the principle of democratic self-government).

THE DEMOCRATIC CORPORATION

The democratic corporation extends democratic principles from the communities where people live to the communities where people work. Political democracy embodies certain principles such as the one-person, one-vote rule, and a democratic firm embodies that fundamental rule.

Democracy is a method for people to govern themselves, not a method for property-owners to govern their property. The democratic franchise is "people-based," not property-based or capital-based. Hence in a democratic firm, the people hire the capital, not vice versa. And if labor hires capital, then the residual net income, after the deduction of all costs (including the cost of interest on capital), is a return to labor, not a return to capital.

In a conventional corporation, the *traditional bundle of ownership rights* can be analyzed into (Ellerman, 1982, ch. 12):

- the voting rights,
- the profit or residual claimant rights, and
- the rights to the net book value (assets minus liabilities).

Let the first two rights, the voting rights (e.g., to elect the board) and the rights to the residual net income or profit, be called the *membership rights*.

A *democratic firm* can be defined as a firm where the membership rights are personal rights attached to the functional role of working in the firm.

The assignment of the voting rights to the functional role of working in the firm, and thus to being managed by the management, realizes the application of the democratic principle to the firm. The second set of rights, the residual claimant rights, represent the net value of the positive and negative fruits of the labor of the people working in the firm. Hence the assignment of the residual claimant rights to the functional role of working in the firm realizes the old labor principle that people should appropriate the fruits of their labor (see Ellerman, 1985).

In a democratic firm, the third right to the net asset value should remain a property right which ultimately accrues to the worker-members. Some worker-managed firms such as the Yugoslavian self-managed firms or the common-ownership firms in England deny that net asset right. The value of the assets minus the liabilities is held collectively without individual claims. But it represents the past fruits of the workers' labor which was reinvested in the firm so there seems to be little rationale for the workers to forfeit any recoupable claim on that property.

There are now legal forms available which recognize the workers' rights to the reinvested fruits of their past labor. Worker cooperatives using a design pioneered by the Mondragon cooperatives in Spain (Ellerman and Pitegoff, 1983; Ellerman, 1984, 1986b) have an internal capital account for each member which keeps track of the capital ultimately due back to the member. The employee stock ownership plan or ESOP can be restructured in a democratic manner to form a democratic ESOP with the democratic and cooperative attribute of one-person, one-vote. In a democratic ESOP, the ESOP capital accounts play a role similar to the internal capital accounts in the Mondragon-style worker cooperatives.

It should be noted that the equality of votes in a democratic corporation does not imply equality of pay or equality of capital investment. In a democratic firm and in a democratic political organization, capital is a hired resource; there is no capital with votes attached to it. One cannot "Take Stock in America"; one can only take bonds. Citizens may only invest capital in a political democracy by loaning capital to it, e.g., by purchasing municipal bonds, treasury notes, or U.S. Savings Bonds. Thus citizens can have equal voting rights with quite different amounts of invested capital since the votes are quite separate from the capital. For the same reason, worker-members have equal voting rights but can have different capital investments in a democratic firm. This could not be true if the democratic corporation were legally structured as a piece of property.

In the democratic corporation, the membership rights are personal rights attached to the role of working in the firm--so the workers hold those rights because they work in the firm. By contrast, in a conventional corporation, the ownership rights (the shares of stock) are transferable property rights which can be owned by anyone regardless of whether they work in the firm or not. In the democratic firm, labor hires capital (even the workers' own capital) so the ownership structure is labor-based; the membership rights are attached to the role of working in the firm. Who owns a democratic firm? The workers have the ownership rights, but not as ownership rights. The rights are held as personal rights.

The transformation of the corporate voting and profit rights from property to personal rights entails a fundamental transformation in the nature of the corporation. The conventional corporation is the only major human organization in present-day society which has owners who may buy and sell it as a piece of property. Indeed, a corporation is often thought of as a piece of property, a chunk of capital, like a machine, a building, a parcel of land, or a sum of money. But this is most peculiar. A corporation is an organization; a machine, a building, a plot of land, or an amount of financial capital are not. A corporation has a built-in governance system, members (stockholders) who vote to elect representatives (directors) who, in turn, appoint governors (managers) to govern the affairs of the organization. Machines, buildings, and other chunks of property have no governance system.

Other institutions and organizations are not conceived of as property at all. Universities, hospitals, churches, and other nonprofit corporations are not property. Labor unions, clubs, and other unincorporated organizations are not property. The units of city, state, or national government are not property. All these are human organizations. All have a system of governance with certain members who vote directly or indirectly to select the governors or managers of the organization. All these organizations own property, but none are themselves property. None have owners who may buy or sell the organization. The capitalist corporation is the peculiar institution of our time.

Democratic theory, which embodies the inalienable rights arguments descending from the Enlightenment, does not stop at the corporate gates. It implies the abolition of the modern economic *pactum subjectionis*, the employer-employee contract, which lies at the foundation of the conventional corporation. The inherent autonomy and dignity of the person entails that, instead of being rented by a company, work and participation in a corporation should automatically qualify a person as a member of the company. That transforms the traditional corporation into the democratic corporation where the membership rights are allocated as personal rights rather than sold as property rights. Thus the corporation itself is transformed from a piece of property into a democratic social institution.

References

Batt, F. 1967. *The Law of Master and Servant*. Fifth edition by G. Webber. London: Pitman.

Berle, A. and Means, G. 1932. *The Modern Corporation and Private Property*. New York: MacMillan Company.

Cassirer, E. 1963. *The Myth of the State*. New Haven: Yale University Press.

Catterall, H. T. (ed.). 1926. *Judicial Cases Concerning Slavery and the Negro*. Vol. III. Carnegie Institute: Washington, DC.

Chayes, A. 1966. *The Modern Corporation and the Rule of Law. The Corporation in Modern Society*, edited by E. S. Mason. New York: Atheneum.

Dahl, R. A. 1985. *A Preface to Economic Democracy*. Berkeley: University of California Press.

Davis, D. B. 1975. *The Problem of Slavery in The Age of Revolution 1770-1823*. Ithaca: Cornell University Press.

Diderot, D. 1967. *The Encyclopedia: Selections*, edited and translated by S. Gendzier. New York: Harper Torchbooks.

Ellerman, D. 1982. *Economics, Accounting, and Property Theory*. Lexington, MA: Lexington Books.

_____. 1983. "A model structure for cooperatives: worker co-ops and housing co-ops," *Review of Social Economy* 41:1 (April), 52-67.

_____. 1984. "Entrepreneurship in the Mondragon cooperatives," *Review of Social Economy* 42:3 (December), 272-294.

_____. 1985. "On the labor theory of property," *The Philosophical Forum* 16:4 (Summer), 293-326.

_____. 1986a. "The employment contract and liberal thought," *Review of Social Economy* 44:1 (April), 13-39.

_____. 1986b. "Horizon problems and property rights in labor-managed firms," *The Journal of Comparative Economics* 10:1 (March), 62-78.

Ellerman, D. and P. Pitegoff. 1983. "The democratic corporation," *The Review of Law and Social Change* 11:3, 441-472.

Gierke, O. von. 1957. *Natural Law and The Theory of Society: 1500 to 1800*, trans. E. Barker. Boston: Beacon Press.

_____. 1966. *The Development of Political Theory*, trans. B. Freyd. New York: Howard Fertig.

Goodell, W. 1853. *The American Slave Code in Theory and Practice*. Reprinted in 1969. New York: New American Library.

Hobbes, T. 1651. *Leviathan*. Reprinted 1958. Indianapolis: Bobbs-Merrill.

Justinian. 1948. *The Institutes of Justinian*, trans. T. C. Sandars. London: Longmans, Green, and Co.

Marx, K. 1977. *Capital*. Volume I, trans. B. Fowkes. New York: Vintage Books.

Nozick, R. 1974. *Anarchy, State, and Utopia*. New York: Basic Books.

Rousseau, J. J.   1755.   "Discourse on the origin of inequality," in *The Social Contract and Discourses*, trans. G. D. H. Cole.   Published in 1973.   London: J. M. Dent & Sons.

Samuelson, P. A.   1976.   *Economics*, 10th edition.   New York: McGraw-Hill.

Tobin, J.   1970.   "On Limiting the Domain of Inequality," *Journal of Law and Economics* 13 (October).

Wills, G.   1979.   *Inventing America: Jefferson's Declaration of Independence*.   [1978]   Vintage edition.   New York: Vintage Books.

PART IV:

CONCLUSION: THE PROSPECT FOR SOCIAL
ECONOMICS

12

SCIENCE, SELF-CORRECTION AND VALUES: FROM PEIRCE TO INSTITUTIONALISM

Malcolm Rutherford

> *The value theory of institutional economics, which may also be called instrumental value theory (and is in the general tradition of C. S. Peirce, William James, and John Dewey), views value determination as a process involving continuously testing a technique (used in an effort to implement values) against the consequences of the use of that technique . . . . But, at the same time that the quality or the value of the technique is being tested, the value itself is subject to reappraisal in the light of the consequences of the effort to implement it. Thus, values themselves are reappraised against the consequences of trying to give them effect. . . .*

The value theory, then, is that values are created and identified (instrumentally determined) in a process involving self-correcting (or self-adjusting) value judgments.

--Wendell Gordon (1980, pp. 43-45)

Democracy stands for the procedure by which alone all the other values can be achieved . . . . The essence of democracy is . . . the process by which majorities are formed . . . . Voting has democratic significance only to the degree that it registers the free choices of an informed electorate . . . . The self-government of peoples is a possibility only because it is possible for large numbers of people--in effect, whole communities--to arrive at common conclusions . . . . The confusion that is so often manifest in the democratic process is the confusion of learning. Conditions change, and it is not immediately apparent to anybody--certainly not to all--in what direction operational efficiency lies . . . . Nevertheless in all such cases the democratic process is a process of learning the truth and operating accordingly, and the unanimity towards which the process aims is that of the universality of science and technology.

--Clarence Ayres (1961, pp. 282-285)

INTRODUCTION

The lengthy passages quoted above perfectly display the major characteristics of what might be called the "standard" institutionalist treatment of processes of valuation.[1] The first and most obvious characteristic is the naturalism of the approach. Values are seen as being determined, appraised, reappraised, and modified in a continual process of instrumental and experimental investigation no different from the process of inquiry found within natural science. This follows Dewey's explicit denial that "as judgments, or in respect to method of inquiry, test, and verification, value-judgments have any peculiar or unique features" (Dewey, 1946, pp. 258-259; see also Dewey, 1939). Furthermore, the application of scientific methods is also taken to be relevant to the formation of *social* values. Here, again following Dewey, there is an explicit identification of a democratic community with a "scientific" community of inquiry (Gouinlock, 1972, p. 354). A second feature, as the passages from Ayres make abundantly clear, is the associated claim that the application of scientific methods to the democratic discourse over values aids powerfully in the settlement of belief and the creation of a broad consensus on social values and appropriate social policy. The third and last characteristic is the view of the scientific method as, in some largely undefined sense, self-corrective. Self-correction is a particularly important attribute for scientific methods to possess given the institutionalist enthusiasm for the application of a scientific, experimental, approach to social policymaking. It cannot, of course, be claimed that scientific methods will always result in successful social experiments. Such social experimentation, therefore, is not justified on the grounds that science can never mislead or is always reliable, but on the grounds that science is self-corrective, meaning, presumably, that errors (adverse consequences) will be discovered in a timely fashion and successfully corrected.[2]

This treatment of questions of value derives from the American pragmatic tradition in philosophy. There can be little doubt that John Dewey exerted the most direct influence on Ayres and later institutionalists, but it has also been argued that a continuity of ideas runs from the work of C. S. Peirce through Dewey to Ayres and beyond (Hill, 1978, 1979, 1986; Liebhafsky, 1986). This chapter seeks to investigate some aspects of Peirce's view of science--in particular the ability of science to "settle belief" and its self-corrective nature--that appear to have come through (although *not* in any straightforward manner) to the modern institutionalist view of science and its applicability to matters of social value and policy. In this, many of the issues surrounding the naturalism of the institutionalist approach to valuation will not be dealt with. Discussion of the naturalistic position and its problems has already been extensive (see Geiger, 1958; Gouinlock, 1972; Rutherford, 1981; Lutz, 1985), while other aspects of the institutionalist viewpoint have been much less closely examined.

SCIENCE AND THE SETTLEMENT OF BELIEF

In a recent paper H. H. Liebhafsky argues that Clarence Ayres reached the "result Peirce reached in 1878 by concluding that scientific method was the best method of fixing belief" (1986, p. 19), and goes on to quote Ayres' view that "when we seek to determine whether anything is good or bad, or whether any act is right or wrong, we are seeking clear and certain knowledge of its causal bearing on the life process of mankind" (Ayres, 1961, p. 122). Peirce's views on science and its ability to settle belief are not, however, quite as clear as Liebhafsky seems to suppose.

In the investigation of Peirce's views on science and the settlement of belief two of his essays have particular significance: "The Fixation of Belief" (1877) and "How to Make our Ideas Clear" (1878). The first essay begins from "the proposition that the agitation of a question ceases when satisfaction is attained with the settlement of belief, and then only, goes on to consider how the conception of truth gradually develops from that principle under the action of experience" (Peirce, 5.564).[3] Peirce argues that inquiry is the attempt to overcome doubt and achieve a state of belief. His focus is on the establishment of a stable belief. Once a stable belief has been achieved, inquiry comes to an end. Peirce then considers how man has been led to the adoption of the scientific method as the best method for settling belief, and this involves him in a consideration of various prescientific methods and the difficulties that led to their abandonment. What Peirce presents purports to be an evolutionary sequence.

The first method is that of tenacity, the method of dogmatically continuing to believe whatever one already believes (Peirce, 5.377). This method of fixing belief, however, runs into a difficulty in that "the man who adopts it will find that other men think differently from him, and it will be apt to occur to him, in some saner moment, that their opinions are quite as good as his own, and this will shake his confidence in his belief" (Peirce, 5.378). The idea that another's opinion may be as good as one's own arises from the basic social impulse in man and cannot be avoided "unless we make ourselves hermits." The problem, therefore, becomes one of "how to fix belief, not in the individual merely, but in the community" (Peirce, 5.378).

The need for the fixing of belief on the level of the whole community leads to the adoption of the next method, the method of authority. Historically, the fixing of belief by authority has had much greater success than the method of tenacity. For the "mass of mankind" who are content to be "intellectual slaves" there is no more effective method than this (Peirce, 5.380). The problems that arise with the method of authority are first, that no institution can regulate *all* beliefs and some other method will be used to settle belief in those cases, and second, that some men will have contact with other societies and come to realize that it is the "mere accident" of their birth and upbringing that "has caused them to believe as they do and not far differently" (Peirce, 5.381). For these reasons a "new method of settling opinions must be adopted, that shall not only produce an impulse to believe, but shall also decide what proposition it is which is to be believed" (Peirce, 5.382). This gives rise to the *a priori* method.

For Peirce, the method *a priori* is the method of choosing a belief on grounds of it being "agreeable to reason." This method does not usually or generally take account of observed facts. It is the method employed throughout the history of metaphysics (Peirce, 5.382). The *a priori* method does have an intellectual respectability the methods of tenacity and authority lack, but, despite this, "its failure has been the most manifest" (Peirce, 5.383). This failure can be seen in the fact that "metaphysicians have never come to any fixed agreement." The method results in opinions having the character of tastes or fashions that swing back and forth (Peirce, 5.383). Thus "to satisfy our doubts . . . it is necessary that a method should be found by which our beliefs may be determined by nothing human, but by some external permanency--by something upon which our thinking has no effect." This, according to Peirce, is the "method of science" (Peirce, 5.384).

Peirce's concept of science and his argument that scientific methods can settle belief are based on his acceptance of the existence of an objective reality. Thus, "by taking advantage of the laws of perception, we can ascertain by reasoning how things really and truly are; and any man, if he have sufficient experience and he reason enough about it, will be led to the one True conclusion" (Peirce, 5.384). The establishment of a stable belief by scientific methods is possible only because science leads ultimately to the truth. The great problem with this is that while, in Peirce's work, science does lead to the truth, it does so only over the very long run.

Peirce's long run perspective is made very clear in his 1878 essay. Here Peirce places repeated emphasis on the truth as that belief which will be *ultimately* arrived at and agreed to by all if only the process of investigation is carried on for long enough and pushed far enough (Peirce, 5.407). In a noteworthy passage Peirce argues:

> Our perversity and that of others may indefinitely postpone the settlement of opinion; it might even conceivably cause an arbitrary proposition to be universally accepted as long as the human race should last. Yet even

that would not change the nature of the belief, which
alone could be the result of investigation carried sufficiently far; and if, after the extinction of our race, another
should arise with faculties and disposition for investigation,
that true opinion must be the one which they would
ultimately come to. "Truth crushed to earth shall rise
again," and the opinion which would finally result from
investigation does not depend on how anybody may
actually think. But the reality of that which is real does
depend on the real fact that investigation is destined to
lead, at last, if continued long enough, to a belief in it
(Peirce, 5.409).[4]

These passages indicate that the settlement of belief via the use of
scientific methods is something that may take an *indefinitely*, even *infinitely*,
long time. This makes Peirce's whole discussion of the superiority of
science in settling belief and its evolutionary adoption over other,
nonscientific, methods entirely problematic. As pointed out by Skagestad,
"while science in its mature stages achieves relative stability for numerous
beliefs, it achieves this result by initially casting doubt on our habitual
beliefs; hence science is a far more unsettling method of forming opinion
than any of the three others mentioned by Peirce" (1981, p. 37). Science
may unsettle belief in the short run and only settle it again in the very
(infinitely) long run. Science cannot, on the argument that it leads
eventually to the truth, be thought of as a superior method for fixing
belief in the here and now or in the immediate future.

Peirce does make one other argument for the superiority of
scientific methods in fixing belief, and this is the purely empirical point
that "experience of the method has not led us to doubt it, but, on the
contrary, scientific investigation has had the most wonderful triumphs in
the way of settling opinion" (Peirce, 5.384). This short run success,
however, is not a necessary consequence of the method, and although it
would be true to say that in the natural sciences the scientific method has
had success in "resolving disputes and temporarily establishing shared
meaning" (Sederberg, 1984, p. 27), the same success cannot be claimed in
the social sciences. One of the reasons for this difference is the difficulty
of isolating social scientific research from political, economic, and ethical
interests and concerns. In other words, the position taken by institutionalists that the application of science to social issues can create a value
consensus out of diversity may often, in fact, be exactly reversed, with the

intrusion of science into matters of social interest leading to disputes over the meaning and adequacy of scientific methods and findings. As shall be seen below, this latter possibility was of great concern to Peirce.

SCIENCE AND THE SELF-CORRECTIVE THESIS

The notion of scientific methods as self-corrective is also one that much interested Peirce. Self-correction is obviously linked to Peirce's arguments concerning the long-run ability of scientific methods to lead to the truth. Although Peirce did not originate the self-corrective thesis (SCT), he did understand that the thesis was not simply self-evidently true (Laudan, 1973, p. 287).

Peirce argues that self-correction is a characteristic of all reasoning, and particularly of scientific reasoning. Furthermore, self-correction applies both to the correction of conclusions and to the correction of premises (Peirce, 5.575, 5.579, 5.582). The idea of self-correction would seem to imply not only the discovery of error but also some notion of improvement. Laurens Laudan (1973, pp. 279, 300) has argued that to be more than trivial the SCT must imply:

(1)   Scientific method is such that, in the long run, its use will refute a theory T, if T is false;

and also:

(2)   Science possesses a method for finding an alternative T' which is closer to the truth than a refuted T;

or, at the least:

(2')   Science processes techniques for determining unambiguously whether an alternative T' is closer to the truth than a refuted T.[5]

For Peirce the scientific method consists of induction (by which he means the processes involved in testing a hypothesis), deduction and also abduction or retroduction (the processes of generating and provisionally adopting hypotheses). On deduction Peirce recognizes that errors in reasoning may go long undiscovered: "Errors of reasoning in the first book of Euclid's Elements, the logic of which book was for two thousand years subjected to more careful criticism than any other piece of reasoning without exception ever was or probably ever will be, only became known after the non-Euclidean geometry had been developed." Discovery of errors in reasoning, then, need be neither sure nor swift, although once discovered they can be quickly corrected (Peirce, 5.577). Similarly, on abduction, Peirce has to admit that "retroductive inquiries" tend to be "theatres of controversy." These controversies "do get settled, after a time, in the minds of candid inquirers; though it does not always happen that the protagonists themselves are able to assent to the justice of the decision. Nor is the general verdict always logical or just" (Peirce, 5.578). Peirce is thus forced to conclude that the "marvellous self-correcting property of Reason" is "essential, intrinsic, and inevitable only in the highest type of reasoning, which is induction" (Peirce, 5.579).

Peirce's case for the SCT, thus, depends on his case for the self-corrective nature of induction. Induction is to be understood in a broad way as the various methods of empirical testing. The self-corrective nature of induction is constantly asserted by Peirce,[6] but, despite this, all Peirce actually demonstrates is that empirical testing can expose error, not that induction (in general) can correct or improve on any mistaken hypothesis. The one possible exception to this is in the case of simple quantitative induction. In this case Peirce is dealing with an estimate arrived at from a random sampling procedure. He argues that repeated sampling will, over the long run, lead to estimates that gradually (although irregularly) come closer to the true value (Peirce, 2.770). However, the method of quantitative induction is *not* seen by Peirce as a particularly important one, and it is obviously the case that the logic of the argument concerning quantitative induction cannot be transferred to other forms of empirical testing.

In terms of the various statements of the SCT given above, it is clear that Peirce sustains neither (2) nor (2'). His arguments for the self-corrective nature of induction (and science in general) appear to come down only to statement (1): That the inductive investigation of a theory, if persisted in long enough, will result in the refutation of that theory if it is false. That Peirce could only provide support for the SCT in such a trivial form is not surprising given the extent of his fallibilism and his very long run perspective on the attainment of truth. Peirce fully supported the view that any currently accepted theory may prove to be false, and it is quite clear that he did not believe that the history of science was a history of continuous or smooth convergence to the truth. The path to the truth may be both devious and long.

In Peirce's system, then, self-correction is not a process of short-run improvement or correction, but a process that operates via the falsification of incorrect hypotheses, and only in the infinitely long run will such a process necessarily converge on the truth.[7]

SCIENCE AND SOCIAL POLICY

Peirce's arguments concerning the SCT have been variously interpreted. Laudan (1973) argues that they represent a failure by Peirce to achieve his goals of defending science against skeptical criticism and of maintaining the view of science as a "progressive enterprise." On the other hand, and of particular interest in the present context, Skagestad claims that Peirce never intended a general defense of the scientific enterprise, but only a defense of "pure" scientific research against "those who would make science subservient either to religious dogmas or to technological or political goals" (1981, p. 200). For this purpose the SCT in its trivial version was exactly what Peirce required. In Skagestad's words, "not only did he not need a decision procedure for short-run self-correction; such a decision procedure would actually have defeated his purposes by guaranteeing immediate practical utility and thereby delivering science into the hands of his opponents" (1981, p. 206).

Peirce's arguments against a utilitarian view of science are several. If science is looked upon as "an instrument for a practical end," certainty or firm belief in the proposition to be applied is required. This attitude militates against probabilistic reasoning and against scientific progress which is brought about by *doubt*. Doubt tends to "paralyze action" but "the scientific spirit requires a man to be at all times ready to dump his whole cartload of beliefs, the moment experience is against them." Thus "the real character of science is destroyed as soon as it is made an adjunct to conduct" (Peirce, 1.55). Furthermore, the utilitarian point of view is a narrow one, concentrating attention to what appears to have the greatest practical importance, but practical importance does not necessarily coincide with importance for scientific understanding. In Peirce's view it is impossible to serve both theory and practice: "that perfect balance of attention which is requisite for observing the system of things is utterly lost if human desires intervene" (Peirce, 1.642). Finally, science is fallible and is self-corrective only over the long term. From a scientific point of view even an idea that is "grossly mistaken" may aid in the ultimate discovery of truth (Peirce, 1.644) and highly unlikely ideas are often worth pursuing (Peirce, 1.120).   What is required for practical purposes is reliable knowledge, and scientific knowledge may often be unreliable. Peirce argues that it is "because of this utterly unsettled and uncertain condition of philosophy at present, that I regard any practical applications of it to religion and conduct as exceedingly dangerous . . . . I do not say that philosophical science should not ultimately influence religion and morality; I only say that it should be allowed to do so only with secular slowness and the most conservative caution" (Peirce, 1.620).

Peirce was sharply critical of men such as Karl Pearson who argued that science should be directed toward the "welfare of human society," "social happiness," and "social stability." Peirce considered such ideas to be entirely wrongheaded, tending to make science subservient to whatever particular content might be read into phrases such as "the welfare of human society" or "social stability," and encouraging the belief that it is those who deal with applications, and not the theoreticians, who are the true scientists (Peirce, 8.141-143). For Peirce, science involved the search for truth regardless of where that search may lead, and he argued that the scientist must be prepared "to look the truth in the face" regardless of whether it supported some prior notion of the social interest. What "the true interest of society" might actually consist of Peirce regarded as an "excessively difficult problem," but one that would be best approached indirectly by allowing pure science to take its own course (Peirce, 8.143).

Peirce's views on the importance of separating pure science from concerns over immediate policy application were also linked to his arguments concerning the importance of instinct, common sense, and traditional morality in directing conduct. Traditional rules of conduct have evolved out of long experience and are not to be lightly discarded on the basis of some currently held, but quite possibly false, scientific theory. As Peirce noted, the lower animals who rely on instinct rarely get the important things wrong. In contrast, when men start to rationalize about their conduct, traditional rules may break down with little to replace them (Peirce, 1.57; 1.649): "Truly, that reason upon which we so plume ourselves, though it may answer for little things, yet for great decisions is hardly surer than a toss-up" (Peirce, 1.649). Peirce, of course, was not arguing that science could not, in principle, address questions of morality and conduct. His point was simply that science was fallible and would reach truth only in the long run. In the short term, traditional morality and standards of conduct are likely to be the more reliable guide:

> It is a damnable absurdity indeed to say that one thing is true in theology and another in science. But it is perfectly true that the belief which I shall do well to embrace in my practical affairs, such as my religion, may not accord with the proposition which a sound scientific method requires me provisionally to adopt at this stage of my investigation. Later, both the one proposition and the other may very likely be modified; but how, or which comes nearer to the ultimate conclusion, not being a prophet or a magician, I cannot yet say (Peirce, 6.216).

This point deserves emphasis. Peirce did want to preserve science from interference from religious or political ideals, and also wanted to preserve religious values from premature abandonment on the basis of criticism from scientists claiming knowledge of the social interest, but there can be little doubt that, over the long term, Peirce thought that science both could and would have implications for values. Nevertheless, for science to be able to discover the truth and settle belief, it must be allowed to proceed undeflected by immediate concerns over issues of social value.

In his later work Peirce argued for a "scientific metaphysics," but his views on science and values did not alter in any fundamental way. For Peirce, religion should approach science with confidence, "accepting all the results of science, as scientific men themselves accept them, as steps toward the truth, which may appear for a time to be in conflict with other truths but which in such cases merely await adjustments which time is sure to affect" (Peirce, 6.433). On the side of science, "what is to be its goal is precisely what it must not seek to determine for itself . . . . Teleological considerations, that is to say ideals, must be left to religion; science can allow itself to be swayed only by efficient causes; and philosophy, in her character of queen of the sciences, must not care, or must not seem to care, whether her conclusions be wholesome or dangerous" (Peirce, 6.434). Even in his essay "Evolutionary Love" (Peirce, 6.287-317), where he criticizes the economists' "Gospel of Greed" and puts forward instead the "Gospel of Christ," that social progress comes from "every individual merging his individuality in sympathy with his neighbors" (Peirce, 6.294), Peirce ultimately appeals and defers to the final outcome of the process of scientific investigation (Peirce, 6.317). Thus, in the end, science will indeed speak to matters of religion and conduct, but science, if it is to ever arrive at the truth, must be guided only by "nature's strong hand" (Peirce, 6.434).

PEIRCE AND INSTITUTIONALISM

From the foregoing it is clear that although some of Peirce's terminology has come through into institutionalist writings, the view of science and its potential for fixing belief, creating consensus and short-term application to social problems that is found in Peirce's work differs markedly from that found within modern institutionalism.

The most significant difference is to be found in Peirce's very long-run perspective. Science fixes belief and generates consensus only in the long run, science is self-corrective only in the long run, and science does not, therefore, provide a reliable basis for short-term social engineering. As a part of this, Peirce does not see science in purely instrumental terms. Science is justified not by any practical benefits it may confer, but by its long run search after truth. Furthermore, the pursuit of practical, instrumental objectives can distort and damage the true scientific enterprise as well as resulting in the premature abandonment of traditional values and modes of conduct. Later institutionalists appear to have adopted Peirce's ideas of science as capable of fixing belief and as self-corrective in nature, but have applied these ideas in a short-run context in order to justify a scientistic approach to issues of social value and social policy that Peirce himself would have rejected.

This transition from the antiscientism of Peirce to the exaggerated scientism of Ayres and many later writers has been noted elsewhere (Mirowski, 1987). Arguments that in Peirce's hands were a defense of tradition against the intrusion of science into practical life have been turned to the purpose of proclaiming the superiority of science over traditional norms and conduct. It is, of course, true that institutionalists such as Ayres take a more purely instrumental view of science than Peirce, but even within such an instrumentalist viewpoint there is no convincing argument that instrumental tests can do more than indicate success or failure. Even here, and particularly where social experiments are concerned, such tests may mislead due to the length of time it can take for some consequences to appear, and suffer from the extreme difficulty of identifying the particular consequences of any given value or policy change in a world that is not otherwise constant. Moreover, the discovery of some adverse consequence does not, in itself, indicate how to correct for that failure. Short-term self-correction is in no way assured.

Similarly, an instrumentalist approach to science does not imply an ability to generate a consensus over the short term. Ayres' analogy between the choice of values and the mechanic's choice of the right tool (Ayres, 1962, pp. 212-219) would seem to require a very well-specified objective, very clear criteria of success or failure, and the ability to conduct decisive tests. The fact that everyone may agree that a wrench of certain size and type is the best tool for tightening a specific bolt in specific circumstances does not then imply that science can readily create agreement over something as complex as the values that will best serve some objective as ill-defined as the "life process." Even with reference to physical science, modern discussion of the philosophy of science tends to emphasize the plurality of research programs, the existence of incommensurabilities, and the impossibility of conducting decisive tests between different programs. These problems can only be compounded in the social sciences. In many respects Peirce is closer to this modern philosophy of science than either Dewey or Ayres (Mirowski, 1987).

As one final point, it has been claimed that Peirce's concept of the *summum bonum*, the unlimited community of reasoned and reasonable conduct, is closely linked to Dewey's and Ayres' stress on the continuum of inquiry and of progress "toward a reasonable society" (Liebhafsky, 1986, p. 19). While not denying this link, there is a crucial difference. For Dewey, and particularly for Ayres, what is reasonable is what is in line with the current state of scientific knowledge. For Ayres what is not legitimized by science is without meaning or worth (Ayres, 1949). Peirce, on the other hand, spent considerable effort on arguing exactly for the reasonableness of maintaining nonscientific beliefs due to the fallibility of scientific knowledge. For Peirce what it is reasonable to believe for short-term practical matters does not necessarily coincide with the "best" available scientific ideas.

CONCLUSION

The links between Peirce and later institutionalists, at least as far as their views on the nature of science and its short run applicability to matters of social value and policy are concerned, are not as clear as has sometimes been supposed. The institutionalist who sees in science a self-correcting tool for the immediate guidance of social policy finds no ally in Peirce, but neither does the dogmatist who would simply ignore science or deny that its methods provide, over the long term, the only sure path to the truth.

Peirce's point of view is not a simple or easily explicable one. Science, for Peirce, can only be properly or effectively pursued as *pure* science, free from concerns over the social implications of any particular hypothesis. On the other hand, religion, as a guide to values and conduct, should not ignore science. This does not imply that religion should respond to or immediately adopt whatever theory is currently in scientific vogue, but it does imply the--in some ways much deeper--acceptance of the scientific method as the only available method capable of *ultimately* settling belief:

> Religion is a practical matter. Its beliefs are formulae you will go upon. But a scientific proposition is merely something you take up provisionally as being the proper hypothesis to try first and endeavor to refute. The only belief you--as a purely scientific man--have about it is that it is adopted in accordance with a method that must lead to the truth in the long run (Peirce, 6.216)

Notes

[1] There is a distinction to be drawn between the institutionalist view of "genuine" processes of valuation based on the scientific model, and ceremonialism--the adoption of "false" values without scientific validity. The former is being dealt with here.

[2] Self-correction is a major theme in Gordon (1980). For another example see Liebhafsky (1971).

[3] All references to Peirce are to his *Collected Papers*, by volume and paragraph numbers.

[4] This clearly contradicts the view sometimes expressed that Peirce defined truth simply in terms of the consensus of scientific opinion. Peirce defines truth in terms of what will *ultimately* be agreed to as a result of inquiry, not in terms of the results of an opinion poll of scientists taken at any finite point in time. See Nissen (1966, pp. 87-100). In one place Peirce defines truth as "that concordance of an abstract statement with the ideal limit toward which endless investigation would tend to bring scientific belief" . . . (Peirce, 5.565). For extensive discussion of this point see Skagestad (1981).

[5]Laudan calls (1) and (2) together the strong version of the SCT, while (1) and (2') constitute the "weak" version (1973, p. 300).

[6]See for example, Peirce (1.67, 2.775, 2.780, 5.576, 6.100).

[7]The only reason Peirce gives for believing that the truth may be obtained in some finite period of time is an innate human ability of "guessing right." Thus "it is certain that the only hope of retroductive reasoning ever reaching the truth is that there may be some natural tendency toward an agreement between the ideas which suggest themselves to the human mind and those which are concerned in the laws of nature" (Peirce, 1.81). Again, "it is a primary hypothesis . . . that the human mind is akin to the truth in the sense that in a finite number of guesses it will light upon the correct hypothesis" (Peirce, 7.220). This argument, however, does not constitute a *methodological* rational for the SCT. See Laudan (1973, pp. 294-295).

References

Ayres, C. E.   1949.   "The value economy," in *Value: A Co-operative Inquiry*, edited by R. Lepley.   New York: Columbia University Press.

_____.   1961.   *Toward a Reasonable Society*.   Austin: University of Texas Press.

_____.   1962.   *The Theory of Economic Progress*, 2nd ed.   New York: Schocken.

Dewey, J.   1939.   *Theory of Valuation*.   Chicago: University of Chicago Press.

_____.   1946.   *Problems of Men*.   New York: Philosophical Library.

Geiger, G. R.   1958.   *John Dewey in Perspective*.   New York: Oxford University Press.

Gordon, W.   1980.   *Institutional Economics*.   Austin: University of Texas Press.

Gouinlock, J.   1972.   *John Dewey's Philosophy of Value*.   New York: Humanities Press.

Hill, L. E.   1978.   "Social and institutional economics: toward a creative synthesis," *Review of Social Economy* 36 (December), 311-323.

_____.   1979.   "The metaphysical preconceptions of the economic science," *Review of Social Economy* 37 (October), 189-197.

_____.   1986.   "Pragmatism, instrumental value theory and social economics: comment," *Review of Social Economy* 44 (October), 193-195.

Laudan, L.   1973.   "Peirce and the trivialization of the self-correcting thesis," in *Foundations of Scientific Method: The Nineteenth*

Century, edited by R. N. Giere and R. S. Westfall. Bloomington, Indiana: Indiana University Press.

Liebhafsky, H. H. 1971. *American Government and Business*. New York: Wiley.

_____. 1986. "Peirce on the *summum bonum* and the unlimited community; Ayres on 'the criterion of value'," *Journal of Economic Issues* 20 (March), 5-20.

Lutz, M. A. 1985. "Pragmatism, instrumental value theory and social economics," *Review of Social Economy* 43 (October), 140-172.

Mirowski, P. 1987. "The philosophical bases of institutionalist economics," *Journal of Economic Issues* 21 (September), 1001-1038.

Nissen, L. 1966. *John Dewey's Theory of Inquiry and Truth*. The Hague: Mouton.

Peirce, C. S. 1934-58. *Collected Papers*. (8 volumes). Cambridge, MA: Harvard University Press.

Rutherford, M. 1981. "Clarence Ayres and the instrumental theory of value," *Journal of Economic Issues* 15 (September), 657-673.

Sederberg, P. C. 1984. *The Politics of Meaning*. Tucson: University of Arizona Press.

Skagestad, P. 1981. *The Road of Inquiry: Charles Peirce's Pragmatic Realism*. New York: Columbia University Press.

13

AN ESSAY ON THE NATURE AND SIGNIFICANCE OF SOCIAL ECONOMICS

Mark A. Lutz

As noted in the Preface, the conception of the present book has from the very beginning been deeply rooted in a point of view that regards contemporary social economics as a highly pluralistic field of inquiry. It would seem, accordingly, that any meaningful attempt to better comprehend it will have to come to grips with its characteristic inner diversity. Today, pluralism is the very key, the nuts and bolts of modern social economics, and even more certainly, the glue that has been holding it together. At the same time, especially in the present context, we need to recognize that there can be some diversity in the concept and meaning of "pluralism" itself. In particular, we will here distinguish between a "strong version" and a more "moderate version" of pluralism. One is epistemological *and* ontological, the other merely epistemological.

The perspective of a "strong" pluralism can, for example, be found in the work of Warren Samuels, both in this volume and elsewhere (1977).

Diversity in social theory and social economics simply reflects an irreducibly complex and *intrinsically* diverse social reality "out there." Therefore, Samuels, for example, is led to prefer an "open-ended 'matrix' approach to the study of schools and strands of thought." His is a vision of "let the hundred flowers bloom," and "don't even try to discover the real, true or 'best' principles of anything, including social economics." More specifically, how can we aim at a "reconstruction of society on a sound ethical and moral base," if we ought to doubt that such a base even exists in the first place. There may be none, or there may be more than one. Furthermore, anybody who wishes to deny this in pretending his (or her) chosen approach is better or even "the best" by some supposedly more objective, universal, or (pardon the expression) "absolute" set of criteria, reveals a propensity to differentiate oneself in a way that both deprecates and excludes others (Samuels, 1977, p. 287). Operating on the a priori principle [a discovered truth?] that there are no discoverable universal truths, no pragmatists can be expected to participate wholeheartedly in the hunting down of a phantom. Instead, the "true" principles of social economics would only be a figment of the soul, and so would be any serious proposal recommending criteria for a meaningful evaluation of alternative normative approaches. It would also follow that any attempt to the contrary would never amount to anything more than a counterproductive imposition.

One problem with this view, so it would seem, is that it can be rejected on its own grounds, the kind of *internal* criticism that it generally recommends. It entails an a priori rejection of a monist (meta-)conception of social economics. It could be argued that such an uncritical preconception makes a pluralism in its strong version unnecessarily dogmatic and one-sided. Another problem would be that there really is no good reason to stop at merely four versions of social economics. On what basis could we rule out even 400 and more?

An alternative, more moderate form of pluralism would be more in line with what Bruce Caldwell calls "methodological pluralism," a plurality of methods in proceeding toward the attainment of knowledge of the *one* reality "out" there. According to this alternative, there is nothing wrong with a belief that "deep down" and within a particular context, there does exist a true, right, "best" (possible) way to reconstruct society on a sound and ethical base. But, and here we paraphrase Caldwell's view (1982, p. 245) on methodology, even though such a sound basis exists, we can never be sure we have discovered it, even if we have. Still, just because we can never be sure that we are moving in the "right direction" does not mean that there is no "right" direction, or "better," or "best" direction.

Social economists prepared to embrace this practical type of "pluralistic monism" will be troubled by a proliferation of mutually conflicting ethical views and prescriptions for social reconstruction. Responding, they seek to overcome the existing diversity by striving for a more unitarian normative framework. They travel the long road toward eventual discovery of a sound and unified social economics, wherever the road will take them. Their method is a relentless, open-minded critical (including *self-critical*) approach. Diversity, in contrast to the strong version of pluralism, is not seen as necessarily an ultimate and unchangeable fact of (and intrinsic to) the world; rather, pluralism is held dearly as a means toward discovering an underlying monism: a conception of authentic social economy, one that, to paraphrase C. S. Peirce, we can eventually all agree on.

This brings us to another aspect of Caldwell's methodological pluralism, one that also strongly emerges in Malcolm Rutherford's portrait of Charles S. Peirce. In the name of pluralism we have to proceed by questioning one operative presupposition of our time: the almost unquestioned authority of science as the only (or certainly the "best") way to "settle belief." In other words, genuine pluralism and scientism do not readily mix. In particular, we have to be more cautious when told that the application of scientific methods to the discourse over values aids powerfully in the creation of a broad consensus on social values and the social policies they would imply. For example, disputes are likely to arise over the meaning and adequacy of empirical findings. Therefore, as Malcolm Rutherford reminds us, when it comes to matters of morality and theology, we do well to keep science and morality more separate. This would also seem to entail a recognition that, at least for the time being, we had better make room for both scientific *and* traditional knowledge in these matters. What is important for both domains, however, is a critical attitude; in this we must follow C. S. Peirce and be willing "to look truth in the face" and "dump our whole cartload of beliefs the moment experience is against them."

If this notion of a pluralist-monist social economics will be labeled by some as "idealism," or even "Thomism," so be it. It surely constitutes the basic approach that this book, for better or for worse, is intended to promote. The road to progress in social economics is not likely to be a straight one, but it is paved by a better mutual understanding and genuine dialogue. And in this vein, the most promising vehicle of progress is a strong and pluralist *organization*, an Association centered around Annual Meetings and a responsive journal. It is also for this reason that in this concluding essay special emphasis will be given to a more organizational perspective that focuses in large part on the development of our current Association as manifested in its main forum, the *Review of Social Economy*.

THE EVOLUTION OF AMERICAN SOCIAL ECONOMICS

Although the term "social economics" may not be that familar with many, perhaps even most, contemporary economists, it nevertheless can pride itself on a long and fascinating history, summarized by Tom Nitsch at the beginning of this book. He demonstrates how the concept social economics was used primarily in France and other countries of continental Europe, and to a somewhat lesser extent in Great Britain. At the same time, it always lacked precise meaning. Some understood it positively, others primarily normatively. To some it was a secular enterprise, to others it was an economics inspired by the Catholic faith and Papal social doctrine. Interestingly enough, social economics *today* is a largely North American phenomenon imported from nineteenth century Europe and with newly invigorated roots stemming from the German Historical School.

Probably one of the first American social economists was George Gunton who directed an Institute for Social Economics in New York and also edited a magazine called *The Social Economist*. He published two books on the subject: his *Principles of Social Economics* (1897) and, together with Hayes Robbins, the shorter *Outlines of Social Economics* (1900). To Gunton, social economics concerned itself not only with industrial prosperity but also with the social welfare of the people and the "laws and conditions which govern it." His ultimate goal was social progress defined as moral development of the people, and he trusted that it would be enhanced by industrial prosperity which he considered "the soil in which all the superior phases of social life grow." Similarly, "Moral improvement, social culture, intellectual advance, justice and integrity, have their roots in the subsoil of industrial welfare" (1900, p. 4). More specifically "instead of a system of 'commodity' economics which justifies human degradation as a means of cheapening wealth" he upheld "a system of social economics which shows that the most effective means of promoting the industrial welfare of society on a strictly equitable basis, must be sought in influences which develop the wants and elevate the social life and character of the masses" (Gunton, 1897, p. x).

George Gunton may not have had an association with a college or university, but the general themes he emphasized (an economics of social welfare compatible with moral development, a social economy that elevates rather than degrades the worker) continue to resonate to this day.

Slowly but surely the idea of a social economics also managed to start taking hold in academia itself. Due to the term being increasingly used by foremost scholars, such as Wesley Clair Mitchell, in connection with the new works of the Austrian Friedrich von Wieser and the Swede Gustav Cassel, it got increasingly established after World War I. For example, it was to figure quite predominantly in the work of American economists Frank Fetter (as pursuing justice and social welfare and as contrasted with the conventional business economics) as well as with Thomas Carver (as an economics to promote general well-being and recognized as a subdiscipline of political economy standing on an equal footing with public finance).

But the real boost to the concept of an independent and academically respectable social economics undoubtedly came with John Maurice Clark's celebrated *Preface to Social Economics* ([1936] 1967). The fact that the book was published on the heels of Clark's presidency of the American Economic Association may have futher enhanced the prestige of the still "new" field. Realistically, the relative impact of Clark's book needs to be also seen in the context of the events taking place at that time. For one, the prolonged world depression must have undermined much of the confidence with which economists followed the road of orthodox theory and so cleared the way for a more open-minded assessment of any alternative approach, J. M. Clark's social economics included. Perhaps more importantly, orthodox economics, under the new leadership of the British Lionel Robbins, took a turn toward becoming even more orthodox and sterile. In his highly influential *Essays on the Nature and Significance of Economic Science* (1932), Robbins successfully undercut the basis of any kind of legitimate and academically respectable value-directed social economics. In the concluding chapter of his book, for example, after debunking the possibility of interpersonal comparisons of utility, the following statement about an alleged incompatability of economics and ethics appears:

> In recent years, certain economists, realising the inability
> of Economics thus conceived, to provide within itself a
> series of principles binding upon practice, have urged that
> the boundaries of the subject should be extended to

> include normative studies. Mr. Hawtrey and Mr. J. A.
> Hobson, for instance have argued that Economics should
> not only take account of valuations and ethical standards
> as given data . . . , but that also it should pronounce
> upon the ultimate validity of these valuations and
> standards. 'Economics', says Mr. Hawtrey, 'cannot be
> disassociated from Ethics' (p. 149).

True, Professor Robbins did grant the legitimacy of an "applied economics"
that argues from different value assumptions, but only as long as it is cast
out of the "neutral area of science" and relegated to "the more disputable
area of moral and political philosophy" (Robbins, 1932, p. 151). Against
this background, Clark's sonnet for a recognition of something other than
the 'Euclidian' static, deductive, equilibrium approach was bound to fall on
many receptive ears:

> Alongside of Euclidian Economics is another large body
> of ideas, which some writers distinguish as the 'art' of
> political economy, or 'applied economics', in spite of the
> fact that it is chiefly other principles than those of the
> economic Euclid which are here applied. It may broadly
> be called 'social economics' as distinct from the deductive,
> static economics of price, exchange value and distribution
> (Clark [1936], 1967, p. 42).

And Clark goes on to mention as examples of valuable contributions in
that field, the work of H. Sidwick, J. S. Mill, J. B. Clark, T. D. Carver, J.
A. Hobson, and T. Veblen.[1] In retrospect, we can only speculate that for
many American economists interested in the solution of social problems,
Clark's designation of social economics may have been much more
attractive than Robbins' alternative classification of "moral and political
philosophy."

The next big step in the formation and consolidation of American
social economics is also rooted in yet quite another development of the
1930s. In 1931 Pope Pius XI proclaimed his celebrated encyclical *Quadragesimo Anno* in which, among other issues, he addressed critically the
negative effect both a pure market-dominated society and a state-directed
economy have on the quality of life. He deplored these depersonalizing
influences tending to produce "anomie" or social alienation and a feeling
of "homelessness." In that context, the "Principle of Subsidiarity" was first

officially offered as a structural antidote to the problem. It appears quite certain the Church may have nudged a fair number of Catholic social scientists and economists to worry more about the relation of their work to official Catholic social doctrine. Not surprisingly, *Quadragesimo Anno* was followed by some initial discussion of a Catholic Economic Association and in 1940 by a statement of the American Catholic Bishops on "The Church and the Social Order." In 1941 it led to the founding of a Catholic Economic Association by Father Thomas Devine and 40 other academic economists from 30 colleges and universities (Buckley 1984). Its principal aim was to bring the principles of Christian ethics into contact with economic reality. Thanks to the helpful assistance of Joseph Schumpeter, the Association soon succeeded in becoming affiliated with the American Economic Association. And, a little more than a decade later, in the year 1970, the Association opened its membership to non-Catholics and also changed its name to its current Association of Social Economics.[2]

The events of the late 1960s now set the stage for the various more secular followers of J. M. Clark as well as other sympathizers to associate with an organized academic group. In the process, different strands began to emerge and to combine in weaving the pluralistic fabric of contemporary social economics. Today, the Association of Social Economics counts several hunderd academic economists drawn primarily from American and Canadian universities. At the same time, social economics continues to be a recognized field of specialization in many economics graduate schools.[3]

So much for some of the historical highlights of the process of evolution of social economics in this part of the world. Before we get down to the speculative business of discussing the future prospects of the discipline, it will be beneficial to broaden somewhat the strand-related discussion contained in Part II of this book by further inquiring into the contemporary nature, meaning, and significance of the concept social economics.

THE SUBJECT MATTER AND SIGNIFICANCE OF MODERN SOCIAL ECONOMICS

The transformation of the Association of Catholic Economics into the new Association for Social Economics brought with it a need to better grasp the meaning of the concept of social economics. The first to try to do so was George Rohrlich in his "Challenge of Social Economics" published in 1970. He did so by relying heavily on an earlier book edited by Walter Hagenbuch (1958). There the following four "categories of concern and activity" were singled out: social economics as (1) a branch of applied economics--the application of economic theory to social problems; as (2) a branch of applied statistics: the numerical measurement of the extent and constitution of social problems; as (3) study of the social causes of economic behavior labeled 'economic ecology'; and as (4) the study of the social consequences of economic behavior, also known as "welfare economics." Honoring the general perspective of Jean Maurice Clark, Rohrlich stressed as belonging to Hagenbuch's first category the meeting of nonmarket human needs (health, education, and welfare), the application of the overhead cost concept to labor, and the recognition that there is value to society independent of market valuations. Under the second he mentioned, among other issues, the need to come to grips with qualitative implications of economic outcomes, while under the remaining two categories he included concerns about the environment, what he called the "disinvestment in man" and the role of the social economist as a social policy adviser working from a welfare economics informed by nonmarket values to society.

Some years later, Warren Samuels (1977, p. 287), in a timely pluralistic spirit, pictured social economics as a "serious inquiry into the valuational premises, implications, and status of alternative modes of economic organization and policy. Although not independent of positive inquiry, such an economics would tend to specialize in the study of the ethical or moral dimension of economic organization, life and behavior."

Next came Bill Dugger's 1977 celebrated articulation of what he understood the very backbone of social economics to consist of: value-directed, ameliorative, activist, holistic, and viewing society as an organic whole. It is fair to say that it has survived as the single most comprehensive and successful attempt yet, and was also used as a decisive criterion in Lewis Hill's discussion of the contemporary instrumentalist strand in the present volume. Nevertheless, the exercise to clarify the concept was to continue.

Steve Worland (1978) characterized social economics by three "generic propositions": it being (1) deliberately policy oriented; (2) social in the sense of making allowance for the impact of economic activity, institutions, and policy on the total social order and individual psychological well-being; and (3) being intrinsically connected with ethics and moral philosophy in an effort to "delineate in some fashion the properties of the good life."

At the same time E. K. Hunt (1978) enumerated three distinguishing criteria that would define social economics. First, it recognizes that actual economic behavior is a complex intersection of innate traits of human nature and a cultural socialization process. Second, it is distinctly normative with universal human need satisfaction serving as the standard of evaluation. Third, it addresses primarily the issues of historical evolution of economic institutions, their adequacy and probable future development, and finally, the possibilities of (gradual or radical) institutional change to help in the actualization of the innate human potential.

Similarly, Ron Stanfield (1978) regarded social economics as "a perspective which is needed to allow economics to reform itself" by focusing on how society reproduces itself not only economically but also socially and culturally. In the process he stressed the the individual as being the result of the socialization process and the need to recreate the person by institutions of social control devoid of illegitimate power. From this vantage point, the primary research interests are to be centered on the social stratification of power, social problems arising from a lack of appropriate "social reproduction" of society and the appropriate integration of economy and society.

Kendall Cochran (1979) saw the essential role of the social economist in their rejection of the marketplace as the final arbiter of social values and their acceptance of some responsibility to help define and develop those values.

Severyn Bruyn (1981), seeking to integrate the Marxist with the solidarist strand, proposed to make a distinction between the more bureaucratic and centralized state-dependent political economy with a newly emerging more decentralized, mutualist, and self-governing social economy concerned with finding the social links connecting the organizations of production and consumption. After echoing much of what Proudhon had said more than a century earlier, Bruyn asserts that social economics studies "how economies function in the final analysis for human fulfillment."

Arnold McKee (1984) also sees social economics as something more than a supplement and extension of positive economic analysis to distinctly social areas of the economy, such as welfare institutions. He understands it as a "re-fashioning of conventional economics to take in values, welfare and enquiries reaching beyond that important but insufficient goal of allocating scarce means efficiently to competing ends," as a merging of values and economics. McKee maintains that "economic analysis becomes, in effect, superimposed on a social philosophy underpinning and giving direction to it" (p. 1).

Vardaman R. Smith (1984), in an effort to integrate the viewpoints of Dugger, Samuels, Hunt, and Stanfield, comes up with "the four tenets" of social economics: pluralist, value-directed, holistic, and conceptualizing of society as an organic whole.

Finally, Kenneth Stikkers (1987) echoes both Dugger and Smith when observing that social economics views the economy as one aspect of an organic social whole, rather than merely one unit of society, in large part detachable from that whole. He also reaffirms the general view stressed by Worland, McKee, and others, that social economics sees normative issues as at least equally important for economics as empirical ones, and concludes "that economics is as much a branch of ethics as it is a social science" (Stikkers, 1987, p. 224).

So much for a chronological survey of the alternative views of the criteria, generic propositions, and tenets defining social economics, as published by its own practitioners in the *Review* during the last two decades. Quite interesting, and certainly encouraging, is the apparent fact that none of these alternative characterizations is in any direct mutual conflict; rather they supplement, even reaffirm each other.

Against the background of these various views, we may venture yet another, hopefully all-inclusive, conceptualization of the term:

> Social economics is an economics centered around and directed by certain basic value premises or ethical postulates. It critically examines the mutual interaction between economic valuations (including observed individual psychological dispositions), economic activity (including work, consumption, technological innovation), and economic institutions (including uncoordinated, free market mechanisms, and financial institutions; ownership of property and rules of appropriation; social relations of production and the wage system) in the light of those basic value premises. It can be seen as a kind of "social" or "human" welfare economics with a strong orientation towards identifying and solving social problems through ameliorative action in the form of proposing new economic policies or, when necessary, a more radical restructuring of social institutions. In the process the market is rejected as a final arbiter of social values and instead priority is given to a non-

reductionistic, holistic ethos intrinsically related to a conception of society as an organic whole.

The above paragraph is offered here as yet another tentative characterization seeking to articulate the various themes of 10 contemporary social economists without giving undue emphasis to any particular one. At the same time, while being in language sensitive to the concerns of the instrumentalist strand, it allows for an interpretation of social economics as an essentially *normative* economic discipline, an art that can be juxtaposed to its conventional counterpart: neoclassical welfare economics. We are now prepared to do so in reference to Ezra Mishan's view of "normative economics."

Mishan sees the term 'political economy' as generally associated with the specific advice given by one or more economists to governments or to the public at large either on broad policy issues or on particular proposals. If, however, such advice rests on judgments of values and judgments of facts which are particular to the writer(s) and not necessarily shared by other economists or by the community at large, he would describe it as "personal political economy," the kind of "stuff that appears in newspapers, magazines, bank reviews, pamphlets and popular books" (Mishan, 1982, p. 13). In contrast, he depicts 'welfare economics' as a body "of prescriptive generalizations resting on *widely accepted* value judgements and assumptions of economic behavior" (Mishan, 1982, p. 13; emphasis added). Its basic ethical premises would and should command a consensus in the particular society for which it is intended. They are, he notes, the premises "particular to the Western type liberal democracy."

Besides political economy and welfare economics, Mishan prefers a somewhat broader concept for prescriptive economics which he calls "normative economics" and which goes beyond covering the norms of allocation and distribution in also taking account of *equity* (where "equity" has no direct or necessary relation to distribution) (Mishan, 1982, p. 20). Since ethical norms are more social than political, he naturally prefers the term "normative economics" to the (more common) one of "political economy." So equipped, he can then propose to modify the otherwise utilitarian calculus of his neoclassical welfare economics in several respects: cash transfers are preferable to transfers in kind because they treat recipients of charity as responsible beings in a more dignified manner; it allows us to ignore spillover effects arising from "unwarrantable prejudice, from envy, from spite or from sadism" and other "morally objectionable reactions to the fortune or misfortune of others" (Mishan, 1982, p. 231;

1981, p. 403). Above all, in Mishan's normative economics, the welfare of future generations together with the effects of irrevocably destructive environmental practices enter to overrule propositions merely based on observable individual values and behavior.

Yet, in spite of all these modifications, Mishan cannot let go of the entire apparatus of prescriptive generalizations cranked out by the new welfare economics. In particular, he wants to cling to the proposition that social welfare is the sum of individual choices, a methodological individualism according to which "there is no abstraction such as the general good" to be considered in addition to the welfare of individuals who comprise society (Mishan, 1981, p. 8). One has to wonder on what basis his expressed concern for future generations is not flatly contradicted. Similarly, he fully accepts the maxims that "only the individuals' own valuations of [a] change in question are to be used and that with respect to a choice as between alternative economic situations, the Pareto criterion [both actual *and potential*] is to be employed as a ranking device" (Mishan, 1982, p. 230), in spite of his earlier admission that the maxim of "potential Pareto improvement" is not a "compelling value judgment" and is "ethically unsatisfactory" (Mishan, 1981, pp. 11, 18). Once again, one has to wonder how this fits in with his insistence that "society is bound to reject prescriptive economics or measures that flow from the adoption of ethical premises that it rejects" (Mishan, 1981, p. 18). Finally, Mishan uncritically accepts the axioms and behavioral assumptions of positive economics, including one-dimensional Rational Economic Man. This again seems to be inconsistent with his granting normative economics an ethical foundation where "each individual is not merely a utility maximiser in the usual economic sense, or not so at all times." He explains: "Without invoking the 'veil of ignorance' metaphor of Rawls (1971), we may suppose that he also makes moral decisions impelled by a sense of right, which can run counter to the requirements of his utilitarian calculus" (Mishan, 1981, p. 5).[4] That there is a problematic tension between maximization and ethical commitment was pointed out by Amartya Sen back in 1977 (Sen, 1977) and repeated more recently (1985).

In conclusion, it can be said that by its very nature social economics, far from being yet another set of "private" political economics, has much in common with the general type of economic analysis advocated by Mishan under the name of normative economics: a social welfare economics grounded in a social welfare function that is raised not upon a political but upon an ethical base. Once we move away from a social welfare function conceived as a purely political construct and rely more on social ethics, the nasty wrinkles involving Arrow's Impossibility Theorem begin to be ironed out (see Bonner, 1986). All this speaks for the intrinsic superiority of a normative economics over utilitarian welfare economics. With respect to Mishan, on the other hand, his problem may be that his normative economics remains somewhat of a halfway house, being merely grafted on to the conventional "new" welfare economics with its positivistic overtones.

In a quite different manner, a meaningful social economics should take Mishan's idea of normative economics to its logical conclusion. It would flatly reject the notion of abstract atomistic Economic Man, at least for purposes of prescription, and replace that misleading abstraction with a more social and ethical conception of the person. Moreover, it would consistently, and flatly, reject methodological individualism and replace it with the method Mark Blaug calls "institutional holism." Finally, and not unrelated, it would reject Lionel Robbins' injunction against interpersonal comparisons of utility and welfare. Is it not true that any value-directed economics that denies the need and possibility for such comparison is hopelessly out of tune with the most basic ethical premises commanding a consensus in our contemporary culture and society? Such a fatally sterilized body of prescriptive economics deserves to be depicted "as welfare economics with the welfare left out" (J. M. Clark, 1957, p. 59). In contrast, social economics puts the welfare back into welfare economics and does so by removing the artificial ingredients of methodological individualism, atomistic Economic Man, and the emasculating injunction against interpersonal comparisons of well-being. After all this surgery and enrichment, it may be proudly portrayed as a holistic normative economics aspiring to be recognized as a healthy and strong alternative to mainstream prescriptive economics. Accordingly, we may speculate that as the theoretical flaws of individualistic welfare economics will increasingly manifest, and as social and environmental problems grow in intensity in the face of helpless and insensitive economic advisors, students and the public at large may be very much encouraged to turn to social economics for inspiration and knowledge. To be prepared for such an event, to be able to offer an equally comprehensive but more meaningful alternative, therein lies the real significance of modern social economics.

So much for the "form" of social economics, but what about its content? Here we immediately enter the ante-chambers of more segmented and often jealously defended territory. In other words, just about everybody will readily agree with Oscar Lange's recognition of social economics as yet another branch of economic science with a meaning he described as follows: "The use of resources empirically observed may be compared with the 'ideal' use and measures may be recommended to bring the actual use into closer correspondence with the ideal one" (Lange, 1945-46). But, consensus in such formal terms only sets the stage for disputes regarding these ideals. In other words, if social economics is "value-directed," what are the values that direct it? What are its aims, basic values, or goals?

It is our conviction that even here, underneath the pluralistic diversity, there dwells a significant degree of unity. There are several basic value premises that are shared by most, if not all of its practitioners, regardless of the specific strand they identify with. Equally significant, these basic ideals differentiate social economics clearly from its neoclassical counterpart, and two of them do so in a manner that follows logically with a rejection of methodological individualism, i.e., its affirmation of an organic social welfare representing something more than a mere aggregation of individual welfare. The two basic ideals are the goals of regenerating or "reproducing" community and the goal of "reproducing" or better, "sustaining" the natural environment. Let us begin by taking a closer look at both of them.

The value of *community*, or the regeneration of the "community spirit" is explicitly affirmed by Marc Tool's explication of instrumental value theory, as well as the very basis of the word "communism," the Marxist goal of history where a new federalism of communes and free-associated producers will come to prevail. Moreover, much of Marx's concept of alienation and commodity fetishism is, of course, intrinsically related to a system of social relations devoid of community. Although given somewhat less explicit emphasis and often lost in the maze of more practical concerns, the ideal of community could be recognized as an ideal on the distant horizon for the social economists of the humanistic tradition. Today, after E. F. Schumacher had called for a more human scale and community-oriented economics, it ranks very high on their social agenda as well. Last, but anything but least, we believe to be on quite safe ground in asserting that a concern for community and the spirit of social solidarity has been a most basic value premise for the Catholic social economists.[5]

The basic value of community, of course, relates to and also reflects more generally a concern for culture as well. At the same time, it is helpful to go a step further by distinguishing the concept of community from that of society. Here we refer to the pioneering work of Ferdinand Toennies who contrasted *"Gesellschaft"* with *"Gemeinschaft."*

In the former, "society," atomistic individuals are held together by the external bonds of a (political) state and use-related contractual relationships; in the latter, "community," the bond is more internal, more social, and rooted in interpersonal relationships, fellowship, and a commonly felt purpose. As one social economist put it recently, "community is based upon co-feelings, co-experience, and organic principles, it is a 'natural' form of association; while to the extent that society is based upon organizational structures created through mechanistic principles of human reason, it is an 'artifical' form of association" (Stikkers, 1988, p. 7). A marvelous quote by Max Scheler is then offered to drive the point home:

> In fact, "society" is not the inclusive concept designating all the "communities" which are united by blood, tradition and history. On the contrary, it is only the *remnant*, the *rubbish* left by the inner *decomposition* of communities. Whenever the unity of communal life can no longer prevail, whenever it becomes unable to assimilate the individuals and develop them into living organs, we get a "society"--a unity based on mere contractual agreement (Scheler, 1961, p. 166).

The reference here to communal life developing individuals into living organs serves to remind us of the intrinsic bond between social economics' "institutional holism" and its preference of authentic community over atomistic society.

The other ideal or basic value premise, being *environmental sustainability*, has entered social economics only during the last 15 years. Ever since George Rohrlich's 1973 article calling for an integration of social ecology and economics, the *Review* has been increasingly devoting space to such issues as the entropy law (Georgescu-Roegen, 1977; Gowdy, 1980), the energy crisis (Hill, 1983), solar energy (McDaniel, 1981, 1983), conservation (Daly, 1985) and, perhaps more radically, the need of endowing natural species (redwoods, whales, etc.) with legal rights (Chan, 1988). This "environmental movement" within social economics has been so powerful that Bill Waters considered it necessary to identify it as an "additional vein" appropriately labeled "resources economics." But scholars such as Lew Hill, Bruce McDaniel, John Gowdy, and Herman Daly also tend to remind us that the concern for ecologically sustainable economic growth is shared by social economists of different persuasions and backgrounds. In any case, the compatibility of identifying such nonreducable categories as "the environment" or "future generations" with the commonly held rejection of methodological individualism should not be overlooked.

It should come as no surprise that, therefore, the spokesmen for conventional orthodox approaches to economics and the economy continue to ignore the problems of stratospheric ozone depletion, climate change, acid rain, endangered species, hazardous substances, and the destruction of tropical forests as brought to our attention recently by the Brundtland Commission Report (1987), a study that is likely to figure prominently in the upcoming United Nations Conference on "Sustainable Development" scheduled to take place in Canada in 1992. Social economics by its very constitution is able to recognize the fundamental importance of such a concern, and so also prepared to offer guidance when future events will compel the long overdue public attention to this increasingly urgent issue. Herein, once again, lies the ultimate significance of a normative or "value-driven" social economics.

Besides the shared ideals of regenerating or "reproducing" community and environmental sustainability, we may add two more in order to bring out better the "cardinal unity" underlying the contemporary pluralism of modern social economics.

The first of the two pertains to the goals of economic activity and derives from the view of economic agents as persons. Unlike the neoclassical perspective centering around an abstract, static, atomistic, and one-dimensional Rational Economic Man with the explicit aim to maximize his consumption measured in quantitative terms, social economists of all persuasions unite behind a multidimensional conception *of the person* that is qualitative and dynamic. As Clark, one of the fathers of American social economics, already observed in his *Preface*, the aim of economic activity is not consumption but *the goal of human fulfillment*, the "well-rounded development and use of human faculties" (Clark [1936], 1967, p. 25). In this he merely echoes what has long been held by Marxist, Solidarist-Catholic, Instrumentalist, and Humanistic economists. True, the exact content of human fulfillment remains a matter of debate, but all agree that, whether rooted in biology, genetics, "Creation," or otherwise, there is some social (and more authentic) human aspect which is sensitive to elements of the social environment. It can be discouraged, "stunted," "degraded," or "alienated," by means of exploitative social institutions or "social structures of sin" (e.g., the unrestrained profit motive, unresponsive bureaucracy, etc.). In contrast, there are institutions conducive "to the whole person as he lives the whole life" (Hill, 1978), as well as social structures (e.g., "*Lebensgemeinschaften*" (life-communities)) where a person can develop his or her fullness of life (H. Briefs, 1983, p. 214). Depending on whether we understand the basic value premise of "life fulfillment" in relation to some psychological "self-realization," or some theological "destiny of the individual soul," the goal of moral development and human dignity will obviously lead to somewhat different social economic perspectives and consequences, but for the present purpose this is less central. What matters here is that the social economist is more interested in the development of full human personality than he is in the mere satisfaction of the consumer's hedonistic wants and preferences.

Intimately connected with the third ideal is the fourth goal: *the intrinsic value of work*. It's a theme that runs through all strands and obviously derives from the shared view of the person as an essentially social being that fulfills, realizes, or enobles itself in the very process of creative social activity. Once again, this is very much in contrast to neoclassical mainstream economics viewing the worker primarily as an input of production function, as a "human resource," and because of it as a mere commodity to be sold to the highest bidder in the labor market. Of all social economists, nobody deserves more credit to have pointed this out early on and in no uncertain terms than Karl Marx. Today all social economists, but especially the members of the solidarist and humanistic strands, would also uphold the need for unalienated work.[6]

We can conclude this section with the optimistic note that there seems to exist fundamental premises that give social economics in its modern pluralistic garb a more unified framework and some substance. We stand united in opposition to modern positive economics based on consumption-oriented, atomistic Rational Economic Man. We share a strong conviction that a meaningful economics capable of addressing social problems needs to be value-directed or normative, and guided by such basic ideals as community, environmental sustainability, human fulfillment, and meaningful work.

REFLECTIONS ON THE PROSPECTS OF SOCIAL ECONOMICS

Much of what has been said so far, here as well as elsewhere in this book, goes far in building a framework for assessing the future prospects of our discipline. In this concluding section we will first survey a small sample of some of the current (internal) tensions and basic differences between the various strands and attempt to do so in a spirit of open-mindedness and goodwill. Such a challenging task will be undertaken in the hope and with the expectation that a greater awareness of these fundamentally divisive issues may lead to an enhanced mutual understanding and tolerance, while also stimulating further discussion conducive to greater reconciliation and integration. The issues selected here pertain to the human image, determinism, property, and capitalism. Thereafter, I shall raise some further questions involving our future as a viable and strengthened organization capable of making a significant imprint in the twenty-first century.

As a useful starting point, we may ponder the following statement attributed by Goetz Briefs to Walter Lippman: "All our difficulties, all our confusion, stem from the fact that we no longer know who Man is." To which Goetz Briefs adds: "we no longer know whether we are persons or individuals" and as a result "the flood of social philosophies that has broken over us since the end of the eighteenth century has conjured up a dangerous polarization between absolute individualism and absolute collectivity" (G. Briefs, 1983a, p. 234). This, in a nutshell, is the position underlying Catholic social doctrine. It can also be seen to set the stage between the viewpoints of socialism and instrumentalism on the one hand, and solidarism and a neo-Kantian humanism on the other. The gulf that separates us here is not so much one of ideology but of two clashing world views. One is inspired by the Renaissance, the other marked by the Enlightenment.

Starting with the Enlightenment, we have the triumph of Locke's nominalist epistemology entailing a new view of Man and social theory. Man was seen as having a material and individual entity and with a purpose defined within the sphere of the practical and useful. As Richard Hooley put it: "Man, as an individual is distinguished from other individual entities by the practical matter of which he consists"; and being a small part of a more important whole, he (or she) is reduced to "an insignificant eddy in a confluence of ethnic, economic, historical and social forces with a pattern of behaviour bound by their laws" (Hooley, 1954, p. 157). Human choice occurs within an array of material ends within a context of compelling material circumstances. Accordingly, human understanding proceeds by analyzing these circumstances with the tools of modern social science, more particularly, by psychology and sociology.

The older world view that this new perspective set out to replace attributed to Man a substance composed of matter (resembling the animal) and spirit (resembling God). While the material aspect testifies to our experience as individuals, it is the spiritual aspect that makes us feel as *persons*, that gives us personality and the distinctly human capacity of free will identifying with a reality transcending our individuality. It is also this spiritual quality in Man that empowers us to apprehend (though rational speculation) the common good and to pursue it in (undetermined) volition. According to this view, the person is a moral and spiritual being with a unique place and purpose in a meaningful universe. Man, as a person, has, by his very nature, dignity and is *intrinsically* valuable. Similarly, the very essence of the human being cannot be understood by confining one's search to uncovering relevant material causes, or by science alone, but even more so by means of a reliance on philosophy, more specifically "philosophical anthropology." Both Renaissance humanism and scholastic thought share in this perspective, but so do also, to various degrees, many modern existentialist and phenomenologists and other "post-liberal" thinkers.[7]

Closely connected with the question of "who is Man?" is not only the issue of determinism but also epistemological and methodological questions, (empiricism versus rationalism), the nature of rationality, truth, and the question of ethical relativism. These are all fundamental and important questions that have long been debated by philosophers of all ages, and no end is yet in sight.[8] Many of these questions are also directly relevant to social economics.[9] Whether we like it or not, we cannot ignore them, and to the extent that they defy empirical resolution relying on observation and experiment they have to be resolved by rational argument and introspection. Ultimately, the choice between alternative positions and viewpoints will have to be made according to what makes human experience more meaningful and more intelligible. With this in mind, let us now take a brief look at the issue of determinism.

Determinism can be understood as a view that everything in the world has been caused by preceding factors. A strict interpretation rules out any notion of "self-determination," i.e., internal or self-causation, but insists that any human activity, including individual thoughts, is to be found in causes which are external to the self.[10] In general, such a perspective finds much support in science demonstrating that the physical universe is indeed governed by stable, dependable, and predictable laws of nature. It becomes even more compelling if Man is seen, following Darwin, as a creature of nature (only), and once the Cartesian split of body and mind is rejected. Moreover, according to this view, there is no scientific reason why mental and physical activity cannot both be regarded as subject to essentially the same kind of (natural) laws. Finally, psychology and sociology have, undoubtedly, established that much of human conduct is determined by external factors including social and cultural ones. It follows that a rejection of determinism would also entail the rejection of most of modern social science.

As one would expect, opponents of determinism have traditionally been found among philosophers, not scientists. They point to the logical inconsistency of strict determinism on primarily epistemological grounds: if everything is determined, so is also the thinking of the social scientist and their judgments as to what is true or what works. But this renders their findings and beliefs, including their belief in determinism utterly meaningless.

As an example of determinism we may quote one of Marx's famous passages underlying dialectical materialism:

> The phantoms formed in the human brain are also necessarily sublimates of their [material] life process which is empirically verifiable and bound to material premises. Morality, religion, metaphysics, all the rest of ideology and their corresponding forms of consciousness, thus no longer retain the semblance of independence. They have no history, no development; but men, developing their material intercourse, alter, along with their real [i.e. social] existence, their thinking and the products of their thinking. Life is not determined by consciousness, but consciousness by life (quoted in Stikkers, 1987, p. 225).

More specifically, it is the "modes of production," or economics, that are believed to determine metaphysical and philosophical speculation. However, it was, among others, Juergen Habermas (1971) who pointed out the epistemological problem that such an "offical" view of Marx would convey. In this context, one scholar, himself highly sympathetic to Marx, observes:

> Through acquaintance with the economic base of a given society, its superstructure can be inferred in quasi-deductive fashion. Psychology and sociology are unneccessary sciences, since their results can be reached through economics. *If this is Marx's view, he cannot claim truth for it, since it is determined by his social context* (Rockmore, 1978, p. 68, emphasis added).

and concludes:

> Habermas is perfectly justified in signaling the epistemo-
> logical weakness of this form of Marxism. For *economic
> determinism*, like the behaviorism of which it is a mere
> variant, *is intellectually indefensible*. Since there is no place
> for the thinker within the theory, it is reflexively inconsis-
> tent (Rockmore, 1978, p. 69; emphasis added).

Most probably, this problematic form of Marxism is also what many of us
learned as the official and only version. It certainly is also the one that
helps to give Marxist social theory a high degree of rigorous and scientific
precision. In any case, Marx may have been misunderstood by both friend
and foe. In support of such assertion, we may quote from his *German
Ideology*: "consciousness can sometimes appear further advanced than the
contemporary empirical relationships," implying a less determinist and
more *interactionist* model of the superstructure-base relation. Moreover,
such an interactionist interpretation was also recommended by Engels in
1890 (Rockmore, 1978, p. 68) and now it appears to be accepted by E. K.
Hunt as well.

Parallel to this (re)interpretation of dialectical materialism is the
whole literature on Marx's Sixth Thesis on Feuerbach traditionally cited to
the effect that Marx broke with all conceptions of human nature in 1845.
There we are told that "the human essence is no abstraction inherent in
each single individual" but that it is in reality simply "the ensemble of
social relations" to be "comprehended only as 'genus,' as an internal, dumb
generality which merely naturally unites the many individuals" (Tucker,
1972, p. 109). One is tempted to conclude that if human nature is a set
of social relations, then we are indeed reduced to "an insignificant eddy in
a confluence of social forces," and as such determined by them. But,
again, 'not true,' says the Marxist Norman Geras (1983). He devotes an
entire book to this issue and finds the belief that historical materialism
entailed a denial of human nature is an old fixation, which the Althusser-
ian influence in this matter has fed upon. Instead, argues Geras, the Sixth
Thesis must be read in the context of Marx's work as a whole, particularly
his later writings which are informed by an idea of a distinctly human
nature that fulfills both explanatory and normative functions.[11]

The recent emphasis on interactionism as observed in Marxian
scholarship is good news for social economics since most of us hold to
various degrees an interactionist viewpoint (see also Stikkers, 1987). Now

that the "determinism issue" has cooled somewhat, it should also move us a little closer together when addressing the still hot and burning question of "what is Man?"

Turning now to capitalism, specifically the contemporary American "mode of production," we will briefly survey the question of ownership of the means of production and the perceived need for ameliorative action. Beginning with the legitimacy of private property of the means of production, we seem to have two opposite views, both argued in the name of human fulfillment. To the reader of this book, there appears to be an unresolved tension between the socialist Marxism of E. K. Hunt and the solidarist affirmation of private enterprises by Ed O'Boyle. Somewhere in between, we find the less committed positions of the instrumentalist Hill and the humanistic stance in the tradition of Hobson and Schumacher. Let us zero in on the two extremes.

Ed O'Boyle objects to the Marxian emphasis on socializing the means of production as the way to a better social economy. To him a mere change in ownership will not necessarily guarantee a better society; to the contrary, it would deprive workers and capitalists alike of a natural human right and by implication also interfere with human development of both groups. But later, in his comments on Hunt's contribution, O'Boyle modifies his position when he grants that "the right to private property is not absolute," but subordinate to the common good compelling that the needs of all be adequately met. For example, in a case where private property only serves its owners to the detriment of the employees, remedial action is indicated either in the form of state intervention, or preferably by "socializing" (i.e., moralizing) Man.

Not surprisingly, E. K. Hunt, who had to base his comments on O'Boyle's initial and more uncompromising exposition, was moved to entirely reject the whole of solidarist tradition because of their "anti-social" doctrine of the naturalness of property. In the process he raises some questions that appear to have been provoked by a misunderstanding of the natural law doctrine in general, and the place of Pope Leo XIII's *Rerum Novarum* in Catholic social thought more in particular. Some clarification here is called for.

First, without wanting to touch on the confusing intricacies and complexities of Natural Law doctrine, it should be clear in answer to Hunt's question that not all positive laws are natural. Quite the contrary: Natural Law reasoning claims to be prior and more valid than positive, or "civil" law. For this very reason, it is held as a standard by which to assess in moral terms existing constitutions and legal codes. In other words,

Natural Law was always meant to serve as a universal, normative criteria. Now, because the moral law is conceived as essentially eternal and unchanging, there is a priori no problem in rooting it in insights of the Middle Ages, provided the reasoning underlying them has remained solid.

But, we now get to a second and more important point. Pope Leo's views on property can be considered to be of questionable origin. In a recent important contribution, A. M. C. Waterman demonstrates that the Thomistic (middle-age) theory is at great variance with Leo's doctrine proclaimed in 1891, which instead has been to a very large extent influenced by Locke and the French Encyclopedists and their 1789 declaration of Human Rights. So, for example, it has been argued by Sousberghe and Viner that the French Revolution seriously disrupted the Intellectual life of European Catholicism and that it was the Lockean Jesuit Taparelli d'Azeglio who not only reconstructed it in his own way but also had an (indirect) hand in preparing the first draft of *Rerum Novarum*. Waterman then observes that the Sousberghe-Viner hypothesis "explains what is an unquestioned novelty in Catholic doctrine: the labor theory of appropriation. In the process, we also learn how the 'Lockean' elements of *Rerum Novarum* came to be distorted into an unequivocal theory of a 'sacred and inviolable' natural right to 'private ownership'" (Waterman, 1982, p. 107). We are further informed that *Rerum Novarum* was issued in response to the rise of Marxist social democratic parties in Western Europe, and that it was composed only months after a wave of anarchist violence that culminated in the assassination of Czar Alexander II of Russia (Waterman, 1982, p. 103). In other words, the document has to be understood within the special historical circumstances that it was written. As such, *Rerum Novarum* cannot really be taken to speak for the entire Catholic Natural Law tradition; certainly St. Thomas (like Gratian before him) held that community of goods is according to Natural Law.

Inadvertently but also unfortunately, Ed O'Boyle ends up misleading the uninformed reader and his critic when, after quoting Pope Leo to the effect that "private ownership must be preserved inviolate," he observes that: "Directly in line with *Rerum Novarum* are two other papal letters: Pius XI's *Quadragesimo Anno* (1931) and John Paul II's *Laborem Excercens* (1981)." He thereby creates the impression that there has been little or no change in the Church's position on the property question. Yet, in *Laborem Excercens* a new theme first encountered in the earlier *Quadragesimo Anno*, recommending that workers share in the ownership and management of the industries, was greatly enhanced and extended: "When man works, using all the means of production, he also wishes the fruit of his work to be used by himself and others, and he wishes to be able to take part in the very work process as a sharer in responsibility and creativity at the workbench to which he applies himself." Its author, Pope John Paul II, is even understood to argue that "ultimately workers should be the owner of the giant workbench at which they labour" (Baum and Cameron, 1984, pp. 46-47). As a side note, we may also mention here that earlier, Pope Paul VI in his *Octogesimo Adveniens* (1971) accepts Marxism as a form of social analysis, as a sociology of oppression that can be very useful in the struggle for justice (Baum and Cameron, 1984, p. 24). The ancient Roman wisdom, *Tempora mutantur and nos mutamur in illis*, also seems to apply to what Pope Pius XI referred to as "the Chair of Peter, that sacred depository of all truth." However this may be, enough has been said on the topic of property to indicate that here, too, old and profound differences among social economists are no longer beyond reconciliation.

When examining the more general and concrete issue of capitalism as a satisfactory socioeconomic system, it is fair to say that all strands find ample room for improvement. Few, if any, social economists appear comfortable with the status quo. In fact, this disenchantment may very well be a primary identifying character trait and rallying force of social eonomists as a community of concerned scholars.

The Marxists, as well as Kantian humanists such as Ellerman, proclaim the most radical gospel, one grounding his opposition in the labor theory of value, the other in the labor theory of property.[12] Their ends-in-view are almost identical, especially with a contemporary interactionist Marxism that no longer discounts the cooperative movement as little more than a misguided bourgeois utopian socialist effort seeking to patch up a moribund capitalism. Nevertheless, the burden of proof remains on humanistic thinkers to demonstrate feasibility and viability of workers cooperatives in a global capitalist system.

Perhaps in many ways the instrumentalist perspective concerned with the solving of practical and immediate problems ends up by its very nature being the least radical, resting more content with traditional liberal ideology enriched by a powerful, effective corporate welfare state guided by skilled indicative planners. The success of Sweden and some other European welfare states certainly validates much of their vision of rendering capitalism less inhuman. Yet at the same time, workers' self-management and cooperatives remain relatively unimportant goals.[13] Similarly, it is not clear just how prominently concerns over the alienation of labor are allowed to color their view of the "life process" under capitalism.

The solidarist's aim has always been to create a third way that transcends the limitations not only of socialism but also of capitalism. Yet, the newest constructs seem to be a rather timid modification of capitalism as we know it: a Eucken type "social market economy," combining private property with free associations and a concern for the common good.[14] Workers' self-management has so far never been a major item on the solidarist platform (H. Briefs, 1984, p. 297). Instead, like the instrumentalist social reformers, they strongly affirm trade unions, but quite unlike them, have some hesitations about certain features implied by the concept of a strong and centralized welfare state.[15] Moreover, one could wish it was a little more clear exactly what solidarists mean and intend by their distinctive proposal: "the establishment of forums or councils in the economic order midway between the state and private enterprise." It definitely sounds like industrial councils or cartels aiming at the common good, not group profits.[16] As such it is not easy to envision how they fit into competitive capitalism, and one is tempted to say that such "restructuring" from below will ultimately prove ineffective or else impossible.[17]

Nevertheless, the principle of subsidiarity, as argued, for example, so beautifully by Johannes Messner (1951) is a concept that all social economists may want to take to heart and mind. If there is to be more cross-fertilization between the strands, the idea of a subsidiary state has to be seen as a most distinctive and attractive flower in the Catholic-solidarist garden.

On the other hand, O'Boyle's repeated emphasis on moral exhortations can be seen as the least convincing part of a solidarist reform strategy. Unlike the current Pope, he does not put much emphasis where more properly it seems to belong: the combatting of the structures of "social sin," i.e., institutions that promote individual moral decay and error (or "sin"). One gets the impression that O'Boyle is not sufficiently "interactionist" in his social analysis. In this regard, solidarists like him may have something to learn from John Hobson, and perhaps even more from Karl Marx.

In conclusion, we may end this discussion on the optimistic note that social economists do have more in common than is generally assumed. Often our fraternal fights are based on a lack of understanding about the other side. With an increase in interstrand communication, we should be able to correct this somewhat and so be able to look forward to greater cohesion and more strength in the years and decades ahead.

In ending this chapter, I will now take the liberty to make some more personal observations and speculations about the prospects of our discipline. This will be done by raising three or four delicate questions that will be offered as food for thought for the reader to ponder. As we go along, it should be understood that one of the primary concerns underlying the conception and editing of this present book has been a strong desire to present social economics in a manner that is also intelligible to conventional economists. Such exposition will hopefully render our alternative approach more understandable to others and perhaps more attractive to some. With this in mind, let us briefly focus on some basic questions that we can expect will be asked by the more seriously interested outsiders. In anticipating a few of those here, we may want to supply some tentative answers.

Question 1: *How does social economics relate to regular micro-macro economics?* Based on what has been said here and elsewhere, most of us would reply that with the notable exception of (the new) welfare economics, our approach is essentially complementary. Rather than rejecting the entire mainstream edifice, we seek to overcome some of its obvious basic limitations by extending or broadening its scope and in "deformalizing" and "deindividualizing" its method. It is primarily modern welfare economics that maintains irreconcilable differences with contemporary social economics, while other fields (e.g., development economics, neoclassical "hydraulic" Keynesianism) may or may not be seen to conflict as seriously.[18]

Question 2: *How does social economics differ from political economy?* In particular, if by political economy we mean "the study of the effects of various mechanisms and systems of mechanisms, used (or useable) by societies to operate their social economy" (Phelps, 1985, p. 27). Here we may point out that the difference pertains to the nature of "the effects" studied. Rather than just limiting ourselves to consider material "reward structures" or impacts on the aggregate "wealth of nations," social economy is more interested in the effects pertaining to human well-being, social welfare, and social justice.[19] Moreover, we can refer to the fact that there has historically been an effort, particularly in nineteenth century France, Germany, and Austria, to deemphasize the connotation of a bureaucratic, political, or state-centered economics, and focus instead on a more generic approach that gives room for more decentralized community decisionmaking and human action in an ethical

context.[20] The approach recognizing a social principle in resource allocation has been particularly germane to the solidarist school, but it has also
had some appeal to Marxists (Bruyn, 1981, 1984) and practitioners of the
modern human-centered school (Lutz, 1987).

Question 3: *If social economics has indeed an identity of its own, if
it is unique enough to warrant attention, what is the difference between it and
the economics practiced by members of the Association of Evolutionary
Economics or the Union of Radical Political Economy?* This is a serious
and difficult question warranting more discussion. Let us take the
example of instrumentalism: if the instrumental value theory of evolutionary economics, as Lewis Hill assures us, totally qualifies as social economics by meeting the test of Dugger's criteria, we have here clearly more
than a mere intersection, or overlap, of two different sets of economics.
Logically, the two are either identical, or one is the subset of another. If
so, would it not follow that the division between the two Associations now
appears somewhat artificial, wasteful, and counterproductive? Why not
merge into an Association of Evolutionary Social Economics, or with
respect to Marxist socialism, create a Union of Radical Social Economy,
in short URSE? Personally, I trust that there must be some distinct
differences that still need to be spelled out; otherwise our own Association, in spite of the upcoming 50th anniversary, would be merely "just
another" association with no distinct agenda of its own.

There is, of course, another way to answer the question and
address this seemingly thorny issue. Why not look at it this way: social
economics is not so much a school of thought as it is an applied discipline
studying certain questions (e.g., the valuation process) comparable to, let
us say, the history of economic thought. Nothing precludes practitioners
from approaching their specialized subject in a highly pluralistic manner,
from different point of view, as happens, for example, in the History of
Economics Society. Seen in this manner, our Association would then be
essentially a forum for different strands of value-directed economics, perhaps some sort of sophisticated debating society. It need not always stay
this way, of course, since in time one of the approaches or "strands" may
gain a large enough following that would enable it to "capture" the *Review*
as well as the entire organization and, in the process, effectively crowd the
others out. The result would be a uniformity gained through competitive
struggle in the marketplace of ideas.

Regardless of this happening or not, such an alternative perspective does not enchant me. There is an essential problem with the analogy
to the History of Economics Society. The problem is that mainstream

mainstream economists of the highest reputation (e.g., George Stigler) are actively participating in that group giving it thereby automatically a sufficient amount of legitimacy and organizational strength. Yet, in our own Association, on the other hand, such is clearly less the case, and accordingly, we cannot take its long-term survival and development for granted, at least as long as Lionel Robbins remains Lord and his positive economics continues to be taught as the alpha and omega of scientific economics. Realistically, under such circumstances, social economics would be bound to remain a marginal enterprise relegated to the sidelines of economic thought and policymaking of the future.

Would it not, under the circumstances, appear more promising to sort out our differences, to enter more into a constructive dialogue among ourselves in order to build a more coherent and independent school, a new paradigm, or a progressive research program with a solid philosophical core and a sturdy "protective belt"? Naturally, such efforts at integration have to be seen as a highly ambitious undertaking, but it also implies a high degree of intrinsically interesting and meaningful work ahead. This is the real challenge to contemporary social economics. We cannot afford to ignore it. The present book is intended to serve as preliminary scaffolding for such a construction, while fully aware that the real book on social economics has yet to be written. True, we already have a "Preface" penned by J. M. Clark, and we also have, thanks to Tom Nitsch, the beginning of a comprehensive history, but the real text, consisting of a true and common substance, still eludes us. Only if that real substance can be better grasped, pinned down, and developed are we really prepared to gain the most when, under the pressure of external events, neoclassical economics starts to crumble. It is in this respect that I would like to see understood the true significance and the real prospect of twenty-first century social economics.

Notes

[1]For a more direct answer of Clark to Robbins see his 1950 article "Economic Means--to What End? A Problem in the Teaching of Economics," reprinted in Clark (1957, pp. 12-38).

[2]As a significant side note we may also mention that the chief alternative designation considered was Association for Normative Economics. In fact, a survey of the membership conducted in April of 1969 revealed that there was more support for the combination of

Association for Normative Economics or Normative Economic Association than for the third alternative presented, Social Economics Association (see *Review of Social Economy*, March 1970, p. 134). From this evidence one could conclude that the traditional Catholic core of the Association that went on to constitute the backbone of the contemporary "Catholic strand" was leaning toward a primarily normative interpretation of social economics.

[3]The seventh edition of the Economic Institute's *Guide to American Graduate Education, Agricultural Economics and Doctorate Degrees in Business Administration* (Boulder, CO, 1984) lists over 30 North American universities where some kind of postgraduate instruction in social economics is offered.

[4]He rejects the Rawlsian "moral geometry" since it operates on the assumption of self-interested prudence rather than ethical beings "seeking to guide their thoughts and actions by moral precepts alone" (Mishan, 1981, p. 131).

[5]Not surprisingly, the intrinsic importance of community is also recognized in the short statement of our association's Aims and Objectives. The special concern is also indicated by a special issue of the *Review* dedicated to the topic of Community in Enterprise. There, in an introductory essay by George Rohrlich titled "Community--The Submerged Component of Economic Theorizing," we can also take note of his revealing comment on the treatment of community in neoclassical economics: "Insofar as community has remained in the picture at all, its residual role has changed to explaining 'deviant' economic behavior that clearly defies the homo homini lupus mold which is deemed 'normal.' In this vein, some current economic theorists have felt called upon to explain away even those seemingly rare occasions when such 'atypical' human behavior has been observed beyond any doubt (notably in extremis, e.g., in natural catastrophes and comparable collective emergencies) as a selfish ruse, mere make-believe" (Rohrlich, 1984, p. 224). And he refers to Douty's "theory of postdisaster coopera-tion" (Douty, 1972). According to Rohrlich, social economics, far from "explaining community away," lets it reemerge and assume a strongly directing influence.

[6]All this raises the more controversial issue of the wage system in general as elaborated by the Kantian social economist David Ellerman in this book and elsewhere (see Ellerman, 1983, 1986, 1988), but this would bring us prematurely onto the slippery grounds of unresolved issues, both clouding and energizing the contemporary scene in social economics.

[7]For a revival of interest in the soul, triggered by the computer revolution involving a machine-centered mentality, see the book by William Barrett (1987). For an account affirming free will, see the book by John Eccles and Daniel Robinson (1984).

[8]For interesting treatments of some of the issues involved, see R. F. Baum (1974), Rosenthal (1984, pp. 115-173), the book edited by John Ladd (1973), and, more fundamental-ly, Mortimer J. Adler's wellknown challenge (1985).

[9]A case in point is Haney's (1913) discussion of what constitutes the true "social point of view" in economics.

[10]A less strict interpretation of determinism would equate it with self-determinism understood as determinism of the organism in its interaction with its natural environment. Determinism is then not to be contrasted with freedom but with accident and chance (see

Randall and Buchler, 1942). According to this view, the human organism would not be any more determined than that of a flower or a mushroom.

[11]It is not clear whether such revisions also extend to some of the more belligerent statements also to be found in *German Philosophy*; claims that not only must have irritated (and mislead) the venerable Pope Leo, but others as well. Take this one as an example:

> The sum of productive forces, capital funds and social forms of inter-course, which every individual and generation finds in existence as something given, is the real basis of what the philosophers have conceived as 'substance' or 'essence of man', and what they have deified and attacked: a real basis which is not in the least disturbed, in its effect and influence on the development of men, by the fact that these philosophers revolt against it as "self-consciousness" and the "Unique" (Tucker, 1972, p. 129).

[12]See especially Ellerman (1985). For two recent pro-Marxist views on worker self-management coming from prominent members of the Association, see Bruyn (1984) and Elliott (1984).

[13]See, for example, the somewhat hesitant endorsement of the principle in the recent work of Dugger (1987).

[14]For a short description of Walter Eucken's views, see Karsten (1986); for more detail, see Mueller-Armack (1978).

[15]It is, for example, commonly held that Pope Pius XI's *Quadragesimo Anno* was composed, at least in part, in direct opposition to the British Beveridge Plan, the first blueprint of a modern welfare state (Ward, 1954). For other solidarist qualms concerning the welfare state see Rauscher (1978).

[16]And we are also told in Pesch's *Lehrbuch* that cartels received sympathetic sanction (G. Briefs, 1983b, p. 256).

[17]Perhaps there is some potential in regional groups (e.g., united Chambers of Commerce and Labor) aiming at promoting the local economy, but there are too few viable examples of such new organisms to take the idea too seriously. Alternatively, it may be seen as a new version of Proudhon's proposed federalism (which sees economic structure as a federation of work groups, called Agrarian-Industrial Federation, within a decentralized political structure), being more of an anarcho-syndicalism than a model of capitalist free enterprise.

[18]Based on J. M. Clark's distinction that contrasts social economics with the static, deductive, equilibrium type *Euclidian Economics* of the mainstream, a strong case can be made that social economics is by its very nature more in tune with post-Keynesian economics than the reigning macroeconomic orthodoxies.

[19]But answers like this raise new questions: What about the pragmatic *political economy* of Adolph Loewe? Is *that* social economics, and if not, why not?

[20]One branch or strand of these earlier social economists developed with Wieser into the contemporary neo-Austrian school of economic thought focusing in their own way on what they conceive to be "natural" social interactions. See also the history of the "secular positive" approach to social economics as outlined by Nitsch in this book.

References

Adler, M. J. 1985. *Ten Philosophical Mistakes*. New York: Macmillan Publishing Company.

Allett. J. 1981. *New Liberalism: The Political Economy of J. A. Hobson*. Buffalo: University of Toronto Press.

Althusser, L. 1969. *For Marx*. New York: Random Press.

Ayres, C. 1944. *The Theory of Economic Progress*. Chapel Hill, NC: University of Carolina Press.

Barrett, W. 1987. *Death of the Soul*. New York: Anchor Books.

Baum, G. and D. Cameron. 1984. *Ethics and Economics*. Toronto: James Lorimer and Co.

Baum, R. F. 1974. "Popper, Kuhn and Lakatos: a crisis of modern intellect," *The Intercollegiate Review* (Spring), 99-110.

Blaug, M. 1980. *The Methodology of Economics*. New York: Cambridge University Press.

Bonner, J. 1986. *Introduction to the Theory of Social Choice*. Baltimore: Johns Hopkins University Press.

Briefs, G. 1983a. "Person and ethos: person and individual in European thought," *Review of Social Economy* 41:3 (December), 228-234.

_____. 1983b. "Catholic social doctrine, laissez-faire liberalism, and social market economy," *Review of Social Economy* 41:3 (December), 246-258.

Briefs, H. 1983. "Goetz Briefs on capitalism and democracy," *Review of Social Economy* 41:3 (December), 212-227.

_____. 1984. "Solidarity within the firm: principles, concepts and reflections," *Review of Social Economy* 42:3 (December), 295-317.

Brundtland, G. H. et al. 1987. *Our Common Future: World Commission on Environment and Development*. New York: Oxford University Press.

Bruyn, S. 1981. "Social economy: a note on its theoretical foundations," *Review of Social Economy* 34:1 (April), 81-84.

_____. 1984. "The community self study: worker self-management versus the new class," *Review of Social Economy* 42:3 (December), 388-412.

Buckley, L. 1984. "Early years of the Association for Social Economics," *Forum for Social Economics* (Spring), 63-83.

Caldwell, B. 1982. *Beyond Equilibrium*. Boston: George Allen and Unwin.

Carver, T. N. 1919. *Principles of Political Economy*. Boston: Ginn and Co.

Cassel, G. 1932. *The Theory of Social Economy* [1918], trans. S. L. Barron. New York: Harcourt, Brace and Co.

Chan, A. 1988. "Adapting natural resources management to changing societal needs through evolving property rights," *Review of Social Economy* 46:1 (April), 46-60.

Clark, J. M. 1957. *Economic Institutions and Human Welfare*. New York: Alfred Knopf.

_____. 1967. *Preface to Social Economics*. [1936] Reprint. New York: Augustus M. Kelley Publ.

Cochran, K. 1979. "Why a social economics," *Review of Social Economy* 37:1 (April), 121-132.

Daly, H. E. 1985. "The circular flow of exchange value and the linear throughput of matter-energy: a case of misplaced concreteness," *Review of Social Economy* 43:3 (December), 279-297.

Douty, C. 1972. "Disaster and charity: some aspects of cooperative economic behavior," *American Economic Review* 62:4 (September), 580-590.

Dugger, W. M. 1977. "Social economics: one perspective," *Review of Social Economy* 35:3, 299-310.

_____. 1987. "Democratic planning and worker ownership," *Journal of Economic Issues* 21:1 (March), 87-99.

Eccles, J. and D. Robinson. 1984. *The Wonder of Being Human: Our Brain and Our Mind*. New York: The Free Press.

Ellerman, D. 1983. "A model structure for cooperatives: worker co-ops and housing co-ops," *Review of Social Economy* 51:1 (April), 52-67.

_____. 1985. "On the labor theory of property," *The Philosophical Forum* 16:4, 293-326.

_____. 1986. "The employment contract and liberal thought," *Review of Social Economy* 44:1 (April), 13-39.

_____. 1988. "A Kantian person/thing principle in political economy," *Journal of Economic Issues*, 22:4 (December), 1109-1122.

Elliott, J. 1984. "Recapitulations and prospects: worker ownership and self-government," *Review of Social Economy* 42:3 (December), 433-438.

Fetter, F. 1915. *Economic Principles*. New York: The Century Co.

Georgescu-Roegen, N. 1977. "A bioeconomic viewpoint," *Review of Social Economy* (December), 361-375.

Geras, N. 1983. *Marx and Human Nature: Refutation of a Legend*. London: N.L.R. Verso Editions.

Gowdy, J. 1980. "Bioeconomics: a comment," *Review of Social Economy* 38:1 (April), 95-97.

_____. "Radical economics and resource scarcity," *Review of Social Economy* 39:2 (October), 165-180.

Gunn, B. 1987. "Capitalism and consumption vs. competruism and conservation," *Forum for Social Economics* (Spring), 27-44.

Gunton, G. 1897. *Principles of Social Economics*. New York: G. P. Putnam's Sons.

Gunton, G. and H. Robbins. 1900. *Outlines of Social Economics*. New York: D. Appleton & Co.

Habermas, J. 1971. *Knowledge and Human Interests,* trans. J. Shapiro. Boston: Beacon Press.

Hagenbuch, W. (ed.) 1958. *Social Economics*. Cambridge Economic Series. Cambridge, UK: The University Press.

Haney, L. 1913. "The social point of view in economics," *Quarterly Journal of Economics* (November), 115-139.

Hill, L. E. 1978. "Social and institutional economics: toward a creative synthesis," *Review of Social Economy* 36 (December), 311-324.

_____. 1983. "The energy crisis: requiem for the growth-oriented economy," *Review of Social Economy* 41:2 (October), 97-108.

Hobson, J. A. 1927. *Economics and Ethics*. London: D. C. Heath.

Hooley, R. 1954. "Comment: the challenge of legal supremacy," *Review of Social Economy* 12:2 (September), 156-160.

Hunt, E. K. 1978. "Normative foundations of social theory: an essay on the criteria defining social economics," *Review of Social Economy* 36:3 (December), 285-310.

Karsten, S. 1986. "Pastoral economics within the framework of a social economy," *Forum for Social Economics* (Fall), 45-58.

Ladd, J. (ed.). 1973. *Ethical Relativism*. Belmont, CA: Wadsworth Publishing Company.

Lange, O. 1945-46. "The subject matter of economics," *Review of Economic Studies* XIII.

Loewe, A. 1965. *On Economic Knowledge*. New York: Harper & Row.

Lutz, M. A. 1987. "Philosophical anthropology and social economics," paper presented at December meeting of the Association of Social Economics in Chicago.

Marx, K. 1970. *The German Ideology* [1846], C. J. Arthur, ed. New York: International Publishers.

Marx, K. and F. Engels. 1975-76. *Collected Works*. Volumes 1-6. London.

McDaniel, B. A. 1981. "Solar energy and social economy," *Review of Social Economy* 39:2 (October), 181-196.

_____. 1983. "Solar energy and the politics of first and second best," *Review of Social Economy* 41:1 (April), 12-24.

McKee, A. 1984. "Market failures and the place of government in social economy," *Review of Social Economy* 42:1 (April), 1-15.

Messner, J. 1951. "Freedom as a principle of social order: an essay in the substance of subsidiary function," *The Modern Schoolman* 28:1 (January), 97-110.

Mishan, E. J. 1981. *Introduction to Normative Economics*. New York: Oxford University Press.

_____. 1982. *What Political Economy Is All About*. New York: Cambridge University Press.

Mueller-Armack, A. 1978. "The social market economy as an economic and social order," *Review of Social Economy* 36:3 (December), 325-331.

Phelps, E. 1985. *Political Economy: An Introductory Text*. New York: W. W. Norton and Co.

Randall, J. and J. Buchler. 1942. *Philosophy: An Introduction*. New York: Harper & Row.

Rauscher, A. 1978. "The necessity for and limits of the social welfare state," *Review of Social Economy* 36:3 (December), 333-348.

Rawls, J. 1971. *A Theory of Justice*. Cambridge, MA: Harvard University Press.

Robbins, L. 1984. *An Essay on the Nature and Significance of Economic Science*. [1932] 3rd edition. London: Macmillan Press.

Rockmore, T. 1978. "Marxian man," *Monist* 61:1 (January), 56-71.

Rohrlich, G. 1970. "The challenge of social economics" in his ed. *Social Economics for the 1970s*. Cambridge, MA: Cambridge University Press, pp. 3-23.

_____. 1973. "The potential for social ecology for economic science," *Review of Social Economy* 31:1 (April), 31-39.

_____. 1984. "Community--the submerged component of economic theorizing," *Review of Social Economy* 42:3 (December), 221-230.

Rosenthal, P. 1984. *Words and Values (Some Leading Words and Where They Lead Us)*. New York: Oxford University Press.

Samuels, W. 1977. "Reflections on social economics in a diverse and open economics," *Review of Social Economy* 35:3, 283-291.

Scheler, M. 1961. *Ressentiment*, trans. W. H. Holdheim. New York.

Schumacher, E. F. 1973. *Small Is Beautiful*. New York: Harper and Row.

Sen, A. 1977. "Rational fools: a critique of the behavioral foundation of economic theory," *Philosophy and Public Affairs* 6, 317-344.

_____. 1985. "Goals, commitment and identity," *Journal of Law, Economics and Organization* 1:2, 341-355.

_____. 1987. *On Economics and Ethics*. New York: Basil Blackwell Ltd.

Sen, A. and B. Williams. 1982. *Utilitarianism and Beyond*. New York: Cambridge University Press.

Smith, V. 1984. "Marx's social ontology, his critical method and contemporary social economics," *Review of Social Economy* 42:2 (October), 143-169.

Stanfield, R. 1978. "On social economics," *Review of Social Economics* 36:3 (December), 349-362.

Stikkers, K. 1987. "Max Scheler's contribution to social economics," *Review of Social Economy* 45:3 (December), 223-242.

_____. 1988. "Goals, values and community in the social economy," *Forum for Social Economics* (Spring), 1-12.

Toennis, F. 1963. *Community and Society*, trans. C. Loomis. East Lansing, MI: Michigan University Press.

Tucker, R. (ed.). 1972. *The Marx-Engels Reader*. New York: W. W. Norton.

Viner, J. 1963. "Possessive individualism as original sin," *Canadian Journal of Economics and Political Science*, 548-559.

Ward, R. J. 1954. "Welfare economics, planning, and the individual," *Review of Social Economy* 12:2 (September), 122-134.

Waterman, A. M. C.   1982.   "John Locke's theory of property and
    christian social thought," *Review of Social Economy* 40:2 (October),
    97-115.
Wieser, F. von.   1927.   *Principles of Social Economy* [1914], trans. F.
    Hinrichs and with a preface by W. C. Mitchell.   New York:
    Adelphi Co.
Worland, S.   1978.   "On the uncertain future of social economics," *Review
    of Social Economy* 36:2 (October), 127-135.